SimCity 2000™

Power, Politics, and Planning

SECRETS OF THE GAMES
Now Available from Prima

COMPUTER GAME BOOKS
SimEarth: The Official Strategy Guide
Harpoon Battlebook: The Official Strategy Guide
JetFighter II: The Official Strategy Guide
The Official LucasFilm Games Air Combat Strategies Book
Sid Meier's Civilization, or Rome on 640K a Day
Wing Commander I and II: The Ultimate Strategy Guide
Chuck Yeager's Air Combat Handbook
Ultima: The Avatar Adventures
Ultima VII and Underworld: More Avatar Adventures
A-Train: The Official Strategy Guide
PowerMonger: The Official Strategy Guide
Global Conquest: The Official Strategy Guide (with disk)
Falcon 3: The Official Combat Strategy Book (with disk)
Gunship 2000: The Official Strategy Guide
Dynamix Great War Planes: The Ultimate Strategy Guide
SimLife: The Official Strategy Guide
Populous: The Official Strategy Guide
Stunt Island: The Official Strategy Guide
Prince of Persia: The Official Strategy Guide
X-Wing Collector's: The Official Strategy Guide
Empire Deluxe: The Official Strategy Guide
F-15 Strike Eagle III: The Official Strategy Guide (with disk)
Lemmings: The Official Companion (with disk)
Secret of Mana Official Game Secrets
The 7th Guest: The Official Strategy Guide
Myst Revised and Expanded: The Official Strategy Guide
Return to Zork Adventurer's Guide
Microsoft Flight Simulator: The Official Strategy Guide
Strike Commander: The Official Strategy Guide
Might and Magic Compendium: The Authorized Strategy
Guide for Games I, II, III, and IV

How to Order:
Individual orders and quantity discounts are available from the publisher, Prima Publishing, P.O. Box 1260BK, Rocklin, CA 95677; phone (916) 632-4400. For Quantity orders, include information on your letterhead concerning the intended use of the books and the number of books you wish to purchase. For individual orders, turn to the back of the book for more information.

SimCity 2000

Power, Politics, and Planning

Nick Dargahi

Michael Bremer

Prima Publishing
P.O. Box 1260BK
Rocklin, CA 95677

Library of Congress Catalog Card Number: 94-80099
ISBN: 0-7615-0075-8

Project Editor: Kip Ward

94 95 96 97 BB   10 9 8 7 6 5 4
Printed in the United States of America

Table of Contents

Part III: Planning—City Design and Scenario Solutions ...259

Chapter 11   A Survey of Cities 261

Chapter 12   Disasters for Fun and Profit...............................281

Acknowledgments

I would like to thank all the people who were instrumental in bringing this project to fruition. At Prima, Stefan Grünwedel was an extremely able project editor on the original book (he cracked his whip judiciously, but with great aplomb), Bob Campbell successfully turned my prose into King's English, Marian Hartsough created the book design and layout, Ocean Quigley gave his Michelangelo touch to the graphics, Roger Stewart landed me the job writing the book, Diane Pasquetti was a great factotum, and James Alton performed a very thorough technical edit that corrected my many errors.

Special mention needs to be made of James Alton's numerous contributions throughout the book. His MaxiANC city (population 9,325,541!) is featured prominently in the color insert of this book, and his independent testing of the program revealed many surprises about the *SimCity* model. *SimCity* veteran Kevin Endo also deserves credit for being the first to discover how to create new scenarios. Jerry Moore was helpful in providing us with timely new tips for the updated version of this book. His Rubigger city, with its world record breaking population of 9,395,128, is also featured in the color insert of this book.

Many thanks go to my family—including Xenia, Kira, Milou, Ali, and Alec—who provided me with life-support while I was tethered to my computer. To Adriene goes my appreciation for encouraging my work.

—Nick Dargahi

This book would have been real stinky without the help and support of everyone at Maxis—from Jeff and Will and Joe on down—and the Prima Patrol: Ben, Roger, Rusel, Ocean, Stefan, Marian, and the rest of the crew. Special thanks go to all the Maxoids who answered lots of questions and/or let themselves be interviewed: Don Walters, Will Wright, Fred Haslam, Jenny Martin, Chris Weiss, Alan Barton, Jon Ross, and Daniel Browning— and to everyone who worked on *SimCity 2000* from first concept through tech support and customer service. Good work, gang!

—Michael Bremer

Introduction

SimCity is back—and it's bigger and better than ever!

A major part of the appeal of the original *SimCity* and now *SimCity 2000* is that we already know all about them. We know what cities are, because we've lived in them—in one form or another, from a tiny town of a dozen people to a bustling metropolis of millions—all our lives. So, unlike other games, we approach *SimCity* as lifelong experts in the field.

We all know by experience the things that a city needs: a place to live, a place to work, a place to shop, a way to get around, some utilities, and all the other things that we've taken for granted our whole lives. We all know the problems and challenges that cities and the people in them face every day.

We also know by experience that cities are never "finished." They change with the times and with the people who live in them. Every one of us has witnessed this, whether it was your favorite climbing tree that was bulldozed to make way for apartment buildings, your old beloved neighborhood crumbling into decay, or a new city center with gleaming new skyscrapers. Like us, like any organism, cities change and evolve to survive in a changing environment.

While we know this instinctively and experientially, it is hard to really grasp it on an intellectual level because of the time scale at which change happens. These simulation games let you step back out of the city and out of time and watch and learn—and poke around to see what happens.

One of the major things that pushes change in cities is new technology. The invention of the bicycle alone (cheap transportation) allowed cities to double in size. The telephone let it grow even further. The automobile lead to the creation of the suburb. New sources of power and water and sewage systems allowed cities to grow ever larger and more dense. With the level of technology increasing every day, with space travel and undersea exploration, we can only guess and dream about what cities will become.

And like the city it simulates, *SimCity* has grown and changed with the times. Evolving in response to survival needs, features have been added, new platforms have been mounted, and the sound and graphics capabilities of today's computers have been more fully exploited in *SimCity 2000*.

There are limitations to the growth of real cities. Sometimes you can't change something any more, or at least not fast enough. Sometimes there isn't room for expansion. Sometimes you have to pack your bags, move out of town, and build a new city. *SimCity* had the same limitations. It had reached the end of the line for slow growth. So, taking into account all the features and functions that the designers wanted to add, plus all the suggestions received from many thousands of players, a new *SimCity* was founded.

The result, *SimCity 2000*, is a masterpiece. A near-perfect combination of simulation technology, entertainment value, and lesson in reality. Requiring much more powerful hardware than its predecessor (now called *SimCity Classic*), it pushes the limits of today's home computers, challenges your thinking skills, and enhances your city designing and creating abilities.

This book will guide you through the tools and techniques of playing with *SimCity 2000*. It will show you how to win the scenarios, take you on a tour of the inner workings of the simulation behind the game, introduce you to the people who created the program, and leave you with a taste of things to come.

And there is more to come. *SimCity 2000* may be the state of the art in city simulations—for now—but times change, cities change, technology changes as computers grow in power, players grow in sophistication, and *SimCity* will grow and change, too. There will be new add-ons, new versions on new computers, and a number of other surprises. But as long as we're human, there will always be cities. It will always be fun to design, create, and rule your own cities; and it will always be fun to play with *SimCity*.

So read on. Enjoy yourself—play, create, have fun.

ABOUT THIS BOOK

This book is presented in four parts:

Part I: Power—Controlling *SimCity* gives you a quick once-over to get you started playing *SimCity 2000*, then proceeds to explain in detail how to use all the tools in the City Toolbar, use all the tools in the Terrain Toolbar, deal with the city budget, make the most use of your maps, and customize the simulator to conform to your city-building tastes.

Part II: Politics—SimCitizens, City Councils, and Hidden Agendas begins by filling you in on those lovable—yet demanding—citizens of SimCities (the Sims), as well as neighboring cities and SimNation. It also covers the newspaper system, the city council, and ordinances. Then it reveals all the "Easter eggs" and secrets that are hidden in *SimCity 2000*—and goes even beyond that with ways to modify the game play and the cities that even the programmers never thought of!

Part III: Planning—City Design and Scenario Solutions presents and critiques a number of different cities for design, functionality, and fun. It tells you how to deal with disasters and beat all the scenarios. And it tells you how to re-create real cities from maps—even where you can get the maps.

Part IV: The Making of *SimCity 2000* tells the saga of the creation of a great computer game—the process and the people. It delves inside the simulation model and explains, from the inside out, exactly how everything works. You'll also be treated to truth, predictions, and rumors about the future of *SimCity 2000*, and you'll learn how to use the *SimCity Urban Renewal Kit* (aka "*SCURK*") to print your cities, design new building types, and create your own cities without money worries.

In addition, Appendix A gives you tips for setting up the DOS version of *SimCity 2000* and *SCURK* so that they can run under OS/2 and Windows 3.1 as DOS applications. Appendix B covers special Windows installation tips, while Appendix C discusses the contents of the new *SimCity CD-ROM Collection*.

PART

I

Power—Controlling *SimCity*

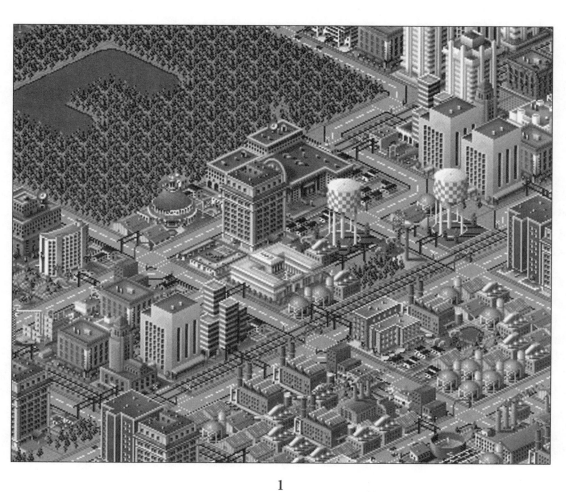

C H A P T E R
1
Playing *SimCity*

In this chapter, you will be given a guided tour of how to play *SimCity 2000* and be introduced to some of its amazing new features. If you already have a basic understanding of the game and how to play, you may want to skip this chapter. But if you're new to *SimCity 2000*, or would like a quick introduction, then this chapter is for you.

With *SimCity 2000*, you have much more flexibility and control in charting the growth of your city, but with this extensive new repertoire of tools and features comes added responsibility. To keep things under control, you will need to have a better understanding of how things work, and be more vigilant and attentive to emerging developments. As with *SimCity Classic*,[1] the success or failure of your city depends on what actions you, as mayor and city planning commissioner, decide to take. The many facets of urban life that can make a city bearable or unbearable are simulated with great exactitude, and so you must continually respond to the ever-changing dynamics of city development. How do you attract new industries to your city to provide badly needed jobs? How do you increase the housing supply without creating a real estate slump? How do you balance the need for industrial development against the need to preserve the environment? These and many other questions are what this book is designed to answer.

---

[1]The original *SimCity*, first released in 1989, has been renamed and repackaged as *SimCity Classic*.

WHAT IS *SIMCITY*?

SimCity 2000 is a type of entertainment/educational software described as a *system simulation*, a program that attempts to represent or reproduce "real-world" conditions and phenomena under the governance of strict rules or laws.

The simulator is a tool that enables users to model real-world conditions and see what kinds of outcomes can be predicted from different scenarios. By identifying and observing elementary processes and how they interact, programmers have succeeded in modeling very complex systems. In the case of *SimCity*, each tile or block of land contains dynamic variables that represent elements of city life such as traffic, crime, pollution, and population. These variables change as events occur in adjacent blocks.

For example, when pollution goes up in a particular block due to industrial development, this makes the area less attractive, so land value variables fall. If there is also a lack of police coverage, the crime variable is nudged up a factor for adjacent blocks, and the population tends to migrate out. The *SimCity* algorithm calculates changes in these variables for each tile of land, and then updates the visual appearance of the buildings to show what is happening internally. When you see your buildings crumbling or turning black—indicating abandonment—you know something is amiss, and you must take corrective action. Other subtle effects can be observed in *SimCity*'s many feedback mechanisms, such as the graphs windows, budget window, and newspapers, all of which convey important information about your city's progress.

SimCity creates a highly detailed artificial model of urban city life. The simulation demonstrates the potentially successful or disastrous consequences of city planning decisions. The system model itself is extremely complex, using special new algorithms called "micro-simulations" and "cellular automata" that accurately portray the organic processes going on in an actual city. Because there is no specific opponent, *SimCity* offers a noncompetitive environment in which to explore, experiment, and create new types of cities. You can make your own goals, or you can attempt to master the five built-in scenarios, tackling specific problems such as fires, economic recession, flooding, crime, pollution, traffic, earthquakes, hurricanes and tornadoes, urban riots, nuclear meltdowns, and more.

Unlike many other computer simulations and games, there is no one way to win or succeed in *SimCity*, so you needn't fear that you will soon be bored after discovering how to "beat the machine." There are a myriad of paths to accomplish your goals, which are only limited by your imagination. Random elements, such as disasters or economic recessions, introduce uncertainties into the game, so that you can never be too complacent or carefree about your city's safety. Starting from scratch, you can create a thriving megalopolis from a scrubby village, all the while fine-tuning the process of growth. Along the way, you can attempt to rectify intransigent problems before they become insurmountable, and you, as mayor, are turned out of office by an irate citizenry.

NEW FEATURES OF *SIMCITY 2000*

SimCity 2000 differs from its mighty predecessor, *SimCity Classic*, in the following ways:

- Three-dimensional graphics; with mountains, foothills, valleys, lakes, streams, waterfalls, and buildings.

- A three-dimensional isometric view of your city, with three different zoom levels, and a rotatable 360° panoramic view to see behind mountains and buildings. Customize your view by selecting just what you want to see, whether it be zones only, infrastructure (such as roads, rails, tunnels, small parks, and power lines), just the underground (subway lines, subway stations, water pipes, and water pumps), or just your city's public buildings (police stations, fire stations, educational facilities, bus depots, rail depots, water pumps, treatment plants, water towers, arcologies, piers, hospitals, zoos, large parks, marinas, stadiums, prisons, churches, and power plants).

- New zone sub-types. You can now zone high- or low-density commercial, industrial, and residential zones. Zones can now be made any size by clicking and dragging the mouse where you want to zone. Although you can drag a zone over any existing road, power line, or rail line, the land underneath this infrastructure will remain de-zoned. Also, if you place a road or rail over a previously zoned area, the land underneath the road or rail will become de-zoned. In *SimCity 2000* (unlike in *SimCity Classic*), power lines must connect empty adjacent zones, but (as in *SimCity Classic*) power is transmitted from building to building. Roads and tracks impede power transmission through a zone, and must be bridged with power lines.

- Altitude. There are now 31 levels of altitude, from 50 feet all the way to 3,050 feet, with each tile level representing an altitude change of 100 feet. Sloped land, such as hillsides, will display the average elevation between the level land below it and the level land above it. Cities can now be built on mountains, plains, valleys, or gorges.

- An underground view of your city for the purpose of viewing subterranean water pipes, tunnels and subways, and subway stations.

- A built-in terrain editor allows you to terraform coasts, mountains, lakes, and rivers; to raise and lower terrain; to increase or decrease sea levels; to place trees and forests, and much more.

- A new water distribution system. Lay pipes, place pumping stations, build storage tanks, and construct desalinization plants to supply water to your SimCitizens.

- Emergency services. Dispatch services to battle fires, contain riots, and fight crime.
- New power plant types including gas, oil, solar, wind, hydroelectric, microwave, and fusion power, as well as the original coal and nuclear power plant options.
- Rewards for city growth and achievements. Depending on your success, a mansion, statue, llama dome, military base, or arcology can be built.
- Trains, subways, depots, and stations. The subway and aboveground train network can be linked via special intermodal transfer junctions. Train tracks act differently in *SimCity 2000* than in the *Classic* version: The Sims can use trains and subways only if they are within three blocks of a depot or station; it's not enough for them to be within three blocks of the tracks.
- Bus depots
- Freeways and freeway interchanges
- Tunnels for vehicular traffic
- Suspension bridges, causeways, and lift bridges
- Grammar schools and colleges
- Hospitals (new health model in *SimCity 2000*)
- Libraries
- Museums
- Prisons
- Military bases
- Large parks
- Zoos
- Marinas
- Customized stadiums with your choice of sport and team names .
- Sign posts that allow you to quickly name and identify different parts of your city.
- A query tool to provide instant information on any building, zone, tile, or infrastructure for your planning purposes. Find out exactly what is going on in any part of the city by simply clicking on the object you're interested in.
- Construction tools for planting new trees and creating ponds, lakes, rivers, and streams.
- Extensive new maps and graphs of city demographics, for evaluating your city's growth patterns.

- City ordinances you can enact to beautify the city, encourage tourism, promote education, or increase public safety and health, along with other measures.
- New budget advisors to help you decide what to do.
- Means to micro-manage your budgeting and tax collection, allowing you to selectively raise or lower expenditures on any item in the city budget, set different tax rates for commerce, industry, and residential zones, and tap new sources of revenue, such as sales taxes, income taxes, legalized gambling, and parking fines.
- $10,000 bonds you can take out to finance your city's development.
- On-screen newspapers that report your city's problems and reveal how successfully the populace thinks you are doing your job.
- New kinds of disasters, such as volcanoes, urban riots, pollution, and a new monster attack.
- An expanded economic model, in which you trade and compete with up to four neighboring off-screen cities. If your city's business environment and quality of life decline, the neighboring cities will lure your citizens and industries away.
- Means to discourage and encourage different kinds of industry, depending on what kind of economy you wish to emphasize. By selectively raising and lowering tax rates on the steel and mining, textiles, petrochemical, food, construction, automotive, aerospace, finance, media, electronics, and tourism industries, you can exert a powerful influence on what kind of city develops.
- Five new scenarios: Oakland Firestorm 1991; Flint, Michigan Recession; flooding in Charleston, South Carolina; Dullsville; and a Hollywood monster attack. An add-on product, *Volume 1: Great Disasters and the Great Cities*, included as part of the *SimCity CD-ROM Collection*, add additional new scenarios to challenge your skills as mayor.
- Improved display. The program runs in 640 × 480 SVGA 256-color display mode on the PC and in 256 colors on the Macintosh. The Windows and Macintosh versions of *SimCity 2000* can display as large a window as your screen resolution permits. Although at present, the Windows version of *SimCity 2000* can only be run with a display driver of 256 colors, Maxis is working on an update that will allow you to run the program with higher color resolutions.
- Vastly improved sound effects and music. *SimCity 2000* supports the new General MIDI Wave Table Synthesis sound cards on the PC, as well as all common FM sound cards. With a MIDI Wave Table Synthesis sound card, individual instruments can be heard, creating the effect of a "live" orchestra.

- The ability to import cities from *SimCity Classic* into *SimCity 2000*.
- A new on-screen help system. Hold down the Shift key and then click on any button or tool for an on-screen explanation of what it does and how it works.
- An enhanced Toolbar. The Toolbar has pop-up submenus for many tools, allowing you to access multiple functions. Simply click and hold down the mouse button over any tool to see if it has a submenu.
- Pop-up and tear-off windows. Some Toolbar buttons, when pressed, cause small pop-up windows to appear on screen (some of these windows—particularly on the Macintosh—remain open only as long as you are holding the mouse button down).

  These pop-up windows can be expanded and moved to any convenient location on screen. You close them by clicking on the Close Window button, located at the upper-left corner of the window's title bar. New windows include:

  - A Population window to survey age ranges, life expectancies, and education levels.
  - An Industry window to survey different types of industries, assess national demand for products of different industries, and set tax rates to encourage or discourage selected industries.
  - A Neighbors window to view neighboring cities and compare their growing populations to your city's population.
  - A Budget window: Vastly expanded from *SimCity Classic*, this window gives you complete control over budgetary matters.[2]
  - A Graphs window that allows you to chart the changes in city size (total population), residents (non-working population), commerce (number of people employed), industry (number of people employed), traffic (density of congestion), pollution, average land values, crime, power capacity (percent of free capacity left), water (percent of free capacity left), health levels, education levels, unemployment, Gross National Product (GNP), national population (in entire SimNation), and federal rate (prime interest rate for credit and loans).
  - An Ordinances window to set various city ordinances regarding public health and safety, education, finance, promotion, and other

---

[2]Although you can set global industry tax rates in the Budget window, if you want to selectively raise or lower taxes on a particular industry type, you must do so in the Industry window.

issues. You can select this window from the Windows menu, or from within the Budget window.

◆ A Maps window that allows you to display a particular aspect of your city. By selecting one of the available buttons in this window, you can see a mini-map display of your city that shows vital information about that subject. Graphically view city form, roads, rails, traffic density, powered and unpowered areas, the water system, population density and rate of growth, crime rate, police coverage, pollution, land values, and other aspects of city life. There is also a new Map-Mode view that superimposes your map view on the City window, thereby allowing you to see cartographic information displayed directly on your city. This view allows you to visually inspect crime rates, land values, pollution levels, police or fire station coverage, and other values with great precision.

STARTING A NEW CITY

In this part of the chapter, you will actually open and create your first SimCity, learning as you go. Although you won't learn how to use all the available tools during this session, you will learn the essentials for creating your cities.

Before you can begin, you must have installed *SimCity 2000* to your hard disk. If you have not yet installed the program, refer to your manual for the proper installation procedure. Assuming all is well, if you are running the DOS version,[3] type **SC2000**. If you are running the Windows or Macintosh version, simply click twice on the SC2000 icon on your Windows or Macintosh desktop. You should see an opening screen similar to that pictured in Figure 1-1.

Figure 1-1
Opening screen for *SimCity 2000* (Macintosh version)

Depending on whether you have sound capabilities or not, you will hear the opening strains of *SimCity*'s music. At this point, if you click on your mouse button, you will see your name appear on screen as you registered it during the installation. Clicking once

---

[3]If you are running the DOS version of *SimCity 2000* under OS/2, or Windows 3.1, see the Appendices for advice on optimum settings.

again will bring up the Startup Menu screen, as shown, where you will ordinarily decide whether to load a previously saved city, start a new city, terraform a city, or try your hand at winning one of the scenarios.

For now, let's choose Start New City by clicking on this button. You will next see your city being terraformed automatically for you. After this process has been finished, you will be prompted to choose your city's name, starting year, and challenge level. For your city's name, type in **MyCity**. If you are running *SimCity 2000* on a DOS-based machine, the filename for your city will be based on the first eight characters of your city's name.[4] The three levels— Easy, Medium, and Hard—simply refer to the amount of money you start with, the economic difficulty level, and the propensity for disasters to occur. At the easy level, you start out with $20,000, the neighboring economies are clamoring for industrial products from your city, and you will experience few disasters. The year

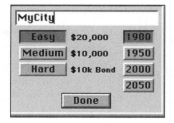

you start your city determines what kinds of technology and city infrastructure you have available to use, and the kind of economy that exists for the period. In the year 1900, for example, you will not be able to build nuclear power plants or highways—since they have not yet been invented—and the economy tends to grow more slowly than in later years. For the sake of simplicity, let's choose Easy and the year 1900, as shown, even though it is easier to build a bigger city in the year 2000. To continue with game startup, click the Done button.

Your next screen will display the city's main newspaper. You can click on any article that might interest you, and see it enlarged so that you can actually read the text.

Figure 1-2 shows a newspaper article that has been zoomed in for reading. Note that many of the articles are silly and have no bearing on your city. Others, however, tell you important things such as "City Experiences Drought," or "Citizens Up in Arms Over Tax Increase." When you are done reading the newspaper, close it by clicking on the close box in the upper-left corner of the window.

---

[4]You can actually type in a city name of up to 30 characters, which will be displayed at the top of your City window. But for DOS machines, only the first eight characters are used to name the disk file, and those eight characters can include only the letters *A* through *Z*, the numbers *0* through *9*, and the following special characters: _^$-!#%& {}@`'(). No other characters are permissible. Furthermore, the DOS filename cannot contain spaces, commas, backslashes, or periods.

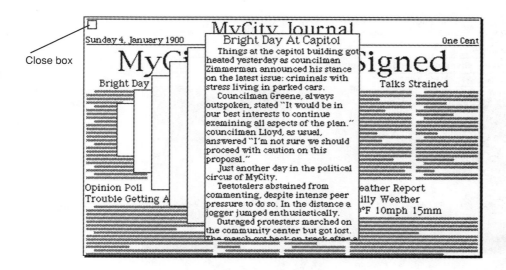

Close box

Figure 1-2
Reading the
newspaper

Figure 1-2
Reading the
newspaper

THE CITY WINDOW

Once the city newspaper is off the screen, you will be presented with the City window, in which you will do all your building and zoning. In the DOS version, the City window may be sized abnormally small; to increase it to full screen width, simply click on the zoom box button at the top right-hand corner of the window. Your screen should appear as in Figure 1-3.

Looking at your City window, you will see a Toolbar with assorted button icons on your left, as well as a title bar at the top of the window that displays the city name, date, and how much money you have left in your city treasury. A Zoom Box for quickly maximizing or minimizing your City window's size is located at the upper-right corner, and at the right and bottom edges you will see scroll bars for scrolling the map image. The Resize button, at the lower right-hand corner, is used to customize the size of the City window. To resize the City window, simply click and drag the Resize button to a position where you want the window's lower-right corner to be.

At the very top of the screen, you will see various pull-down menus that allow you to access the Simulator's controls. Accessing these menus and commands is easy: Simply click on the menu name and then drag the mouse cursor to the command you wish to activate. Click on the menu command if you wish to have it executed immediately.

Notice that the month that is displayed in the City window's title bar changes every so often. This tells you that the simulation is actually running, and that time is slipping by. Each January, the City's budget must be reviewed and approved, and the budget window will appear on screen. If,

City toolbar   Status window   Year and date   Name of your city   City funds   Title bar   Menu bar

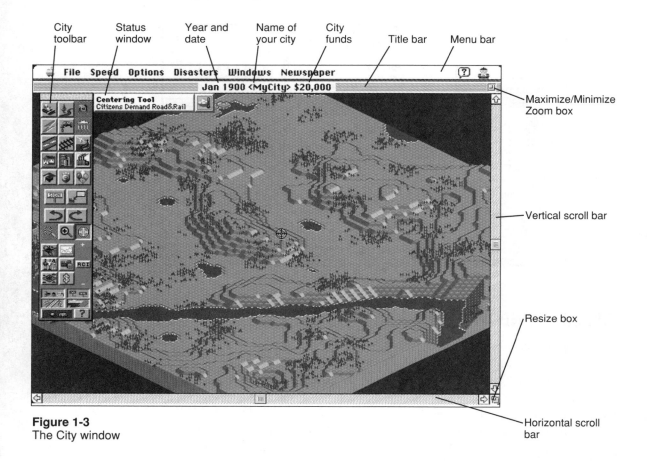

Maximize/Minimize Zoom box

Vertical scroll bar

Resize box

Figure 1-3
The City window

Horizontal scroll bar

during this initiation to *SimCity*, the Budget window appears on screen, don't be alarmed. Simply click on the Done button and it will vanish. You can recall the Budget window at any time by selecting it from the **Windows** menu or by clicking on the Budget icon located on the Toolbar. Likewise, if the Newspaper suddenly appears, you can get rid of it by clicking on the close box, and instantly recall it by selecting it from the Newspaper menu.

Now examine your City window. In it you will see bare landscape, sprinkled with patches of forest and interspersed with areas of water and mountains. As you gaze at your landscape, keep an eye out for a nice flat parcel of land where you can found your city. Ideally, the site will be near water, so that you can pump water efficiently for your city's water system, and also so that you can establish a seaport in the future.

Your city is divided into blocks, or "tiles," of land, each measuring 200

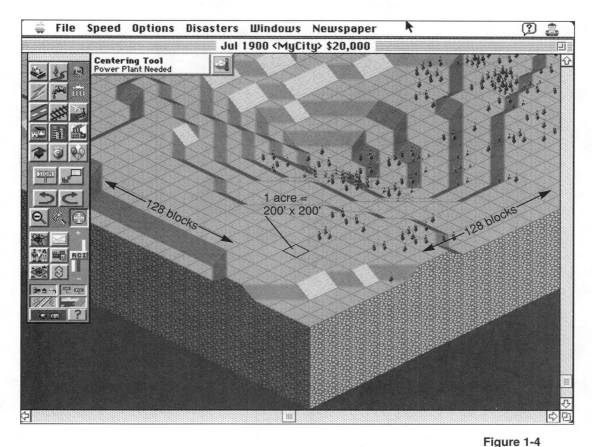

Figure 1-4
City size: Each tile or block of land equals roughly one acre (200 feet by 200 feet); the city's maximum size is 128 blocks by 128 blocks (16,384 acres)

feet by 200 feet, approximately one acre, as you can see in Figure 1-4.[5] The dimensions of your city are 128 blocks by 128 blocks, or about 16,384 acres.

USING THE TOOLBAR

The Toolbar, as shown on the following page, is a floating palette of icons in a special window that you see on the left edge of your screen. Through this control, you can operate all the building and zoning tools in *SimCity 2000*, and call up various maps, graphs, views, and other information about your

---

[5]An acre of land measures exactly 208.7 feet by 208.7 feet, or 43,560 feet^2 (4,840 yards^2 or 4047 meters^2). In *SimCity*, however, each parcel of land measures 200 feet by 200 feet, just shy of an actual acre.

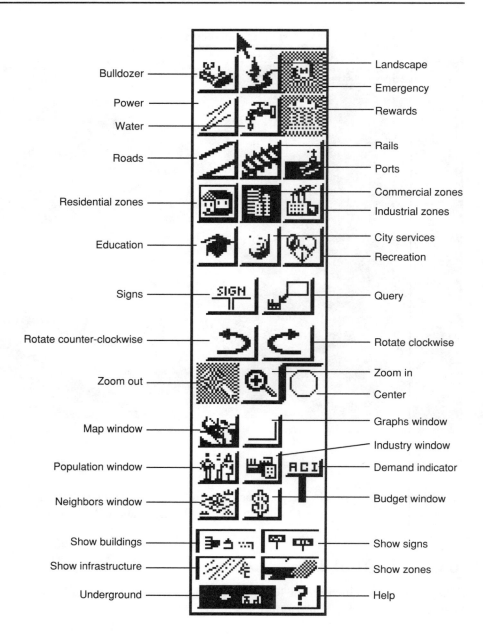

Bulldozer — Landscape

Emergency

Power — Rewards

Water

Roads — Rails

Ports

Residential zones — Commercial zones

Industrial zones

Education — City services

Recreation

Signs — Query

Rotate counter-clockwise — Rotate clockwise

Zoom out — Zoom in

Center

Map window — Graphs window

Industry window

Population window — Demand indicator

Neighbors window — Budget window

Show buildings — Show signs

Show infrastructure — Show zones

Underground — Help

city. All the functions of the Toolbar are listed here, but in the event you forget what an icon tool does, there is a built-in help feature that brings instant context-sensitive help on screen. To activate the help feature, simply hold down the Shift key and then click on any button in the Toolbar. This will cause a miniature text box to appear with a description of the button. The built-in help feature can be applied to any of the buttons, keys, or functions you see in *SimCity 2000*.

Clicking and holding down the left mouse button in the DOS version of *SimCity* (for the Macintosh version simply hold down the mouse button) on any of the top five rows of buttons in the Toolbar (except for those that are "ghosted" or unavailable) activates a submenu that allows more choices. For example, clicking and holding down the mouse button on the Bulldozer icon causes a pop-up menu to appear that allows you to select one of five different kinds of bulldozing. Elsewhere on the Toolbar are buttons that bring up tear-off windows or graphs, or that affect the kinds of objects displayed in the main view of the City window.

You'll notice that two of the buttons are ghosted, meaning that they are unavailable for use, as indicated by their washed-out appearance. The Emergency and Rewards buttons are not currently active, but they become so when certain events occur. When a disaster strikes, the Emergency button is activated, and you can click on it to dispatch the police or fire department to the scene of the trouble. If you have a military base, then you can also dispatch the military using this button. Only when your city reaches a certain population size does the Rewards button light up, enabling you to build a statue, a Mayor's mansion, and other goodies.

You can move the Toolbar anywhere on screen by simply clicking and dragging the top border of the Toolbar's window.

Let's look at some of the viewing functions that are available on the Toolbar. You can zoom in and zoom out your view of the city window using the Zoom buttons. There are three different zoom levels. When zoomed all the way in, you will see maximum detail in buildings and other objects, but your field of view will be limited. At the medium zoom, you can see more of your city, but with not quite as much detail as full zoom in. At full zoom out, you'll be able to see most of your city all at once, but you won't be able to see much detail. Using the rotation buttons, you can cause your city to rotate 360° in 90° increments, thereby allowing you an unobstructed view of your city from all angles. Quickly scrolling the map large distances is a snap, using the Center tool.

To zoom in for a closer look, click the Zoom In button on the Toolbar. Since there are three possible zoom levels, you may be able to click the Zoom In button once more for an especially magnified view of your city.

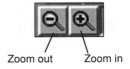

Zoom out   Zoom in

To zoom out, click the Zoom Out button, also on the Toolbar. If you are already zoomed in to maximum magnification, you should be able to click the Zoom Out button twice to obtain the farthest-away view of your city. The full zoom out allows you to get the widest possible view of your city environs, while the full zoom in allows you to see individual blocks of a particular neighborhood.

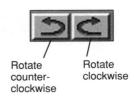

Rotate counter-clockwise   Rotate clockwise

On the Macintosh, to scroll or pan the map view in any direction, simply select the Center tool and then click and hold down the mouse button while you drag the Center icon in any direction. The map will scroll in the direction you move the Center icon.

In the DOS and Windows version of *SimCity 2000*, you can quickly center the map by clicking on the right mouse button while the cursor is over the map, regardless of which tool you have currently selected.

You can rotate your city view by clicking on the Rotate Counter-Clockwise button and Rotate Clockwise button on the Toolbar.

The Center tool is used to reposition your city view quickly to anywhere in the city. Although you can use the scroll bars to move the city view, the Center tool provides a much simpler and easier way to view a distant part of your city quickly. To use this tool, simply select it and then click anywhere on the map where you want to center your view. On the Macintosh, you can also drag the Center icon anywhere on your map, and the map will scroll in that direction.[6] For example, to scroll right without using the scroll bars, simply select the Center tool, move the Center icon over the map, and then click and hold down the mouse button while you drag the Center icon in the direction you wish the map to scroll.

THE STATUS WINDOW

The Status window located next to your Toolbar displays important information about your city. This floating window, like the Toolbar, can easily be moved anywhere on your screen by clicking and dragging the top of the window. The Status window displays the current tool you have selected on the

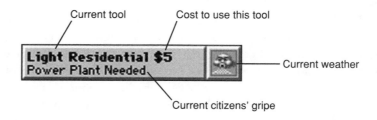

Toolbar and the cost of using that tool. An icon in the Status window tells you what current weather conditions are like, and a message line warns you of the city's most pressing needs, as well as impending disasters. You should periodically glance at the message that is displayed to find out what your SimCitizens are demanding.

---

[6]In the DOS version of *SimCity 2000*, the scrolling technique of dragging the center tool to pan the map view was purposely disabled, due to programming bugs that were encountered.

DESIGNING YOUR CITY

SimCity 2000 possesses many of the characteristics and design guidelines of its predecessor, *SimCity Classic*. Although it has a much greater repertoire of tools and features than *SimCity Classic* does, *SimCity 2000*—at its most basic level—functions in much the same way as the original. As in *SimCity Classic*, for example, to make a functioning city in *SimCity 2000* you will need to create the following:

- Residential zones for the Sims to live in
- Industrial zones for the Sims to work in
- Commercial zones for the Sims to trade, shop, and conduct business
- A power plant to furnish electricity for the city
- Power lines to connect the power plant with the zones and buildings
- Transportation links—such as roads, rails, subways, and highways— for the Sims to travel between work, home, and shops

Later, once you have established these basic conditions, you can add:

- Different zone density types
- Bus stations
- A water system
- Airports and seaports
- Police and fire stations
- Colleges and schools
- Hospitals and prisons
- Museums and libraries
- Sign posts for naming different boroughs of your city
- Stadiums, marinas, zoos, and parks
- Custom landscaping, created by adding trees, forests, and water, or by clearing, raising, or lowering terrain
- Arcologies and rewards for certain city achievements and population thresholds

Let's build our first city using these basic guidelines. We will start by first placing residential zones, and then constructing a power plant and power lines to connect the zones. Using the Bulldozer, we will learn how to correct any mistakes we make, and then we will proceed to build industrial and commercial zones, along with roads to link them. Afterwards, we'll undertake a new waterworks program to help supply our city with fresh water.

A Word from Our Sponsors on Zoning

Zoning in *SimCity 2000* is slightly different from zoning in *SimCity Classic*. For one thing, *SimCity 2000* zones are no longer a fixed size. They can be made any size, shape, or form, and they can be mapped over hills, mountains, gullies, valleys, trees, and forests. You can plop down a single zone by clicking on a single tile, or you can click and drag any size rectangular or square zone. Zones can be placed over preexisting infrastructure, including (but not limited to) roads, rails, buildings, power lines, and previously placed zones. When you place a zone over a previously existing zone, as long as there are no buildings on the existing zone, the zone changes to the new zone type. For example, you can zone over existing residential zones with commercial zones, but only if they have no buildings. Of course, you can always bulldoze a zone with buildings on it, allowing it to be converted to a different zone type.

Zones can also be "de-zoned" by using the Bulldozer's **De-Zone** command. This will cause the zone to revert to bare land. Again, any buildings or structures on the land must first be removed before the de-zoning can take place.

Placing Residential Zones

Our first order of business is to provide the Sims with a suitable place to live. Look at your map, zooming out to a whole view of your city, to spot some flat land that is, preferably, near water. *SimCity* places a high value on land near water, and this makes it more attractive for people to move in. Although hilly terrain is considered more valuable than flat terrain, to simplify things here we will use flat land. Once you have spotted Nirvana-by-the-Water, center the map by clicking the Center tool on the land where the zone is to be placed. Then click the Zoom In button until your view is zoomed in as close as you can get.

Now click the Residential Zones icon:

and select the Light Residential density option in the pop-up menu:

(hold down the mouse button while you do this — don't let go — or else the pop-up menu will disappear). You will see the cursor change into a picture icon of a house. Notice that your Status window now shows that you have selected the Light Residential Zone tool, and that the cost for zoning one tile would be $5. Position the cursor over the map where you wish to zone, and then click and drag this icon over the land you wish to cover.

Don't worry about zoning over hills and trees—this is perfectly OK to do. You can even zone over small bodies of water, previously zoned areas that are not as yet built up, roads, rails, and power lines. As you zone over preexisting structures, the buildings and infrastructure will remain as they were, but empty zones will be rezoned.

The density of the zone governs what kind of housing is permissible. Generally, the higher the density, the more people. With the Light option that we have selected, only single-family dwellings will be allowed in the zoned area, so the type of housing that will be created is of a more suburban nature. Later, when you wish to create a more urban setting, you can select **Dense**.

Figure 1-5 shows the placement of the residential zone as you click and drag the Residential Zone tool over the map. Notice that as you increase the size of the zone, the total cumulative cost, which is displayed inside the zone, also increases. While holding down the mouse button, you can increase or decrease the size of the zone, but once you decide your zone is the right size, release the mouse button. You should hear a "popping" sound, if you are equipped with a sound card or have a Macintosh, indicating the placement of the zone, represented as a colored green area filled with a dot-like matrix pattern. If you hear a harsh sounding beep or buzz, and you don't see the zone, then your zone was not placed, due to either an improper location or a lack of funds.

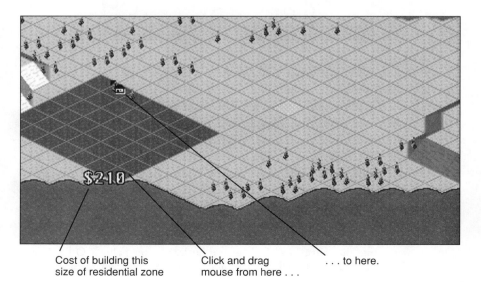

Cost of building this size of residential zone

Click and drag mouse from here . . .

. . . to here.

Figure 1-5 Zoning for residences. As you increase the size of the zone, the total cost displayed increases.

Even though you now have a zone into which the Sims can move, you still need to provide power and other necessities before they will migrate in.

Constructing a Power Plant

To power up the residential zone you have just created, you will need to build a power plant and construct power lines to the zone. Click and hold down the mouse button while selecting the Power icon on the Toolbar: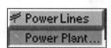

As you do so, you will see a pop-up menu listing two options: **Power Lines** and **Power Plant**. Select the **Power Plant** option and release the mouse button.

You must now decide what kind of power plant to build. The power plants that are listed range from primitive coal-powered plants to advanced fusion reactors, but you may not see the more advanced power plants in this dialog box until your technology progresses to a higher level. For now, select the Coal Power plant, which costs $4,000 and provides 200 megawatts of electricity. If you want more information on each power plant type, click on the INFO button above each icon:

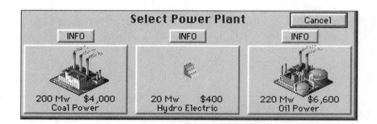

Next, move the cursor over the map to a location that is near (but not too near) your residential zone, like the site shown in Figure 1-6. The coal power plant is a heavy polluter, and so you want to avoid having it near your residents, who will complain bitterly and blame you for its consequences.[7] The square shadow area that moves over the map as you move your cursor represents the exact position for the power plant if you click the mouse button. Unlike zones, the power plant can be placed only on level terrain, so make sure the shadow marker is on a flat surface before you click the mouse button. If you try to place a power plant in a prohibited location, such as

---

[7]Only power plants that burn fossil fuels or use nuclear power pollute. Other power plants, such as the solar, wind, hydroelectric, and microwave power plants produce no pollution whatsoever.

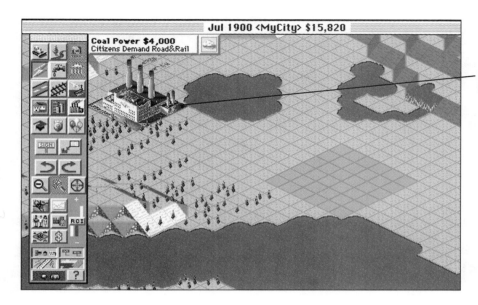

New coal
power plant

Figure 1-6
Constructing your
power plant

over water or partially on a hill, you will hear an angry beep and nothing will happen. You can place the power plant (or any other building) over trees and forests, since the simulator will automatically clear the land before construction begins.

When you place your power plant, you will hear a jackhammer-like sound, telling you that construction is proceeding without a hitch.

Connecting Power Lines between Residential Zones and a Power Plant

Your next step is to connect the power plant to your residential zone. To do this, again select the Power icon on the Toolbar. This time, however, when you hold down the mouse button, select the **Power Line** submenu option and then release the button. If you have done this correctly, you will see that your currently selected tool in the Status window is the Power Line, and that the cost for laying it over land is $2 per block (over water it costs $10 per block).

Move the cursor over the map and place it right next to the power plant. Hold down the mouse button and then drag the cursor directly over to your residential zone, releasing the mouse button when you reach the zone. If there is nothing but flat land between your power plant and the residential zone, you will see power lines and poles erected along the path you have just traced, as in Figure 1-7. As the power lines are placed, you will hear a "hum-

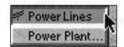

Figure 1-7
Let there be light

From time to time, watch your power lines for an alternating yellow-and red-flashing power symbol. This tells you that power is not flowing through the line as it should. Either there is a break in the line, or your power plant is overloaded and you must add another power plant to supplement your generating capacity.

ming" electrical discharge noise, telling you the line was properly placed. If, however, your path crossed any mountains, rivers, or other objects, it may have been blocked, and you will have to construct the power line tile by tile where the obstruction exists. It is possible to build power lines over water and over hills, but it is trickier over hills, since some slopes cannot have power lines placed on them. In mountainous terrain, you may need to rotate your map to get a better vantage point from which to place the power lines, since the slope on the opposite side of a hill may not be visible to you.

After your power line is placed to the residential zone, observe the tops of the poles for a flashing red-and-yellow power symbol. If there is no such symbol, then power is flowing smoothly between the power plant and the zone. But if you do see the symbols, then you must investigate where the break in the power line is, and reconnect the interrupted portion of the line. When power is restored, the flashing power symbols should disappear.

Be sure that you construct the power lines *into the zone itself.* The closer the Sims are to the power line, the faster they will move in, so you can speed the pace of construction by building a network of power lines *inside* the zone. Power is transmitted from building to building but cannot cross roads, rails, water, undeveloped zones,[8] or zone boundaries without a power line. Also, if you build a road inside a residential zone, the divided residential zone must have a power line to connect the unpowered half of the zone to the powered half. You *must* build power lines between zones in order for power

---

[8]Without power line connections, new buildings will crop up in an undeveloped zone only if they are adjacent to powered buildings.

to be transmitted, with one exception: If there are two buildings opposing one another on a zone boundary, those buildings will transmit power across the boundary.

Unlike *SimCity Classic*, there is *no power loss* from power lines due to line resistance. This is a bit unrealistic in the real world, of course, but this is how it is in *SimCity 2000*.

To summarize:

- Power is transmitted from building to building[9] or via power lines.
- To expedite growth, power lines can be built inside a zone.
- The Sims will merely convert the power lines to buildings when they need to.
- Power lines need to be built across roads, rails, and empty zones in order for power to be distributed.
- There must be an unbroken chain of power lines from a power plant to zones and buildings for power to be transmitted.
- There is no power loss from power lines.

Bulldozing Your Mistakes

Because you will inevitably make mistakes or make changes in your land-use policies, you will need to know how to use the Bulldozer. The Bulldozer allows you to:

- Demolish/Clear all buildings, zones, or objects
- Level terrain
- Raise terrain
- Lower terrain
- De-zone previously created zones

To use the Bulldozer, you must first select which type of work you want done from the Bulldozer submenu options. The procedure for selecting the submenu commands is always the same: Hold down the mouse button on the Bulldozer icon, and then move the pointer over the pop-up submenu command you wish to activate. Release the mouse button, move the pointer over the map, and click the mouse button over the terrain, buildings, infrastructure, or zones that you wish to bulldoze.

On the Macintosh you can summon the Bull-dozer while using any other tool by pressing and holding down B. You can bulldoze on the PC in this way by holding down the Ctrl key while clicking the mouse.

---

[9]Any public structure that you build, including water pumps, marinas, and water towers, will transmit power. Only small and large parks do not transmit power.

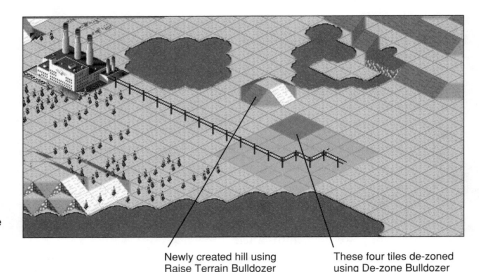

Figure 1-8
The art of bulldozing: clearing and raising the elevation of terrain

Newly created hill using
Raise Terrain Bulldozer

These four tiles de-zoned
using De-zone Bulldozer

Let's first try de-zoning a small portion of our residential zone by using the **De-zone** Bulldozer, and then try elevating some terrain by using the **Raise Terrain** Bulldozer. First, select the **De-zone** option under the Bulldozer's submenu, and then drag the pointer over some residential zones. Figure 1-8 shows the effect of de-zoning one corner of your residential zone. Next, try using the Raise Terrain Bulldozer: Select the Raise Terrain option under the Bulldozer's submenu and then click the mouse pointer on some nearby terrain. You will see a new hill crop up where you clicked the mouse pointer, as shown in Figure 1-8. In order to bulldoze or demolish any structures, trees, or buildings, use the Demolish/Clear Bulldozer. If you want, you can try bulldozing a few trees or power lines, but be sure to replace the power lines you do destroy.

By the same token, you can lower terrain by selecting the **Lower Terrain** command, and you can level terrain so that it is uniformly flat by selecting the same command. The **Level Terrain** Bulldozer "locks in" whatever altitude level you initially click on the map, and it will raise or lower terrain to match this altitude as you drag the Bulldozer around the map.

Creating Zones for Industries

A city without industry and commerce will not survive long. Therefore, your next order of business is to create a zone where industry and factories can be established, thus jump-starting the local economy. As a general principle, industrial zones should not be placed side by side with residential zones, for they emit pollution and tend to depress land values. A wise course of action might be to buffer the residential and industrial zones from each other with parks or commercial zones, but the separation should be more than three blocks, if at all possible.

Industrial zones, like residential zones, have two zone densities: Light and Heavy. Different kinds of industries are encouraged or discouraged by the zone type you choose. For example, heavy industrial zones include such industries as steel mining, textiles, and aerospace, whereas light industrial zones can include industries such as electronics, finance, and media. Before deciding which kind of industry you wish to push on your city, you should consider the availability of technology and the chronological year. It wouldn't do, for example, to build light industry exclusively in the year 1900, expecting that a booming electronics industry will spawn. If the technology has not yet been invented, then you cannot expect industry to exploit it. Therefore, in 1900, it might be more appropriate to emphasize high-density steel, automotive, and textiles production.

Select the Dense Industrial zone type by clicking on the Industry tool, and while holding down the mouse button, pick the **Dense** option. After you release the mouse button, notice that the Status window shows the price to zone each tile of heavy industrial land— $10.

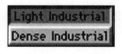

Looking at your map, choose a section of your city that is relatively flat and within easy transportation range of your residential zones. Click and drag over the map a rectangular swath of land that is approximately equivalent in size to your residential zone.[10] Note that the cost increases as you stretch the zone ever larger. You might try something like the layout shown in Figure 1-9.

Don't forget to add power lines to connect the industrial zone to the residential zone, as pictured in Figure 1-10.

---

[10]For simplicity's sake, in this example we are not following the zone ratio rule of $R = I + C$, where R is the number of tiles contained in your residential zones, I is the number of tiles contained in your industrial zones, and C is the number of tiles contained in your commercial zones. Normally, you would want to create an industrial zone that is half the size of your residential zone, and then follow up by building a commercial zone that is also half the size of your residential zone. This $R = I + C$ ratio would then be properly balanced.

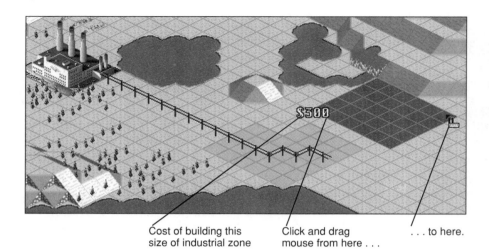

Figure 1-9
Let's go industrial!

Cost of building this   Click and drag   . . . to here.
size of industrial zone   mouse from here . . .

Figure 1-10
Don't forget to add
power lines.

Extend power lines
into industrial zone

Zoning Commercial Districts

To complete the zonal triad, you will need to build commercial zones so that
the Sims can shop, perform services, and conduct other business.

As with residential and industrial zones, there are Dense Commercial
and Light Commercial zones. For this exercise, we'll go ahead with building
a Dense Commercial zone, so hold down the mouse on the Commercial
Zones icon and select the Dense option.

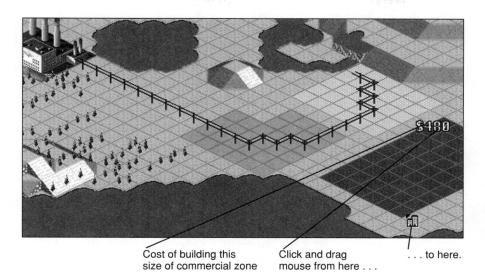

Cost of building this
size of commercial zone

Click and drag
mouse from here . . .

. . . to here.

Figure 1-11
Planning for a
Walgreens and K-mart

After moving the pointer over the map, locate a convenient flat spot near your residential zones for a future Walgreens and K-mart. Click and drag a rectangular zone, similar in size to the residential and industrial zones you previously created, as shown in Figure 1-11.

Don't forget to add power lines to provide needed electricity for the zone. Connect your power lines to the commercial zone by linking them to the power lines that are already functioning in the industrial and residential zones.

Building Roads to Link Your Zones

There remains but one step to complete before the Sims will move in *en masse*. You must build roads and/or other transportation links between the three different zones types. The Sims will not be happy until they can travel to and from one zone type to the other two. For example, Sims in a residential zone will attempt to journey to an industrial zone, return, and then travel to a commercial zone. If the Sims are frustrated by impediments, they will give up and your zones will not develop. This also means that if traffic is heavy and you are experiencing traffic bottlenecks, those Sims who have trouble getting from zone to zone will leave town, and their domiciles, places of commerce, and industry will wither away. When this happens, you will notice that your buildings turn black or charcoal gray and shrivel up, eventually decaying away altogether.

Click and hold down the mouse button on the Roads icon and you will see a pop-up submenu appear with the following choices:[11]

- Road
- Tunnel

Since you are mostly interested in simple road links at this time, select the Road option.

Roads, highways, and rails can be laid directly over empty zones, but it is better to plan ahead and build your transportation infrastructure first, *before* zoning. If you build your transportation on top of your zones (in other words, after you have already zoned), you will needlessly waste money on the zones that become "de-zoned" underneath the road, rail, or highway tiles. To simplify matters here, we have purposely ignored this economic truth, but you should be aware of it when building your own cities.

In order to be effective, no zone or building should be farther than three blocks away from a road, rail depot, or subway station. *SimCity 2000* does not allow the Sims to travel farther than three blocks to any road, rail depot, or subway station. If this distance is exceeded, the trip will fail.[12]

Unlike *SimCity Classic*, rails do not allow zones to use them directly. Any Sim wishing to travel by rail *or* subway must first travel to a train depot or subway station to embark or disembark. The three block-tile transportation-range limit rule applies here, too. Thus, to use the subway or train directly, the Sims must find a station or depot that is *less* than three blocks from them.[13]

With this design consideration in mind, you shouldn't build zones that are larger than six tiles in width, without an intervening road. A tile size of 6×4, 6×5, 6×6, 6×7, or longer is OK for zones, but—ideally—each zone tile would like to access two roads. Figure 1-12 shows one possible road layout for your city.

One ideal zone layout would have you carve up your zones into a cookie cutter-shaped pattern of 6 x 6 blocks, circumscribed by roads. This way, each zone tile would be served by at least two roads.

---

[11]The Highway, Onramp, and Bus Station options will not be visible on this menu just yet. They have not been invented.

[12]In some cases where you have high-density zones, there is an exception to the three-block rule. If you have a building that is four tiles or larger, where at least one tile of the building is within three blocks of a road, subway station, or rail depot, the building can prosper even though the other tiles inside it are farther than three blocks from the nearest road, railroad depot, or subway station.

[13]There is an exception to this three-block rule for subway stations and railroad depots: If you build road connections to the station or depot, those Sims farther than three blocks away who can reach the road can also use the station or depot.

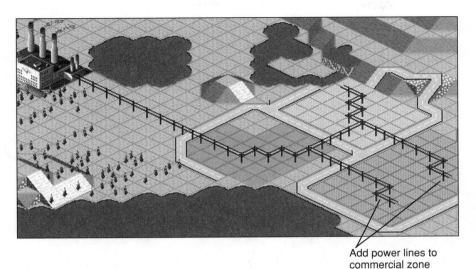

Figure 1-12
No zone should be farther than three blocks from a road, rail, or subway station.

Add power lines to commercial zone

You should start to see some construction activity after your roads have been completed. Notice how buildings appear, sometimes disappear, and then are replaced by dark, abandoned buildings. This sequence of events tells you that the Sims have moved in, found something not to their liking, and moved out, leaving an abandoned derelict building. Your job is to try to entice them to stay, and you do this by making the city attractive for them. For instance, you provide access to jobs, transportation, power, water, convenient shopping, good education, police and fire protection,[14] and recreational facilities.

A Bridge over Troubled Waters

Because you will often need to cross water to link your city with other transportation, you will need to know how to build a bridge.

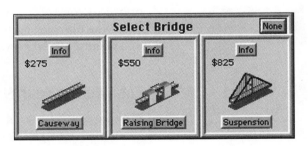

To build any road bridge, simply select the Road tool and then click and drag across the water channel. If you have done this correctly, you will see a dialog box of bridge options pop up on screen. Each bridge type has its advantages and disadvantages with regard to ship traffic, building costs, and maintenance costs.

---

[14]Fire protection does not have a direct effect on city growth. In the event of a disaster, however, your city will benefit from having emergency crews available for damage control.

Figure 1-13
Constructing your
bridge

Causeway bridge. Note that the addition
of roads has caused a building boom.

Of the three different bridge types, one or more may not appear in this
dialog box because the length of the water channel is either too long or too
short for the bridge type in question.

Let's bridge the gap across the river that divides your city. Select the
Road menu suboption under the Road tool and then click and drag the
pointer across the water. You should immediately see the Bridges dialog box
asking which bridge you wish to choose from. For now, select the Causeway
bridge to construct the bridge shown in Figure 1-13. If you are confused
about the different bridges, click the INFO button to obtain more information about the relative merits and demerits of the three bridges.

Engineering Your Water System

Without a proper water and sewage system, no city can ever really flourish
and grow into a great metropolis. Though you needn't bother with a water
system for a small village, if you want your city's population to grow larger,
you will need to provide for water and sewage.

Water is distributed through large water mains and smaller water pipes.
The small pipes are automatically constructed under buildings that both you
and the Sims build. The large water mains, however, can be built only by

you, and they will connect to the smaller pipes automatically if they are in close proximity. *SimCity 2000* has an underground view of your city, which you can easily bring up on screen by clicking the Underground button on the Toolbar. This view allows you to see all water pipes, both large and small, as well as your subway system.

Click the Underground button now to see the subterranean view of your city. Click it once again to return to your normal aboveground view of the city.

To build a complete water system you will need:

- Pipes to distribute the water
- Pumps to pump the water out of wells, rivers, and aquifers; pumps also circulate the water in the pipes
- Water towers to bank excess water for periods where water demand soars, or when there is a drought

Later on, when you have accreted more technology, you can build water desalinization facilities to expand the supply of water, and treatment plants to reduce water pollution.

Let's build some pipes and pumps now to establish your first local water supply and distribution network.

Laying Water Pipes

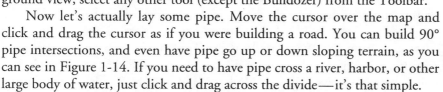 While in the Toolbar, click and hold down the mouse button on the Water icon till you see the **Water** submenu shown below. Select the **Pipes** command. Notice that once you have selected **Pipes**, the City window shows the underground view of your city. To return to the aboveground view, select any other tool (except the Bulldozer) from the Toolbar.

Now let's actually lay some pipe. Move the cursor over the map and click and drag the cursor as if you were building a road. You can build 90° pipe intersections, and even have pipe go up or down sloping terrain, as you can see in Figure 1-14. If you need to have pipe cross a river, harbor, or other large body of water, just click and drag across the divide—it's that simple.

One word of advice: You may want to build your water pipes underneath your roads, since they more or less parallel all development in the city.

Constructing Water Pumps

To get water flowing through your new pipes, you must build water pumping stations. These facilities have two simultaneous functions: They pump water out of the ground, and they circulate the water through the pipes.

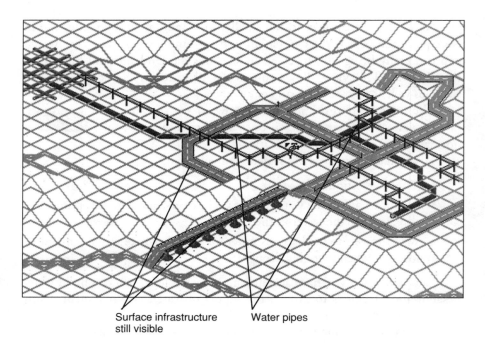

Figure 1-14
The subterranean view
of your city while laying
water pipes

Surface infrastructure   Water pipes
still visible

Since they rely on motors that require electricity, water pumps must be connected to power lines in order to work.

Water pumps introduce new water into your water system, and the amount of water they produce is a function of their location and the current weather. When placed next to a lake or river, pumps produce two to five times[15] as much water as a land-locked pump or a pump placed on a saltwater coastline. You can easily check the output of your water pumps, or check on the salinity of nearby water, by using the Query tool on the Toolbar.

Go ahead and build a few water pumps by selecting the **Water Pump** command from the Water tool on the Toolbar. You can place the water pumps in either the aboveground or underground view of your city; to switch between views, click the Underground button. Be sure to place water pumps on or adjacent to your water pipes, and also make sure that you connect them to your power grid. If all goes well, you will see water pulsating through your water mains in the underground view of your city (as in Figure 1-15), although you may not see the pulsating pipes right next to your water pump. The reason for this will be explained in Chapter 2. When finished building the water pumps, return to the aboveground view of your city.

---

[15]The more water surrounding the pump, the more water the pump can deliver.

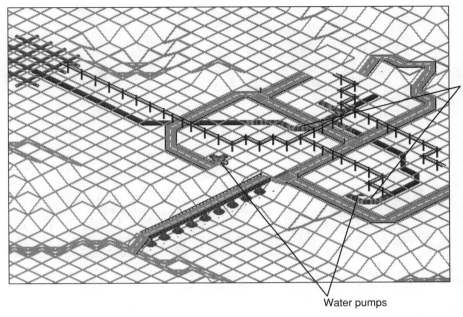

Notice pulsating water
flow in pipes here.
These pipe sections
are the only ones with
water actually flowing
through them.

Figure 1-5
Water pumps produce
water, but need to be
connected to power
lines and pipes to
function.

Water pumps

Using the Query Tool

SimCity 2000 offers a new tool to spy on each block of your city. The Query
tool on the Toolbar allows you to get specific information about any object,
block, or building in *SimCity* by simply clicking on it. Thus, for example,
you can click on the Police Department and find out whether it has power,
how much crime there has been, and how effective the police department has
been in apprehending criminals. In the same way, you can investigate any
zone's or building's land value, crime level, availability of water and power,
and many other tidbits of information.

To access the Query tool, click on its icon and then click on any block,
building, or object on the map. A Query text box will then open,
giving you vital information about the object you clicked on.

UNDERSTANDING FUNDING AND BUDGETING

SimCity 2000 prompts you to set your city's yearly budget each January
using a special Budget window, although you can easily make changes on a
monthly basis if you so wish. In the budget window, you can set your tax
rates, and allocate money for education, money for police and fire protec-

You can also bring up
the Query text box
shown in Figure 1-16,
while using any other
tool, by simply holding
down the Shift key and
clicking on the map.

Figure 1-16 Click the
Query tool on any
object on the map. You
will see a Query text
box open, revealing
vital statistical information about the object.

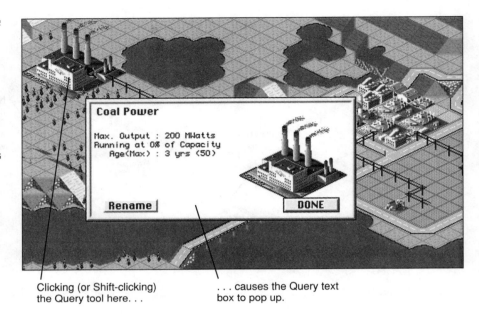

Clicking (or Shift-clicking)
the Query tool here. . .

. . . causes the Query text
box to pop up.

tion, money for health, and money for transit maintenance. You can also
pass ordinances that affect your city.

You can wait until January for the Budget window to open, or you can
open the budget window at any time by clicking on the Budget icon on the
Toolbar (you can also open it from the **Windows** menu). If you don't want
to be bothered by the Budget window opening each year and would rather
have things stay as they are, you can toggle the **Auto-Budget** command on
the **Options** menu. The Budget window closes automatically after two minutes have elapsed, as graphically depicted by the hourglass symbol emptying
its sand in the upper-left corner of the window. The two-minute timer is
reset whenever the simulator detects any activity on your part.

For now, open the Budget window, as pictured in Figure 1-17, by clicking on the Budget tool.

In the Budget window there are eight departmental categories, each with
an Advisor icon and Book icon. The Police, Fire, Health & Welfare, Education, and Transit Authority departments each have arrow buttons for
increasing or decreasing the amount of funding. Normally you will want to
keep budgeting all departments at 100 percent of their yearly request, but in
times of economic hardship, you can reduce funding to save money. The
Property Taxes department also includes arrows for separately increasing or
decreasing the tax rates on industry, commerce, and residences. To access
these arrows, you must first click on the Property Tax Book icon in the row

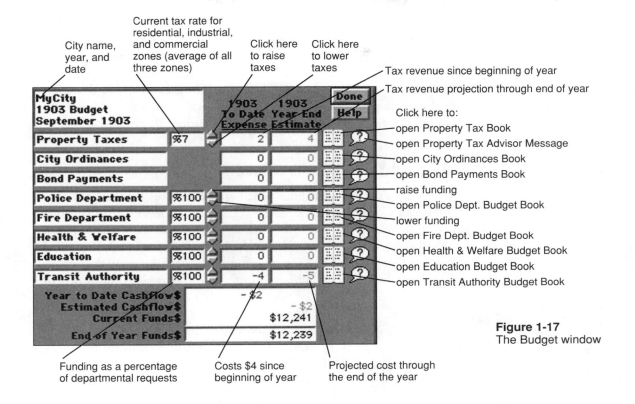

City name, year, and date

Current tax rate for residential, industrial, and commercial zones (average of all three zones)

Click here to raise taxes

Click here to lower taxes

Tax revenue since beginning of year

Tax revenue projection through end of year

Click here to:
open Property Tax Book
open Property Tax Advisor Message
open City Ordinances Book
open Bond Payments Book
raise funding
open Police Dept. Budget Book
lower funding
open Fire Dept. Budget Book
open Health & Welfare Budget Book
open Education Budget Book
open Transit Authority Budget Book

Funding as a percentage of departmental requests

Costs $4 since beginning of year

Projected cost through the end of the year

Figure 1-17
The Budget window

that lists Property Taxes, and then, when the book opens up, select the up or down arrow button to raise or lower taxes for each zone category.

If you are unsure about what each department does, you can summon instant on-screen explanations by holding down the Shift key and clicking on the department name.

The first column of budget numbers show the current year's expenses and revenues, whereas the second column shows the estimated budget figures through the end of the fiscal year, using projections of current policies. At the bottom of the window, you can see a summary of your cash flow, along with calculations for your End of Year fund balance. Obviously, the more red ink you see, the higher the probability that you will run out of money and will have to take out a bond.

If you click on the Advisor icon, which looks like a question mark, you can get free advice from the head of each department on what you should do.

Let's consult with your Mayoral Advisors from every department to see what kind of advice they have to offer. Click on each Advisor icon and see what they have to say.

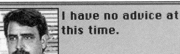

As long as we are tinkering around with the budget, let's go ahead and lower taxes to encourage some growth (a fundamental precept of "supply-side economics"). Click on the down arrow next to the 7 percent tax rate, until your tax rate is 5 percent. If your computer comes equipped with a sound card or you have a Macintosh, you will be greeted with a thunderous cheer from the populace. Conversely, if you raise taxes, you will hear a chorus of boos and catcalls from your irate constituents.

Bailing Out Your City with a Bond

Yes, *SimCity 2000* now includes deficit spending! You too can imitate the U.S. Federal Government's largesse by taking in less money than you spend and then financing the difference with bonds. Of course, you are obligated to pay the yearly interest on the bonds, but you can avoid paying off the principal as long as you like (or can afford to!). Each January, the accumulated interest from each bond is subtracted from your city's funds, whether or not your city has enough money to cover the interest. If you don't have enough money at the end of the year to pay off the interest, you will show a negative balance, indicating a budget deficit. You are allowed a deficit of as much as $100,000 before you are deposed as Mayor and lose your city.[16]

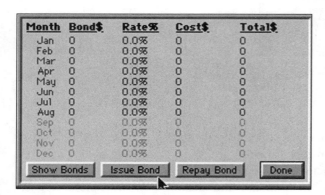

Bonds can be taken out only in $10,000 increments, and the interest that is charged varies from year to year. The interest rate, based on the Federal Prime Interest Rate, fluctuates with changes in the economy and your city's infrastructure value.

To take out a bond, follow these steps:

1. Open the Budget window.
2. Click on the Bond Payments Book button.
3. In the Bonds window (shown above), click the Issue Bond button.
4. When prompted to accept the interest rate, click Yes.

---

[16] If you have not saved your city when this happens, you will lose it forever, since Sim-City does not give you chance to save your city when you go bust.

5. Click the Done button to exit the Bonds window and return to the Budget window.

6. Back in the Budget window, note that you now have $10,000 that you didn't have before.

7. Exit the Budget window by clicking the Done button.

Good! Now you have learned how to handle your basic budget needs. In later chapters, we will delve into the other intricacies of the Budget window.

The Demand Indicators

If you have ever played *SimCity* before, you will recognize the Demand Indicators on the Toolbar. These three bar graphs show you the relative demand by the Sims for more residential, commercial, and industrial zones. The higher the bars on the positive side of the graph, the more demand there is for that particular zone type. Likewise, the lower the bars on the negative side of the graph, the less demand there is for the respective zone type. These three indicators probably constitute the most important barometer of your city's health, since they instantaneously show whether your city is growing or declining.

If you see that the residential column is on the positive side of the graph, but that the commercial and industrial columns are on the negative side, then you know that you need to build more residential zones and fewer commercial and industrial zones, since there may now be a glut of the latter two.[17]

THE THIRD ESTATE: NEWSPAPERS

A new feature of *SimCity 2000*, the newspapers announce important events, explain new discoveries, chronicle disasters and weather conditions, and report on many other topics of interest. You can subscribe to up to six newspapers in a large city, but generally one newspaper at the start up of a new

---

[17]The Demand Indicator is only a rough gauge of your zone balances. For example, if the Demand Indicator shows a negative demand for commerce and industry, it may be caused by the lack of an airport or seaport and not have anything to do with whether or not you have a surplus of industrial and commercial zones. Instead, for a more accurate count of your zone ratios, use the Graphs window to check on the exact residential, commercial, and industrial zone populations. If the ratios are in the correct proportions, you should have $R = C + I$, where R = residential zone population, C = commercial zone population, and I = industrial zone population.

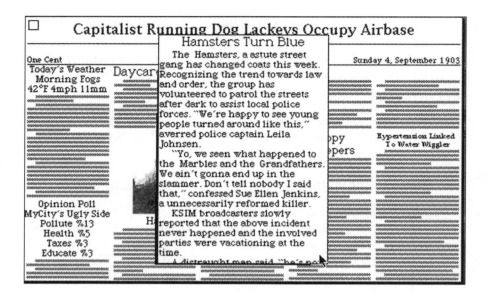

Figure 1-18 Reading the newspaper

city is sufficient reading. To bring up the newspaper, select it from the **Newspaper** menu. You close the Newspaper window by clicking on the close button on the upper-left corner of the newspaper. There are several delivery options: either a full subscription, which gives you a newspaper twice a year, or only Extras, which gives you a newspaper only when something dramatically new occurs or something new has been invented.

Bring up the newspaper for reading now by clicking on the **Newspaper** menu, and select one of the newspapers listed. When it appears (as in Figure 1-18), you can read any article by clicking on it to zoom in and see the fine print. When you are done, close the newspaper by clicking on the upper-left button in the window.

SAVING YOUR CITY TO DISK FOR LATER PLAY

Saving your city to disk is important if you wish to play your city at some later time. To save your city, open the **File** menu and select the **Save City As** option.

In a moment, the Save As dialog box will appear on screen. Enter the name of your city. By default, your city will be stored in the SC2000

directory on the PC, or the *SimCity 2000* folder on the Macintosh; if you
need to, you can change the directory to which the city is stored by clicking
on a directory name in the list box. Remember, the DOS filename can

include only eight characters, and certain punctu-
ation marks are not acceptable in the name. Click
the Save button and then quit the game by selecting **Quit** from the **File** menu.

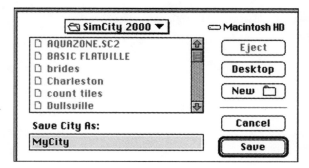

   The next time you save your city, you can
choose the **Save City** option in the **File** menu.
Choosing this command will cause your city to be
saved automatically using the current name of
your city in the previous directory location. If you
want to rename the city or save it to a different
directory, use the **Save City As** option under the
File menu.

   Congratulations: You have created your first viable city! In the next
chapter, you will be introduced to each individual tool and how it is used.

C H A P T E R

2

Tools of the Trade

Most of your activity in *SimCity 2000* takes place in the City window using the tool icons found on the Toolbar. This chapter guides you through the 34 icon tools, and acquaints you with their use and misuse.

MAKING SELECTIONS

To select an icon, point and click the pointer on the 3-D icon button so that it looks depressed. When you click on one of the 17 tool icons at the top of the Toolbar, the pointer in the City window will assume the profile of the button you selected. As you move the pointer around the screen, a shadow will follow it showing exactly where the intended building or object will be placed. For example, when you select the City Services button (it looks like a police badge) and choose the Police station, the pointer changes into a police badge. When you move the pointer, a tan rectangle will follow closely, showing exactly where the police department will be placed if you click the mouse button. Figure 2-1 shows the Toolbar and identifies all the icon buttons.

You can move the Toolbar anywhere on screen by clicking and dragging the top bar. If you forget what a particular button does, you can instantly summon on-screen help by holding down the Shift key and then clicking on the button in question.

The buttons on the top five rows of the Toolbar each have submenus from which you must specify the tool you wish to use. To access these submenus, click and hold down your mouse button on the Toolbar button. Before releasing your mouse button, wait for a pop-up menu to appear from which you will select one of the tools.

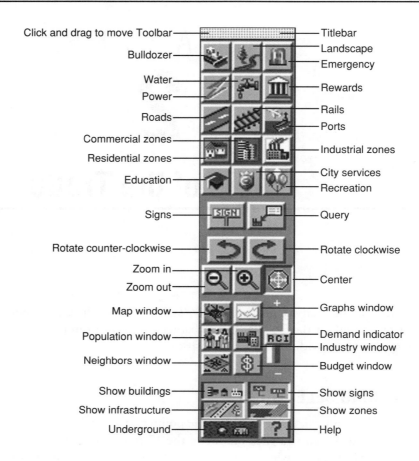

Click and drag to move Toolbar —
Bulldozer —
Water —
Power —
Roads —
Commercial zones —
Residential zones —
Education —
Signs —
Rotate counter-clockwise —
Zoom in —
Zoom out —
Map window —
Population window —
Neighbors window —
Show buildings —
Show infrastructure —
Underground —

— Titlebar
— Landscape
— Emergency
— Rewards
— Rails
— Ports
— Industrial zones
— City services
— Recreation
— Query
— Rotate clockwise
— Center
— Graphs window
— Demand indicator
— Industry window
— Budget window
— Show signs
— Show zones
— Help

Figure 2-1
The *SimCity 2000*
Toolbar

You may notice that two of the buttons on the Toolbar, the Emergency and Rewards buttons, are ghosted out and are unavailable for use. This is because there are no emergencies to report and you have not earned any rewards yet. Rewards are triggered by achieving certain population and city size goals.

UNDERSTANDING MICROSIMS

Microsims are localized simulations that track local statistics. They are updated once a year in January, and they exist for most of the special types of buildings and zones you can build in *SimCity 2000*. The information that they keep track of is available for you to see when you click the Query tool on any building or Microsim-based object. Only 150 Microsims are allowed per city.[1] Although you can build more than 150 such Microsim-based buildings and structures, localized statistics will not be kept for objects beyond the 150th, even though their global effects will still be felt in the simulation.

Microsims are available for:

- Power plants
- City hall
- Hospitals
- Police departments
- Fire departments
- Schools
- Colleges
- Prisons
- Zoos
- Statues
- The mayor's house
- Water treatment plants
- Desalinization plants
- Arcologies
- Llama domes
- Bus stations
- Rail stations
- Subway stations
- Parks
- Museums
- Libraries
- Marinas

USING THE STATUS WINDOW

The Status window (Figure 2-2), located next to your Toolbar, displays important information about your city. This floating window, like the Toolbar, can be easily moved anywhere on your screen by clicking and dragging the top of it with the mouse. The Status window displays the current tool you have selected on the Toolbar and the cost of using that tool. An iconic display in the Status window tells you what the current weather conditions are, and there is a message-and-recommendation line that informs you of the city's most pressing needs. You should glance periodically at the message that

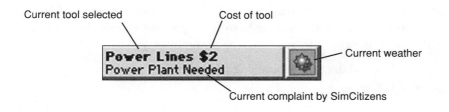

Current tool selected

Cost of tool

Power Lines $2
Power Plant Needed

Current weather

Current complaint by SimCitizens

Figure 2-2
The Status window tells you the cost of your currently selected tool, the current weather conditions, and demands being made by your citizens.

[1]Arcologies are excepted, being limited to 140 in the DOS version of *SimCity 2000*. In the Macintosh Version 1.1 and the Windows Version 1.0, this limitation is removed, and you can build more than 140 arcologies, with an attendant increase in population.

Table 2-1 Weather Conditions as Displayed in the Status Window			
Weather Icon	**Description**	**Weather Icon**	**Description**
	Snow		Chilly weather, low temperatures, wind chill
	Hot day		Overcast day
	High winds		Rain
	Clear skies, beautiful weather		Tornado
	Cold front, temperatures dropping into the thirties		Hurricane
	Fog		

is displayed to find out what your SimCitizens are demanding. Table 2-1 gives a description of each of the weather icons that is displayed in the Status window.

USING THE TOOLS

All building and zoning tools are found on the Toolbar. When you click and hold down the mouse button while selecting any of the top 15 icons on the Toolbar, a pop-up submenu opens to reveal more choices. After highlighting the menu option you want, you select the appropriate zone or object you wish to build by releasing the mouse button. To actually place the zone, building, or object on the map, move the mouse pointer over your City window, and then click the mouse button. If you are zoning; bulldozing; or building roads, rails, subways, pipes, or power lines, you can:

- Click and drag the mouse pointer to work on a larger area
- Click on each individual tile

Using the Bulldozers

There are five types of bulldozers in *SimCity 2000*. Each bulldozer performs a specialized function and has different costs associated with it. Bulldozers are used to clear land or destroy buildings and infrastructure; raise, lower, and level terrain; and remove previously established zones.

To access the Bulldozer submenu, hold down the mouse button while selecting the Bulldozer tool from the Toolbar. As you do this, you will see a pop-up menu appear to the right of the icon button.

When you use the Bulldozer, it costs you money. Table 2-2 shows the relative costs per tile of land for each bulldozer type.

Table 2-2 Bulldozing Costs

Action	Cost
Demolish/clear	$1 per tile
Level terrain	$25 per tile
Raise terrain	$25 per tile
Lower terrain	$25 per tile
De-zone	$1 per tile

Demolish/Clear Bulldozer

The Demolish/Clear bulldozer removes and clears all buildings, infrastructure (roads, power lines, rails, bridges, tunnels, water mains, subways, and so forth), trees, and rubble. It will also fill in or cover up shallow streams and ponds, but it will not fill in land along coasts or larger bodies of water (unless you created the water with the Landscape/Water tool). Operating the bulldozer is simple: after selecting the Demolish/Clear command from the Bulldozer menu, just click and drag on the map or click on any object to begin bulldozing. There is also a much easier way to bulldoze on the Macintosh or PC. On the PC, simply hold down the Ctrl key and then click the left mouse button on any object. (You can do this while any other tool is selected!). On the Macintosh, hold down the B key and click the mouse button.

There is a special technique used for removing underground objects such as subways and water mains. Here's how:

1. Select the Underground tool from the Toolbar. You will see an underground view of your city.

2. Select the **Demolish/Clear** command from the Bulldozer submenu, and then click the mouse button to start bulldozing. If you prefer, you can bulldoze on the PC by holding down the Ctrl key and then clicking the left mouse button, or on the Macintosh by holding down the B key and clicking.

Level Terrain Bulldozer

Use this special bulldozing tool as a means to level uneven terrain, or to create bay fill or landfill for water. Here's how to use it:

1. Select the **Level Terrain** command from the Bulldozer submenu.

2. Choose a tile that is close to the area you wish to level, and that is at the altitude you want.

3. Starting from this tile of land, click and drag the bulldozer icon towards the mountains, gorges, valleys, or water that you wish to bring to this altitude.

The Level Terrain bulldozer will automatically clear the land of all trees, roads, power lines, and buildings in the area that you are raising or lowering. It will not bulldoze land at the same elevation as your starting point. For this you must still use the Demolish/Clear bulldozer.

Raise Terrain Bulldozer

The Raise Terrain bulldozer allows you to sculpt land by making mountains and hills rise out of seemingly flat land. Each click of the mouse button causes a pyramid-shaped mound of land to rise beneath the bulldozer cursor. Note that as you raise your mini-mountain with each click, it becomes more and more costly. This is because the cost for elevating each land tile increases with the area of your pyramid. Figure 2-3 and Table 2-3 show the geometric increase in cost as you increase the height of the mountain by 100 feet with each successive click of the Raise Terrain bulldozer.

When you use the Raise Terrain bulldozer, watch out for nearby buildings and structures. If you use this bulldozer tool next to previously built structures, they will be destroyed, and you will have to rebuild them. Remember that raising one tile of land actually affects *at least eight* tiles around it, making them slopes, and causing buildings or structures sitting on them to be bulldozed.[2]

Figure 2-3
The cost of a mountain increases geometrically as the height increases.

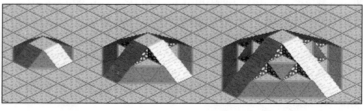

One click   Two clicks   Three clicks

[2]Actually, when you raise more than one tile of terrain, even more surrounding tiles around the base of the raised area are affected, causing buildings and structures farther away to be pulverized. Therefore, exercise caution when raising terrain in urban areas.

Table 2-3 Costs of Using the Raise Terrain Bulldozer

Number of Mouse Clicks	Altitude Gained (Feet)	Number of Tiles Elevated	Cost ($)
1	100	1	25
2	200	5	125
3	300	13	325
4	400	25	625
5	500	41	1,025

As you can easily see, the cost of lowering, raising, and leveling terrain gets more prohibitive with each successive 100-foot change in altitude. The moral here is this: Do your terraforming in terrain-editing mode before you create your city, or you will quickly go bust.

Lower Terrain Bulldozer

The Lower Terrain bulldozer allows you to lower the altitude of selected tiles of land. If you lower the selected land too much, however, you will go below the water table, and the hole will fill up with water. As with **Raise Terrain**, if you click on a selected tile more than once, the cost of lowering the land's altitude will increase geometrically with each additional click. Note that each click of the Lower Terrain bulldozer lowers the altitude of the land by 100 feet.

As with the Raise Terrain bulldozer, if you use the Lower Terrain bulldozer next to previously built structures, they will be obliterated and you will have to rebuild them. Remember that lowering one tile of land actually affects *at least eight* tiles around it, making them slopes, and this will cause structures sitting on them to be bulldozed down.[3] Table 2-4 details the costs associated with this tool.

De-Zone

As the name implies, the **De-Zone** command is used to remove any previously created zones. You can, however, de-zone only empty zones—zones

---

[3]When you lower terrain by more than one tile, even more surrounding tiles around the base are affected, causing buildings and structures farther away to be pulverized. Therefore, excercise caution when lowering terrain in urban areas.

Table 2-4 Costs of Using the Lower Terrain Bulldozer			
Number of Mouse Clicks	Altitude Lost (Feet)	Number of Tiles Lowered	Cost ($)
1	100	1	25
2	200	5	125
3	300	13	325
4	400	25	625
5	500	41	1,025

that have no buildings on them. If a zone is occupied, you must bulldoze it clear before you can de-zone it, except in the case of rubble. You can use the De-Zone bulldozer to remove large areas of rubble to help extinguish fires. See the Chapter 10 for information on how to do this.

Here is the procedure for removing zones:

1. Pull down the **Speed** menu and select **Pause**. You need to do this because the simulation moves so quickly that, by the time you bulldoze clear the zone, the Sims will rebuild it.
2. Select the Bulldozer tool and choose **Demolish/Clear** from the pop-up submenu.
3. Bulldoze the zone clear of any buildings.
4. Select the Bulldozer tool, and choose **De-Zone** from the pop-up submenu.
5. Click and drag the De-Zone tool over the zone you wish to remove, and then release the mouse button.

This technique will remove any type of zone. If, on the other hand, you wish merely to rezone an existing zone, just drag the new zone over the old zone, but only if the old zone is first cleared of buildings and structures.

Landscaping

Click and hold down the mouse button on the Landscape tool and you will see two options: Trees and Water. Both tools allow you to add landscape features to the land. Table 2-5 shows the costs of each.

Table 2-5 Landscaping Costs

Landscape Feature		Cost
	Trees	$3 per click
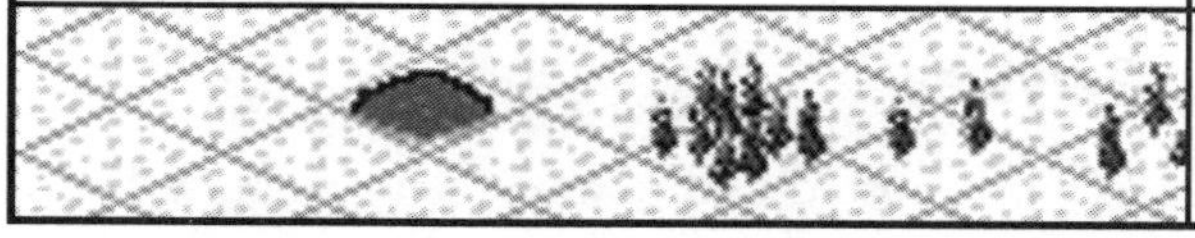	Water	$100 per tile

Trees

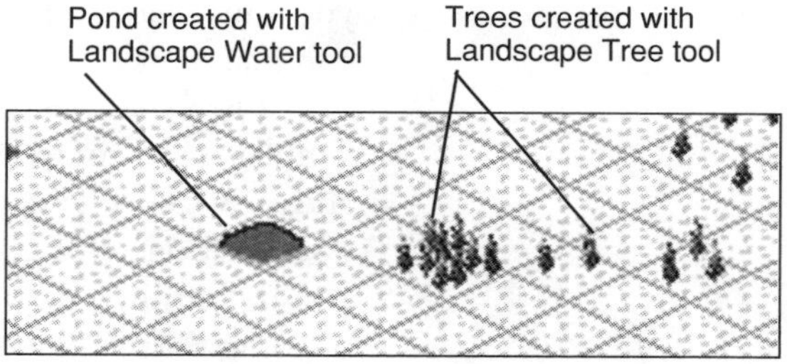

Each click on the Trees tool on the map adds another tree or two to the land, and costs $3, as you can see in Figure 2-4. Trees add to land values, and this makes the city more attractive for your residents to live in. Don't click more than six or seven times on any particular tile, since you can't add any more trees than this, but you will nonetheless get billed $3 a pop for the attempted tree planting. You can either add trees individually or add forests collectively.

Pond created with
Landscape Water tool

Trees created with
Landscape Tree tool

Figure 2-4
Adding trees and
water to your city

There is a secret "Magic Eraser" effect that you can get by using the Trees tool. To access this function, select the Trees tool and then click and hold down the mouse button. Next, press Shift, and move the mouse pointer around the map to erase any building, object, or zone. Using this technique, you can reduce the size of polluting power plants or overlap some buildings. Unfortunately, the output of the power plant is reduced in proportion to the number of tiles you erase. The Magic Eraser seems to work best on arcologies: You can erase the arcology and reduce its negative influences, but still keep the arcology population.

Water

By using the Water tool, you can create lakes, waterfalls on hills, ponds, rivers, and streams. This tool is especially handy when you want to increase the capacity of your water pumps. If you surround a water pump with water, it will double or even triple its output over what it would be on dry land.

If you want to build a hydroelectric facility on a hill where there is no

water, use this tool to create the waterfalls necessary to run the generators, as pictured at right.

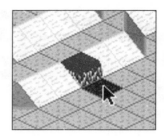

Creating water raises land values for nearby
zones and buildings. Water can also be used as a
way to block the passage of fires.

Providing Emergency Services

The Emergency button is usually ghosted and unavailable for use. When a
disaster occurs somewhere in the city, the button becomes activated, allowing you to dispatch firefighters, police, and the military (if you have a military base that is not a missile silo) to the scene of the calamity. Of course,
you must have built a police or fire department before you can use this
command.

When the Emergency tool becomes active at the onset of a disaster, the
simulator's chronological clock stops. Although you can still zone or even
add new police and fire stations, the newly added zones and buildings will
not function until the disaster is over. Thus it does no good to combat an
already burning fire by adding additional fire stations, and you can't suppress
ongoing riots by building new police stations.

Dispatching Emergency Units to Disasters

To dispatch the fire department, the police department, or the military,
simply:

1. Click and hold the mouse button on the
   Emergency tool, and then select the
   department you wish to send from the
   pop-up submenu.

2. Scroll the map to the scene of the
   disaster by clicking on the red
   arrow in the Status window.

Click here to go to the
scene of the disaster

3. Move your mouse pointer to where you want to move your emergency
   crews, and then click the mouse button. You will see an icon for your
   police, fire, or military force placed on the map, like the fire crew icons in
   Figure 2-5.

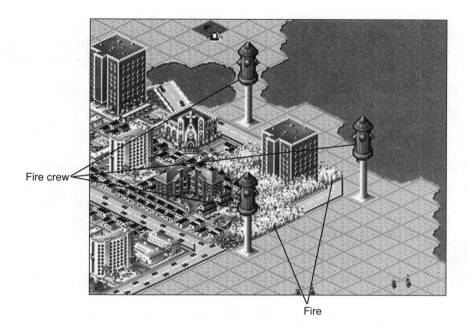

Fire crew

Fire

Figure 2-5
Dispatching the
fire department
to a roaring fire

You are allowed to place one emergency crew per police station or fire department. If have more than one fire department, for example, clicking on the map a second time will summon a second fire crew icon onto the map. For military bases, you are allowed to dispatch five military crews per army base, two crews per air force base, and three crews per navy base (but none for the missile silo). After all your emergency crews have been dispatched, clicking again elsewhere on the map will move the very first icon crew that you placed at the beginning of the emergency to the new location.

SimCity 2000 allows a maximum of 33 emergency crews to operate simultaneously in a city. Trying to place more than this number will not have any effect on the simulation.

Note that you cannot place your emergency crews right on top of the tiles of land that are experiencing the disaster; you can only place them adjacent to the tile. The basic strategy for containing any disaster is to surround the site with emergency crews, placing each icon as close to the disaster as possible. Some hilly terrain is inaccessible to your emergency crews, so you will have to work around that. It doesn't usually matter if there is road access to the area. As each disaster tile is forced back by the onslaught of your emergency crews, you will need to reposition each crew to douse the flames, contain the riot, or whatever.

When crews are battling fires, it makes no difference whether there are water mains nearby or not. The only thing that will stop a fire dead in its tracks are water tiles (which you can add using the Landscape tool!), fire crews, and bare land.

There is no cost for dispatching police, firefighters, or the military.

Providing Power

Using the Power tool, you build power plants and power lines, which are absolutely vital to the growth of your city. Without power, none of your zones will develop, and most buildings will not function properly. Power distribution in *SimCity 2000* is not based on zones but rather on individual tiles. A tile is powered if:

- It is a power plant
- It is next to a tile with a power line that has power (diagonals don't count)
- It is next to a developed tile that has power; this includes any building, but not bare zones, rails, roads, or big or small parks

Power Is Not Automatically Distributed throughout a Zone

If you run power to just one corner of a new zone, then only that corner of the zone will have power. Once construction starts in that corner, the tiles next to the construction will have power. Power radiates out to the entire zone as construction occurs on a block-by-block basis.

Sometimes it may seem that buildings are developing in opposite ends of the zone you created, even though there is no power there. If there is a high-enough demand for the kind of zone you just created, then sometimes construction will take place in parts of the zone even before power reaches them—as long as some other part of the zone has power. This does not mean that the far reaches of the zone have power; it just means that the construction crews are gambling that power will reach them by the time they finish construction.

If you add some building or zone to the side of the zone opposite the power, that new building or zone will not have power until there's an unbroken chain of development or power lines stretching to it.

Power Lines

Power lines serve as conduits for electricity between your power plants and all zones and buildings. They can be run only in straight lines, and at 90-degree angles, but not on diagonal branches of 45 degrees. You can build power lines over mountains, hills, and slopes, as well as down gullies, gorges, and valleys.

Power lines are needed to transfer power between undeveloped zones, inside undeveloped zones, and across roads and rails that divide zones. Power is also transferred directly from building to building, so you don't need to build a power line across a zone boundary if two buildings are straddling the boundary side by side.

Expedite Zone Development by Extending Power Lines inside Zones

Even though a power line enters a zone, it does not distribute power throughout the zone. The Sims will build their first buildings next to the nearest power lines, or even convert the power lines into buildings, but they will not develop elsewhere in the zone until there is an adjacent powered building or power line. One trick to speed up development for zones is to extend power line sub-branches inside a zone (as was done for Figure 2-6) so that the Sims will have more access to the power lines.

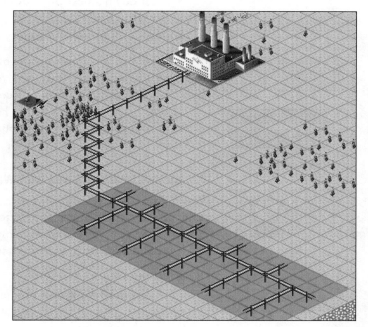

Figure 2-6
To expedite zone development, extend power lines inside the zones.

Building Power Lines over Land

Here's how you build a power line over land:

1. Click and hold down the mouse button while selecting the Power tool.
2. In the pop-up menu, select the **Power Line** option.
3. Move the pointer over the map and then click and drag over the route you wish to place the power line. As you do this, you will see a shaded portion of tiles trail your pointer as it moves. This represents the intended path for your power lines. When you release the mouse button, the individual poles and wire will be erected. Note that the total cost is displayed next to the starting location for your power line.

If the power lines have a flashing red-and-yellow power symbol over them, no power is flowing through the line yet. In order for your power lines to function, they must be connected to a functioning power plant with adequate power capacity. Sometimes during game play you will notice your power lines flashing the power loss symbol, even though your lines are connected to a power plant. When this happens, it is because your power plant is overburdened, and cannot meet your city's electrical demands. There are three solutions to this problem:

- Build new power plants
- Tear down an existing power plant, and replace it with a more powerful one
- Demolish or unhook zones from the power grid

Unlike the previous version of *SimCity*, *SimCity 2000*'s power lines cause no loss of power from line resistance. Therefore, you needn't worry about excess lines causing an unnecessary drain on your power plant.

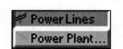

If you make a mistake while laying power lines, press and hold down Shift before releasing the mouse button. This action will prevent the power line from being placed on the map.

Building Raised Wires over Water

Power lines over water, which are called raised wires, have yearly maintenance charges, which are subtracted from your transportation budget for bridges. The yearly maintenance cost is $2 per 10 tiles of raised wire per year.

To build a power line over water:

1. Select the Power Lines tool.
2. Click and drag the mouse pointer over the water.
3. In the dialog box that appears, click the **Raised Wires** button (or select **None** if you change your mind about building the wires). There is also an Info button you can click for more information on the use of raised wires.

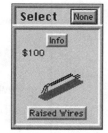

4. The overhead raised wires will be built, as shown.

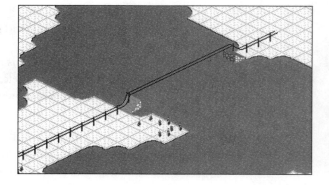

Raised power lines, like normal land-based power lines, are constrained to straight paths; they cannot travel diagonally. Also, they cannot have 90-degree intersections with other power lines.

A Trick to Run Power Lines over Water

There is a neat trick you can perform to conduct electricity over water without having unsightly raised wires. Here's how to do this:

1. Using the Power Lines tool, build a raised power line over some water.
2. Using the Demolish/Clear bulldozer, click the bulldozer on the wires above the water, *but not on the approaches to the raised wires.*
3. When the power lines disappear, you can cover over the approaches with water, using the Landscape/Water tool. Even though the power lines are no longer visible, they still conduct electricity across the water!

Power Costs

Table 2-6 shows the relative costs of laying power lines over land, and raising power lines over water.

Power Plants

There are nine power plants to choose from in *SimCity 2000*; however, some of the more sophisticated power plants will not become available for your use until a certain year and level of technology have been reached.

Table 2-6 Power Costs

	Power	Cost ($)	Yearly Maintenance Fee ($)
	Power lines	2 per tile	0
	Raised wires (across water)	10 per tile	2 per 10 tiles

Table 2-7 Number of Power Plants Needed by Zone Size

Zone Size	Total Number of Blocks (Tiles)	Total Amount of Energy Needed (Mega-watts)	Number of Coal Power Plants Needed	Number of Hydro-electric Power Plants Needed	Number of Oil Power Plants Needed	Number of Gas Power Plants Needed	Number of Nuclear Power Plants Needed	Number of Wind Power Plants Needed	Number of Solar Power Plants Needed	Number of Micro-wave Power Plants Needed	Number of Fusion Power Plants Needed
1 x 1 zone	1	0.33	1	1	1	1	1	1[a]	1[b]	1	1
10 x 10 zone	100	33.33	1	2	1	1	1	9	1	1	1
20 x 20 zone	400	133.33	1	7	1	3	1	34	3	1	1
30 x 30 zone	900	300.00	2	15	2	6	1	75	6	1	1
50 x 50	2500	833.33	5	42	4	17	2	209	17	1	1

[a]The number of windmill power plants needed will most likely be greater than what appears in this table. This is because we are assuming optimum weather conditions, and with low wind conditions the power output will drop. Note that wind generators will produce more power at higher elevations.

[b]The number of solar power plants needed will vary depending on weather conditions.

Each tile of developed zone needs about one-third megawatt (MW) of electricity, so you need to plan which power plant would be appropriate for your needs. For example, a developed zone with 100 blocks or tiles in it will require 33.33 MW of power. (To arrive at this figure, multiply 0.3333 MW times 100 blocks to get 33.33 MW). This means that you can easily satisfy the power consumption demands by building one coal power plant (which will produce 200 MW, leaving an unused excess capacity of 166 MW), or alternatively two hydroelectric power plants (which together will produce 40 MW, leaving an unused excess capacity of six MW). Table 2-7 shows the number of power plants needed for various zone sizes.

In the table, note the large number of wind power plants needed to supply even small zones. You can easily check how many tiles of zones you have by bringing up the Analysis text box while inside city hall. To do this, click the Query tool on the City Hall and then click on the Analysis button.[4]

---

[4]The city hall is a reward that you can build only after your population has reached 10,000 people.

Using AutoPurchase (or AutoReplace)

Power plants, with the exception of the hydroelectric and wind power plants, have a useful life span of only 50 years, after which they crumble. (The hydroelectric and wind power plants never fail.) If your plant is reaching retirement age, you should plan on saving enough money to buy its replacement. If you have **No Disasters** selected from the **Disaster** menu, when your power plant needs to be retired the simulator will automatically rebuild it, provided of course that you have enough cash on hand to pay for it. This process is called "auto-purchase," since the simulator automatically takes care of bulldozing and rebuilding your power plant for you. If you have **Disasters** enabled or you don't have enough money to pay for the power plant, then the AutoPurchase (also sometimes called AutoReplace) function will be switched off, and no new power plant will be built to replace the 50-year-old one.

Fossil-fueled power plants produce much air pollution, and should thus be placed far away from residential, commercial, and industrial zones. They act much like heavy industrial zones and, as such, tend to cause the Sims to move away. It is best to place them near the edges of the map, so that half their pollution gets absorbed by your neighbors.

Each power plant has its advantages and disadvantages, as you can see in Table 2-8. The coal- and oil-fired plants are environmentally dirty, but they produce cheap electricity. Hydroelectric plants are efficient, safe, environmentally benign, and just as cheap to construct per megawatt of electricity as coal power plants, but they can be built only where there are waterfalls.[5] What's more, each hydro plant puts out very little power, so you must build many facilities to generate lots of power. On the other hand, since hydro plants don't wear out after 50 years, they are a more cost-effective investment in the long run.

Natural gas power plants are cleaner than their coal- and oil-powered brethren, but they are more expensive to build, and don't become available till 1950. Like hydro power, natural gas plants generate small amounts of power, so many plants must be built to produce large quantities of energy.

Nuclear power, only available after 1955, is costly to build and incurs the risk of dangerous meltdowns and radiation contamination. But, considering the cost per megawatt, nuclear power is cheaper than natural gas power, and compares favorably with oil-fired plants.

---

[5]You can create waterfalls using the Landscape Water tool on the Toolbar. Just select the Water submenu option and then click the mouse pointer on a slope. After you have done this, you can build the hydroelectric power plant. You should note that some people consider this cheating. In the real world, hydro power is only available where nature has created the opportunity for it to exist.

Table 2-8 Power Plant Efficiency and Comparison Chart

	Type	Zone Size	Year Available[a]	Megawatts	Pollution Index	Life Span (Years)	Land Value ($)	Cost ($)	Cost per Megawatt
	Coal	4 x 4 tiles	1900	200 (serves 606 zoned tiles)	50	50	4,000,000	4,000	20
	Hydro-electric	1 tile	1900	20 (serves 60 zoned tiles)	0	Unlimited	400,000	400	20
	Oil	4 x 4 tiles	1900	220 (serves 666 zoned tiles)	25	50	6,600,000[b]	6,600	30
	Gas	4 x 4 tiles	1950	50 (serves 151 zoned tiles)	10	50	2,000,000[b]	2,000	40
	Nuclear	4 x 4 tiles	1955	500 (serves 1,515 zoned tiles)	2[c]	50	15,000,000[b]	15,000	30
	Wind	1 tile	1980	4 (serves up to 12 zoned tiles, but power output depends on weather and elevation of generator)	0	Unlimited	100,000[b]	100	25
	Solar	4 x 4 tiles	1990	50 (serves up to 151 zoned tiles, but depends on weather)	0	50	1,300,000[b]	1,300	26
	Micro-wave	4 x 4 tiles	2020	1600 (serves 4,848 zoned tiles)	0	50	28,000,000[b]	28,000	17.50
	Fusion	4 x 4 tiles	2050	2500 (serves 7,575 zoned tiles)	2c	50	40,000,000[b]	40,000	16

[a]Some of the power plants become available at slightly different times than those listed. The years shown should be used as a good approximation of availability, not an exact time.

[b]In the initial release of *SimCity 2000*, the land value is not correctly reported for this power plant.

[c]Independent testing results show that pollution from nuclear fission and fusion power plants is so negligible that you don't need to worry about it.

Wind power, a technology that becomes available only after 1980, is relatively cheap and safe but puts out little power, and is subject to adverse weather conditions and altitude considerations. (You get better power output when the generators are placed on mountain tops.)

Solar power, available only after 1990, is pollution-free but produces limited amounts of power, and it is not a reliable source of energy on cloudy or foggy days. The cost per megawatt for solar power plants is slightly better than for oil and nuclear power plants, and much better than for gas-fired plants. By combining solar and wind power, you can produce a more steady and reliable flow of electricity, because while one energy source is hampered by the weather, the other can take up the slack.

Microwave power, available only after 2020, is electricity collected from orbiting solar arrays and beamed down to earth via microwaves. The microwave power plant has a giant parabolic collector dish that focuses the incoming microwave beam and then converts it to electricity. As a cheap source of electricity, microwave power plants are second only to fusion power plants in efficiency, but they do take a huge investment of cash to build, and they sometimes pose a risk to your city when the dangerous microwave beam misses its intended target on the ground.

Fusion power is the most reliable and clean source of energy available in *SimCity 2000*, but the technology for it does not become available until 2050, and the initial capital construction outlays are enormous.

As you study Table 2-8, you will notice that the most cost-efficient power plant per megawatt produced is the fusion power plant, at $16 per megawatt. Unfortunately, the fusion power plant is also the most expensive plant to build, costing $40,000. When deciding which power plant type to build, you must take into account what you can afford, and also what is practical.

Like it or not, the environmentally safe wind and hydroelectric plants are limited in usefulness. There are not that many good places where a hydro station will work, unless you create waterfalls on hills using the Water tool. Wind power plants are really effective only at higher elevations, and because of their limited output they cannot supply much megawattage. Furthermore, wind plants take up huge amounts of space; to equal the output of a single nuclear power plant, you would have to build 125 wind generators. In a large city, you simply cannot afford to squander that much land for power generation.

Building a Power Plant

Power plants must be placed on level ground; they can be constructed over previously undeveloped areas and zones, but not over water, hills, or slopes.

Water pipes are built underneath the power plant and can later be connected to your city's water system.

To build a power plant:

1. Hold down the mouse button while selecting the Power tool.
2. In the pop-up submenu, select Power Plants and then release the mouse button.
3. When the Power Plant dialog box opens (Figure 2-7), select the power plant you want by clicking on it.
4. Move the pointer over the city window and find a flat patch of ground to place the plant.
5. Click the mouse to construct the plant.

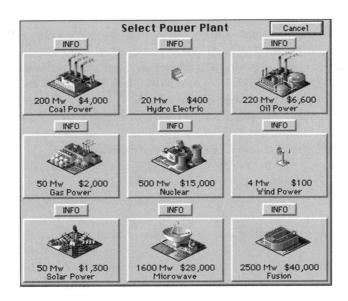

Figure 2-7
Power plant options

Using the Query Function to Check Power Plant Capacity

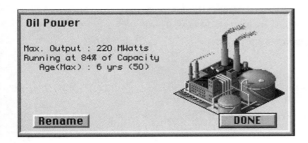

You can easily check to see how much surplus generating capacity your power plant has by selecting the Query tool function and clicking on the power plant. The power plant shown here is operating at 84 percent of rated capacity, meaning that 16 percent of the available energy is not being used and is ready for future growth in the city's electrical demand.

Providing Water

The Water tool is used to build the water supply and sewage system underneath your city. You can build pipes, water pumps, water treatment facilities, storage tanks, and desalinization plants. If you build a city without a water system, it will function, but the population will never really grow. You must also supply power to your water system in order for the water pumps, plants, storage tanks, and treatment facilities to function.

All the water tools are accessed in the pop-up submenu found under the Water tool. The costs, energy requirements, and amount of pollution emitted for each water tool are shown in Table 2-9.

Table 2-9 Water Tool Costs and Environmental Data

	Water Tool	Size	Year Available	Water Output	Number Required	Power Requirements	Pollution Index	Land Value ($)	Cost ($)
	Pipe	1 tile	1900	Not applicable	Not applicable	0	0	0[a]	3 per tile
	Water pump	1 tile	1900	15,000 gallons	Approximately 1 pump per 17 tiles (if the pump is near water, 1 per 38 tiles)	0.3 MW	2	100,000	100
	Water tower	2 x 2 tiles	1900	Stores 40,000 gallons	1 per 61 zoned tiles[b]	1.3 MW	0	250,000	250
	Treatment plant	2 x 2 tiles	1935	Only reduces overall city pollution; does not produce new water	1 per 20,000 population	1.2 MW	10	200,000[c]	500
	Desalinization plant	3 x 3 tiles	1990	105,000 gallons	In lieu of water pumps, 1 per 160 zoned tiles	2.8 MW	0	1,000,000	1,000

[a]Pipes are underground and so don't count towards land value.

[b]See the section "Water Towers" later in this chapter for a more complete explanation of this number.

[c]The land value should be $500,000, but tests reveal that it actually is $200,000.

Pipes

The large water mains are built using the Pipes tool, and when you select this tool, you will see a special underground view of your city. Each building that is built in *SimCity 2000* has its own smaller water pipe delivery system automatically built underneath it, which you can see in the underground view of your city. You don't need to duplicate pipe laying where there are already small pipes linked together, but if there are gaps where the small pipes are not connected, you can bridge them by building a large pipe between them. Figure 2-8 shows part of a working network of large and small pipes.

When you observe your water system in action in the underground view, you will see an animation of surging, pulsating water running through the pipes. Those areas of your city that are not receiving water will show no moving water through the pipes. Pay particular attention to small pipes underneath buildings; if they are getting water they will be pulsating a blue color, but if they are cut off from water they will look like gray pipes. Whether the pipe is large or small, when water is flowing you will see a pulsating blue color.

> You don't have to build water mains everywhere. If you have a series of pipes under buildings, you can just connect those together.

Pulsating bands mean water is flowing

Solid color means water is not flowing

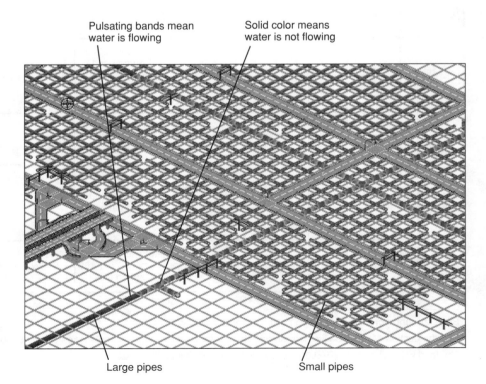

Figure 2-8
Large pipes and small pipes: Large pipes are ones you build using the pipes tool, and small pipes are automatically built by the simulation underneath each building.

Large pipes

Small pipes

Laying Your Water Pipes

To lay a water pipe, follow these steps:

1. Hold down the mouse button while selecting the water tool.
2. In the pop-up menu that next appears, select the **Pipes** command. You will see an underground view of your city.
3. Move the mouse pointer over the map where you wish to lay pipe, and then click and drag. As you move the pointer, a faint trail of black-bordered tiles will follow your pointer, indicating where the pipe will be laid. When you release the mouse button, the pipe will be constructed along the path you have just traced. While dragging the pointer, note that the cost for laying the pipe is displayed next to the starting point for your pipe.

If you make a mistake while constructing your pipe and you haven't yet released the mouse button, hold down Shift and release the mouse button to cancel the operation.

Pipes can be laid in straight segments up and down hills, and underneath rivers and other terrain depressions. Pipes can also be built diagonally, but only on flat land. Intersections and junctions with other large and small pipes are made possible simply by clicking the pipe tool on tiles that are next to these preexisting pipes. You should see some sort of connection if you have completed the link.

Note: You don't need to build large pipes where there are already smaller pipes linked together underneath buildings.

How to Remove Water Pipes

To remove previously laid water pipes, click the Bulldozer tool and select the **Demolish/Clear** option (or hold down the Ctrl key and click). Then click on the Underground button on the Toolbar. Next, click on the individual pipe members to remove them one by one.

Water Pumps

Water pumps act like a combination between a well and pumping plant, and they add needed water to your water system. They must be connected to power and to pipes connected to your city's water distribution network. They also produce a slight amount of pollution.

Water pumps can be built anywhere to produce water. The amount of water they can pump depends on their proximity to water, and how far below the ground the water table is. Thus the higher the elevation of your pump, the less water you'll get; the lower the elevation, the more water you'll get.[6]

---

[6]In early versions of *SimCity 2000*, the pumping capacity of a water pump did not decrease with higher elevation.

If you place a water pump adjacent to water, it produces more water per month than it would in a landlocked region. Therefore, for maximum efficiency, you should build water pumps on riversides, lakeshores, and ponds. Next to saltwater—such as on coastlines—water pumps produce only as much water as landlocked pumps. The more sides of your pump are surrounded by fresh water, the more water is pumped, so it is to your advantage to surround the pumps with water, as in Figure 2-9. Table 2-10 shows the approximate relationship between water pump location and the number of gallons of water produced.

Water Consumption per Tile of Land

Each tile of land consumes, on average, 650 gallons of water per month. Table 2-11 shows the water consumption for various sizes of a zone, along with the number of pumps and water towers needed to meet the water demand.

You can easily check how many tiles of zones you have by bringing up the Analysis text box while inside city hall. To do this, click the Query tool on the city hall and then click on the Analysis button.

Effects of Weather on Water Production

The climate affects the amount of water your pumps produce. When the temperature is hot, such as in the summer, water production can drop off by

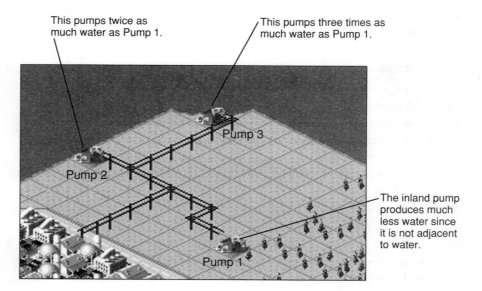

This pumps twice as much water as Pump 1.

This pumps three times as much water as Pump 1.

Pump 3

Pump 2

The inland pump produces much less water since it is not adjacent to water.

Pump 1

Figure 2-9
Water pumps produce more water when surrounded by water.

Table 2-10 Location of Water Pump and Its Effect on Water Production

	Water Pump Location	Average Gallons of Water/Month
	Inland	15,000
	On coast (salt water)	15,000
	One side adjacent to river (fresh water)	36,000
	Two sides adjacent to river (fresh water)	48,000
	Three sides adjacent to river (fresh water)	54,000
	Surrounded by fresh water (all four sides)	62,000

Table 2-11 Water Consumption and Production

Zone Size	Number of Blocks (Tiles)	Gallons of Water per Month Needed	Inland Water Pumps Needed	Water Pumps Next to Fresh Water That Are Needed	Desalinization Plants Needed	Water Towers Needed for One Month's Water Supply
6 x 6	36	23,400	2	1	1	1
10 x 10	100	65,000	5	2	1	2
12 x 12	144	93,600	7	3	1	3
15 x 15	225	146,250	10	4	2	4
20 x 20	400	260,000	18	7	3	7
30 x 30	900	585,000	39	16	6	15
40 x 40	1,600	1,040,000	69	29	10	26
50 x 50	2,500	1,625,,000	108	45	15	41

33 percent of its normal amount. And when it is raining or snowing, water production can increase by the same amount.

Water Is Centrally Distributed

The water model in *SimCity 2000* calculates water distribution by taking all the connected water sources in the city and dumping the resultant water value into the density-weighted center of the city. This is a potentially confusing aspect of the simulation, because when you add new water pumps in a part of the city where water isn't flowing, the new water from these pumps will often show up elsewhere in your city, but not where you intended it. In essence, all water from your pumps that enters the system flows from the "center" of your city outwards in all directions.[7] If you don't have enough pumps introducing new water and circulating it, regardless of where they are placed in the city, you will see spot water shortages. Thus the location of your water pumps really has nothing to do with which parts of your city get water or not.

Water Towers

The water tower is a water reservoir that stores excess water for use when demand exceeds pumping capacity. It acts like a water bank, filling up with water when it is not needed, and releasing it when it is needed. Water towers store from 10,000 gallons to as much as 40,000 gallons of water. In order to fill a water tower, you need to have water pumps or desalinization plants that are creating more water than your city needs. Thus the water towers won't fill until your entire water pipe network is pulsating blue, showing that your water system is fully pressurized.

A water tower can supply water for 62 tiles of zoned land for one month, or for about 15 tiles of zoned land for four months. As mentioned before, each tile of occupied land needs an average of 650 gallons of water per month. During dry weather conditions, when your pumping capacity drops off, the water towers will release their water back into the system.

Water towers are nonpolluting, but they do consume electricity, and so must be hooked up to your city's power supply.

---

[7]By this, we mean that *SimCity* calculates a center of gravity for your city that is based on where the population density is greatest.

Checking How Much Your Water Tower Is Storing

You can easily check to see how many gallons of water your water tower contains by using the Query tool. The number of gallons stored in your tank is updated each month.

Treatment Plants

The treatment plants clean your sewage and discharge waste effluents that are less toxic to the environment than untreated raw sewage. They do not create new water, nor do they act as pumps. Treatment plants only become available after the year 1935. Like water pumps, though, they produce pollution (five times as much) and need power to operate. You also need to connect them to your water system via pipes.

Although treatment plants themselves produce pollution, they actually help to reduce overall city pollution levels by 10 percent to 15 percent. You should build approximately one treatment plant for every 20,000 Sims.

Since the simulation only checks to see whether you have built the treatment plants, but not whether you have connected them to a water system, you can actually lower pollution in your city by building the treatment plants without building any other water facilities!

Desalinization Plants

Desalinization plants, only available after the year 1990, produce fresh water from sea water by distillation. Water is boiled to separate it from the salt, and the steam is collected in a special condenser to be pumped into the city's water system. Each desalinization plant must be placed on a seashore; the plants will not operate on rivers or other bodies of water that do not contain salt water. Use the Query function on the water tiles if you are unsure as to whether the water is salty or not. Unlike water pumps and treatment plants, desalinization plants do not produce any pollution, but they do consume electricity, and need to be connected to your city's power supply.

Each desalinization plant produces approximately two and a half times as much water as a water pump next to a river (that is, they produce over 105,000 gallons of water per month). As with pumps, the more water that surrounds the desalinization plant, the more water pumped. Thus one good strategy to maximize your water production is to build your desalinization plant on an island so that all four sides are surrounded by water. Figures 2-10 and 2-11 show a desalinization plant as part of a complete water system, in above-ground and underground views, respectively.

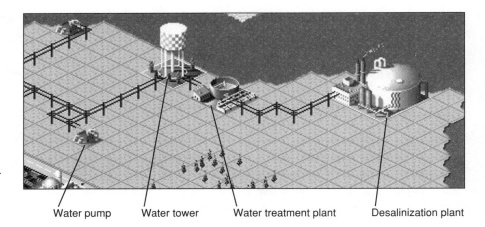

Figure 2-10
Pipes, water pumps, desalinization plants, water towers, water treatment plant: above-ground view

Water pump   Water tower   Water treatment plant   Desalinization plant

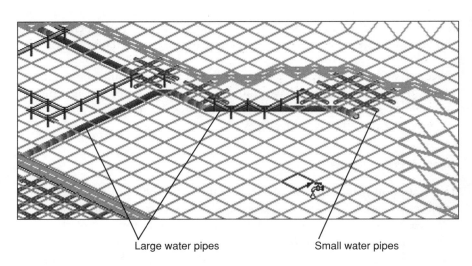

Figure 2-11
Pipes, water pumps, desalinization plants, water towers, water treatment plant: underground view

Large water pipes   Small water pipes

Accepting Rewards

| Mayor's House |
| City Hall |
| Statue |
| Braun Llama Dome |
| Arcologies |

Until your city has met certain population goals, your Rewards tool will be ghosted out and unavailable for use. When it is active, you are allowed to build certain kinds of buildings and monuments that enhance your city's prestige. (They are all detailed in Table 2-12.) As you reach each population plateau at which you are entitled to a new reward, you will be notified in a newspaper article, and the reward will appear in the submenu of the Rewards tool. With the exception of the arcologies reward, you can build only one reward of each type per city. Once you have placed your reward on the map, the reward is removed from the **Rewards** pop-up menu, but if you bulldoze your reward off the map, it will reappear on the **Rewards** menu.

Table 2-12 Rewards for Population Goals

	Zone Size	Year Available	Population Threshold	Pollution Units	Power Require-ments	Land Value ($)	Cost ($)	Reward
	2x2 tiles	1900	2,000	0	2 MW	0	0	Mayor's mansion
	3x3 tiles	1900	10,000	0	3.5 MW	0	0	City hall
	1 tile	1900	30,000	0	0 MW	0	0	Statue in your honor
	8x8 tiles	1900	60,000	2 per military parking lot tile, 2 per military hanger, 6 per each other tile	22 MW	0	0	Military base
	4x4 tiles	1900	80,000	0	2 MW	0	0	Braun llama dome
	4x4 tiles 4x4 tiles 4x4 tiles 4x4 tiles	Plymouth 2000 Forest arco 2050 Darco 2100 Launch arco 2150	> 120,000 Plymouth pop. = 55,000 Forest pop. = 30,000 Darco pop = 45,000 Launch = 65,000	Plymouth = 15 Forest = 10 Darco = 12 Launch = 15	5 MW 5 MW 5 MW 5 MW	100,000,000 120,000,000 150,000,000 200,000,000	100,000 120,000 150,000 200,000	Arco-logies

The Mayor's Mansion

The mayor's mansion is your first reward. If you click the Query tool on the Mayor's mansion, you will hear a cheer if your approval rating is positive, and a boo if your approval rating is negative. Inside the Query text box, you can see your actual popularity ratings. The Mayor's mansion needs to be connected to your power system.

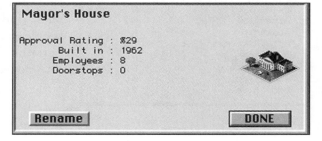

The Statue

The statue doesn't really have any value in *SimCity* other than as a boost to your ego. The statue does not need to be hooked up to your power system.

City Hall

After your city has reached a population of 10,000, you are rewarded with the opportunity to build a city hall. This reward is *very* useful. There is a special land-use analysis tool inside the city hall that you can call up by using its Query function. Make sure you connect the city hall to your power grid.

To access the Analysis tool, after having built the city hall, hold down Shift and then click on the city hall building (or select the Query tool and click on the city hall building). In the Query text box, click the Analysis button. You will see the Land Use Analysis text box open up, as shown below. The information presented in this text box tells you how your land use is allocated, by different categories. You can find out, for example, exactly how many tiles or acres of land are devoted to residential, commercial, industrial, ports or airports, education, health and safety, recreation, arcologies, transportation, power, and water use. This information is presented both in total numbers of acres or tiles of land, and as a percentage of your total *developed* land holdings. Empty or undeveloped zones are not counted in these figures.

One interesting use for this tool is to figure out exactly how much of your city is being used for transportation. Conventional thinking in urban planning has it that no more than 15 to 25 percent of a city's land area should be devoted to streets and railroads. Therefore, if your city has a transportation land use of 30 percent, you'll know that you have built too many roads and that you should find better ways of moving people and goods around. On the other hand, if your transportation land use is below 14 percent and your city is thriving, you are doing *very* well.

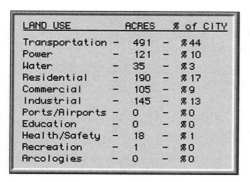

LAND USE		ACRES		% of CITY
Transportation	-	491	-	%44
Power	-	121	-	%10
Water	-	35	-	%3
Residential	-	190	-	%17
Commercial	-	105	-	%9
Industrial	-	145	-	%13
Ports/Airports	-	0	-	%0
Education	-	0	-	%0
Health/Safety	-	18	-	%1
Recreation	-	1	-	%0
Arcologies	-	0	-	%0

The city hall is counted among your Safety/Health zone tiles, while the statue is considered a recreational zone tile. The mayor's mansion and llama dome are not counted as any kind of zone category, while the arcologies have their own separate category. Military bases are not counted, except for the navy base, which seems to be counted as a seaport. Water pipes and subways are not accounted for in any category, since they are underground and don't affect surface land use.

Military Bases

After your population passes 60,000, the government asks for permission to build a military base on your city's soil. The Military reward does not appear in the Rewards submenu, but instead is brought to your attention through a special announcement on-screen. Unfortunately, if you agree to have a base built, you can't choose what kind of base you get. You can get an army, navy, air force, or missile silo base, but it really depends on where your city is built and the kind of terrain. For example, if your city is inland on flat terrain, you may get an air force base like that in Figure 2-12a.

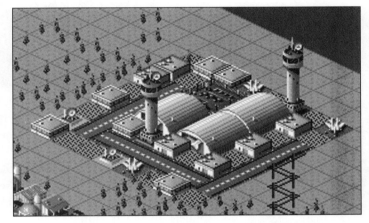

Figure 2-12a
An air force base located on flat terrain.

If it is on mountainous terrain, you may get an army base (Figure 2-12b).

Figure 2-12b
An army base likes hilly terrain.

If your city is on the coast, chances are you will get a naval base (Figure 2.12c).

Figure 2-12c
A navy base is built
on the coast.

Finally, if you are on really mountainous terrain, you'll probably end up with a missile base.

Military bases (except for missile silos) require an 8×8 tile area that is empty and flat. If you haven't got the free land, the government won't build.

Military bases help boost commerce in your city by bringing in lots of soldiers and their families who want to shop. One other good thing about military bases, except for the missile silos, is that you can deploy their troops to help deal with disasters. They also help deter the monster from attacking, and they may even force it to leave sooner than it ordinarily might.

The drawback to having a military base is that it increases crime and traffic congestion, and your economy can become too dependent on them when it comes time to close them.

Missile silos are the least useful to your city, since they have all the bad effects of military bases but don't offer your city any protection or emergency services. This is because they are manned by skeleton crews who are only there to press the nuclear button.

The Braun Llama Dome

This reward is named in honor of Jeff Braun, CEO of Maxis. The reference to llamas is a tribute to *SimCity Classic*'s creator Will Wright, and his abiding interest in Dromedaries. The Llama dome doesn't really do anything.

In the Australian version of *SimCity 2000*, the Llama Dome is replaced with the famous Sydney Opera House (shown in the color section of this book).

Arcologies

SimCity includes, as one of your rewards, giant arcologies. Arcologies are self-contained cities that exist in three dimensions and strive to separate the urban life of humankind from the pristine natural landscape. The idea is to try to preserve as much of the natural environment and ecology without disturbing it through humankind's intrusive developments and urban sprawl.

Although they are supposed to be completely self-contained, arcologies need power from your city's power grid and water from your water system. Arcologies also introduce crime and pollution (but not traffic) into the neighborhoods surrounding them, so you will need to add police protection, put in adequate transportation, and keep your residential zones away from the arcology's nesting site. Arcologies have huge numbers of people in them, and can drastically increase your population. Because of their large propensity to increase crime and their huge populations, arcologies have been likened to huge prisons that warehouse up to 65,000 "criminals." This is not far off the mark!

If you build too many arcologies without mitigating their pollution effects, you will experience a chemical spill disaster. To avoid this scenario, build lots of parks with trees to buffer the pollution, and don't put all your arcologies next to one another. By concentrating them all in one location, you increase the chances for disaster.

There are four types of arcologies: Plymouth Arco, Forest Arco, Darco, and the Launch Arco, designed in the year 2000, 2050, 2100, and 2150, respectively. This means that even if you have the money to build them, the arcologies will not become available for you to build until you pass the year in which they were designed.[8]

Should you want more of a description for each arcology, click on the Info button in the Arcology submenu.

---

[8]The present Launch Arcos will now launch into space in the Macintosh Version 1.1, DOS Version 1.1, and Windows Version 1.0. What you'll see, after you've reached a certain critical number of Launch Arcos, is a message informing you that the arcos are about to launch, and that you will be compensated for their loss. After this, the arcos will blow up one by one.

Arcologies

In the late 1950s and early 1960s, Paolo Soleri, an architect of great vision and utopian idealism, perceived that the conventional notions of planning and development—as conceived by Major Pierre L'Enfant, Le Corbusier, Frank Lloyd Wright, and others—would eventually lead to ecological collapse of the planet. Soleri asserted that the urban sprawl of cities and suburbs would eventually consume so much of the earth's space that the environment would be utterly destroyed. Soleri believed that modern city planning also created a whole host of other problems, such as the long distances and travel times that separated individuals from their institutions and from nature.

By Soleri's definition, architecture and ecology are two parts of the same thing, inseparable in their effect on man. Soleri called this concept "arcology."

Architecture can be defined as the articulation of space so as to produce in the viewer a definite spatial experience. Ecology is the science that studies the interrelationship of organisms and their environments. Arcology was to be a synthesis of these two definitions, a new way of looking at man's need to fit form and design to environmental considerations.

Soleri envisioned a population implosion, whereby the earth's teeming multitudes would abandon their squalid cities in favor of three-dimensional, single-

The Maximum Number of Arcologies

With the release of the Macintosh Version 1.1 and the Windows Version 1.0 of *SimCity 2000*, it became possible to build more than 140 arcos, thereby enabling you to build cities with much greater populations. However, both DOS Versions 1.0 and 1.1 still have a limitation of 140 arcos. You can check to see which version of *SimCity 2000* you have by typing the word **vers** while in the *SimCity* program.

The Maximum Arcologies Number for *SimCity* Version 1.00

Although *SimCity 2000* Version 1.00 allows up to 150 Microsims, you can only have up to 140 arcologies, because some of the Microsims are reserved by the program for other building types. Assuming, then, that you choose to build 140 Launch Arcos (which have the largest population of all the arcos, 65,000 people), you could achieve a population of 9,100,000 people, not counting the Sims that live outside the arcologies. Combining the ground structure, super-high-density, self-contained cities that would allow nature to return to its "natural state," undefiled and unspoiled. These so-called arcologies, as designed by Soleri, were to consist of cities built vertically with many hundreds of levels, providing for millions of people. In some of his designs, densities approached 300 people per cubic acre, or 400,000 people per cubic mile!

The nearest ancestor to the arcology is the ocean liner, that magnificently conceived, highly structured, self-contained city at sea. That Soleri was influenced by ships is incontrovertible—one of his arcologies was suggestively named "Novanoah" (after Noah's ark). Some of Soleri's arcologies were designed to move like giant ships, but most were to be fixed and permanently built into natural sites, such as canyons, mountain ranges, dams, shorelines, and underground as well as undersea. In his book, Arcology: *The City in the Image of Man*,[9] Soleri sketches out his arcology designs and defines his vision of the future, one which includes man living in harmony with nature, not subjugating it. Some critics of his cities, however, have made the point that few people would be willing to live in the kinds of beehives that Soleri has proposed, and because of their immense scale, these cities are intrinsically impractical.

Soleri has attempted a prototypal demonstration of one arcology, called Arcosante (formerly Cosante II), and some construction in Arizona is still going on.

population with the arcology population, your maximum city population is about 9,755,000 people.[10]

Providing Roads

Using the Roads tool, you can build roads, bridges, bus stations, highways, and on-ramps. Roads are the means by which most Sims will move from zone to zone. The operative idea in *SimCity 2000* is that the Sims need to travel successfully between residential, commercial, and industrial zones

---

[9]Soleri, Paolo. *Arcology: The City in the Image of Man*. Cambridge: Massachusetts Institute of Technology Press, 1969.

[10]This population number represents a theoretical maximum. In actual practice, you would not be able to achieve this population due to landform constrants and the need for public facilities such as roads, power plants, schools, and police stations.

before any growth can occur. In short, without transportation between the different zone types, all activity will cease. Just as you must ensure that power is being delivered to each zone and building, you must also make sure that adequate transportation exists for the Sims to commute, shop, and ship their goods. Roads also indirectly contribute to pollution. Pollution is actually tied to traffic, so the heavier the traffic on a road, the more pollution there is.

When you place any kind of road object or structure over pre-existing zone tiles, those zone tiles are erased and replaced by the road or road structure (including bus stations). If you then bulldoze the road or road structure, you will find that the land underneath has reverted to its former unzoned state, barren of any features. As an economy measure, be sure to build your roads, highways, and bus stations *before* you lay out your zones, so that you don't inadvertently "erase" the investment of zoned tiles by paving over them.

When you hold down the mouse button while selecting the Roads tool, a submenu pops open, allowing you to select five different road building options. If your city is started before 1920, you may be able to see only **Roads** and **Tunnels** on the submenu. This is because highways, on-ramps, and bus stations have not yet been invented.

You can build simple two-lane roads and bridges using the **Road** command, or modern high-speed multilane highways and bridges using the **Highway** option. For burrowing underneath mountains, you can use the **Tunnel** command, although it will only build two-lane tunnels that can slow down your highway traffic. The **Onramp** command is used to build on-ramps and off-ramps to connect your roads to your highways. Without on-ramps and off-ramps, no traffic will be able to get on or off the highway. By building bus depots using the **Bus Depot** command, you can alleviate traffic congestion on busy arterial routes. Table 2-13 shows the various costs, power requirements, and land values of the different road types that are possible in *SimCity 2000*.

All roads (including bus stations and bridges) must be maintained yearly by your transportation department. These costs, which are itemized transportation department's account books in the Budget window, are subtracted from your city's treasury. If your transportation system is fully funded, then damage is automatically repaired as it occurs, and no road squares will go bad. But if damage occurs through disasters or other acts of God, you have to lay new road tiles or repair the damaged bridge or highway sections. By the way, you can be a cheapskate and reduce maintenance funding for your transportation department, and then just fix things as they go bad. In the long run, however, this strategy will end up costing you more than just fully funding transportation, because each basic road tile costs $10 to build, whereas maintenance for 10 tiles per year costs you only $1. Bridges and other road tiles have different maintenance costs, as shown in Table 2-13.

Table 2-13 Data for Different Modes of Transportation

	Road Type	Year Available	Advantages and Disadvantages	Pollution Units[a]	Power Require- ments (MW)	Land Value ($)	Maintenance Costs per Year ($)	Construction Cost ($)
	Road	1900	Causes pollution through traffic	0	0	10,000 per tile	0.10 per tile	10 per tile
	Bridges Causeway	1900	Relatively cheap and can be any length, but no ships can pass under it	0	0	100,000 per tile (required bridge ramparts add $20,000 for each bridge)	0.25 per tile plus 0.10 for each end ramp	25 per tile
	Raising Bridge	1900	Cheaper than suspension and can allow ships to pass under, limited to 5–12 tiles length	0	0	100,000 per tile (required bridge ramparts add $20,000 for each bridge)	0.25 per tile plus 0.10 for each end ramp	50 per tile
	Suspension	1900	Most expensive road bridge; allows ships to pass but must be 7 tiles or longer	0	0	100,000 per tile (required bridge ramparts add $20,000 for each bridge	0.25 per tile plus 0.10 for each end ramp	75 per tile
	Highway	1930	Sims can traverse much farther distances than on roads;[b] expensive, however	0	0	60,000 per section	0.80 per section	100 per section (each highway section is 4 square tiles)
	Bridges Highway	1930	Cheaper than reinforced girder highway bridge, but does not allow ships to pass under	0	0	60,000 per section	0.80 per section	200 per section (each bridge section is 4 square tiles)
	Reinforced Girder	1930	Most expensive highway bridge	0	0 MW	400,000 per section	1.80 per section over water, plus 1.60 for both end ramps	300 per section[c] (each bridge section is 4 square tiles)
	Tunnel	1900	Expensive to construct; allows more direct routes between urban centers through mountains	0	0 MW	7,500 per tile[d]	0.20 per tiles[e]	150 per tile
	On-Ramp	1930	Needed for highway entrance and exit	0	0 MW	100,000 per ramp	0.10 per ramp	25 per ramp
	Bus-Depot (2x2 tiles)	1920	Lowers traffic on nearby roads within a 10-block radius; traffic- reducing effect drops off with distance	4	2.22 MW	250,000	2 Month per bus depot ($24 per year)	250 per bus depot

[a]Roads and highways don't give off pollution *per se*, but the traffic that travels on them does, and this can contribute significant pollution to your city.

[b]There is still a bug in the transportation model that prevents the Sims from traveling farther on highways than on roads.

[c]*SimCity 2000* also charges an additional $200 for both end ramps of the reinforced girder bridge.

[d]There is at present a bug in the model that causes each tunnel to be valued at $30,000, regardless of length!

[e]Maintenance costs are incorrectly calculated for tunnels (yes, another bug). In some cases there are no maintenance charges, in others the charges are the same as for roads ($0.10 per tile). Maxis claims that the true cost should be $0.40 per tile, but this is not borne out in tests.

The Maximum Walking Distance

The Sims can travel by foot a maximum of three blocks (or tiles, as shown in Figure 2-13). They cannot cross zone boundaries to travel to another zone unless they travel by road, rail, or subway.[11] In order to travel distances farther than three blocks, they must drive their cars on roads, highways, tunnels, or bridges, or take public transportation such as rails, subways, or buses. This means that if you design a zone larger than 6×6 tiles (for example 7×7 or 8×8 tiles) that exceeds three blocks' walking distance for Sims in the center of the zone, you *must* provide some means of transit for the Sims in the center of the zone such that they need walk no more than three blocks (or tiles) to a road, rail station, or subway station.[12] (Figures 2-14 and 2-15 illustrate a typical case and its solution.) If they can't do this, the zone will simply not develop![13] On the other hand, a zone of 6×7, 6×8, 6×9, or the like is OK, as long as a road surrounds the zone.

With more access to transportation, zones will develop quicker. Thus, if you can design a zone such that there is easy access to *two* roads, the zone will develop more quickly than if there is access only to *one* road.

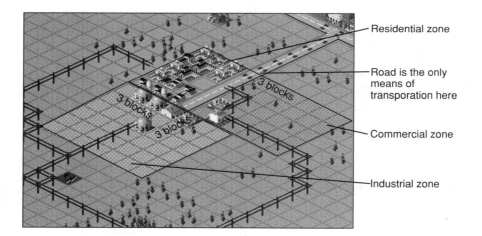

Figure 2-13
Sims can walk only three blocks to nearby transportation.

---

[11]There is an exception to this rule. If there is a subway station, rail depot, or road in a nearby zone, then the Sims can walk three blocks across zone boundaries or even empty terrain to reach the road or stations.

[12]In *SimCity 2000*, unlike *SimCity Classic*, rail lines (including subway lines) cannot be used directly by the Sims. They must first get on or off the line at a rail depot (station) or subway station.

[13]High-density zones can actually develop if they are within four blocks from transportation. This is because buildings that have a footprint of 2×2, 3×3, or larger can develop if part of their structure is within a three-block radius of transportation.

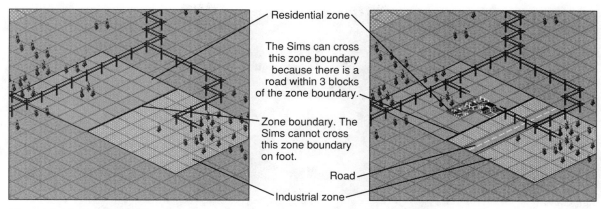

Residential zone

The Sims can cross this zone boundary because there is a road within 3 blocks of the zone boundary.

Zone boundary. The Sims cannot cross this zone boundary on foot.

Road

Industrial zone

Figure 2-14 Normally, zone-to-zone crossings are not permitted.

Figure 2-15 Here a zone-to-zone crossing is permitted because there is a road within three blocks.

Crossing Zone Boundaries

The Sims can cross a zone boundary only if they are on a road, highway, rail line, or subway, *or if there is a road, subway station, or train depot within three blocks of the zone boundary.* In the absence of transportation within three blocks, zone crossings are not permitted.

Intermodal Transportation

Transferring from one mode of transportation to another, such as when a Sim switches from his or her car to a train or subway, or between a train and a subway, is known as *intermodal transportation.* Traveling between roads and highways is not considered intermodal because the Sims don't get out of their cars. Traveling between roads and subway or rail stations is possible only when the road tiles touch the station itself, as in Figure 2-16. Intermodal travel between subway stations and train depots (stations) is possible only if a road connects the two stations. The road connection can be as short as one tile, if that tile borders both stations.

Alternatively, you can create intermodal transportation between rail and subway by building a subway-to-rail junction

Figure 2-16 Intermodal transit between rail and subway stations is possible only when the stations are connected by a road. The road tile can be as short as one block, but it must border both stations.

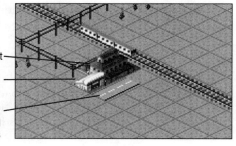

Train depot

Subway station

Road connects subway station to train depot, thereby allowing passengers to travel intermodally between the subway and train lines

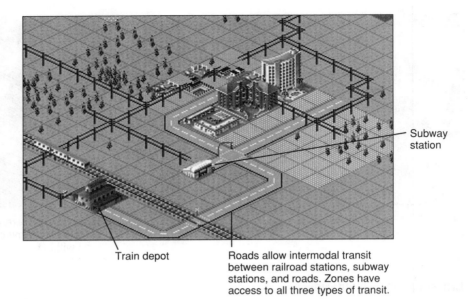

Figure 2-17
Intermodal transit
between roads,
railroad stations, and
subway stations

Subway
station

Train depot

Roads allow intermodal transit
between railroad stations, subway
stations, and roads. Zones have
access to all three types of transit.

(as in Figure 2-17), which connects the tracks of the railroad to an underground passageway leading to your subway line. Use the **Sub<—>Rail** command under the Rail submenu to do this.

Road-Building Strategies

By building zones that are 6×6—or 6×x, where x can be any length—and then surrounding the zones with roads, you can optimize your road network for maximum efficiency. This strategy allows all the Sims in the zone full access to the road, and it allows them to build the largest 3×3 buildings possible. Some different road designs are illustrated in Figures 2-18, 2-19, and 2-20.

Roads

Without roads, growth is all but impossible in *SimCity 2000*.[14] Roads, like rails and subways, allow your Sims to travel from zone to zone, and they

---

[14]You can build a city with only subways and subway stations, or a city with only trains and train depots, but it would be very expensive and hard to do. The *SimCity 2000* model heavily favors roads as a cheap and effective means of transportation (especially when combined with bus stations). The traffic model "flips a coin" to decide whether to use mass transit or not. So at best, there is a fifty-fifty chance that a Sim will use mass transit,

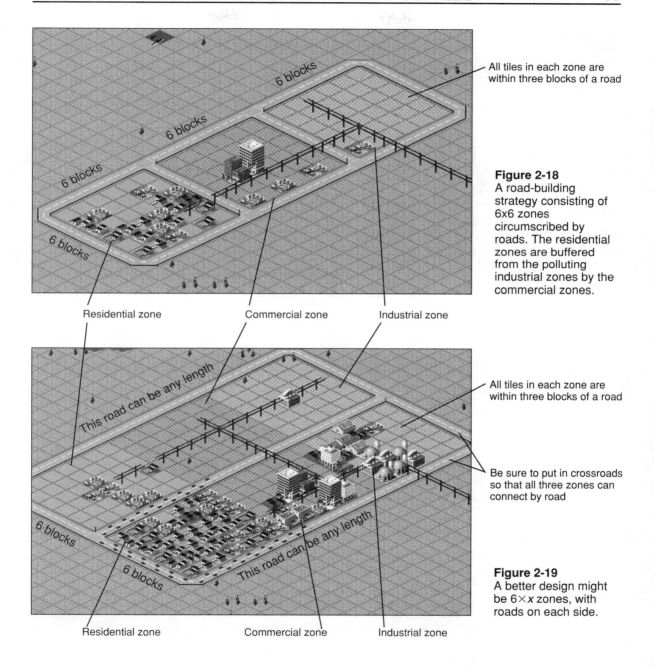

All tiles in each zone are within three blocks of a road

Figure 2-18
A road-building strategy consisting of 6x6 zones circumscribed by roads. The residential zones are buffered from the polluting industrial zones by the commercial zones.

All tiles in each zone are within three blocks of a road

Be sure to put in crossroads so that all three zones can connect by road

Figure 2-19
A better design might be 6×*x* zones, with roads on each side.

whereas when traveling on roads, there is no such decision making. Travel between zones is not permitted unless there is a road, railway depot, or subway station within three blocks.

Figure 2-20
A strategy of
alternating 6×*x* zones

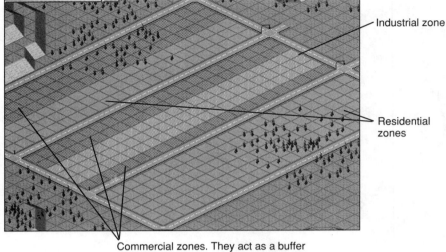

Industrial zone

Residential
zones

Commercial zones. They act as a buffer
between Industrial and Residential zones.

allow greater traveling distances than are possible by foot. The distance the Sims can travel is governed by a "trip generator" that calculates how many tiles the Sims can move from a given number of "steps." Each residential, commercial, and industrial zone attempts to send traffic from its own zone to the other two zone types. If a one-way trip is completed within 100 steps, the trip is deemed successful and the zone prospers. As you can see from Table 2-14, cars take three steps per tile of road traveled, while buses take two steps. Theoretically, this gives a maximum range for cars traveling on roads of 33 blocks, and for buses, 50 blocks. In practice, however, the maximum range is about 24 blocks for both buses and cars, due to other factors that subtract steps from the 100 that are allowed.

Roads can be built over flat land, over mountains and gullies, and over water via three different bridge types. As you can see from Table 2-13, there are yearly maintenance fees associated with each road/bridge type.

Table 2-14 Steps Taken for Each Tile of Road Traveled	
Vehicle Type	**Steps Taken**
Car	3
Bus	2

Roads Versus Rail and Subway Lines

In *SimCity 2000*, roads are the cheapest and most effective mode of transportation to build and maintain. The secret to building fast, efficient traffic arterials in *SimCity* is to build roads with plenty of bus stations. This combination really can't be beat, even with subways and rail lines. For example, rails cost two and one-half times as much to build and four times as much to maintain as roads. Subways, on the other hand, cost ten times as much to build. Furthermore, any SimCitizen within three blocks of a road can make use of it, whereas they can use a subway or rail line only if there is a subway station or rail depot within three blocks. Another bias in the model that favors roads has to do with the way trips are made. If a Sim travels on a road to get to a subway or rail station, he or she flips a coin to decide whether or not to get on the subway or train. Thus there is only a fifty-fifty probability that mass transit will be used, but only if the journey was started on a road. If the trip originates in a three-block radius of the subway station or rail depot, then this coin flipping proposition does not apply and the Sims will take the train or subway. The bias toward roads severely hinders the effectiveness of rail and subway transit.

So what does this all mean to you? Build roads, roads, and roads! Even though we favor mass transit, and hate the idea of recommending that you build more roads, the simple fact of the matter is that roads are a better buy than rail lines and subways. Plus, you can all but remove the pollution problem caused by road traffic by adding bus stations all over.

Roads Create Traffic, Which in Turn Causes Pollution

Roads do not directly create pollution. Traffic is what creates pollution, and the way to eliminate this problem from your roads is to design efficient traffic arterials in connection with your zone layout. You can also build bus stations to help reduce congestion. Building subways and rail lines, unfortunately, lowers traffic levels by only 10 and 20 percent, respectively. Bus stations, on the other hand, can lower traffic by as much as 50 percent on nearby roads.

You can check the amount of traffic on your roads by clicking the Query tool on the road tiles you are interested in. A shortcut method of using the Query tool is to hold down Shift while clicking on any tile on the map. A light amount of traffic could be 70 cars, but anything over 88 cars requires your immediate attention to reduce traffic. (Table 2-15 shows how the different levels are defined.) Traffic congestion can be eased by building bus stations, and by constructing subways and railroad lines, all of which woo the Sims out of their cars.

Table 2-15 Road Traffic Definitions	
Definition	**Number of Cars**
No traffic	0–43
Light	44–88
Heavy	> 88

How to Build a Road

To build a road, follow these steps:

1. While selecting the Road tool, hold down the mouse button and select the **Road** option when the pop-up submenu opens.
2. Place the pointer over the map and then click and drag where you wish to "draw" your road. Notice as you do so that the total cost for placement is displayed alongside your road, and that this number will change as your road gets longer or shorter:

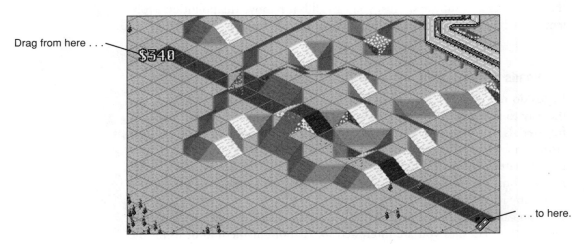

Drag from here . . .

$340

. . . to here.

"Undo" Your Road or Highway by Pressing the Shift Key

Sometimes when building roads or highways, you will discover that you have made a mistake that you would like to undo. If you have not yet released the mouse button, you can remove your road, and not be charged for it, by pressing Shift and then releasing the mouse button.

Building Off-Map Road Connections to Neighboring Cities

If, while building a road, you drag the road off one edge of the map, you will be asked whether you want to establish a neighbor road connection for $1,000. If you click on the Yes button, a road will be built all the way to your neighbor's city off that edge of the map. Figures 2-21 through 2-23 show the sequence.

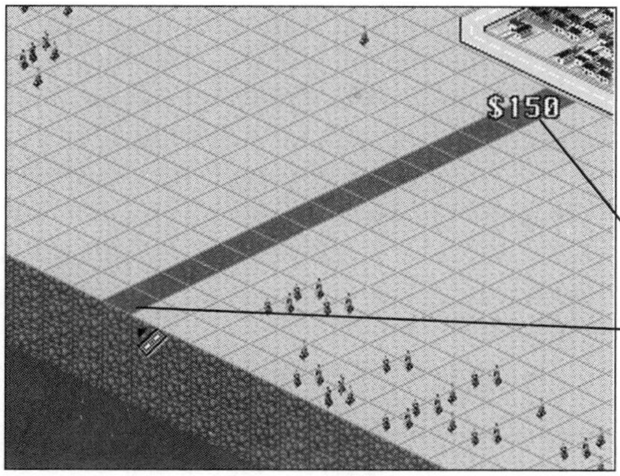

Road connections to your neighbor cities help your commercial zones but not your industrial or residential zones.[15] They are not as effective at boosting commerce as airports. When you build the road connection, the simulation kicks a commerce multiplier into the equations for calculating economic growth. Since this multiplier only affects commerce, a road connection is a waste of money early on in the development of a city, when you are still trying to develop industry.

Only one road connection is necessary for the multiplier to kick in, but if you build more than one road connection (by more than one road connection, we mean adding new road connections off the other three edges of the map), they will hasten the development of your neighboring cities, thereby increasing the GNP (gross national product) of your nation. The more prosperous your neighbors are, the more likely they will be to buy your products and trade with you, so it is to your advantage to encourage multiple road connections.

Figure 2-21
To begin building your off-map road connections, drag the road tool off the edge of the map.

Drag from here . . .

. . . to here

Figure 2-22
The dialog box asks you if you wish to spend $1,000 to construct the off-map road connection.

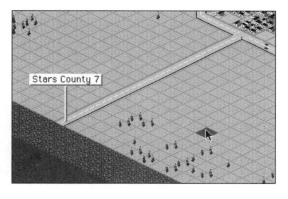

Figure 2-23
The road connection is complete.

---

[15]Unfortunately, the effects of road connections on commerce seem very weak. Perhaps this will be fixed in a future revision.

It does not help commerce in your city to build multiple road connections to the same neighboring city off the same edge of the map. You will, however, need to build a highway or railroad connection to allow your industry to trade with the neighbor cities.

One way you'll know that it's time to build an off-map road connection is that the Sims will display a message in the Status window stating, "Commerce demands a connection." Be sure you build a road connection, not a highway or rail connection, for this purpose.

Building Road Bridges

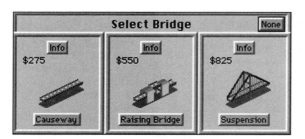

Figure 2-24
The three road bridges: causeway, raising bridge, and suspension bridge.

There are three types of road bridges, as shown in Figure 2-24. To construct a bridge, all you do is click and drag your road tool icon to the edge of the water where you wish the crossing to be. Immediately, you will see a dialog box similar to Figure 2-24, which displays the bridge types that are possible for the crossing you have selected. Road bridges cannot intersect with other bridges.

Highways

Highways, available after 1930, have double the traffic capacity of roads, and they allow the Sims to travel farther than they can by road.[16] The distance the Sims can travel is governed by a "trip generator" that calculates how many tiles the Sims can move from a given number of "steps." Each residential, commercial, and industrial zone attempts to send traffic from its own zone to the other two zone types. If a one-way trip is completed within 100 steps, the trip is deemed successful and the zone prospers. As you can see from Table 2-16, both cars and buses take one step per tile of highway trav-

Table 2-16 Number of Steps Taken per Highway Tile Traveled	
Vehicle Type	**Steps per Tile**
Car	1
Bus	1

---

[16]There is a bug in the present version of *SimCity* that limits highway travel to about 20 blocks, the same maximum distance as for road travel.

eled. Theoretically, this gives a maximum range of 100 blocks for cars and buses traveling on highways.[17] Highways allow greater amounts of traffic to flow in urban areas than do roads.

To build a highway, follow this procedure:

1. Select the Road tool, and while holding down the mouse button on it, select the **Highway** option.

2. Move the cursor over the map to where you wish to start your highway.

3. Click and drag the pointer over the route you want the highway to follow. You will see the associated cost for your actions displayed alongside your cursor.

4. When building curves, simply drag the Highway tool diagonally at 45-degree angles to the existing highway. When you release the mouse button, the curve will be built.

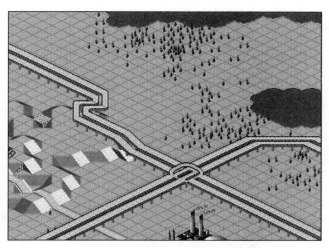

When highways intersect, they create cloverleaf intersections like the one in Figure 2-25.

For highways to be of any use to you, you must build on-ramp and off-ramp connections to your roads. In *SimCity*, both on-ramps and off-ramps are built using the **Onramp** command under the **Roads** submenu.

Figure 2-25
Building highways

Building Highway Bridges

Highway bridges, which only become available after 1930, cannot intersect other bridges, and they can only be built straight and level, not on diagonals, nor on slopes of different elevation. Thus the approaches to both ends of the bridge must be on terrain that is at the same elevation.

There are two types of highway bridges: the highway bridge as such and the reinforced bridge. The highway bridge is a little less expensive than the reinforced bridge, but the reinforced bridge allows ship traffic to pass underneath. In order to construct either type of bridge, follow this procedure:

1. Select the **Highway** option from the **Road** submenu.

2. Position your Highway pointer with the mouse so that it straddles the edge of the water and the land where you wish the crossing to be.

---

[17]See previous footnote.

3. Click the mouse button and you will see a dialog box pop up, giving you two bridge choices. (If you have not done this correctly or a reinforced bridge crossing is not possible at this spot, you will see only the highway bridge displayed in the dialog box.)

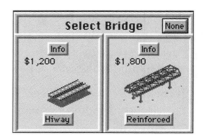

Beware of trying to build highway bridges by clicking and dragging as you would a road bridge — in this case, you will only be allowed to build the highway bridge, not the reinforced bridge. The correct technique to bring up both bridge choices, including the reinforced bridge, is to position the Highway pointer on the shoreline and then click the mouse button, as shown in Figures 2-26 and 2-27. *This is the only way to build a reinforced bridge.*

Figure 2-26 To build a reinforced bridge, you must position the highway pointer on the shoreline, and then click the mouse button.

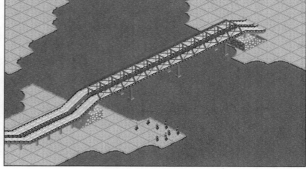

Figure 2-27 The completed bridge

Building Off-Map Highway Connections to Neighboring Cities

When you click the Highway tool on any edge of the map, you will be asked whether you want to establish a neighbor highway connection for $1,500. If you click on the Yes button, a highway will be built all the way to your neighbor's city off that edge of the map. The sequence is illustrated in Figures 2-28 through 2-30.

Highway connections to your neighbor cities help your industrial zones, but not your commercial or residential zones.[18] They are not as effective at

---

[18]Unfortunately, in the present version, the Highway off-map connections don't have as big an impact on industry as they should.

boosting industry as sea-ports, however. When you build the highway connec-tion, the simulation kicks an industry multiplier into the equations for calculat-ing economic growth. Since this multiplier affects only industry, a highway con-nection is a waste of money early on in the development of a city, when you are try-ing to develop commerce.

Only one highway connection is necessary for the multiplier to kick in, but if you build more than one highway connection (that is, if you add new highway connections off more than one edge of the map), it will hasten the development of your neighboring cities, thereby increasing the GNP of your nation. The more prosperous your neighbors are, the more likely they will be to buy your prod-ucts and trade with you, so it is to your advantage to encourage multiple high-way connections (but only one per edge!).

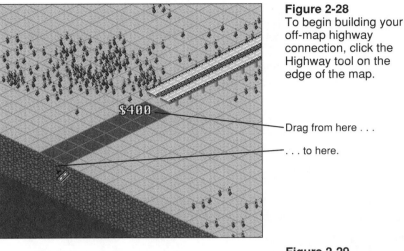

Figure 2-28
To begin building your off-map highway connection, click the Highway tool on the edge of the map.

Drag from here . . .

. . . to here.

Figure 2-29
The dialog box asks if you wish to spend $1,500 to construct the off-map highway connection.

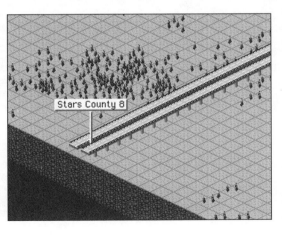

Figure 2-30
The completed highway connection

It does not help industry in your city to build multiple highway connec-tions to the same neighboring city off the same edge of the map. You will, however, need to build a road connection to allow commerce with the neigh-bor cities.

One way you'll know that it's time to build an off-map highway connec-tion is that the Sims will display a message in the Status window stating, "Industry demands a connection." Be sure you build a highway (or rail) con-nection, not a road connection, for this purpose.

Tunnels

You can bore through mountain ranges to build tunnels like the one shown in Figure 2-31 and thus connect different parts of your city more efficiently. If you are connecting a highway to your tunnels, you should link them with on-ramps and off-ramps, and you should seriously consider building two tunnels to handle the additional traffic capacity that the highway offers, as shown in Figure 2-32.

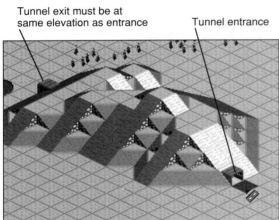

Tunnel exit must be at same elevation as entrance

Tunnel entrance

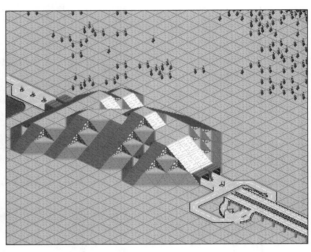

Figure 2-31 Building a tunnel

Figure 2-32 Building tunnel and highway connections. Be sure to add off-ramps and on-ramps between the highway and tunnel. You may also want to consider drilling twin tunnel bores to handle the highway's larger traffic densities.

To build a tunnel:

1. Select the Road tool and hold down the mouse button.
2. In the pop-up submenu, select **Tunnel** and then release the mouse button.
3. Click the mouse pointer on a sloping tile of a hill or mountain. (The entrance to the tunnel must be a slope.)
4. If the exit point of your proposed tunnel is stable and accessible, you will get an engineer's report dialog box informing you of the cost ($150 per tile) and asking you whether to proceed or not. Click the Yes button to allow construction or the No button to cancel.

Tunnels cannot curve, nor can they cross other tunnels inside mountains. They also cannot slope inside the mountain to a different elevation.

On-Ramps

On-ramps, which are needed to connect your highways to your roads, become available only after highways have been invented (1930). You should build both on-ramps and off-ramps (off-ramps are identical in appearance and function to on-ramps) to your highways on both sides of the highway; thus, all told, there should be four ramps (two on-ramps and two off-ramps) to your highway for each road connection.

Before building an on-ramp, you must build your highway and road. The road tiles *must intersect the highway at 90 degrees* before you can construct the on-ramps. This is a constant point of confusion for many *SimCity* enthusiasts. Using the **Onramps** tool, you place each on-ramp to each side of the road, right next to the highway.

Here is a summary of the steps to take when building on-ramps:

1. First build your highway, using the **Highway** command from the **Road** submenu.

2. At the location where you want to build the on-ramps, build a road underneath the highway, intersecting it at right angles. To build the road, use the **Road** command from the **Road** submenu.

3. Next, select the **Onramp** option from the **Road** submenu.

4. Move the cursor over to where the road intersects the highway. On each side of the road right next to the highway, click and place the on-ramp.

5. Repeat the previous step and build on-ramps for the opposite side of the highway. If you have trouble seeing the other side of the freeway, click on the Rotate button on the Toolbar to get a different vantage point.

You must build your highway and road before you can build the on-ramp. The road must intersect the highway at right angles, and the on-ramps must be constructed on each side of the road, as shown in Figures 2-33 and 2-34.

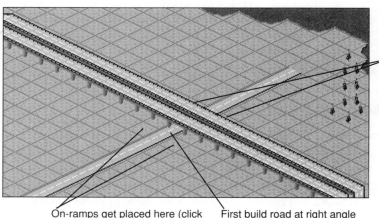

On-ramps get placed here (rotate view to get better viewing angle)

On-ramps get placed here (click Onramps tool on these two tiles).

First build road at right angle (or perpendicular) to highway.

Figure 2-33
Before building an on-ramp, you must build a road intersecting the highway at 90 degrees.

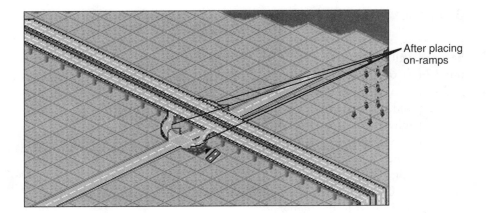

After placing
on-ramps

Figure 2-34
On-ramp construction
in progress

Bus Depots

Bus depots, which only become available after 1920, help to reduce traffic congestion along roads that are within 10 tiles radius of them. The traffic-reducing potential is greatest nearest the bus station, and drops off with

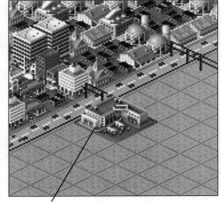

Bus depot

increasing distance. Of all the modes of public transportation, amazingly enough, the bus station is the most effective means of reducing traffic, even beating out rail and subway transit. Each bus depot can cause nearby traffic to decline by as much as 50 percent.

Bus depots need to be maintained on an annual basis by your transportation department. The yearly maintenance fee of $24 ($2 per month) is deducted from your transportation budget under the category of Roads.

Bus depots pollute very slightly, and they need to be hooked up to your power network to function properly. When building a bus depot, you must place it on level ground and along a road.

Traffic Reduction and Distance Relationships

As shown in Figure 2-35, the zone of coverage extends out to about nine blocks. Notice that the bus station affects not only the street that it is on, but also all other streets in its zone of coverage. This zone extends radially.

Although Maxis claims that bus stations reduce traffic up to 25 blocks away, this is not borne out by tests conducted on the simulation. The maximum effective radius seems to be about nine blocks.

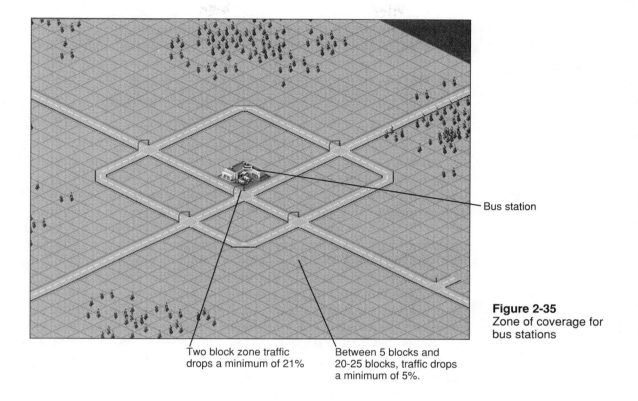

Bus station

Figure 2-35
Zone of coverage for
bus stations

Two block zone traffic
drops a minimum of 21%

Between 5 blocks and
20-25 blocks, traffic drops
a minimum of 5%.

Providing Rail Transport

Using the Rails tool, you can build train tracks, train depots (stations), subway lines, subway stations, and rail-to-subway junctions. Rail lines and subways do not pollute (although their stations do), but they both help to reduce traffic congestion in your city.

When you hold down the mouse button while selecting the Rails tool, a submenu pops open allowing you to select five different rail-building options. If your city was started before 1910, you may see only **Rail and Rail Depot** on the submenu. This is because subways have not been invented.

Train lines will become active once you build station depots alongside the tracks. You can see trains move on the tracks, but only at the lowest zoom level. There are no subway trains that you can see move, but both subways and trains use the same kind of cars.

When you place any kind of rail object or structure (except subways) over preexisting zone tiles, those zone tiles are erased and replaced by the rail or rail building. If you then bulldoze the rail or rail building, you will find that the land underneath has reverted to its former unzoned state, barren of any features. As an economy measure, be sure to build your rail lines and stations before you build your zones, so that you don't inadvertently "erase" the investment of zoned tiles by laying tracks over them. You don't need to bother doing this with subways and subway stations, since they are underground.[19]

Covering the Distance

The distance that Sims can travel is governed by a "trip generator" that calculates how many tiles the Sims can move from a given number of "steps." Each residential, commercial, and industrial zone attempts to send traffic from its own zone to the other two zone types. If a one-way trip is completed within 100 steps, the trip is deemed successful and the zone prospers. Thus, a residential zone will attempt to send a SimCitizen to a nearby industrial zone, allotting him or her 100 steps for the trip. Next, the same residential zone will attempt to reach a nearby commercial zone, again allotting 100 steps for the trip. If both trips are completed, the zone will develop.

As you can see from Table 2-17, traveling by rail or subway takes one step per tile of rail traveled. But four steps are subtracted for passing through train depots and subway stations, thus limiting the range somewhat. Maximum range via rail or subway is theoretically around 92 blocks (subtracting four steps on each end for entering and exiting stations). In practice, however, the maximum range is about 39 blocks, due to other factors that subtract steps from the 100 that are allowed.[20]

Table 2-17 Number of Steps Taken per Rail or Subway Tile Traveled	
Rail/Subway Tile	**Steps Taken**
Rail	1
Railway depot (station)	4
Subway	1
Subway station	4

[19]Subway stations occupy only one tile above ground, so it really doesn't cost you a great deal to sacrifice the investment you put into the zone underneath it.

[20]One factor that subtracts steps is that many Sims have already transferred from another mode of transit and have used up some of their steps before jumping on the railroad or subway.

Crossing Zone Boundaries

Sims can cross a zone boundary only if they are on a road, highway, rail line, or subway, *or if there is a road, subway station, or train depot within three blocks of the zone boundary.* In the absence of transportation within three blocks, zone crossings are not permitted. Table 2-18 shows the costs, effects, and requirements of the different rail options you can build.

Intermodal Rail Transportation

There are three ways to connect your rail or subway lines to other transit modes:

- **Rail/Subway Junction:** You can connect your railroad network directly to your subway lines via a rail/subway junction. This allows the same train cars that roll in your subway to emerge above ground and continue along your rail lines.

Table 2-18 Rail Costs

	Rail Type	Year Available	Pollution Units	Power Requirements (MW)	Land Value ($)	Maintenance Costs per Year ($)	Construction Cost ($)
	Rail on land	1900	0	0	25,000 per tile	0.40 per tile	25 per tile
	Rail bridge	1900	0	0	100,000 per tile (required bridge ramparts add $20,000 for each bridge)	0.25 per tile	75 per tile
	Rail depot (station) (2x2 tiles)	1900	4	2.2	500,000	1.50 per depot	500 per depot
	Subway line	1910	0	0	0ª	0.40	100 per tile
	Subway station (1 tile)	1910	5	0.51	250,000	0.80 per station (the first one is free)	250 per station
	Rail/subway junction (1 tile)	1910	0	0	250,000	0.80 per junction	250 per junction

ªSubways are underground and so don't count toward land value.

- **Rail Depot to Subway Station:** Passengers from a rail depot can transfer to a subway station *only if there is a road tile connecting the rail depot to the subway station.* Even if the rail depot and subway station are side by side, you must still build a single road tile that touches both stations in order for this intermodal transit junction to work.
- **Rail Depot or Subway Station to Road:** The road tiles must actually touch the rail depot or subway station in order for the SimPassengers to transfer between the rail/subway line and their cars.

The Maximum Walking Distance to Transportation

As mentioned previously, all residential, commercial, and industrial zones must be within three blocks of a road, railroad depot, or subway station for any development to occur.[21] For more details on this subject, see the previous section under "Providing Roads." Note that, unlike *SimCity Classic, SimCity 2000* does not allow you to use a rail line (or subway) directly from a zone. You can get on and off rails (or subways) only at designated rail depots (stations) and subway stations. If a tile in any zone type is farther than three blocks from the rail depot or subway station, then you must build a road that allows the Sims to travel from the zone to the station or depot.

Figure 2-36
Rail lines over land and water

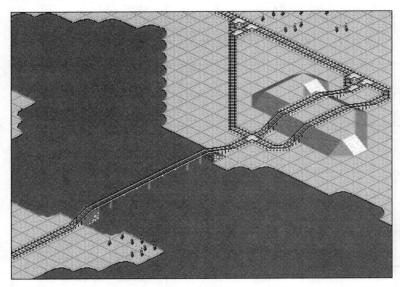

Laying Down Rails

Rail lines (like those in Figure 2-36) are two and one-half times as expensive as roads to build, and they cost four times as much to maintain. Their advantages over roads are that they don't pollute (although the rail depots that are needed to complete a rail system do pollute slightly) and there is never a problem with traffic jams. Since, however, the Sims can get on and off only at rail depots, the effective transportation coverage radius of a rail line

---

[21]High-density zones can actually develop if they are within four blocks of transportation. This is because buildings that have a footprint of 2×2, 3×3, or larger can develop if part of their structure is within a three-block radius of transportation.

is severely dependent on the number of expensive depots you place, and their location.

Unrealistic though it may be, the maintenance costs for rail over water (rail bridges) is less than for rail over land! This may change in a future revision of *SimCity*—apparently it was an oversight in the transportation model.

To build a rail line, follow these steps:

1. While selecting the Rail tool, hold down the mouse button and, when the pop-up submenu opens, select the **Rail** option.

2. Place the pointer over the map, then click and drag where you wish to "draw" your rail line. You will see a shaded portion of tiles trail your pointer as you move it, indicating the intended path the tracks will take. When you release the mouse button, the tracks will be laid. Notice as you move the mouse pointer that the total cost for placement is displayed next to your starting point, and that this number will change as your rail line gets longer or shorter.

"Undo" Your Rail Line or Subway by Pressing Shift

Sometimes, when building rails or subways, you will discover that you have made a mistake that you would like to "undo." If you have not yet released the mouse button, you can remove your rail or subway line, and not be charged for it, by pressing the Shift key and then releasing the mouse button.

Building Off-Map Railroad Connections

If you click the Rail tool on any edge of the map (Figure 2-37), you will be asked whether you want to establish a neighbor railroad connection for $1,500 (Figure 2-38). If you click on the Yes button, a railroad will be built all the way to your neighbor's city off that edge of the map (Figure 2-39).

Rail connections to your neighbor cities help your industrial

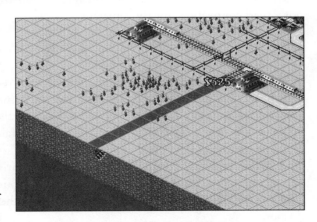

Figure 2-37
To build off-map rail connections, drag the rail tool off the edge of the map.

Figure 2-38
The dialog box asks you whether you wish to spend $1,500 to construct the off-map rail connection.

Figure 2-39
The completed rail
connection

zones, but not your commercial or residential zones.[22] They are not as effective at boosting industry as seaports, however. When you build the road connection, the simulation kicks an industry multiplier into the equations for calculating economic growth. Since this multiplier affects only industry, a rail connection would be a waste of money early in the development of a city, when you are trying to develop commerce.

Only one rail connection is necessary for the multiplier to kick in, but if you build more than one rail connection (by more than one rail connection, we mean adding new rail connections off two or more edges of the map), they will hasten the development of your neighboring cities, thereby increasing your nation's GNP. The more prosperous your neighbors are, the more likely they are to buy your products and trade with you, so it is to your advantage to encourage multiple rail connections (but only one per edge!).

It does not help industry in your city to build multiple rail connections to the same neighboring city off the same edge of the map. You will, however, still need to build a road connection to allow trade with the neighbor cities.

One way you'll know that it's time to build an off-map rail connection is that the Sims will display a message in the Status window stating, "Industry demands a connection." Be sure you build a rail (or highway) connection, not a road connection, for this purpose.

Subways

Subways are underground railroads, which require subway stations to be functional. The only way the Sims can use the subway is if they can find a subway station near enough to where they live to walk or drive to the station. Subways are very expensive to construct and maintain, costing four times as much as rails and ten times as much as roads. They don't occupy surface land, however, except for their 1×1–tile subway stations, and this fact allows you to devote less of your land to transportation purposes. You can use the land that would otherwise have been wasted for other—more productive—purposes.

---

[22]At present, there is a bug in the model that prevents off-map rail connections from boosting industry as much as a seaport. Therefore, seaports are much more effective at boosting industry. This may change in a future revision.

To build a subway line, follow these steps:

1. While selecting the Rail tool, hold down the mouse button, and when the pop-up submenu opens, select the **Subway** option. You will see an underground view of your city immediately.

2. Place the pointer over the map, and then click and drag where you wish to "draw" your subway line. As you move the pointer, a faint trail of black-bordered tiles will follow your pointer, indicating where the subway will be built, as in Figure 2-40. When you release the mouse button, the subway will appear, as in Figure 2-41. Notice as you move the mouse pointer that the total cost for placement is displayed next to your starting point, and that this number will change as your rail line gets longer or shorter.

Click and drag from here . . .   . . . to here.

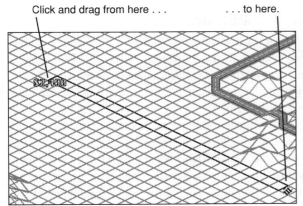

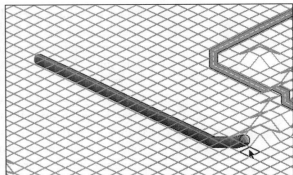

Figure 2-40 After selecting the subway option on the train tool's submenu, you will be presented with an underground view of your city. Click and drag the mouse to place the subway line.

Figure 2-41 The subway line now needs subway stations to become operational.

Subways Cannot Connect with Neighbor Cities Off-Map

Subways cannot be used for direct off-map transportation connections to your neighbor cities. You can build a subway all the way to the city boundary, then build a subway-to-rail connection, and then complete the final leg of the journey to the neighbor cities via rail.

How to Remove Subway Lines

To remove previously laid subway lines, click the Bulldozer tool and select the **Demolish/Clear** option. Click on the Underground button on the Toolbar, then click on the individual tunnel members to remove them one by one.

Rail Depots

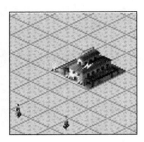

The rail depot is really a railroad station that collects and disperses passengers from your railroad network. In order to function properly, the rail depot needs power, and needs to be adjacent to a rail line. Rail depots emit slight amounts of pollution, but they help to reduce nearby traffic on roads by about 25 to 40 percent. The traffic-reducing potential falls off as the distance from the station increases. Strangely enough, railroad depots reduce traffic more effectively than do subways, but less than bus stations.

At least two Rail depots must be placed alongside your track—and powered—in order for the train system to work its best. You will know your train station is working by the appearance of a train moving on the tracks in the lowest zoom view. When rail depots are unpowered, they will still allow passengers access to the trains, but they won't carry as much traffic.

The Maximum Walking Distance to Rail Depots

When building your rail depots, keep in mind that the three-block-radius walking distance applies to train stations as well as to roads. This means that, in the absence of any connecting or adjacent roads to the rail depot, only those Sims that are within a three-block radius of the station can ride the train.

As explained earlier, by building roads to each depot you can vastly extend the radius within which the Sims in nearby zones can reach the depots. Unfortunately, in the *SimCity 2000* model, if a Sim travels on a road to get to a rail depot, he or she flips a coin to decide whether or not to get on the train. Thus, there is only a fifty-fifty probability that the train will be used, if the journey was started on a road. This reduced probability severely hinders the effectiveness of rail transit. If the trip originates in a three-block radius of the rail depot, then this coin-flipping proposition does not apply, and the Sims will take the train. Figures 2-42 and 2-43 show how a few roads can add to the effectiveness of your rail depots.

How Far Apart Should Rail Depots Be?

Rail depots can be as far apart as 39 blocks, which is the maximum distance the Sims can travel on a rail line without getting off. Since the object of all travel in *SimCity* is for each zone type to "pollinate" the other two zone types, this should be your goal when placing rail depots. Thus, there should be a rail depot *in each of the three zone types*. The majority of all trips should be zone changes, not intrazonal trips. The mark of a successful trip, as gauged by the *SimCity* program, is that it progresses from one zone type to another. Intrazonal trips, or trips inside the same zone, are a waste of time and money, regardless of the travel mode.

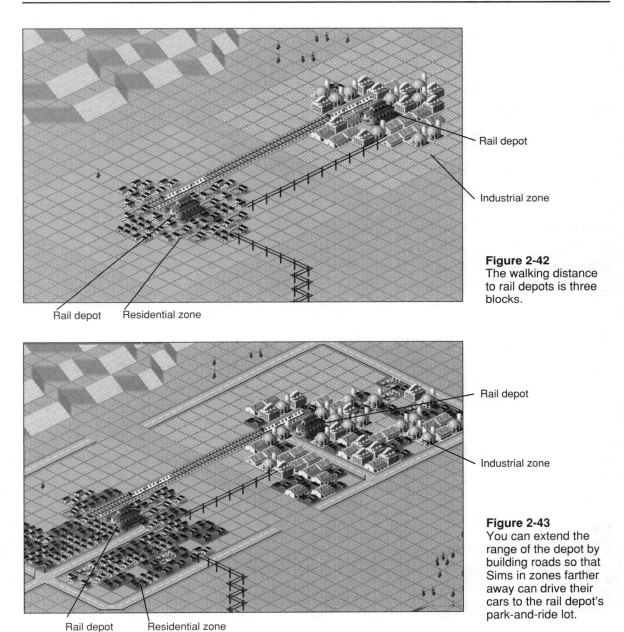

Rail depot

Industrial zone

Figure 2-42
The walking distance
to rail depots is three
blocks.

Rail depot   Residential zone

Rail depot

Industrial zone

Figure 2-43
You can extend the
range of the depot by
building roads so that
Sims in zones farther
away can drive their
cars to the rail depot's
park-and-ride lot.

Rail depot   Residential zone

   If you plan on building a city that depends heavily on rails or subways,
with few or no roads, you need to space your stations at most six blocks apart
in each zone. Furthermore, each depot or station should have access to
another depot in a different zone type that is within the maximum range of

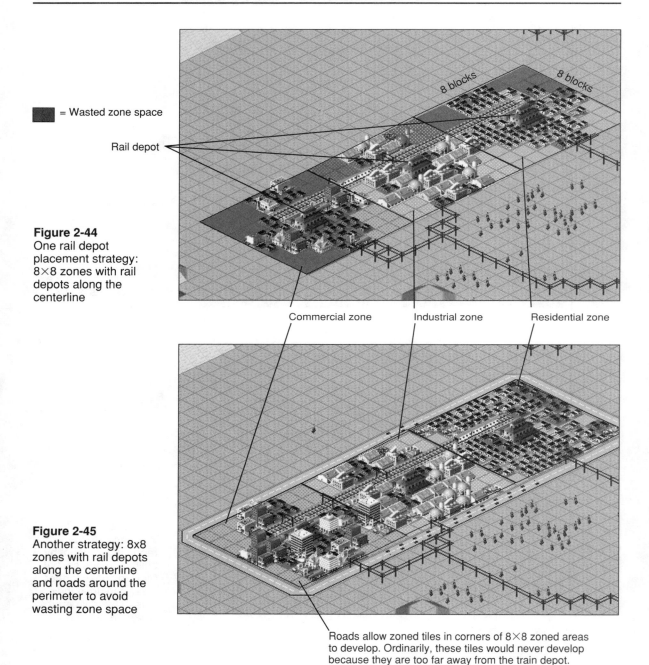

■ = Wasted zone space

Rail depot

Figure 2-44
One rail depot
placement strategy:
8×8 zones with rail
depots along the
centerline

8 blocks

8 blocks

Commercial zone   Industrial zone   Residential zone

Figure 2-45
Another strategy: 8x8
zones with rail depots
along the centerline
and roads around the
perimeter to avoid
wasting zone space

Roads allow zoned tiles in corners of 8×8 zoned areas
to develop. Ordinarily, these tiles would never develop
because they are too far away from the train depot.

rail travel. (The maximum is 39 tiles, but the closer, the better.) Figures 2-44
and 2-45 show two approaches to the station-placement problem.

Subway Stations

Subway stations are needed in order to enter and exit the subway system. The subway line is accessible to the surface only via the subway station, so you must build plenty of stations in order for people to use the system.

Like railroad depots, subway stations emit pollution and need power. They also help to reduce nearby traffic on roads by as much as 10 to 15 percent, with the traffic-reducing potential falling off as the distance from the station increases. In this respect, subways are less effective than trains in reducing traffic, with bus stations still being the best means of relieving traffic arteriosclerosis.

Subway stations must be placed right on top of your subway line, as Figures 2-46 and 2-47 show. They cannot be off to the side by even one block.

The Maximum Walking Distance to Subway Stations

When building your subway stations, remember that the three-block walking-distance rule applies to them. This means that, in the absence of any connecting or adjacent roads to the subway station, only those Sims that are within a three-block radius of the station can use the subway.

As explained earlier, by building roads to each subway station, you can vastly extend the radius within which the Sims in nearby zones can reach the station. Unfortunately, if a Sim travels on a road to get to a subway, he or she flips a coin to decide whether or not to get on the subway. Thus, there is only a fifty-fifty probability that the subway will be used if the journey was started

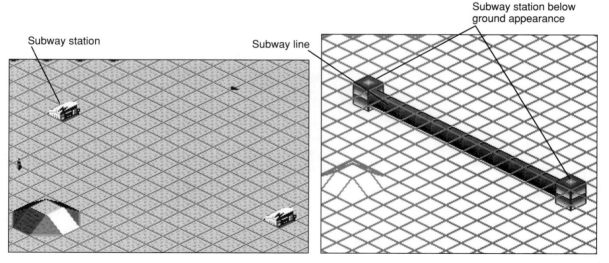

Figure 2-46 Subway stations, an above-ground view

Figure 2-47 Subway stations, a below-ground view, showing placement directly over a subway line

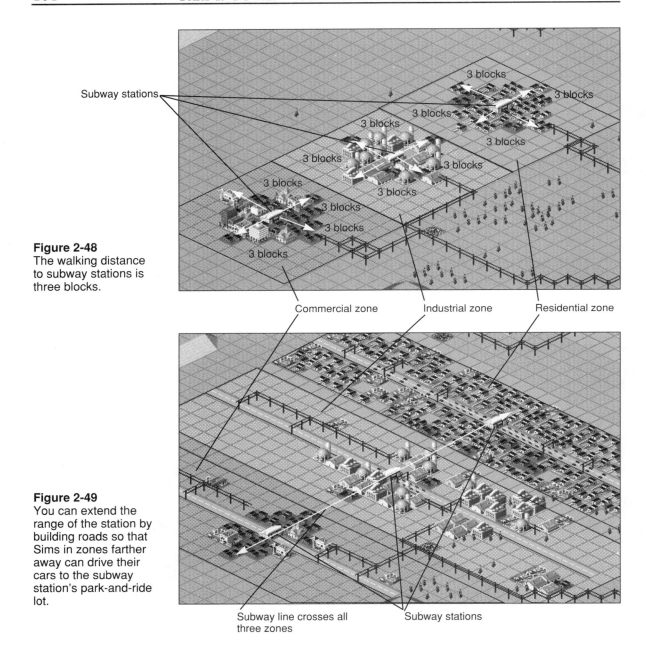

Figure 2-48
The walking distance
to subway stations is
three blocks.

Figure 2-49
You can extend the
range of the station by
building roads so that
Sims in zones farther
away can drive their
cars to the subway
station's park-and-ride
lot.

on a road. If the trip originates in a three-block radius of the subway station,
then this coin-flipping proposition does not apply, and the Sims will take the
subway. The coin-flipping behavior severely hinders the effectiveness of subway transit. Figures 2-48 and 2-49 show the difference a few roads can make.

How Far Apart Should Subway Stations Be?

Subway stations can be as far apart as 39 blocks, which is the maximum distance the Sims can travel on a subway without getting off. Since the object of all travel in *SimCity* is for each zone type to "pollinate" the other two, this should be your goal when deciding where to place subway stations. Thus, there should be a subway station *in each of the three zone types.* The majority of all trips should be zone changes, not intrazonal trips. The mark of a successful trip is when it extends from one zone type to another. Intrazonal trips, or trips inside the same zone, are a waste of time and money on subways; they are better served by roads.

If you plan on building a city with many rails or subways but few or no roads, you need to space your stations at most six blocks apart in each zone, as shown in Figure 2-50, although there is a clever technique for stretching this distance to 12 blocks by using roads, as is illustrated in Figure 2-43 (just substitute the rail depots with subway stations). Each subway station should have access to another station in a different zone type that is within the maximum range of subway travel. (The maximum is 39 tiles, but the closer, the better.)

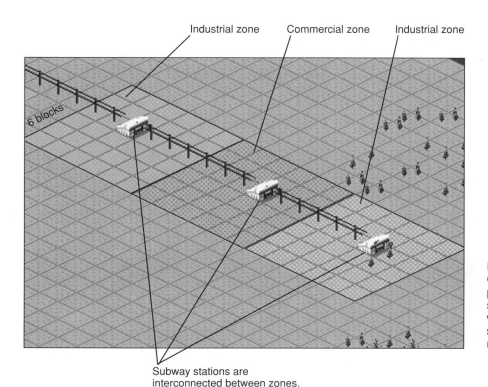

Industrial zone   Commercial zone   Industrial zone

6 blocks

Figure 2-50
One strategy for placing your subway stations: 6x6 zones with subway stations six blocks apart and no roads

Subway stations are interconnected between zones.

Figure 2-51
A different strategy for station placement: $6 \times x$ zones (where x can be any length) with subway stations six blocks apart; are more efficient than 6×6 zones.

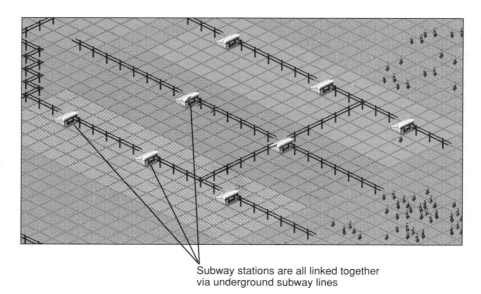

Subway stations are all linked together
via underground subway lines

Subway-to-Rail Junctions

Subway-to-rail junctions allow you to interconnect the subways to your rail lines. You can build the subway-to-rail junction in the above-ground view (Figure 2-52) or the underground view (Figure 2-53) of your city, but in either case, you must have built a rail line or subway *before* you can place the junction on top of it.

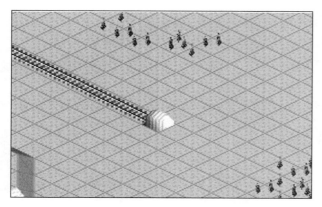

Figure 2-52
An above-ground view of a subway-to-rail junction

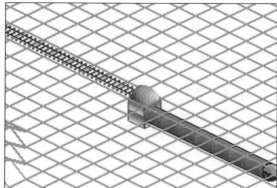

Figure 2-53 A below-ground view of the same junction, showing the need for placement right on top of the subway

Building Ports

Using the Ports tool, you can zone areas for airports to help your commercial zones trade outside your city, and zone areas for seaports to help export your industrial zones export their products. Ports need to be hooked up to your power and water utility conduits in order to function properly, but they don't require transportation links to your zones.[23] For cities of less than 10,000 people, you really don't need to build either kind of port. But once your city reaches a population of 40,000, ports become absolutely essential for further growth. Ports are heavy polluters, with airports being worse than seaports. There are no maintenance costs for ports.

Ports Are Built by the Simulation, Not by You

You can only zone land for ports; you cannot directly build seaports or airports. But you can zone as large an area as you wish for either kind of port. Since ports are very expensive to build, start out with small port zones that are more manageable. All you need to do to build a port is zone the land and then provide power to it. Of course, geographical considerations can deter the development of a port; for example, seaports need to be placed along coastlines and airports need to have a minimum 2×6 parcel on flat terrain before they will appear.

By clicking and holding down the mouse button on the Ports tool, you will see a Ports submenu, revealing two choices: Airport and Seaport. From this menu, select the kind of port you wish to zone, and release the mouse button.

You zone a port just as you would a residential, commercial, or industrial zone. Simply move the mouse pointer over the map and click and drag a rectangular area where you wish the port to develop. As you drag the rectangular area to a larger size, you will see the cost for zoning the port displayed on the map also increase. Table 2-19 shows the relative values, pollution levels, and power costs for each of the two port types.

---

[23]Interestingly enough, the simulation does not check to see if the airport or seaport is connected via rail, road, or subway to your other zones. This means that you can place ports anywhere on your map, and they will function just as if they were at the heart of your city.

Table 2-19 SimCity Speed Comparison

	Zone Type	When Needed	Pollution Units	Power Requirement (MW)	Land Value ($ per tile)	Maintenance Costs ($)	Direct Cost ($)
	Airport zone	> 15,000 people				0 per year for all airports	250 per tile for zoning as an airport (buildings and structures are built by the simulation and cost you nothing)
	Airplanes on runways		10	1	250,000		
	Civilian airplane hanger		2	1	1,000,000		
	Runways		10	0	250,000		
	Warehouses		5	1	250,000		
	Seaport zone	> 10,000 people				0 per year for all seaports	150 per tile for zoning as a seaport (buildings and structures are built by the simulation and cost you nothing)
	Piers		10	1	750,000		
	Crane		5	1	Crane is connected to piers of seaport		
	Port loading zone		10	0	0		
	Loading dock		2	1	600,000		
	Warehouses		5	1	150,000		

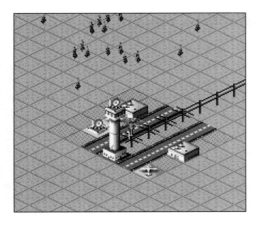

Flying into Airports

Airports boost commerce, but they shouldn't be built until your population reaches 15,000. As mentioned before, road connections off the edge of your city to your neighbor cities are supposed to help commerce grow, just like airports, but this effect seems to be very weak in the *SimCity 2000* Versions 1.00 and 1.1. Airports also require power and water, but they do not require transportation links to the city. This means that your airport can be placed in remote parts of your map, far away from urban centers, without building expensive transportation connections.

Having Trouble Establishing Your Airport?

If your airport is not constructed on your airport zones, there are several possible reasons why. The zone size could be too small. You need a minimum size of 2×5, although 2×6 or larger is preferred. The runway itself takes up five tiles in one direction, and the support buildings fill in the rest.

Enacting pollution-control ordinances can negatively influence airport operations (!).

The location is a poor choice for one of these reasons:

- The nearby terrain interferes with the flight path of aircraft.
- There is not enough level land for the runway to be constructed in the zone.
- The runway orientation (north-south, or east-west) is wrong for your zone. (For example, an airport zone size of 3 vertical tiles by 5 horizontal tiles might not develop, but a zone size of 5 vertical tiles by 3 horizontal tiles will).[24]

The Airport must be situated on level ground.

You haven't supplied power to the zone sufficiently. Add more power lines inside the zone, and when you finally see the runway appear, start removing the excess power lines so that the airport buildings can replace them.

When Commerce Pleads for More Airports, Expand Your Existing Airport

When you learn that the Sims are demanding more airports (as reported in your Status window), it is time to expand your existing airport by another 2×6–tile area to accommodate additional aircraft. It is best to expand your current airport, rather than starting construction on a new airport, because all that's really needed are additional runways. You don't need to duplicate all the support structures, towers, and buildings that make up the original airport.

If you ignore the plea to expand your airport, activity in your commercial zones will slowly grind to a halt.

Avoiding Air Crashes Near Airports

You should avoid having tall buildings built near your runway. This can be done by dezoning areas that are hazardous, or by moving the airport. Gener-

---

[24]A word of advice. If the airport refuses to be built no matter what you do, consider relocating it to another part of your city. Sometimes, *SimCity* decides, for whatever reason, that it doesn't like the site you've picked out, and so it will never build there.

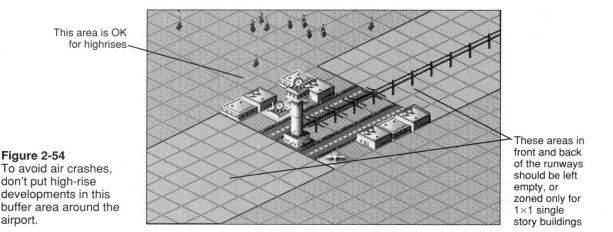

This area is OK for highrises

These areas in front and back of the runways should be left empty, or zoned only for 1×1 single story buildings

Figure 2-54
To avoid air crashes, don't put high-rise developments in this buffer area around the airport.

ally, keep one to three blocks in the front and the rear of the runway clear of all tall obstructions, as shown in Figure 2-54. Small parks, water pumps, trees, and roads are OK, but anything taller could pose a danger to low-fly-ing aircraft. At distances of four to eight tiles, you can zone light density, so that only 1×1–tile low-profile buildings can be built. The height restrictions do not apply to those tiles that are to the side of the runway, but only to those to the front and rear.

Seaports

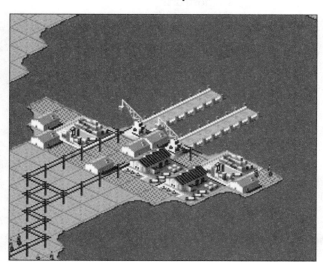

Though this may be obvious, seaport zones should be placed right next to the waterfront, bordering rivers or oceans. If you place the seaport inland, no ships will come by, and the seaport will not be able to perform its assigned task of importing and exporting industrial goods to and from the rest of the world.

Seaports help boost your industry, but are not needed until your population reaches 10,000. Seaports are better at boosting indus-trial growth than highway and rail connec-tions off-map. For a seaport to function properly, it must have power, but it does not require transportation links to your city. This means that your seaport can be placed in remote parts of your map, far away from urban centers, without your building expensive transportation links.

Scaling Seaports

Only one seaport is necessary; in fact, it is wasteful to build more than one seaport, since the simulation checks only to see if one has been built, and if there is enough room for expansion. The seaport will want to expand as your city's industrial base grows, so keep plenty of empty space nearby to enlarge it. From time to time, check on your seaport to see if it has completely filled all your seaport zones with warehouses, piers, and cranes. If it has, you should immediately add some new seaport zones to it. Note that the seaport tiles that are adjacent to the water's edge are the most valuable real estate of all, since they are where the piers are built.

Keep an eye on your Demand Indicator for your industrial zones. If you notice that industrial zones are declining, you should check to see if your seaport is filled to capacity, and needs to be expanded.

Having Trouble Building Your Seaport?

When zoning your seaport, be sure to create a waterfront space for the loading docks and piers, and a large space behind the waterfront area for warehouses and storage yards. If you don't zone your seaport land with ample warehouse and storage space, the port will not function at full capacity. The actual capacity of your seaport is based on the number of docks you have, but the warehouses behind are also an important adjunct to its operation.

If your seaport is not functioning properly, you will not see or hear the ship in the channel, and no cranes, piers, or warehouses appear. Some of the reasons for this trouble are these:

- The ship is blocked from approaching the port by a causeway bridge or some other obstruction.
- The seaport is not situated on level ground.
- You haven't supplied sufficient power to the seaport zone. Add more power lines, and when you finally see the pier develop, start removing the excess lines so that seaport buildings can replace them.
- The seaport zone size is smaller than 1x3 tiles.
- If you have situated your seaport on a river, the water must flow all the way to the edge of the map. Without such a passage, there is no way for the ships to travel to neighboring cities.

Creating Residential Zones

All residents must find or build homes in the residential zones. There are two kinds of residential zones, light and dense, which you select from the Residential Zones tool's submenu. The basic difference between the two zone densities is that light densities allow only 1x1 sized buildings with low population densities, light traffic, and high land values, while the dense zones allow building sizes up to 3×3 with higher population densities, lower land values, and higher traffic levels.[25] There is no pollution associated with either residential zone density, except for the pollution caused by traffic on nearby roads.

One common source of frustration for neophyte mayors is that they can't get their residential zones to develop. Here are the most common reasons:

- No power lines are *inside* the zone. Power lines must be connected, without gaps, to a power plant.
- There are no road connections to nearby industrial zones and commercial zones. It is not enough to have the zones border one another. You *must* build some form of transportation between each zone, whether it be road, rail, or subway.

The Correct Zone Ratios

When building residential zones, the correct ratio of residential zones to commercial and industrial zones is as follows:

Residential zone tiles = Commercial zone tiles + Industrial zone tiles

The ratio of commercial tiles to industrial tiles changes during the course of the game. Early on, you will want to emphasize industry over commercial development. As your population approaches 100,000, you will want to have equal numbers of commercial and industrial zones. When your city has developed sufficiently into a large exporting economy (past, say, a population of 100,000), you should change the ratio to favor commercial over industrial. In all cases, the number of residential zone tiles should equal the combined number of commercial and industrial zone tiles. Table 2-20 shows the changing relationship between industry and commerce based on population.

---

[25]There is an unfortunate bug in the *SimCity* model that prevents high land values from being associated with low-density zones, and low land values from being associated with high-density zones. This should be fixed in a future revision.

Table 2-20 The Proper Ratio of Industrial Zones to Commercial Zones	
Population	Ratio
20,000 and less	3:1
60,000	2:1
100,000	1:1
150,000	1:2
200,000 and greater	1:3

The Demand Indicator on the Toolbar tells you which zone types are most in demand. Don't try to follow its results with knee-jerk reactions, because there is some time delay and what you see may well have changed internally. Use it as a rough guide to what you need to do.

Building Residential Zones

To build a residential zone, follow these steps:

1. Select the Residential Zones tool and hold down the mouse button.
2. In the pop-up menu, choose the **Light** or **Dense** zone option, then release the mouse button.
3. Move the cursor over the map, and click and drag the mouse. As you move the mouse, you will see a shaded rectangle of tiles follow your cursor; this shows you how large your zone will be when you release the mouse button. Notice that the price for building the zone is displayed next to your starting point.
4. When you are satisfied that the zone is the right size, release the mouse button. If you have made a mistake, you can hold down the Shift key before releasing the mouse button to cancel your actions.

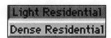

If you zone over an area with buildings on it, nothing will happen and you won't be charged a penny. Likewise, if you zone over an existing empty zone of the same type and density, nothing will happen and you will not be charged. But if you zone over an empty zone of a different type *or* density, the zone will change, and you will be charged for it. Table 2-21 details the different residential zone types.

Table 2-21 Residential Zone Density and Building Parameters

Zone Density	Population	Cost per Tile to Zone ($)	Description
Light 1x1 buildings	10 people per acre	5	Low traffic, low population, and high land values[a]
Dense 1x1 buildings	10 people per acre	10	High traffic, high population, and low land values[a]
2x2 buildings	Low density: 80 people (20 people per acre); High density: 120 people (30 people per acre)		
3x3 buildings	360 people (40 people per acre)		

[a]At present, there is a bug in the program that affects the land value–land density relationship.

Removing and Rezoning Residential Zones

Zones can be removed entirely with the De-Zone bulldozer tool. But you must first rid the zone of any buildings. If, on the other hand, you wish to merely rezone an existing zone, you can just drag the new zone over the old zone, but only if the old zone is first cleared of structures.

Light Residential Zones

Traffic in light residential zones is less than traffic in dense residential zones.[26] With the lower population densities, the quality of life is better, and you earn more tax revenues because the land values are higher. Unfortunately, your population is limited to about 10 persons per acre, and this tends to limit the potential size of your city.

The only buildings that are allowed in light residential zones are 1×1-tile single-family dwellings. These consist of three types: lower-class homes, middle-class homes, and luxury homes. Each class of homes has four different building styles. The cost for building light residential zones is $5 per tile.

---

[26]There is a bug in *SimCity* that causes this relationship to be reversed. It should be fixed in an update, but probably won't be.

Dense Residential Zones

Traffic is worse in dense residential zones than it is in light residential zones. Also, land values are lower, due to greater congestion, which tends to depress your tax revenues. Balanced against these twin evils, your population densities are much higher, and this fact tends to counter the effect that lower land values have on your tax revenues. With higher populations, your tax revenues will be higher.

Any 1×1 buildings on one-acre parcels contain 10 people. There are two classes of 2×2 buildings: low-density and high-density. (Don't confuse these classes with zone densities; these are just subtypes within the **Dense Residential** zone type.) For the low-density 2×2 buildings, the population added is 80 people, or 20 people per acre, while the high-density 2×2 buildings have 120 people, or 30 people per acre. For each 3×3 building, the population increases by 360 people, or 40 people per acre. The cost for building each tile of dense residential zone is $10.

Churches

Churches, which can pop up in residential zones and occupy 2×2 tiles, have no people in them, and don't add to your population. What's more, they are more of a nuisance than a help in *SimCity 2000*, since they occupy valuable real estate, and frequently pop up where you least want them. Furthermore, the land they absorb is converted to empty land, so when you bulldoze them, you'll have to rezone the land again. Churches offer nothing to your city, except their aesthetic architecture. The number of churches your city gets is determined by the number of zones you have. When you drop below a certain ratio of churches to residential zones, the simulation adds a new church to any available residential 2×2 plot of land that it can find.

Which Zone Density Should You Build?

In making the choice between light and dense zones, you must figure out whether higher population or higher land values will best maximize your income stream.[27] Then choose light residential zones if land value is more important, or dense residential zones if population is more important.

Dense residential zone buildings have three sizes: 1×1 tile, 2×2 tiles, and 3×3 tiles. (The maximum size is 3×3 tiles.) There are eight different kinds of residential buildings sized 2×2, and four different kinds of 3×3 buildings.

For maximum efficiency, build dense residential zones in block sizes of 6×6 or 6×x (where x can be any length).

---

[27]Tax revenue is based on a combination of population and land values.

The larger 3×3 buildings consist of apartment buildings and condominiums, and the medium-sized 2×2 buildings consist of cheap apartments, so-so apartments, nice apartments, and condominiums.

Since you will want to allow room for the 3×3 buildings to crop up, you should plan your roads, rails, and other infrastructure to allow unimpeded zone blocks of at least 3×3, 3×x, 6×6, or 6×x (where x can be any number of tiles).[28] Because the Sims can walk three blocks to transportation, it is actually more efficient to build 6×x zones, because you then avoid unnecessary duplication of transportation services.

Creating Commercial Zones

In order for the Sims to shop or conduct routine business, they must have commercial buildings. These buildings can be built only in the areas of your city designated as commercial zones. You build commercial zones by selecting the Commercial Zones tool, holding down the mouse button, and then choosing which zone density you want in the pop-up menu. If you want dense commercial zones, select **Dense**, or if you want light commercial zones, select **Light**. The basic difference between the two zone densities is that light densities allow only 1×1 buildings with low population densities, low traffic, and high land values, while the dense zones allow building sizes up to 3×3 with higher population densities but with lower land values and higher traffic levels. There is no pollution associated with either commercial zone density, except for the pollution caused by traffic on nearby roads..

The growth of commercial zones can be boosted by the addition of road connections to your neighboring cities,[29] or by the construction of an airport. These connections further trade between your city and the neighboring city. In either case, you will be alerted to the need for either an airport or an off-map neighbor-city connection by a message in the Status window.

Commerce is heavily favored only when your city has grown past a population of 100,000. This is because you no longer need to develop an external export market for your industry but can consume your internally produced goods yourself. Your commerce takes the predominant role in the city, as your industry slows down. Thus, when your city reaches a large size, you need to restructure the industry-to-commerce zone ratio to favor commerce. Gradually, as your city grows larger, you will increase the ratio to three commercial zones for each industrial zone, although the combined

[28]It is also possible to design 12×12 zones. See Figure 2-43.

[29]This does not work right in the current release.

total of industrial and commercial zones should still equal the total number of residential zones. For a discussion of the relationship between commercial, residential, and industrial zones, see the previous section, "Creating Residential Zones."

Building Commercial Zones

To build a commercial zone, follow these steps:

1. Select the Commercial Zones tool and hold down the mouse button.
2. In the pop-up menu, choose the **Light** or **Dense** zone option, then release the mouse button.
3. Move the cursor over the map and click and drag the mouse. As you move the mouse, you will see a shaded rectangle of tiles follow your cursor; this shows you how large your zone will be when you release the mouse button. Notice too that the price for building the zone is displayed next to your starting point.
4. When you are satisfied that the zone is the right size, release the mouse button. If you have made a mistake, hold down the Shift key before releasing the mouse button to cancel your actions.

If you zone over an area with buildings on it, nothing will happen and you won't be charged a dime. Likewise, if you zone over an existing empty zone of the same type and density, nothing will happen and you will not be charged. But if you zone over an empty zone of a different type *or* density, the zone will change, and you will be charged for it. Table 2-22 shows the costs and other factors associated with the various zones.

Light Commercial Zones

Only 1×1 buildings are allowed in light commercial zones. There are eight different types of 1×1 commercial buildings; they include two gas stations, a bed-and-breakfast establishment, a convenience store, a small office building, a larger office building, a warehouse, and a toy store. For each of these building types, there exists a population of 10 people per acre.

As in other light-density zones, traffic in light commercial zones is less than traffic in dense commercial zones.[30] Land values are higher as well. It costs $5 per tile to zone light commercial zones.

---

[30]There is a bug in *SimCity* that causes this relationship to be reversed. It should be fixed in a bug update, but we doubt it.

Table 2-22 Commercial Zone Density and Building Parameters

Zone Density	Population	Cost per Tile to Zone ($)	Description
Light 1×1 buildings	10 people per acre	5	Low traffic, low population, and high land values[a]
Dense 1×1 buildings	10 people per acre	10	High traffic, high population, and low land values[a]
2×2 buildings	Low density: 80 people (20 people per acre); High density: 120 people (30 people per acre)		
3×3 buildings	360 people (40 people per acre)		

[a]At present, there is a bug in the program that affects the land value–land density relationship.

Dense Commercial Zones

Dense commercial zones, which consist of banking conglomerates, real estate firms, and financial services, have more traffic and lower land values. Dense commercial zones can have higher population densities than light zones, and this fact helps increase revenues from your tax collections. It costs $10 per tile to zone dense commercial zones.

Which Zone Density Should You Build?

In making the choice between light and dense zones, you must figure out whether higher population or higher land values will best maximize your income stream.[31] Choose light commercial zones if land value is more important, or dense commercial zones if population is more important.

 For maximum efficiency, build dense commercial zones in block sizes of 6×6 or 6×x (where x can be any length).

---

[31]Tax revenue is based on a combination of population and land values.

Dense commercial zone buildings have three sizes: 1×1 tile, 2×2 tiles, and 3×3 tiles. (The maximum size is 3×3 tiles.) As mentioned in the previous section, there are eight different 1×1 commercial buildings. In addition, there are 10 different kinds of commercial buildings sized 2×2 and 10 different kinds of 3×3 buildings. The 2×2 and 3×3 buildings consist of shopping centers, grocery stores, office buildings, resort hotels, office parks, office towers, mini-malls, "theatre squares" (modeled after Maxis Headquarters in Orinda, California—you will see the Maxis marquee prominently emblazoned on the corner edifice of a theatre square), drive-ins, parking garages, historic office buildings, and KSIM corporate headquarters skyscrapers.

The 1×1 buildings have 10 people per acre, and there are two classes of 2×2 buildings: low-density and high-density. (Don't confuse this kind of density with zone densities; these are just subtypes within the **Dense Commercial** zone type.) Low-density 2×2 buildings add 80 people, or 20 people per acre, while high-density 2×2 buildings have 120 people, or 30 people per acre. For each 3×3 building, the population increases by 360 people, or 40 people per acre.

Since you will want to allow room for the 3×3 buildings to crop up, you should plan your roads, rails, and other infrastructure to allow unimpeded zone blocks of at least 3×3, 3×x, 6×6, or 6×x (where x can be any number of tiles).[32] Because the Sims can walk three blocks to transportation, it is actually more efficient to build 6×x zones, because you then avoid unnecessary duplication of transportation services.

Creating Industrial Zones

Industry is vital to your city's economy. Without it, there would be no jobs for your residents and they would be forced to move away. In short, without a thriving industrial base, your city will wither away or simply not develop at all. All industrial enterprises must be located in industrial zones, which you establish by using the Industrial Zones tool. When you select this tool, a pop-up menu will open and you must decide whether you want to build a light or dense industrial zone. Select Light if you want light industry or Dense if you want heavy industry. All industrial zones emit pollution, with the light-density zones producing less than the dense zones. In fact, industrial zones are the primary source of pollution in *SimCity*. Also, industrial zones tend to assume low land values and high crime rates, so they need plenty of police stations and parks to counteract these negative attributes. It

---

[32]It is also possible to design 12×12 zones. See Figure 2-43.

also helps to separate your industrial zones from residential and commercial zones because the intensity of pollution falls off with distance from the source.

The growth of industrial zones can be boosted by the addition of highway or rail connections to your neighboring cities, or by the construction of a seaport.[33] These transportation systems further trade between your city and the neighboring city. In either case, you will be alerted to the need for either a seaport or an off-map connection to a neighbor city by a message in the Status window.

Industry is heavily favored in the early growth of any city, because you must develop export markets for your goods before you can build an internal economy based on commerce. Thus, when starting out with a small city, you should build three times as many industrial zones as you do commercial zones, although the combined total of industrial and commercial zones should still equal the total number of residential zones. For a discussion of the proper ratios of commercial, residential and industrial zones, see the earlier section, "Creating Residential Zones."

When you build an industrial zone, the kind of industry that develops is dependent on the industries that are in highest demand in the SimNation. You can see which industry is most in demand by checking the Industry window's Demand graph.

Building Industrial Zones

To build an industrial zone, follow these steps:

1. Select the Industrial Zones tool and hold down the mouse button.
2. In the pop-up menu, choose the **Light** or **Dense** zone option, and then release the mouse button.
3. Move the cursor over the map and click and drag the mouse. As you move the mouse, you will see a shaded rectangle of tiles follow your cursor; this shows you how large your zone will be when you release the mouse button. Notice too that the price for building the zone is displayed next to your starting point.
4. When you are satisfied that the zone is the right size, release the mouse button. If you have made a mistake, you can press and hold the Shift key before releasing the mouse button to cancel your actions.

---

[33]The off-map highway and rail connections do not significantly help industry in the current release of *SimCity 2000*. They are supposed to, however.

If you zone over an area with buildings on it, nothing will happen and you won't be charged a nickel. Likewise, if you zone over an existing empty zone of the same type and density, nothing will happen and you will not be charged. But if you zone over an empty zone of a different type *or* density, the zone will change and you will be charged for it.

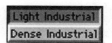

Tip: Lackluster industrial zones are sometimes given a big boost by building residential zones nearby.

Industrial zones' pollution is figured by zone density, the size of the buildings, and industry type. The basic pollution levels for light industrial zones versus dense industrial zones is given by Table 2-23.

The Eleven Industries of *SimCity 2000*

There are 11 different industries that can develop in *SimCity 2000*'s industrial zones. They are listed on the next page:

Table 2-23 Industrial Zones and the Pollution They Emit

Industrial Zone Type	Pollution Units	Population	Cost per Tile ($)	Description
Light industrial 1×1 tile buildings[b]	6	10 people per acre	5	Low traffic, low population, and high land values[a]
Dense industrial 1×1 tile buildings	6	10 people per acre	10	High traffic, high population, and low land values[a]
2×2 tile buildings[c]	12 and 18	80 people (20 people per tile) for warehouses; 120 people (30 people per tile) for factories		
2×2 tile buildings[c]	24	360 people (40 people per tile)		

[a]At present, there is a bug in the program that affects the land value–land density relationship.

[b]Light industrial zones only develop 1×1 tile buildings.

[c]Dense Industrial 2×2 zones have two different pollution levels, which depend on the kind of industry that develops in the zone.

- Steel mining
- Textiles
- Petrochemicals
- Food

- Construction
- Automotive
- Aerospace
- Finance

- Media
- Electronics
- Tourism

Zone Requirements for Each Industry

Of these 11 industries, some prefer dense industrial zones, while others prefer light industrial zones, so if you are planning on emphasizing one of the latter class of industries in your economy — say, finance — then you should establish light industrial zones and avoid dense industrial zones. (Although finance can exist in either zone type, it thrives best in light industrial zones.) Table 2-24 shows the zone preferences and effects of each industry type.

By using the Industry window's Tax Rate button, you can selectively raise or lower taxes on any of the 11 above-listed industries. Thus you can encourage or discourage a particular industry merely by raising or lowering its taxes. In the Industry window, you can also check the relative industry ratios as a percentage of total industrial activity, and you can see what the total national demand for each industry is.

Light Industrial Zones

Certain industries prefer the light industrial zone. You can determine which ones by Shift-clicking on each industry in the Industry window to view the industry description or by consulting Table 2-24. As mentioned earlier, pollution is usually less (about six units per tile) in light industrial zones that in dense industrial zones (which can range up to 24 units for a 3×3 factory). And as in the other light-density zones, traffic congestion is less in the light industrial zones than in dense industrial zones.[34]

Light industrial zones allow buildings that are no larger than one tile in size. There are four kinds of 1×1 industrial buildings: two warehouses, one chemical storage facility, and an industrial substation. A 1×1 building has a population of 10 people.

You should be aware that selective taxation of individual industry categories (in the Industries window) as well as enactment of pollution control ordinances can affect the development of certain industries. It costs $5 per tile to zone light industrial zones.

---

[34]There is a bug in SimCity that causes this relationship to be reversed. It should be fixed in a bug update, but will it?

Table 2-24 Industry Zone Requirements

Industry Type	Pollution Level	Industrial Zone Density Preference	Industry's Effect on City
Steel mining	Heavy	Dense	A major source of employment, it can be stifled by enactment of the Pollution Control Ordinance
Textiles	Heavy	Dense	A major source of employment, it can be stifled by enactment of the Pollution Control Ordinance
Petrochemicals	Heavy	Dense	A high tech industry, it needs a city with a high educational (EQ) level to be properly staffed—it can be stifled by enactment of the Pollution Control Ordinance
Food	Light	Light or dense	Workers don't need high education levels
Construction	Light	Light or dense	Employs few people and relies primarily on out-of-town workers
Automotive	Heavy	Dense	Requires a work force with high education levels and can be stifled by enactment of the Pollution Control Ordinance
Aerospace	Heavy	Dense	Employs many people but requires a work force with high education levels
Finance	Light	Light	Requires a work force with high education levels
Media	Light	Light	Requires a work force with high education levels
Electronics	Medium	Light or dense	Can employ huge numbers of people but requires a work force with high education levels
Tourism	Light	Light or dense	Thrives in cities with lots of tourist attractions such as zoos, marinas, and stadiums; high crime can ruin tourism

Dense Industrial Zones

Certain industries prefer the heavy industrial zone. You can determine which ones by Shift-clicking on each industry in the Industry window to view the industry description, or by consulting Table 2-24. Pollution is heaviest in this type of zone, but many more workers can be employed in each building.

Buildings that you will see in this type of zone include factories, construction sites, chemical storage facilities, warehouses, and industrial substations. You will see all sizes of industrial buildings: 1×1, 2×2, and 3×3 (the largest size). The 1×1 industrial buildings have a population of 10 people, the 2×2 buildings have a population of 120 people (30 per acre) for factories and 80 people (20 per acre) for warehouses, and the 3×3 factories have a population of 360 people (40 per acre). For a discussion of the relative merits of light versus dense zones with regard to your city's finances, see the previous section, "Dense Residential Zones."

Be aware that selective taxation of the individual industry categories (in the Industries window), along with enacting pollution control ordinances, can affect the development of certain industries.

It costs $10 per tile to zone dense industrial zones.

 For maximum efficiency, build dense industrial zones in block sizes of 6×6 or 6×x (where x can be any length).

Dense industrial zone buildings have three sizes: 1×1 tile, 2×2 tiles, and 3×3 tiles. (The maximum size is 3×3 tiles.) As mentioned before, there are four different 1×1 industrial buildings. In addition, there are eight different kinds of industrial buildings sized 2×2, and six different kinds of 3×3 buildings. Both the 2×2 and 3×3 buildings consist of factories, chemical processing plants, and warehouses.

Since you will want to allow room for the 3×3 buildings to crop up, you should plan your roads, rails, and other infrastructure to allow unimpeded zone blocks of at least 3×3, 3×x, 6×6, or 6×x (where x can be any number of tiles).[35] Because the Sims can walk three blocks to transportation, it is actually more efficient to build 6×x zones, because then you then avoid unnecessary duplication of transportation services.

Providing Education

Using the Education tool, you can build schools, colleges, libraries, and museums. Despite what you might think, it doesn't matter where these Microsims are placed. The *SimCity 2000* simulation only checks to see if they are there, not where they are located. Each of the educational institutions you can build either elevates or sustains the education quotient (EQ), of your city. The EQ is the measure of the education your population has received and retained, and it is broken down by age groups. The EQ that most affects your city is that of your work force, ages 20 to 55. By elevating the EQ through educating your young people, you enable your work force to be highly skilled and prepared for the high-tech jobs of tomorrow.

---

[35]It is also possible to design 12×12 zones. See Figure 2-43.

Table 2-25 School and College Effect on EQ	
Educational Institution	EQ Boosted to This Level
School	90
College	140

EQs, which can be viewed in the Population window, range from zero (brain-dead) to 150. Normal EQs for the various amounts of schooling that you have provided for the Sims are listed in Table 2-25. The average EQ for all the Sims is 100. Normal EQ for working-age immigrants to your city is 85, which is about what a high school education offers. The children of new immigrants possess EQs slightly lower than this.

Even after raising your Sims' educational levels, you must still keep them from eroding as the game progresses. After Sims graduate from high school or college, their EQs slowly drop. You can stop this EQ erosion by building libraries and museums, whose sole function in *SimCity 2000* is to maintain high educational levels.

Schools and colleges also tend to degrade over time. The value of education is eroded by a creeping inflation, which can be countered by enacting a Pro-Reading Campaign Ordinance.

Don't neglect the value of education for your children and the future economy of your city. Even though newly arrived residents and their children may have a decent education, in a short time, if nothing is done, education will consist of verbal lore passed down from generation to generation. Children educated this way will achieve only 20 percent of their parents' EQ.

If you believe that everybody should "pull themselves up by their own bootstraps," and that education is a waste of public money, then consider this: cities with a low EQ have a greater chance of both unemployment and rioting. It may cost you more in the long run to neglect educational needs than to attend to them now.

Each school and college costs you money to operate each year. These funds are allocated in your education department's Budget window. Libraries and museums, which help keep your EQs from eroding, don't cost any money to maintain.

The Effect of EQ on Industries

In *SimCity 2000*, education has a bigger effect on city growth than health levels or even industrial population ratios. This is because the EQ is tied directly into the industrial model, influencing the kinds of industries that can thrive.

Your city's EQ affects the economic vitality of certain industries. High-technology industries such as electronics and aerospace get a special growth boost when the population's EQ reaches 130, but they will also get a smaller boost at an EQ of 100.

These industries get a growth boost at an EQ greater than 100:

- Media
- Finance
- Automotive
- Petrochemicals
- Electronics
- Aerospace

These industries get an additional special growth boost at an EQ of 130 or greater, but suffer if the EQ is less than 80:

- Electronics
- Aerospace

Most high-technology industries will grow even with low EQs, but they will receive a growth boost if your average EQ exceeds 100. To reach this EQ, you should build more colleges, but you needn't build enough colleges to serve the entire population. If you build only enough colleges to serve half your population, you can still maintain an EQ of over 100. Thus, for example, if your city has a population of 100,000, you needn't build two colleges; one will suffice, since you need to serve only one-half of 100,000, or 50,000, people, and each college normally serves 50,000 people. Of course, you will still need to build and maintain public schools to prepare students for college.

Building Educational Facilities

To build any educational institution, follow these steps:

1. Select the Education tool.
2. While holding down the mouse button, select the school, the college, the library, or the museum in the pop-up submenu that you see.
3. Release the mouse button.
4. Move the pointer over the map and click to place the facility.

Table 2-26 shows various data for each educational institution.

Table 2-26 Educational Facilities

	Educational Institution	Zone Size	Function	Land Value	Power Requirements (MW)	Maximum Population Served	Maintenance Costs per Year ($)	Construction Cost ($)
	School	3×3 tiles	Boosts EQ rating to 90 for students aged 5–15	250,000	5	15,000 people (maximum of 1,500 students and 60 teachers)	25	250
	College	4×4 tiles	Boosts EQ rating to 140 for students aged 15–25	1,000,000	6.6	50,000 people (maximum of 5,000 students and 210 teachers)	100	1,000
	Library	2×2 tiles	Keeps EQ levels from eroding in work force	500,000	2	20,000	0	500
	Museum	3×3 tiles	Keeps EQ levels from eroding in work force	1,000,000	5	40,000	0	1,000

In School

Schools, which raise EQ levels to about 90, educate both the 5-to-10 and 10-to-15 age groups by giving them a boost of 35 EQ points each. Children in the zero-to-five age group inherit one-fifth of their parents' EQ at birth, which is added to the 35 EQ points they receive in elementary school (ages 5 to 10) and the additional 35 EQ points they receive in high school (ages 10 to 15). Thus children born to parents with an EQ of 100 would have an EQ of 20 at birth (one-fifth of 100 equals 20). When they finish elementary school at age 10, their EQ is raised an additional 35 points to 55. After they graduate from high school, an additional 35 points of EQ is added, for a total of 90 EQ points—still less than that of their parents. To bring the students' EQ higher than this, they must enroll in college.

Each school serves a population of 15,000 people and can have up to 1,500 students and 60 teachers, with the number of teachers based on educational funding and population. In general, a school can never have more teachers than 10 percent of the population. So, for example, if your population is 100, you can have 10 teachers. Each school is graded on how well it educates its students. This grade is derived from the student-to-teacher ratio, with grades of A being awarded for student-to-teacher ratios of 13:1 or less. Failing grades of F are given for student-to-teacher ratios greater than 26:1. Ratios and the resulting grades are detailed in Table 2-27.

Table 2-27 Student-to-Teacher Ratios and Grades for Schools

Grade	A+	A	A–	B+	B	B–	C+	C	C–	D+	D	D–	F+	F
Ratio	13	14	15	16	17	18	19	20	22	23	24	25	26	27

To see how many teachers and students a school has, or what its grade is, click the Query tool on the school. In the Microsim dialog box that pops up, you can view this information, but it will be updated only once a year, in January.

As long as schools are powered, they don't care where they are placed on the map. What's more, you don't need to bother with providing them with transportation access.

To check the EQ of your population, open the Population Graphs window and click on the Education button. If your school grades are bad, you can improve them:

- Build more schools. This adds new teachers to the district, thereby lowering the student-to-teacher ratio.
- Increase educational funding, if you haven't already.

Off to College

Colleges, which serve the 15-to-25 age group, multiply the EQ levels of entering students by 1.5. Thus an entering freshman with an EQ of 90 will have, by the time he or she graduates, an EQ of 135. If these students have children of their own, their children will have one-fifth their EQ, or 27. Picking up another 70 EQ points in grammar school, these kids will graduate from high school with an EQ of 97, seven points better than their parents. As this generational process repeats, eventually the EQ can be raised as high as 150 points for students graduating from college.

Each college serves a population of 50,000 people and can have up to 5,000 students and 210 teachers, the number of teachers being based on educational funding and population.

Like schools, colleges are given a grade based on how well they educate their students. This grade is derived from the student-to-teacher ratio, with grades of A being awarded for ratios of 13:1 or less. Failing grades of F are given for ratios greater than 26:1. For a list of grades for the different ratios, see the previous section on schools. Likewise, if your college's grades are bad, you can either increase the number of colleges or increase the educational funding.

To see how many teachers and students your college has, or what its grade is, click the Query tool on the school you're interested in. In the Microsim dialog box that pops up, you can view this information, but it will be updated only once a year in January. To check the EQ of your population, open the Population Graphs window and click on the **Education** button.

Colleges don't care where they are placed on the map and don't require road or other transportation access. They do require power, however.

Libraries

Libraries, which serve up to 20,000 people, help slow the erosion of EQ points from your work force. The location of libraries does not matter, nor do they need to be connected to your transportation network. They do require power, however. The number of books and the attendance determine the grade you received for the library's performance of its civic responsibilities. This information can be viewed by clicking the Query tool on the library.

Museums

Museums, which are twice as effective as libraries at slowing the erosion of EQ points (but likewise are twice as expensive), serve 40,000 people. As with libraries, the location of museums does not matter, nor do they need to be connected to your transportation network. The number of exhibits and the attendance determine the grade you receive. This information can be viewed by clicking the Query tool on the museum.

Providing City Services

All your city services are provided through the City Services tool. You can build police stations, fire stations, hospitals, and prisons using this tool.

To build any city services facility, follow these steps:

1. Select the City Services tool.
2. While holding down the mouse button, select the police department, the fire station, the hospital, or the prison in the pop-up submenu that you see.
3. Release the mouse button.
4. Move the pointer over the map and click to place the facility.

Table 2-28 shows important data for each of the city services buildings.

Table 2-28 City Services Building Costs

	City Services Institution	Zone Size	Population	Land Value	Power Requirements (MW)	Pollution Units	Maintenance Costs per Year ($)	Construction Cost ($)
	Police	3×3 tiles	Not applicable	500,000	5	0	100	500
	Fire station	3×3 tiles	Not applicable	500,000	4	0	100	500
	Hospital	3×3 tiles	Serves 25,000 people	500,000	5	0	50	500
	Prison	4×4 tiles	Houses up to 10,000 inmates	3,000,000	6.66	10	0 (yes, it's really true!)	3,000

Police

Police departments are good for suppressing crime, and in disasters they can help stamp out riots. Police stations lower crime rates in a 20×20–block radius around them, but the farther away you get, the less effective they are. Their radius of influence is severely diminished if they are not powered. Plan to build your police stations where they will do the most good, such as in industrial zones

By looking at the Map window's crime readout graph, you can easily pinpoint the heart of the crime district. Similarly, in the Map window, you can plot the location and coverage area of all your police departments in your city. This helps you determine where to add new police stations. Don't situate police stations closer than 20 blocks to one another, since you will be overlapping their coverage areas and wasting money on duplication of services (except in the case of arcos, where you may need to overlap police coverage to force down excessive crime). Also, avoid placing police stations on the edge of the map, since half their coverage area will be wasted. Finally, make sure your police department is powered, since without power its effectiveness is diminished. You can check this out for yourself in the Map window, which shows the police department's effectiveness in shades of black and gray; when the police department is at maximum strength, the center of the coverage area will be black.

Land values are also bolstered by the presence of police stations. Using the Query tool on the police station, you can check various Microsim statistics for your police stations to see how they are performing. You can check the number of arrests versus the number of crimes committed, and you can see how many officers the station has on the payroll. Funding decisions you make in the Budget window for the police department affect the number of officers you can hire. The maximum number of policeman per station is 200.

Analyzing your police department statistics (use the Query tool on the police department), you should notice if the number of officers is greater than the number of crimes. If this is so, you are OK. But if there are more crimes than officers, then it is time to add more police stations and, if necessary, to add a prison.

You may notice a doubling in crime rates if the city council legalizes gambling in a municipal ordinance. This is due to the criminal activity that inevitably follows big gambling establishments. Another huge increase in crime will occur when you build arcologies.

Fire Stations

Fire departments put out fires and clean up toxic spills. The presence of a fire station in a neighborhood tends to discourage fires within a 20×20–block radius of the fire station, but the farther away you get, the less effective it is. Fire stations' radius of influence is severely diminished if they are not powered. Fires that occur outside this radius can be fought by dispatching your fire crews using the Emergency tool, but only one crew per fire department can be sent. The maximum number of firemen per fire department is 50, and the maximum number of fire trucks is four. (You can dispatch only one emergency fire crew to fight fires, regardless of how many fire trucks a particular station has.) The numbers of firemen and fire trucks are tied to your city's population and fire department funding levels. The fire response time is randomly generated and is meaningless.

You can check your fire department's coverage area by using the Map window, checking to see where each station is in relation to other stations. Don't situate fire stations closer than 20 blocks to one another, since you will be overlapping their coverage areas and wasting money on duplication of services. Also avoid placing fire stations on the edge of the map, since half their coverage area will be wasted. Finally, make sure your fire department is powered, since without power, its effectiveness is diminished. You can check this out for yourself in the Map window, which shows the fire department's effectiveness in shades of black and gray; when the fire department is at maximum strength, the center of the coverage area will be black.

Hospitals

Hospitals increase the Life Expectancy (LE) for your city. The general health of your city is represented by the LE, and this number changes for each age group. Hospitals have their most direct influence on the youngest Sims; those children from zero to five years of age. When a Sim is born, its life expectancy is set by the level of hospital service, and by various city ordinances. As Sims age, some time is subtracted from their LE, with additional time subtracted in proportion to your city's pollution levels. The higher the pollution, the more years they lose off their LE. You can view the LE for each age group in the Population window. Note that as each generation moves up to the next age group, the LE gets smaller. Newly arrived immigrant Sims will have an average LE of about 65.

One hospital can serve up to 25,000 people. Although there may be only 600 beds in your city, you can actually squeeze in more patients than this, because many patients who have no health insurance will be left on gurneys in the hall. The number of doctors possible is based on population and hospital funding levels, while the number of patients is based on the city's population and the number of beds.

It is very important to prevent your Sims from dying young, which actually increases the burden on your schools and colleges, since they will have to educate more and more young people as the older generation dies off. Therefore, keeping your Sims healthy is crucial to your economic survival.

You can locate your hospitals anywhere in the city, since the simulation does not care where they are; it just checks to see how many hospitals you have. Just make sure the hospital has power and that you build one more hospital for each increase of 25,000 in the population.

 Watch your pollution levels; high pollution depresses the LE of your Sims.

To check on the LE for each age group, open the Population Graphs window and click on the Health button.

Prisons

Prisons house criminals and help increase the efficiency of your police departments. Their overall effect on your city is to lower crime levels, but they can do this only if they are not overcrowded, as reported in the Microsim for each prison. Each prison can contain as many as 10,000 inmates, but each year 25 percent of the prisoners are released on parole to make room for new prisoners. For example, if you have 1,000 prisoners, 250 prisoners will be released each year. If you have less than 250 new prisoners being added to your prison, this is OK, but if you add more than 250 new prisoners the next year, then there will be an increase in your prison population.

Three Strikes and You're Not Out!

Looking at this matter of prison populations further, suppose you have a full capacity of 10,000 prisoners incarcerated in your local gulag. If 25 percent are to be paroled each year, this means that 2,500 prisoners will be let go and you will have 2,500 empty berths. If your police departments arrest more than 2,500, then your prison will overflow and crime will increase in the city.

Prisons: Not in My Backyard!

Location does not matter really, except that the prison emits heavy pollution and should therefore be placed somewhere that it won't bother people. Prisons also tend to depress nearby land values, so it's best to place them out in the boonies somewhere.

Unlike the other city services institutions, prisons don't cost you any yearly or monthly maintenance fees, but they are frightfully expensive to build, costing over $3,000.

Providing Recreation

Under the recreation tool, you can build small parks, large parks, zoos, stadiums, and marinas. Each of these amenities encourages certain aspects of your city. Residential zones and the tourism industry get a boost from the presence of zoos, stadiums, and marinas.

Residential growth reaches a cap at around a population of about 15,000 people. In order to grow beyond this threshold, you need to build some recreation and entertainment facilities, such as stadiums, zoos, and marinas. The more recreational facilities you build, the more residential population you can attract to your city.

To build any recreational facility, follow these steps:

1. Select the Recreation tool.
2. While holding down the mouse button, select the small park, the large park, the zoo, the stadium, or the marina in the pop-up submenu that you see.
3. Release the mouse button.
4. Move the pointer over the map, and click to place the facility.

Table 2-29 shows requirements for the various recreational facilities.

Table 2-29 Recreational Facilities

	Recreational Facility	Zone Size	Land Value ($)	Power Requirements (MW)	Pollution Units	Maintenance Costs per Year ($)	Construction Cost ($)
	Small park	1x1 tiles	20,000	0	0	0	20
	Big park	3x3 tiles	150,000	0	0	0	150
	Zoo	4x4 tiles	3,000,000	6.66	0	50	3,000
	Stadium	4x4 tiles	5,000,000	6.66	4	0	5,000
	Marina	3x3 tiles	1,000,000	4	0	0	1,000

Small Parks

Small parks have a positive effect on land values, improving values by about as much as trees that you place with the Landscape Trees tool, and so they are a boon to areas with low land values. Small parks help promote residential zone growth. They do not conduct electricity to nearby zones and buildings, nor do they require electricity.

Big Parks

Big parks increase land values twice as much as small parks, and they help promote residential zone growth. Big parks do not conduct electricity to nearby zones and buildings, nor do they require electricity.

Zoos

Zoos are a big attraction for visitors to your city and so help the tourism industry. Zoos also give a big boost to the growth of residential zones, but it does not matter where you locate them, since the simulation only checks to see if they exist, not where they are.

From time to time, you may hear a loud animal roar (from the zoo or Nessie). All the information you see in the zoo Microsim is nonsensical and meaningless.

Stadiums

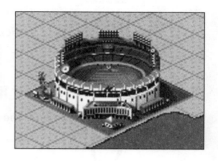

When you build a stadium, you will be asked to choose what kind of sport as well as the name of the team you want to have based at your stadium. As with zoos, the location of the stadium does not matter. Stadiums give a big boost to the growth of residential zones, and they help the tourist industry grow. By building a stadium, you can even improve the rapport between you and your constituents, thereby increasing your popularity.

Marinas

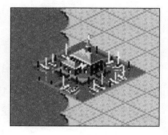

Each Marina has its own sailboat, which will appear after power has been supplied. Marinas must be placed so that they straddle the shoreline. Like stadiums and zoos, marinas give a big boost to the growth of residential zones, and they help the tourist industry grow. For fun, try clicking on the sailboat.

PUSHING THE RIGHT BUTTONS

The buttons, just below the 15 building tools on the Toolbar, allow you to place signposts in your city; query each zone or building's Microsim; rotate and zoom the map; and view various other graphs, maps, and windows.

Signs

With the Sign tool, you can label streets, buildings, and other points of interest in your city. There is no cost for building or removing signposts.

How to Place Signs

To place any signpost:

1. Activate the Sign tool.
2. Click on the map where you wish the sign to be placed.
3. When the sign text box opens, type in the text you want the sign to display and then click the Done button.

How to Remove Signs or Change a Sign's Text

To remove any signpost:

1. Select the Sign tool.
2. Click on the base of the sign you wish to remove.
3. When the sign's text box appears on screen, press the Delete key on your keyboard and then press the on-screen Done button. The sign will disappear.

To change the text in any previously created sign:

1. Select the Sign tool.
2. Click on the base of the sign whose text you wish to change.
3. When the sign's text box appears on screen, backspace over the text you want to replace and then type in the new text. When finished, click Done. The sign will be replaced with the new text.

Queries

The Query tool allows you to inspect each zone, tile, or building, including those with Microsims (specialized microsimulations within the main body of the program). To activate this tool, simply select the button and then click on any part of the map you wish to snoop in. After you click this tool on any object or zone in your city, a text box will open that gives you interesting information about the spot that you clicked.

You can also select the Query tool by holding down Shift and clicking anywhere on the map. The advantage of using this technique is that you don't have to keep reselecting tools from the Toolbar—your last-used tool will still be available when you click the mouse again.

To resume game play and make the text box disappear, you can usually just click your mouse pointer anywhere *inside* the dialog box, or press Esc. In some Query text boxes, however, you have a choice of renaming the building, and so you must decide whether to click the Rename button or the Done button, if you wish to resume game play. For example, you can rename a museum or library, and you can choose a particular sports team to play in your stadium by clicking the Query tool on it and then clicking Rename. The Query Tool doesn't cost you any money to use.

Rotate Clockwise and Rotate Counter-Clockwise

The two Rotate buttons allow you to rotate your view of the city by 90-degree increments. This feature is useful when you have trouble seeing the opposite side of a mountain, or when you are building roads and power lines behind 3-D objects. Simply click either button to shift your view to a different angle. Rotating your city view doesn't cost any money.

From the keyboard, you can press Delete to rotate the map counter-clockwise, or Page Down to rotate the map clockwise.

Zoom In and Zoom Out

There are three different zoom levels in *SimCity 2000*. Use the Zoom In and Zoom Out buttons to select your zoom level. Click on the Zoom In button (with the plus sign) to zoom in for a closer, more detailed look. Click on the Zoom Out button (with the minus sign) to zoom out for a farther, more comprehensive view of your entire city. The Zoom In and Zoom Out buttons don't cost you any money.

From the PC keyboard, you can use Home to zoom in and End to zoom out.

Centering

The Center tool is a wonderful new way to scroll around your city in *Sim-City 2000*. It allows you to pick any spot in your city to center your view in the City window. All you do is select the tool and then click on the spot where you want your view to be centered on screen.

   There are two other ways to use the Center tool on the PC, both of which we highly recommend because they are easier to use:

- Click the right mouse button to select the Center tool instantly, even while using another tool. Your City view will immediately center itself on the present location. And you don't need to pick the tool you were last using again—simply click on the left mouse button to reuse the tool.

- While using the Center tool (however you selected it), hold down the mouse button and drag your mouse. The map will move in the direction you drag. (This method does not work for Version 1.0 on the PC, except in Terrain Edit mode. Because of bug problems, Maxis removed this feature at the last minute for the release of Version 1.0. It may work in future versions, however).

You can make the helicopter crash and burn by clicking on the Center button and then clicking your pointer on the helicopter! The Center button doesn't cost you any money to use.

The Maps Window

The Maps window button opens the Maps window, which you can pop open momentarily or keep on screen. To keep the window on screen, hold down the mouse button and drag the pointer away from the Toolbar. If you don't want to open this window but just want to view it quickly, click the mouse on the Maps window button momentarily; the window will go away

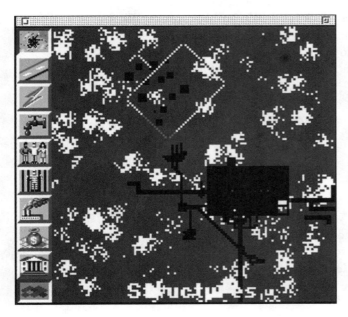

when you release the mouse button. (Don't move the mouse!) You can also open this window from the **Windows** menu.

In the Maps window, you can see a miniaturized version of your city that color codes various data. Click the icon buttons on the left side of the Maps window to activate a particular view. Some of the icon buttons have submenus from which you can select more options. Each of these views is discussed in greater detail in Chapter 5.

The Maps window also has two different sizes that you can toggle by clicking the zoom box at the upper-right side of the window.

There is no cost for using the Maps window.

The Graphs Window

The Graphs window button opens the Graphs window, which you can pop open momentarily or keep on screen. To keep the window on-screen, hold down the mouse button and drag the pointer away from the Toolbar. If you don't want to open this window but just want to view it quickly, click the mouse on the Graphs window button momentarily, the window will go away when you release the mouse button. (Don't move the mouse!) You can also open this window from the **Windows** menu.

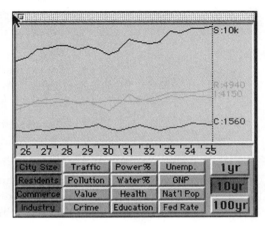

Inside the Graphs window, you can track important statistical information about your city, including population, traffic, pollution, crime, health, water and power coverage, unemployment, health and education levels, interest rates, land values, and GNP.

You'll notice that each graph is shown in a different color and has a letter marker at its right end to help identify it and differentiate it from the other graphs. You'll also see a number that tells you the graph's current value, rounded off to the nearest thousand.

A description of the buttons and their functions follows:

- **City Size**, which is marked with an *S* on the graph, is the sum of your residential, commercial, and industrial zone populations.

- **Residents**, marked with an *R*, shows the combined population of all your residential zones.

- **Commerce**, marked with a *C*, shows the combined population of all your commercial zones.

- **Industry**, marked with an *I*, shows the combined population of all your industrial zones.

- **Traffic**, marked with a *T*, shows the average traffic density of your road network, including buses, but not of your train or subway system. This number represents traffic congestion, not total trips made.

- **Pollution**, marked with a *P*, shows the pollution level in your city.

- **Value**, marked with a *V*, shows the average land value in your city. It takes all your land values in your zoned areas and then sums them up and divides this sum by the number of zoned tiles to obtain an average land value per zoned tile.

- **Crime**, marked with an *X*, shows the crime rate in your city.

- **Power %**, marked with a *p*, shows the remaining power-generating capacity. As it approaches zero percent, you'll have to build more power plants. The percentage reading is confusing; it represents the percentage of power capacity you have surplus.

- **Water %**, marked with a *w*, shows the remaining water-pumping capacity. As it approaches zero percent, you'll have to build add more water pumps or desalinization plants. The percentage reading is confusing; it represents the percentage of water capacity you have surplus.

- **Health**, marked with an *h*, shows the average Life Expectancy of your residents. As their health improves, it goes higher; as their health declines, it goes lower.

- **Education**, marked with an *e*, shows the average Education Quotient of your residents. As their level of education improves, it goes higher; as their educational level declines, it goes lower.

- **Unemployment (Unemp.)**, marked with a *u*, shows the percentage of people that are out of work in your city. It is based on the number that can't find work in your commercial zones and industrial zones. The higher the number, the more unemployed there are. A healthy, vibrant economy should have an unemployment rate of less than seven percent.

- **Gross National Product (GNP)**, marked with a *g*, graphs the total value of goods and services produced by all the economies of SimNation. This number *includes the economies of your neighboring cities.* The higher the number, the larger the market for your exports, and so the better off your industrial zones will be.

- **National Population (Nat'l Pop)**, marked with an *n*, graphs the SimNation's total population, which includes the populations of your city and your neighboring cities.

- **Fed Rate**, marked with a *%*, shows the prime interest rate as set by the SimNation's Federal Reserve Board. This is the interest rate at which your bonds are pegged 1 percent to 2 percent higher.

- **1 Year (1 yr.)**: Clicking on this button causes the graph to show only the last year's changes.

- **10 Years (10 yr.)**: Clicking on this button causes the graph to show the last 10 years' changes.

- **100 Years (100 yr.)**: Clicking on this button causes the graph to show the last 100 years' changes.

There is no cost for using the Graphs window.

The Population Window

The Population window button opens the Population window, which you can pop open momentarily or keep on screen. To keep the window on screen, hold down the mouse button and drag the pointer away from the Toolbar. If you don't want to open this window but just want to view it quickly, just click the mouse on the Population window button momentarily; the window will go away when you release the mouse button. (Don't move the mouse!) You can also open this window from the **Windows** menu.

Inside the Population window, you can view graphs that plot statistical information about your population. A description of the buttons and their functions follows:

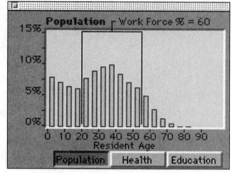

Figure 2-55 Population by age group

- **Population:** This bar chart shows the population distribution by age group, as in Figure 2-55. The bracketed portion of the chart represents the age group of 20-year-olds to 55-year-olds that make up your work force. You'll notice that the total work force as a percentage of your total population is listed at the top of the window.

- **Health:** The Life Expectancy of your population is expressed in bar-chart form by age group, as in Figure 2-56. The bracketed portion of the chart represents the age group of 20-year-olds to 55-year-olds that make up your work force. Notice that the total work force LE is listed at the top of the window.

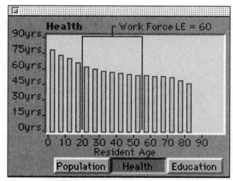

Figure 2-56 Life expectancy by age group

- **Education:** The Educational Quotient of your population is expressed in bar-chart form by age group, as in Figure 2-57. The bracketed portion of the chart represents the age group of 20-year-olds to 55-year-olds that make up your work force. Notice that the total work force EQ is listed at the top of the window.

There is no cost for using the Population window.

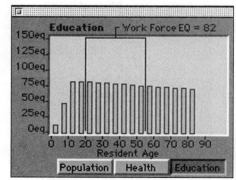

Figure 2-57 Education quotient by age group

The City Industry Window

The City Industry window button opens the City Industry window, which you can pop open momentarily or keep on screen. To keep the window on screen, hold down the mouse button and drag the pointer away from the Toolbar. If you don't want to open this window but just want to view it quickly, click the mouse on the City Industry button momentarily; the window will go away when you release the mouse button. (Don't move the mouse!) You can also open this window from the **Windows** menu.

In the City Industry window, there are three buttons, which allow you to view various statistical graphs and set tax rates for each of your 11 possible industries. This power to set tax rates allows you to discourage or encourage particular industries. For example, you can raise the tax on the steel/mining industry and lower the taxes on the electronics industry. This will have the effect of closing down the high-polluting steel industry yet encouraging the growth of high-technology electronics firms. A complete description of each industry type is given earlier in this chapter under the topic of industrial zones.

The three buttons in the City Industry window perform the following functions:

- **Ratios:** Clicking this button shows the distribution of industries in your city in bar-chart form, as in Figure 2-58.

- **Tax Rates:** Clicking this button brings up a bar chart of industry tax rates, like that in Figure 2-59. You can set any individual industry's

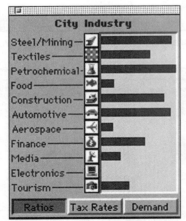

Figure 2-58 The industry ratios bar chart

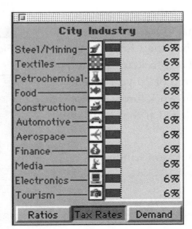

Figure 2-59 Setting the tax rate for individual industries in the tax rate view

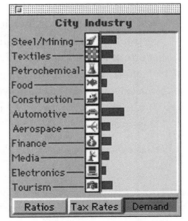

Figure 2-60 The bar-chart view of industry demand by percent in SimNation

tax rate by clicking and dragging its bar. Dragging the bar to the right increases its tax, and dragging it to the left decreases its tax. To drag all the bars at once on the PC, hold down the Alt key while dragging. To drag all the bars at once on the Macintosh, hold down the Option key while dragging.

• **Demand:** Clicking this button causes an Industrial Demand bar chart like the one in Figure 2-60 to appear. This graph shows the demand for each industry's products in the overall SimNation economy. This aggregate demand includes your neighboring cities as well as your own economy.

There is no cost for using the City Industry window

The Demand Indicator

The Demand Indicator tells you whether there is a positive or negative demand for residential (R), commercial (C), and industrial (I) zones. This three-column bar chart graphically shows, by the length and direction of each bar, the need for each type of zone. When a zone bar extends up (positive direction), there is a pent-up demand for that type of zone, and this should be a cue to start putting new zones in your city. The height of the bar tells you the amount of demand: the higher the bar extends from mid-scale, the higher the demand is for that type of zone. When a zone bar extends down (negative direction), there is an overabundance of that zone type and you can take it as a sign not to build any more. The depth the bar dips below mid-scale tells you the relative overabundance of that particular zone type.

There is often a time lag involved while the simulator updates all the zones, so you will not necessarily see instantaneously accurate zone demands. Use this indicator as a guide, but don't respond with a knee-jerk reaction to every quiver of the indicator.

The Neighbors Window

The Neighbors window button opens the Neighbors window, which you can pop open momentarily or keep on-screen. To keep the window on screen, hold down the mouse button and drag the pointer away from the Toolbar. If you don't want to open this window but just want to view it quickly, click the mouse on the Neighbors window button momentarily;

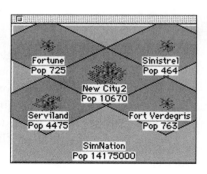

the window will go away when you release the mouse button. (Don't move the mouse!) You can also open this window from the pull-down **Windows** menu.

The Neighbors window displays the population of your neighboring cities, along with your own city's population and a running total of the entire SimNation population. To close this window, click on the button located at the top-left corner. There is no cost for using the Neighbors window.

The Budget Window

By clicking on this button, you bring up the Budget window, in which you make all your city's financial decisions and pass city ordinances. You can also open this window from the pull-down **Windows** menu. The Budget window is discussed in greater detail in Chapter 4. There is no cost for using the Budget window.

New City 2 1935 Budget January 1935		1935 Year End Expense	1936 Estimate		Done Help
Property Taxes	%7	968	980		
City Ordinances		-217	-221		
Bond Payments		-2900	-2900		
Police Department	%100	-100	-100		
Fire Department	%100	-100	-100		
Health & Welfare	%100	-50	-50		
Education	%100	-25	-25		
Transit Authority	%100	-98	-98		

Year to Date Cashflow$	- $2,522
Estimated Cashflow$	- $2,514
Current Funds$	$1,440
End of Year Funds$	- $1,082

Show Buildings

The Show Buildings button toggles on or off the display of all buildings in your City window. You use this button to see what kinds of zones are underneath your buildings, and to remove the visual clutter when redesigning your transportation network in tight quarters. (You can see the effect in Figure 2-61.) You will still see your roads, rail lines, power lines, and other infrastructure in this view. The Show Buildings button doesn't cost any money to use.

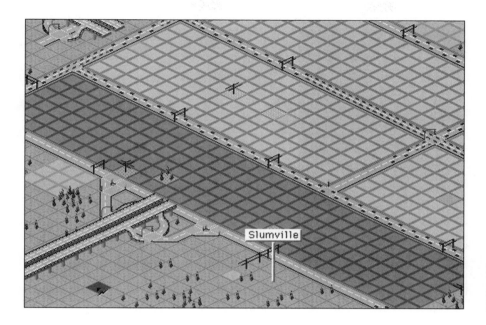

Figure 2-61
The effect on the map
of the Show Buildings
button

Show Signs

The Show Signs button merely toggles off or on the signposts that you have
created with the Sign tool. The signposts are not lost when you toggle them
off; you can redisplay them at any time by clicking the Show Signs button
again. The Show Signs button doesn't cost you any money to use.

Show Infrastructure

The Show Infrastructure button toggles on or off the display of your city's
infrastructure, such as roads, rails, subway and train stations, power lines,
water pumps, and highways. This button works in the normal above-ground
view (as in Figure 2-62) as well as the underground view of your city. The
Show Infrastructure button doesn't cost you any money to use.

Show Zones

While you are in the above-ground view of your city, clicking on the Show
Zones button allows you to view your zones minus the buildings on top of
them, as in Figure 2-63. You will still see all city-owned buildings, like police
and fire stations, power plants, and educational and recreational facilities.

Figure 2-62
The effect on the map when using the Show Infrastructure button

Figure 2-63
Effect on the map when using the Show Zones button

Infrastructure such as roads, power lines, rail lines, and highways remain unaffected and you will still see them on-screen. You won't be able to see the buildings atop port zones or military bases, though. The Show Zones button doesn't cost you any money to use.

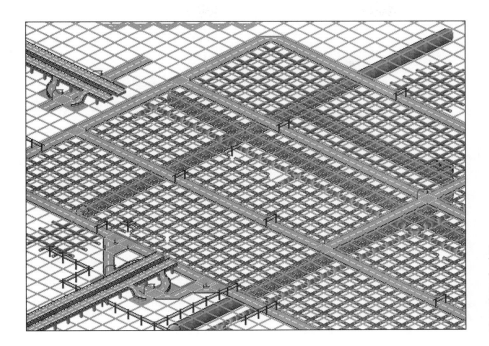

Figure 2-64
The effect on the map when using the Show Underground button with the Show Infrastructure button toggled on

Show Underground

The Show Underground button toggles your view between the underground portion of your city and the above-ground display. In this mode, you can see your pipes, subway lines, subway stations, and subway-to-rail junctures. If your Show Infrastructure button is toggled on, you can also see—in addition to the subways and pipes—your roads, highways, rail lines, power lines, and tunnels, but *not* your rail depots or bus stations, as Figure 2-64 shows. The Show Underground button doesn't cost you any money to use.

Getting Help

By clicking this button, you get a message that tells you how to access the on-screen help feature. All it tells you is that you must hold down the Shift key while clicking on any button or tool to bring up help information.

CHAPTER
3

The Terrain Editor

This chapter describes the use of the *SimCity 2000* Terrain Editor, which allows you to customize your landscape features any way you like. Using the Terrain Toolbar, you can sculpt in such landscape features as mountains, rivers, lakes, forests, and coastlines, and raise or lower the elevation of any terrain. There is no charge for making any modifications to your territory while in terrain-editing mode.

To enter terrain-editing mode when you are just starting up *SimCity*, click the Edit New Map button. Alternatively, if the program is already running, pull down the **File** menu and select **Edit New Map**.

TERRAIN TOOLBAR

When the Terrain Editor opens up, you'll see the Terrain Toolbar and a City window. The Terrain Toolbar (see Figure 3-1) contains all the tools and buttons you need to create any landscape you wish. As with the City Toolbar, you can drag the Toolbar anywhere around your screen by clicking and dragging the top bar.

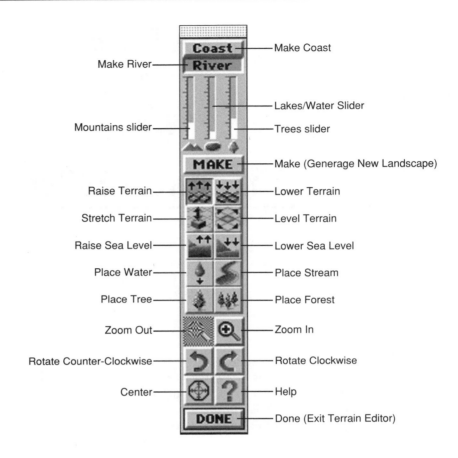

Figure 3-1
The Terrain Toolbar

The following sections describe each tool that is found on the Terrain Toolbar.

COAST

The Coast button is a toggle switch. When it is depressed, you will get a coastline accompanied by a saltwater ocean (before the coastline appears, you need to press the Make button). When the button is released, any coastline you have will be removed when you next press the Make button. Figure 3-2 shows the effect of creating a coastline with the Coast button.

There is an annoying bug in the *SimCity* Terrain Editor that bears mentioning here. If you create a coastline and then change your mind and

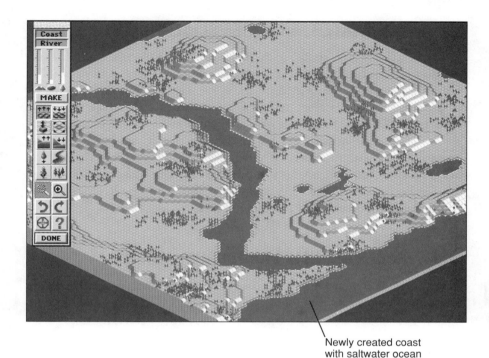

Figure 3-2
Making a coast with
the Coast button

Newly created coast
with saltwater ocean

remove the coast, when you start playing the city in the regular city building
mode, the water that was near the former coastline will be salty. Even if you
have a river or lake passing through the region, the water that overlays the
former coastline will always be salty. In fact, any water that is within 15 tiles
or so of the edge that would have been the coast will be saltwater!

RIVER

Clicking the River button creates a river that flows from one edge of your
map to the other in your next landscape (click the Make button after clicking
the River button to generate the new landscape). If there is a coastline, the
river will empty out into the ocean. The water in the river is fresh, except for
some areas of saltwater intrusion. Those water pumps which are placed along
fresh water will have increased pumping capacity.

MOUNTAIN, WATER, AND TREE SLIDERS

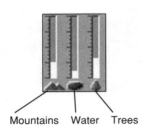

Mountains Water Trees

The Mountain, Water, and Tree sliders let you adjust the amount of the surface area of your terrain that is covered by mountains, water, and trees. Click and drag the sliders up to increase the percentage of your city covered by mountains, water, or trees; or down to decrease the coverage area. The changes to your terrain are made only after you click the Make button.

An apparent bug with the Water slider is that if you have either the Coast or River buttons depressed and the Water slider set to zero, you will still get a lot of lakes when you click the Make button. The only way to keep the Terrain Editor from making lakes is to release both the River and Coast buttons and *then* to set the Water slider to zero.

MAKE (GENERATE NEW LANDSCAPE) BUTTON

The Make, or Generate New Landscape, button creates a new landscape based on the selections you made with the Coast button, the River button, and the Mountain, Water and Trees sliders.

Do not click the Make button *after* making changes to your terrain with any of the Landscape tools below it, otherwise those terrain changes will be wiped clear when the map is regenerated with the Make button. Instead, make your selections for a river, coast, or both, adjust the sliders as you want, and *then* click the Make button. *Only after this* should you go ahead and use the Landscape tools below the Make button.

RAISE TERRAIN

Using the Raise Terrain tool, you can click or drag on the terrain to raise its altitude. If you click on any water with this tool, you will raise the submerged ground above the water level so it becomes dry land.

LOWER TERRAIN

Using the Lower Terrain tool, you can click or drag on the terrain to lower its altitude. If you keep clicking on land with this tool, you will eventually lower the land below sea level and turn the area into an ocean, lake, or river.

STRETCH TERRAIN

With the Stretch Terrain tool you can grab any portion of land and stretch it up or down. To use this tool, click and drag up if you want to create a mountain, or down if you want to create a valley or gully. This tool is better-suited for creating mountains than the Raise Terrain tool described previously.

LEVEL TERRAIN

The Level Terrain tool allows you to flatten the surface of any terrain, bringing up or down the level of nearby land to match your chosen elevation. To use this tool, click the Level Terrain button, then select the land at which elevation you want to create a plateau and click and drag the mouse.

RAISE SEA LEVEL

The Raise Sea Level tool raises the general sea level by one tile. You don't need to click this tool on the map anywhere; simply click the button on the Toolbar.

LOWER SEA LEVEL

The Lower Sea Level tool lowers the general sea level by one tile. You don't need to click this tool on the map anywhere; simply click the button on the Toolbar.

PLACE WATER

Use the Place Water tool to create ponds, lakes, and rivers by clicking on the map.

PLACE STREAM

The Place Stream tool is used to create waterfalls and streams that flow downhill. To use this tool, select the Place Stream button, then click on a mountain or slope where you wish the stream or waterfall to begin. The water will cascade down the slope or hill, seeking the lowest elevation tile it can find in which to terminate.

PLACE TREE

Using the Place Tree tool, you can add individual trees to your landscape. Clicking more than once on a tile adds more and more trees until, finally, the tile is thickly forested. You can also click and drag this tool across many tiles to create forests. To remove trees, hold down the Shift key while clicking this tool on any tile that contains trees.

PLACE FOREST

The Place Forest tool functions much like the Place Tree tool, except it disperses trees over a much wider area with each click. To remove forests, hold down the Shift key while clicking and dragging this tool over the map.

ZOOM OUT AND ZOOM IN

Zoom out

There are two zoom levels in *SimCity 2000*. Use the Zoom Out and Zoom In buttons to select your zoom level. Click on the Zoom Out button to zoom out for a farther, more comprehensive view of your map. When you are zoomed all the way out, you see more of your map.

Zoom in

   Click on the Zoom In button to zoom in for a closer, more detailed look of your terrain. You see less area of the map as you zoom in.

ROTATE COUNTER-CLOCKWISE AND CLOCKWISE

Rotate clockwise

Rotate counter-clockwise

The two Rotate buttons allow you to rotate your view of the city by 90-degree increments. This feature is useful when you need to see a different viewing angle of your map. Click the Rotate Counter-Clockwise button to rotate the map to your left, or the Rotate Clockwise button to rotate the map to your right.

CENTER

The Center tool allows you to scroll your map very quickly, centering your view anywhere in the City window. To center the map at a different location, click the Center tool, then move your cursor to where you want your view to be centered on-screen, and then click the mouse.

There are two other ways to use the Center tool on the PC, both of which I highly recommend because they are easier to use:

- Click the right mouse button to select the Center tool instantly, even while using another tool. Your City view will immediately center itself on the location where you clicked the right mouse button. (And you don't need to pick the tool you were last using again, simply click the left mouse button to continue using it.)

- While using the Center tool function (either by selecting the tool's button or by holding down the right mouse button), hold down the mouse button and drag your mouse.

HELP

Clicking on the Help button brings up a reminder message that you can always summon on-screen help by Shift-clicking on any button in the Terrain Toolbar.

DONE

After completing all changes to your landscape, click the Done button. Your map will be terraformed and then you will be switched into city-building mode.

C H A P T E R
4

Managing Your Money

In this chapter, you will learn how to manipulate your city's finances and learn about the budgeting and funding process. The chapter will conclude with a short overview of several economic theories and their applicability to *SimCity 2000*.

USING THE BUDGET WINDOW

All your funding, budgeting, and city ordinance decisions are made in the Budget window shown in Figure 4-1, which you can open from the Toolbar or from the **Windows** menu. Each January, the Budget window will open automatically (unless you toggle on **Auto-Budget** in the **Options** menu). After about two minutes, as counted by the hourglass in the Budget window, the window will close, but you can reset the counter at any time by clicking anywhere in the window. When you want to close the Budget window, simply click Done. If you are confused about anything, click Help to get a reminder about how to use the context-sensitive help activated by shift-clicking.

As you can see in the Budget window, there are eight rows of figures, each of which covers a particular department. You can Shift-click on any of the department names to get an on-screen description of what the department does. Next to six of the department names, you will see percentage settings, with triangular buttons that you can click to raise or lower the percentage that is shown. Moving further to the right, you can see two columns of numbers: To Date Expense and Year End Estimate (which you won't see in Figure 4-1 since it shows the January Budget window that automati-

157

Hourglass   Percentage   Percentage
             Up button   Down button

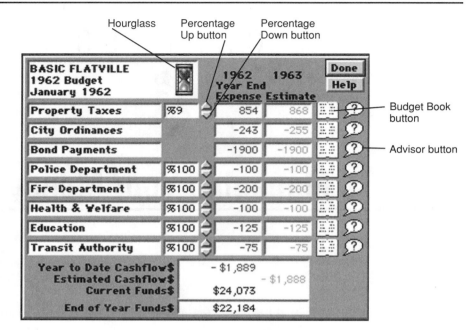

Budget Book button

Advisor button

Figure 4-1.
The Budget window automatically opens each year in January. This window is slightly different in appearance than the Budget window that appears the rest of the year.

cally opens each new fiscal year[1]). The To Date Expense column shows the amount of money that is being spent or earned up to the current month, while the Year End Estimate shows the amount of money you will have spent or earned by the end of the year if you make no further changes to the budget. To the right of these columns, you can see book icon buttons. Clicking on any of these will cause the Budget Book for the department to open up. Inside each Budget Book you'll find a detailed monthly breakdown of expenses and revenues for the department—and for some of the books you'll find additional buttons for customizing your budget further. On the far-right side of the Budget window, you can see a column of balloon buttons with question marks inside them. These are your advisor buttons, and clicking on

[1]The January Budget window that opens automatically each new fiscal year differs slightly from the Budget window that opens each month, with the exception of December's, which has a similar column-labeling scheme. The major difference for the January/December Budget window is that the To Date Expense and Year End Estimate columns are replaced by the labels Year End Expense and Estimate, respectively. Note that the January Budget window that you open manually using the Budget button on the Toolbar is different from the January Budget window that opens automatically each fiscal new year. The manually opened January Budget window has the same appearance as the Budget window that opens from February to November.

one will bring up an advisor for that department. The advisor reports the current status of the department and offers advice on what you should do.

Setting Your Tax Rate

The rate for your property tax, from which you garner your city's income, is assessed on commercial, industrial, and residential zones. The tax is based on land value and population, as shown in the formula below:

Property Tax = Land Value × Tax Rate × Population × Scaling Factor

where *Population* consists of residential, commercial, and industrial zone populations, and *Land Value* represents the average land value. The *Scaling Factor* remains constant and is of no real concern to you.

Thanks to *SimCity 2000* veteran Kevin Endo, who discovered this simple relationship, you can approximate the tax revenue you earn by applying the following formula:[2]

Property Tax = Total City Population × Tax Rate × 1.29

You can set the property tax globally for all three zone types by clicking on the Increase/Decrease buttons in the Budget window, or you can set individual tax rates by clicking on the Increase/Decrease buttons in the Property Tax Book display. Note that the global tax rate, as shown in the main Budget window, is the average of the individual tax rates that appear in the Property Tax Budget Book display, shown in Figure 4-2.

To open the Property Tax Budget Book, click on the Budget Book icon in the Budget window. In this display, you can set the tax rate from zero percent all the way up to 20 percent for your residential, commercial, and industrial zones. Most of the income you derive from taxes is collected through these property taxes, although you can levy a sales tax and garner some gambling tax earnings from the Ordinances display.

In the Property Tax Budget Book, you can see a running total of the amount of tax revenue raised for each zone type. The numbers in red tell you that the corresponding tax

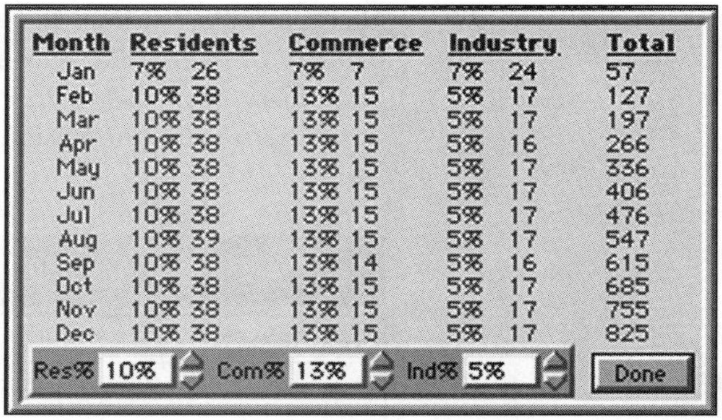

Month	Residents	Commerce	Industry	Total
Jan	7% 26	7% 7	7% 24	57
Feb	10% 38	13% 15	5% 17	127
Mar	10% 38	13% 15	5% 17	197
Apr	10% 38	13% 15	5% 16	266
May	10% 38	13% 15	5% 17	336
Jun	10% 38	13% 15	5% 17	406
Jul	10% 38	13% 15	5% 17	476
Aug	10% 39	13% 15	5% 17	547
Sep	10% 38	13% 14	5% 16	615
Oct	10% 38	13% 15	5% 17	685
Nov	10% 38	13% 15	5% 17	755
Dec	10% 38	13% 15	5% 17	825

Res% 10% Com% 13% Ind% 5%   Done

Figure 4-2.
The Property Tax Budget Book display

[2]This formula works fine in cities without arcologies, but it gives you less-than-accurate results when you have large arcology populations.

revenues have yet to be assessed, and those in blue tell you that those revenues have already been collected. The percent tax for each month and the amount collected for each month are displayed side by side. So, for example, if you change the tax rate to four percent on residential zones mid-year, say in June, you will see the new tax rate displayed for June as 4 percent, and the amount of money collected (or anticipated) will be displayed to its right.

Optimum Tax Rates

Tax rates have a tremendous influence on the economic model for *SimCity 2000.* The higher the tax rate, the less people are inclined to stay. Tax rates from seven to nine percent cause city growth to slow or to increase at a rather sluggish rate, but they *do* allow you to accumulate money for building. Tax rates above nine percent are suicidal: you may initially derive some benefit from increased collections, but you will end up driving the Sims away. Lowering taxes below six percent encourages growth and brings new Sims to your city, but it reduces your income. Table 4-1 shows the effects of the various tax rates. Tax revenues are not available to you till the following January, even though they are collected on a month-by-month basis.

DEFICIT FUNDING

SimCity 2000 now allows you to deficit finance your city operations. What does this mean to you? Well, when you run out of money, you can float $10,000 bonds to generate additional cash. There is no fixed date for which you must repay the bond, but interest will accrue monthly for each bond that is left outstanding, and *this interest must be paid by year's end* (that is, by January of each year). If you don't have enough money to pay the interest in January, then this interest will be added to your deficit, which will show as a negative amount of money for your Current Funds figure. With a nega-

Table 4-1 Tax Rates and Their Effects	
Tax Rate (%)	**Effects**
0–6	Fast growth in all zones, diminished tax revenues
7–9	Slow but gradual growth, tax revenues stable
10–20	All zones decline, population decreases, initially high tax revenues decrease rapidly

tive balance in your treasury, you cannot build or do anything except take out more bonds or raise taxes until you have a positive balance. (You'll notice that the Status window displays the name of each tool in red, thereby telling you that your budget is operating in the red and that you cannot afford the tool in question.) If you allow your deficit to pass the –$100,000 mark, you will be kicked out of office for financial malfeasance, the game will end, and you will lose your city.

Interest Rates and Credit Ratings

Bond interest rates depend on the current Federal Reserve (otherwise called the "Fed") discount interest rate, and you usually end up paying one to two percent above this rate to the bank. Interest rates also depend on your city's "bond rating." This letter grade is issued by a credit agency that evaluates your city's net value, as displayed in the Bond Book's Issue Bonds dialog box. (You must click the Show Bonds button to actually see your city's credit rating.) Other conditions also come into play in determining your city's credit worthiness, such as what the current economic climate is like and how much debt you already carry.

> Unlike in the real world, bonds never mature—that is, they have no fixed date for which the principal must be repaid. Each year, interest is charged on each bond, and this must be paid by January 1st. Theoretically, you need never repay a bond; you can just pay the interest on it indefinitely.

A word of warning is in order here: *once you take a bond out, it is very difficult to pay it off if you have a small or unprofitable city.* The interest rate on the loan will consume much of your city's income, and even if you hope to "grow" your city out of its fiscal hole, you probably will end up paying most of your city's income to the loan sharks. If you have a small city, the best advice to the unwary is *stay away from bonds—they will eat you alive.*[3]

Bond interest, even though it is tabulated on a month-by-month basis, is collected only once a year, in January. Note that the more bonds you take out, the higher the interest rate will go, for two reasons:

- The more indebted you are, the more your credit rating goes down. This makes you a greater risk to the bank.
- You are crowding out other credit seekers and soaking up a lot of the available investment capital. This fact drives rates up as money becomes more scarce.

For example, your credit rating starts out at a very high AAA. This means you are considered an excellent credit risk. You decide to take out a $10,000 bond at five percent interest. After accepting the bond, you check the Show Bonds display and find that now your credit rating has fallen a

---

[3]For medium-to-large cities that have a positive cash flow, taking out bonds can be useful and helpful.

notch to AA. Taking out a second bond, you notice that the interest rate now being offered is six percent. After accepting the bond, you again check your credit rating. This time it has dropped to an A rating. If you continue to take out more bonds, the interest rate will zoom ever higher, and eventually, depending on your city's value, your credit rating will plunge down to an F. At this point, your credit rating is ruined, and you cannot take out any more loans.

The number of bonds you can take out is directly related to your city's value, as shown in the Show Bonds display. You are able to issue an additional $10,000 bond for each $4,000,000 of city value up to a maximum of 50 bonds, or $500,000 of indebtedness. If you try issuing bonds before building any city at all, then you will be allowed to issue only one bond. Once your city value exceeds $4,000,000, you can issue a second bond. By building more public facilities, you increase your city's value so that, for example, if you build a coal power plant that is worth $40,000,000, you can issue up to 10 bonds.

Floating Bonds

To float a bond, click the **Bond Payments** book button in the Budget window to open Bonds Budget Book, shown in Figure 4-3. In this book, you'll see your current interest payments, average interest rate, and current bond amounts outstanding on a month-by-month basis. The interest that you see is an average of all your bonds taken together, while the amount you owe each month represents the combined interest payments for all your outstanding bonds.

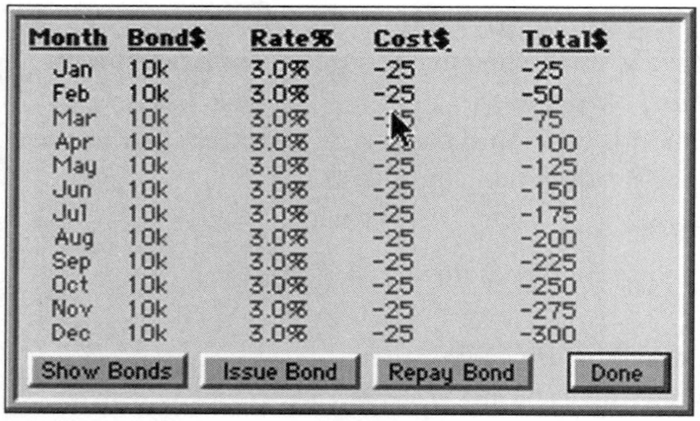

Month	Bond$	Rate%	Cost$	Total$
Jan	10k	3.0%	-25	-25
Feb	10k	3.0%	-25	-50
Mar	10k	3.0%	-25	-75
Apr	10k	3.0%	-25	-100
May	10k	3.0%	-25	-125
Jun	10k	3.0%	-25	-150
Jul	10k	3.0%	-25	-175
Aug	10k	3.0%	-25	-200
Sep	10k	3.0%	-25	-225
Oct	10k	3.0%	-25	-250
Nov	10k	3.0%	-25	-275
Dec	10k	3.0%	-25	-300

[Show Bonds] [Issue Bond] [Repay Bond] [Done]

Figure 4-3.
The Bonds Budget
Book display

Click the **Issue Bonds** button and a dialog box will pop up, asking you to confirm or decline the bond offering at the interest rate being proposed. Click Yes to accept the loan's terms:

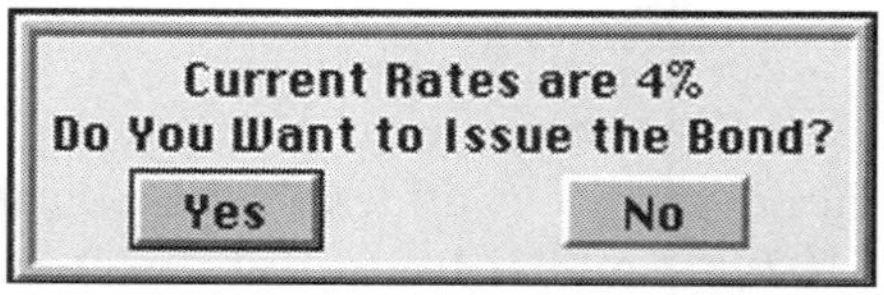

Current Rates are 4%
Do You Want to Issue the Bond?
[Yes]   [No]

To check your city's total indebtedness, click on the **Show Bonds** button. In the Show Bonds display, you'll see listed all your

outstanding bonds, your city's credit rating (AAA to F), the current bond interest rate, the next bond interest rate, and your total city value. The City Value figure is the value of your city's infrastructure and buildings, but *not* the value of buildings that are built by the Sims in the residential, commercial, and industrial zones:

```
Loan Rating:    D          Outstanding Bonds
Total Bonds:    $40,000           3%
Bank Rate%:     2%                4%
Next Bond%:     8%                5%
                                  7%
CityValue: $17,225,000
```

To repay a bond, click on the **Repay Bond** button in the Bond display. You'll see the Repay Bond dialog box open. Click Yes to pay off the particular bond that is shown here.

When you repay bonds, you always pay off the oldest bond first.

To exit the Budget Display, click **Done**.

> **Oldest Bond Rate is 3%**
> **Do You Want to Repay the Bond?**
> [Yes]   [No]

ESTABLISHING FUNDING LEVELS FOR CITY SERVICES

Each of your city services—police department, fire department, health and welfare department, education department, and transit authority—has its own budget book, which you can open by clicking on the appropriate book button in the Budget window. All city service funding levels can be adjusted in the main Budget window by clicking on the Percentage Up or Down button. The transit and education departments, however, have subcategories that you can fund individually. For example, in the transit authority budget book, you can set the funding rates independently for roads, rails, highways, subways, bridges, and tunnels by clicking on the appropriate Percentage Up or Down button. In the education department budget book, you can set the funding levels independently for the colleges or schools also by clicking on the appropriate Percentage Up or Down button. When you set different funding levels within a department, the average of the different percentages is displayed in the main Budget window.

The Police Department

Click the Police Department book button to open the Police Department Budget Book. In this budget display, you can view the amount of money spent to maintain and operate your police department. The financial report breaks down the expenditures month by month, and it shows the number of police stations you have:

Month	Police	Fund	Cost	Total
Jan	1	100%	-8	-8
Feb	1	100%	-8	-16
Mar	1	100%	-9	-25
Apr	1	100%	-8	-33
May	1	100%	-8	-41
Jun	1	100%	-9	-50
Jul	1	100%	-8	-58
Aug	1	100%	-8	-66
Sep	1	100%	-9	-75
Oct	1	100%	-8	-83
Nov	1	100%	-8	-91
Dec	1	100%	-9	-100

To close this display, click your mouse anywhere inside it.

The Fire Department

Click the Fire Department book button to open the Fire Department Budget Book. In this budget display, you can view the amount of money spent to maintain and operate your fire department. The financial report breaks down the expenditures month by month, and it shows the number of fire stations you have:

Month	Fire Dept	Fund	Cost	Total
Jan	2	100%	-16	-16
Feb	2	100%	-17	-33
Mar	2	100%	-17	-50
Apr	2	100%	-16	-66
May	2	100%	-17	-83
Jun	2	100%	-17	-100
Jul	2	100%	-16	-116
Aug	2	100%	-17	-133
Sep	2	100%	-17	-150
Oct	2	100%	-16	-166
Nov	2	100%	-17	-183
Dec	2	100%	-17	-200

To close this display, click your mouse anywhere inside it.

Health & Welfare

Click the Health & Welfare book button to open the Health & Welfare Budget Book. In this budget display, you can view the amount of money spent to maintain and operate your health department. The financial report breaks down the expenditures month by month, and it shows the number of hospitals you have:

Month	Hospital	Fund	Cost	Total
Jan	2	100%	-8	-8
Feb	2	100%	-8	-16
Mar	2	100%	-9	-25
Apr	2	100%	-8	-33
May	2	100%	-8	-41
Jun	2	100%	-9	-50
Jul	2	100%	-8	-58
Aug	2	100%	-8	-66
Sep	2	100%	-9	-75
Oct	2	100%	-8	-83
Nov	2	100%	-8	-91
Dec	2	100%	-9	-100

To close this display, click your mouse anywhere inside it.

Education

Click the Education book button to open the Education Budget Book. In this budget display, you can view the amount of money spent to maintain and operate your schools and colleges. You can individually adjust the percentage funding for schools or colleges by clicking on the Percentage Up or Down button in the Education Budget Book. The two funding numbers — one for colleges, the other for schools — are combined and averaged in the overall education funding indicator in the main Budget window:

Month	School	%	Cost	College	%	Cost	Total
Jan	1	100%	-2	1	100%	-8	-10
Feb	1	100%	-2	1	100%	-8	-20
Mar	1	100%	-2	1	100%	-9	-31
Apr	1	100%	-2	1	100%	-8	-41
May	1	100%	-2	1	100%	-8	-51
Jun	1	100%	-2	1	100%	-9	-62
Jul	1	100%	-2	1	100%	-8	-72
Aug	1	100%	-2	1	100%	-8	-82
Sep	1	100%	-2	1	100%	-9	-93
Oct	1	100%	-2	1	100%	-8	-103
Nov	1	100%	-2	1	100%	-8	-113
Dec	1	100%	-3	1	100%	-9	-125

Schools 100% △▽   Colleges 100% △▽   Done

The financial report breaks down the expenditures month by month, and it shows the number of schools and colleges you have. To close this display, click Done.

The Transit Authority

Click the Transit Authority book button to open the Transit Authority Budget Book. In this budget display, you can view the cost breakdown for maintaining each element of your transportation system—and you can individually adjust funding levels. Thus, for example, you can raise or lower the funding for roads, rails, highways, subways, bridges, or tunnels by clicking on the Percentage Up or Down button:

Month	Road	Hwy.	Brdg.	Rail	Sub.	Tunnel	Total
Jan	-1	-4	0	0	0	0	-5
Feb	-2	-4	0	0	0	0	-11
Mar	-2	-5	0	0	0	0	-18
Apr	-2	-4	0	0	0	0	-24
May	-2	-5	0	0	0	0	-31
Jun	-2	-4	0	0	0	0	-37
Jul	-2	-5	0	0	0	0	-44
Aug	-2	-4	0	0	0	0	-50
Sep	-2	-5	0	0	0	0	-57
Oct	-1	-4	0	0	0	0	-62
Nov	-2	-5	0	0	0	0	-69
Dec	-2	-4	0	0	0	0	-75

Road 100% Hiway 100% Bridge 100%
Rail 100% Subway 100% Tunnel 100%   Done

Bus station maintenance is counted as part of your road maintenance, and maintenance of raised wires (power lines over water) is counted under the bridges category. Subway stations are counted under the subway category, and train depots are counted under the rail category. Without proper funding, your transit system will deteriorate and crumble, eventually shutting down commerce and industry in your city.[4] To exit the Transit Authority Budget Book, click on Done.

ENACTING CITY ORDINANCES

Through the City Ordinances window, you can establish various community programs and city ordinances to benefit your city. You can open this window

[4]Unfortunately, there is a bug in the *SimCity* model that allows you to let your transportation infrastructure fall into disrepair without any affect on population levels. Thus you can get away with not funding transportation, without any significant effect on the city's population! One hopes that Maxis will fix these and other problems with the model in the near future.

Finance			Safety & Health		
1% Sales Tax	✔	13	Volunteer Fire Dept.	✔	-15
1% Income Tax	✔	45	Public Smoking Ban	✔	-2
Legalized Gambling	✔	27	Free Clinics	✔	-22
Parking Fines	✔	22	Junior Sports	✔	-11

Education			Promotional		
Pro-Reading Campaign	✔	-7	Tourist Advertising	✔	-13
Anti-Drug Campaign	✔	-9	Business Advertising	✔	-40
CPR Training	✔	-7	City Beautification	✔	-11
Neighborhood Watch	✔	-15	Annual Carnival	✔	-4

Other			Estimated Annual Cost	
			Finance	109
Energy Conservation	✔	-99	Safety & Health	-51
Nuclear Free Zone	✔	0	Education	-39
Homeless Shelters	✔	-22	Promotional	-70
Pollution Controls	✔	-40	Other	-162

Done	YTD Total$	-36	EST Total$	-196

Figure 4-4.
City Ordinances
display

by clicking the City Ordinances book button or by selecting **Ordinances** from the **Windows** menu.

As you can see in Figure 4-4, there are five categories of programs and ordinances: finance, safety & health, education, promotional, and other. To enact any ordinance or program, simply click on the check box beside the ordinance name. You'll see the estimated cost or income from the program displayed to the right, and a cumulative summary displayed in the bottom-right corner of the window. At the very bottom of the window, the YTD Total$ text box tells you the current amount that has been spent on ordinances and programs since the first of the year ("YTD" stands for *year-to-date*). To its right, the EST Total$ text box gives you the amount that is estimated for the entire year for *all* your programs and ordinances. Table 4-2 describes each ordinance or program in greater detail.

When you are finished with the Ordinances window, click on the Done button.

ECONOMIC MODELS

Most people have no real understanding of how our modern economic system works, and even economists today disagree among themselves over how

Table 4-2 City Ordinances Described

City Ordinance	Description
Finance	
1% Sales Tax	This sales tax is an additional source of revenue, but enacting it tends to inhibit growth in your commercial zones.
1% Income Tax	This additional tax is levied on your residential zones. Although you increase your tax revenues, enacting this ordinance can slow the growth of residential areas.
Legalized Gambling	By encouraging casinos to move in, you can garner additional tax revenues and increase tourism, but the price may be increased crime. Commerce also gets a little incentive from gambling.
Parking Fines	This ordinance causes people to rely more on mass transit, and it hinders commercial development a little, since people find parking difficult. It does bring you additional revenues, but the price may be high: Potential Simmigrants may think twice about moving to a city where cars are discouraged.
Education	
Pro-Reading Campaign	This campaign will increase your overall education levels slightly, which helps the influx of new high-tech industries.
Anti-Drug Campaign	This ordinance reduces crime.
CPR Training	This is an inexpensive way to increase the life expectancy (LE) of your city. (CPR stands for *cardio-pulmonary resuscitation*.)
Neighborhood Watch	This helps reduce crime in residential areas through increased police protection.
Other	
Energy Conservation	By encouraging insulation retrofitting and more energy-efficient appliances, you can give your power plants an additional 15% capacity.[a] This program takes a few years to get up to speed.
Nuclear Free Zone	Costing nothing, this program may attract new residents to your town, but it has a slightly negative influence on industry.[b] With this ordinance in effect, you cannot build any new nuclear power plants, nor can you replace any previously built nuclear power plants with a new one.
Homeless Shelters	This program is expensive, but it decreases the number of homeless, thereby increasing the population available for work in commerce and industry. It also marginally increases land values.
Pollution Controls	Pollution controls tighten up on the uncontrolled emissions from industry. The ordinance lowers overall pollution levels, but it discourages heavy industry from growing, and it can (but doesn't necessarily) suppress airports from taking root in port-zoned lands.

[a]According to independent testing results by James Alton, the power conservation effects are much less than the 15 percent that the programmers claim. Actual results are in the neighborhood of two to three percent additional power capacity.

[b]In actuality, tests conducted with this ordinance in effect showed little effect on industry. What is significant, however, is that with this ordinance in effect, you cannot build any new nuclear power plants or replace any old nuclear power plants.

Table 4-2 City Ordinances Described *(continued)*	
City Ordinance	**Description**
Safety & Health	
Volunteer Fire Department	This economical program promises to save you money in fire protection costs. Although volunteer fire departments can work very well for small communities, this program is no substitute for real fire departments.
Public Smoking Ban	This ordinance increases the LE of your Sims.
Free Clinics	Free public health clinics significantly increase overall LE but will cost you a lot to run.
Junior Sports	Junior sports increase overall LE at moderate expense.
Promotional	
Tourist Advertising	This expensive program is designed to bring in tourists from out of town. Make sure you have plenty of entertainment attractions like stadiums, marinas, parks, and zoos.
Business Advertising	This program promises to bring in new industry to town.
City Beautification	This ordinance is designed to increase the quality of life in residential zones. Although expensive, this program is very useful since it raises land values.
Annual Carnival	This moderately expensive annual event is designed to increase local tourism and commerce.

best to describe its functioning. The development of economies and their expansion in cities is a whole topic unto itself, but we will focus here on briefly describing the main economic theories of our time.[5] Modern economic theory is broken up into two subject classifications: *macroeconomics* and *microeconomics*. Our capitalist economic system can be described in macroeconomic terms and further explained by looking at individual examples in a microeconomic view.

Macroeconomics is the study of whole systems, especially in terms of economic output, national income, inflation, productivity, investment and consumption, recessions, booms, GNP (gross national product), and the

---

[5]For an excellent treatment of the subject, read Jane Jacobs' *The Economy of Cities*, as well as her *Cities and the Wealth of Nations*. In these books, Jacobs makes several important points:

- Economies grow only when new kinds of work are created, not just by expanding existing lines of work.
- The principal means by which new industries are created is when new work is added to older work. Spinoffs and new divisions of labor are what create new wealth. Inefficiencies actually promote duplication of effort, and this creates more new discoveries.
- Large companies get more infertile as they get larger. Paradoxically, useful inventions get ignored by the large companies. Many examples abound of this. For example, the Xerox Corporation, which invented the computer graphical user interface

banking and money supply system. Microeconomics, on the other hand, is the study of individual areas of economic activity, such as prices, supply and demand, monopolies, distribution of income, and rationing.

Today there are several macroeconomic models to describe how our capitalist economy works.

Classical Economics

This theory dominated mainstream economics from roughly 1775 to 1930. It was first advanced by the great English economist Adam Smith (1723–1790) in his seminal book, *The Wealth of Nations*. Its principles were these:

- *Laissez-faire is best for the market.* The market system is best left alone; government intervention always makes things worse. This idea is often called laissez-faire economics.

- *The market is self-regulating.* Each person works for his or her own selfish interest, with no thought of others. Since everybody is competing with everybody else on an equal footing, a manufacturer who tries to charge more than others will not be able to find any buyers. Similarly, a worker who asks for more than the going wage will not be able to find work. And an employer who tries to pay less than competitors will not be able to find workers to fill the jobs. The market is thus *self-regulating*.

- *The market has an invisible hand.* The market will always produce what society wants. If consumers want more pots than pans, for example, the price of pots will soar, while the price of pans will drop. Manufacturers will rush to expand their pot-making business to make hefty profits, while employers in the disfavored pan business will reduce production and lay off workers. Thus the *invisible hand* of the market controls how production is allocated.

---

and the mouse, ignored the technology that revolutionized personal computing. Early in this century, the electric typewriter was turned down by large typewriter companies, ignored, and finally bought by IBM. The rest of the story is history.

- A city grows in three stages: (1) It starts by increasing exports; (2) it increases imports; (3) it produces the imports itself, substituting its own industrial output; and (4) a large import multiplier effect kicks in and a thriving commercial economy, based on locally produced goods, takes root. It is interesting to note how closely the *SimCity 2000* model parallels this growth process: in the beginning, industries grow but commerce takes a back seat; at the midpoint in the city's evolution, commerce and industry are equal; at the final stage, commerce takes over and industry plays a smaller role.

- Increasing divisions of labor help increase capital wealth. Productivity is what creates new wealth in society. In other words, capital wealth, as measured in machinery and equipment, will only increase when worker output, or productivity, improves. The way to increase productivity is to *increase the division of labor.*

Marxism

Karl Marx (1818–1883), the great political revolutionary and economic thinker, established a theory of economics in his monumental book, *Das Kapital.* In this book he outlined his main belief—that capitalist society was headed for a cataclysmic confrontation with the working class, because the ever-increasing accumulation of capital and wealth by the upper classes would impoverish and worsen the lives of the workers. His basic principles were these:

- *Class struggle between haves and have-nots will increase under a capitalist economy.* Contrary to Adam Smith's view of capitalism growing steadily and in harmony with society, the capitalist market forces of exploitation would cause class tensions, antagonism, and instability in society.

- *Profits are produced principally by the labor of the working class.* The accumulation of wealth by the elite is principally brought about by the labor of the working class. Marx described the process by which a given sum of capital—money sitting in a bank or invested in a firm—yields a profit. A sum of money M is used to hire a work force, build a factory, and buy machinery and raw materials. The labor of the workers increases the value of the raw materials, and these are sold, creating a new, larger sum of money M'. The profit is $M'-M$, and this is principally brought about by the labor of the workers.

- *The capitalist system is inherently unstable:* Adam Smith originated the idea that growth is an inherent characteristic of capitalism; but Marx believed that growth is wavering and uncertain. Eventually, Marx believed, the capitalist system would fall apart for two important reasons. The first is that the size of business firms will steadily increase as the consequence of boom and bust economic cycles. With each crisis, smaller firms go bankrupt and are gobbled up by surviving firms. Thus a trend towards big business is an integral part of the capitalist system. The second is that of the increasing *proletarianization* of the labor force. As businesses get larger and larger, more and more small business people and workers will be squeezed out of the economy. This occurs when, for example, small shops are forced out of business by huge discount chains that can afford to practice predatory pricing tactics. Thus the social structure that will emerge will be that of one very rich capitalist clique, and a large majority of proletarianized (propertyless) workers.

Keynesian Economics

The English economist John Maynard Keynes[6] (1883–1946) is often described as the engineer of capitalism repaired. During the upheaval of the worldwide depression in the 1930s, the "self-regulating" economy, as described by Adam Smith, was in tatters. The laissez-faire policies of governments with regard to the economy did not work; the depression only got worse and worse. In the United States, President Hoover told the nation that if people would only wait just a little while longer, "Prosperity is just around the corner." And so people waited and waited. Instead of prosperity returning, the stock market crashed, and one-half the value of all production simply disappeared overnight.

Over 25 percent of the labor force was unemployed, and over one million families found their mortgages foreclosed and soon lost their homes. Nine million savings accounts were lost when many banks closed down for good. What was one to do? Most economists of the time were at a loss to explain what was happening. Against this background of economic chaos predicted by Marx, Keynes wrote and published his great book, *The General Theory of Employment, Interest, and Money*, which was to change the course of capitalist society forever. The central message of his book was this:

- *There is no "self-regulating" market:* In other words, you could have economic conditions whereby unemployment would increase, wages would fall, and capitalists would be unable or unwilling to make investments to employ unused production and labor capacity.

- *Government intervention and spending are an appropriate and vital tool for restoring a depressed capitalist economy.* This revolutionary concept was instrumental in bringing about a sea of change in government policies in the United States and elsewhere. Keynes provided a blueprint for recovery in his book. The depressed economy, he said, was caused by inadequate aggregate demand. People were just not buying enough goods and services to employ the entire labor force.

---

[6]The name *Keynes* is probably the most mispronounced name in economics. It should be pronounced *canes*, not *keens*.

The only entity big and strong enough to counter this force was government. Governments should spend money in any way that got money into the hands of the people. Once the people had money, they would go out and spend it, buying products and creating a demand for increased factory production. This in turn would cause more workers to be hired, and so the economy could be brought back on the road to recovery. But how was government to obtain the money to do this? Keynes said that it didn't matter—governments could borrow it, thereby causing budget deficits, or even just print it! Nothing improper about deficits, said Keynes, and printing money would not cause inflation because in a depression, the economy *deflates*. All that mattered was priming the economic pump, and so governments needed to spend money in whatever way they could.

The Monetarist School

This school of economic thought believes, as its principal tenet, that most economic problems can be attributed to the rate of growth of the money supply. When the money grows too slowly, we have recession; when it grows too fast, we have inflation. Milton Friedman, one of the monetarists' great proponents, did exhaustive quantitative studies to show that there was a link between the rate of growth of the money supply and the rate of increase of prices. The monetarists say that if you increase the money supply by less than three percent a year, the amount of credit and capital available for investment will shrink and the economy will contract. Most monetarists reject Keynesian fiscal theories because they think that when the government spends more money than it takes in, it inevitably crowds out investment funds in the private sector that would otherwise be available for productive uses.

Their chief battle cry today is the Balanced Budget Amendment to the U.S. Constitution, since that would prevent the government from practicing Keynesian policies. As a prescription for the economy's health, monetarists call for the Federal Reserve to increase the money supply by three to four percent a year. In 1979, the Federal Reserve announced that they would adopt the monetarist policy. They did this for three years, which brought under control the double-digit inflation rates of the 1970s, but at horrific cost. First, interest rates went through the roof in 1980, causing a recession, and then the prime rate shot up to 20 percent. A year later the Fed eased up on the money supply but then tightened it again when inflation worries resurfaced. Again interest rates shot up, this time above 21 percent! It was clear by this point that the monetarists' day was over. Their theories did not work, and so the Fed adopted a new policy: supply-side economics.

Supply-Side Economics

Sometimes referred to disparagingly as "voodoo economics" (first in 1980 by presidential candidate George Bush), supply-side economics became the rallying cry of the Reagan Administration in the 1980s—and, ironically, the torch was carried by President George Bush in 1988. The guru of supply-side economics was the economist Arthur Laffer, whose "Laffer Curve" purported to show that if you lower taxes enough, people will have an incentive to work harder and increase their incomes. As more and more people earn more, predicted the Laffer Curve, the government would get more and more tax revenue to offset that lost by the tax cuts. Supply-side economics is a variation of laissez-faire, and its principal tenet is that if you lower taxes, you will increase aggregate supply—the total amount of goods and services produced. The more you lower taxes, the more production goes up and prices fall. As more people work and earn more money, tax revenues increase, and this will make up the shortfall caused by the initial tax cut.

By the late 1980s and early 1990s, it became evident that the promise of supply-side economics was false. It did not lead to a rapid expansion of the economy, as promised, and so, like the Bush administration, it was ignominiously jettisoned into the flotsam of history's other failures.

In *SimCity 2000*, you can try out the following economic theories:

- **Classical Economics.** The market is always right. Allow the natural Darwinian evolution of industry. Those industries that survive will do so because they are the fittest. Practice laissez faire in economic policies—in other words: hands off! Keep taxes and spending stable, and your economy will grow in a sustained way without booms or busts.

- **Keynesian Economics.** For a *SimCity 2000* example, the *SimCity* government finances expansion of the city to fuel economic growth. Use deficit spending by taking out bonds as necessary to prime the economic pump.

- **Monetarism.** For a *SimCity 2000* example, strictly monitor the growth of the economy. Allow only three percent growth per year to avoid economic booms and busts.

- **Supply-Side Economics ("Voodoo Economics").** For a *SimCity 2000* example, lower all taxes and hope that the resulting economic boom will cause tax revenues to increase. You'll try to "grow" your way out of your city's problems.

C H A P T E R
5

Interpreting Your Maps

This chapter gives you useful information on how to use and interpret your various city maps as viewed in the Map window. The Map window allows you to select one of ten buttons to call up and display a map mode depicting some aspect of your city. The different map modes provide detailed cartographic information about population, zones, transportation links, traffic, pollution, power coverage, water coverage, crime, land values, and city services. Inside each Map Mode window, you'll see a miniaturized replica of your city which gives you an overview of the entire city.

HOW TO OPEN THE MAP WINDOW

There are two ways to open the Map window: you can click the Map Window button on the Toolbar or you can select **Map** from the **Windows** menu. From the Toolbar, you can open the Map window permanently by clicking the Map Window button:

and then, while holding the mouse button down, drag the Map window away from the Toolbar. Or you can display the Map window momentarily by clicking and holding down the mouse button on the Map Window button. The Map window will pop up on-screen and remain there for as long as you hold down the mouse button. When you release it, the Map window will vanish.

The Map window has two different default sizes. When it is first opened, the Map window is small, but you can expand it to a larger and easier-to-read size by clicking on the Zoom box, located at the top-right corner of the Map window. You can reposition the Map window anywhere on-screen by clicking and dragging the title bar at the top of the window. To close the Map window, simply click on the Close box, located at the top-left corner of the window.

USING THE SELECTION RECTANGLE TO REPOSITION YOUR CITY VIEW

There is a selection rectangle inside the Map window which tells you what area your current City window view is showing (see Figure 5-1). The size of this rectangle changes as you zoom in and out of your City window view because your field of view changes accordingly. For example, when you are zoomed all the way in, you can only see a small portion of your city, though each block is magnified to its maximum size. The selection rectangle inside the Map window will shrink to reflect the reduced viewing area you see in the City window. By clicking inside the Map window, you can reposition

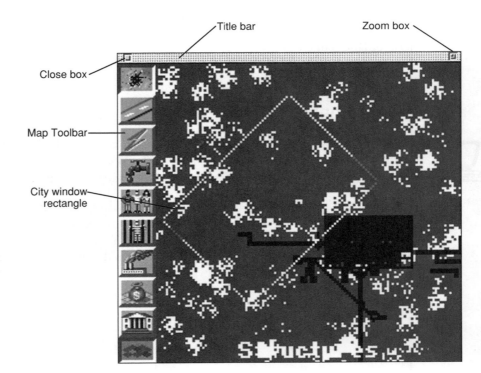

Figure 5-1
The selection rectangle inside the Map window. When you click inside the Map window at a specific location, the rectangle will jump to that new location; your City window will also scroll to that position.

the selection rectangle. It will center itself on the map location where you clicked. The City window will then redraw to show the area where the selection rectangle has been moved. This map-scrolling technique is very useful for when you are trying to visually tie together cartographic information you see in the Map window to the actual view of your city in the City window.

Terrain features are color-coded in the Map window's display. Water is blue and trees and forests are green, while the land is different shades of brown, depending on elevation; the lighter the shade of brown, the higher the elevation.

THE MAP TOOLBAR

On the Map Toolbar you will find buttons that allow you to display the different maps (see Figure 5-2). At first, when you pop up the Map window using the Map button on the Toolbar, you won't see the Map Toolbar. But when you "tear off" the map (meaning you drag it away from the Toolbar), you'll see the Map Toolbar become available. The Map window "remembers" your last map selection, so you can open and shut the window frequently without having to re-click the buttons on its toolbar.

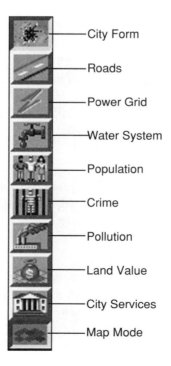

City Form

Roads

Power Grid

Water System

Population

Crime

Pollution

Land Value

City Services

Map Mode

Figure 5-2
The Map Toolbar

Five of the buttons have submenus that pop up when you hold down the mouse button while selecting them.

City Form

The City Form map gives you a view of your entire city limits. When you click the City Form button, a submenu will pop up, letting you decide between displaying structures or zones. Selecting the Structures option lets you see the buildings and city infrastructure, while selecting the Zones option lets you see all your different zone types and how they are distributed on the map. Green represents residential zones, blue represents commercial zones, and yellow represents industrial zones.

Roads

When you click the Roads button, the submenu that pops up will give you three choices—Roads, Rails, and Traffic.

If you select Roads, you will see the map display your entire road network. If you select Rails, you can see your entire rail network. The Traffic option shows the traffic densities for different parts of your city. With the traffic density map display, the denser the traffic, the darker the shade of gray.

Power Grid

Clicking the Power Grid button enables you see your power grid in the city. Unpowered zones will show up in red, while powered zones will appear in yellow. The power lines themselves are colored white.

Water System

Clicking the Water System button enables you to see your water supply system. Zones without water show up in red, while zones with water appear yellow. The water lines themselves are colored white.

Population

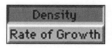

Selecting the Population button causes a submenu to pop up, giving you two map options to pick from—the Density button and the Rate of Growth button.

The Density map shows the relative population densities, with greater population appearing as darker shades of gray, and smaller populations appearing as lighter shades of gray. The Rate of Growth map reveals the areas where population is increasing or decreasing. Those areas that have the greatest rate of growth appear green, while those areas where population is declining show up as red.

Crime

Clicking the Crime button causes a submenu to pop up with three options to choose from to get the Crime Rate map, the Police Power map, and the Police Depts. map.

The Crime Rate map shows the relative amount of crime in each area of your city in different shades of gray. The higher the crime rate, the darker the shade of gray. The Police Power map displays the effective police coverage area for each police station. Areas that have very strong coverage appear black, while those areas that have weaker coverage appear in lighter shades of gray. Since you want to avoid overlapping strong coverage areas, you can use this map to quickly determine where to build new police stations. You can also quickly see where each police station is located by using the Police Depts. map. In this map, each police station is marked by a white square.

Pollution

Clicking the Pollution button lets you see the areas with highest pollution and where they are located. Dark shades of gray tell you that pollution is heaviest, while lighter shades of gray tell you that pollution is light.

Land Value

Clicking the Land Value button lets you see what areas of the city have high land values. The darker the shade of gray, the more valuable the land.

City Services Map

Clicking the City Services button causes a submenu to pop up with four options to choose from to get the Fire Power map, the Fire Depts. map, the Schools map, and the Colleges map.

The Fire Power map displays the effective fire coverage area for each fire station in different shades of gray. Areas that have very strong coverage appear as dark grays, while those areas that have weaker coverage appear in lighter shades of gray. You can use the information displayed in this map to determine where to build new fire stations, without needlessly overlapping coverage areas. You can also quickly see where each fire station is located by using the Fire Depts. map. In this map, each fire department is shown pictured as a white square. The Schools and Colleges maps show you the location of each school or college, which you will see marked on the map as a white square.

Using the Map Mode Button

The Map Mode button is nifty because it allows you to toggle the City window between Map mode and its normal display mode. Figure 5-3 shows the City window *before* clicking the Map Mode button. When this button is toggled on, the information you see displayed in the Map window is simultaneously displayed in the City window, and the buildings and infrastructure will

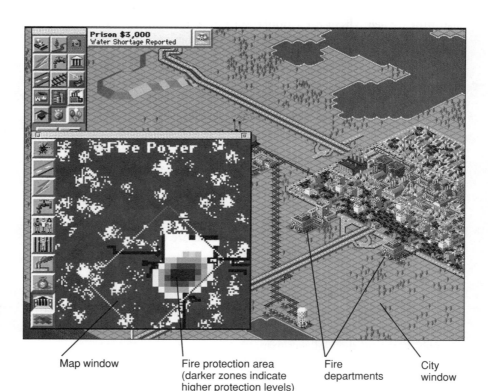

Figure 5-3
City window *before* clicking the Map Mode button.

Map window   Fire protection area   Fire   City
                    (darker zones indicate   departments   window
                    higher protection levels)

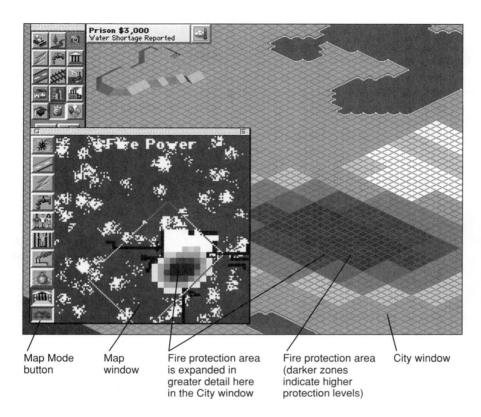

Figure 5-4
City window *after* clicking the Map Mode button. The darker squares indicate areas of highest fire protection, since this is the current Map mode that has been selected here.

Map Mode button

Map window

Fire protection area is expanded in greater detail here in the City window

Fire protection area (darker zones indicate higher protection levels)

City window

vanish, as shown in Figure 5-4. The advantage to having the map information displayed in your City window is that you can see greater detail in the cartographic information presented by the Map window. Because it is too small, the Map window really can't display the same kind of information with the resolution that the City window can. To toggle this switch off to resume your normal City window view—with the buildings and infrastructure again visible—click once more on the Map Mode button.

When in Map mode view, the different densities are displayed in the City window as shades of blue, so that darker blues indicate areas of greater density, while lighter blues indicate areas of lower density. When displaying population rate of growth in the City window, you will see green tiles with plus signs inside them to indicate positive growth and red tiles with negative signs inside them to indicte negative growth.

CHAPTER

6

Customizing the Simulator

Using the pull-down menus in *SimCity 2000*, you can customize the game environment for either the Macintosh or the PC. You can control the speed of the simulation, turn on or off disasters, switch on or off automatic budgeting, choose the frequency of newspaper deliveries, and turn on or off music and sound effects. All of the changes you make to the menu options are saved in your city file, so you don't have to reset them when reloading a favorite city. Most of these menu commands and options are *toggles;* that is, they can only be switched on or off. When the toggle is on, you'll see a check mark next to the menu's option name.

CUSTOMIZING YOUR DISPLAY

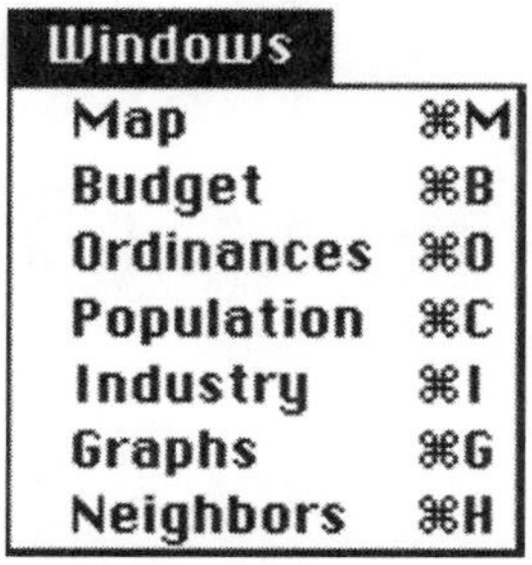

In the Windows or Macintosh version of *SimCity 2000*, you can resize your City window to as large as your screen display permits. In the DOS version of *SimCity 2000*, your City window is limited to a 640×480 screen resolution, although you can resize it to any size smaller than this.

Windows	
Map	⌘M
Budget	⌘B
Ordinances	⌘O
Population	⌘C
Industry	⌘I
Graphs	⌘G
Neighbors	⌘H

All windows and graphs can be opened from the **Windows** menu, shown at right, or they can be opened by clicking their buttons on the Toolbar.

The Ordinance display can be opened quickly and directly from the **Windows** menu or you can go through the two-step procedure of opening the Budget window and then clicking on the Ordinance Book button to open it. You can leave open any window, graph, or map view—except the Budget window (or the Ordinance Display)—while you play with your city. For example, you can leave open the Neighbors window and watch your city population be displayed graphically on screen. Or you could leave open the Graphs window and watch as a particular city trend, such as crime, is graphed month by month.

Unfortunately, you cannot save the location of your map and graphs windows with your city file. This means that each time you start up your city, you will have to reopen any graph or window and position it where you want it.

ADJUSTING THE SPEED OF *SIMCITY 2000*

Through the **Speed** menu you can adjust the rate at which time passes in *SimCity 2000*, or you can pause the simulation.

Of the three speed options on this menu, **Cheetah** speed is the fastest, **Llama** is medium speed, and **Turtle** crawls like a snail (or a turtle, for that matter!). Select **Pause** to freeze the simulation; to restart the simulation, select any of the three speed options. The Windows version of *SimCity 2000* runs best on a Pentium class PC with a PCI or local bus video accelerator card. Because of the complexities of the Windows environment, the Windows version of *SimCity* is ten times slower than its DOS counterpart, despite the inclusion of the new Wing drivers from Microsoft.

The DOS version of *SimCity 2000* on the PC runs best on a 486 running at 66 MHz with a local bus video card interface and local bus SVGA (Super VGA) Video Accelerator Card. Since this simulation is fairly complex and has a sophisticated graphics display, it will tax the abilities of older 386 PCs based on older ISA bus technology and older Macintosh II's. With most DOS-based PCs, the speed bottleneck is video; with ISA buses you don't have the video bandwidth to send Super VGA images fast enough to the screen. local bus PCs have a wider bandwidth, allowing faster data transfer between the PC and the video card. The CPU, or central processing unit, is commonly referred to as a "386" or "486," which are abbreviations for the 80386 or 80486 microprocessors, respectively, and the name local bus refers to a new kind of expansion slot in the latest PCs, which allow super-fast video cards to have faster access to the CPU. The clock speed at which a PC runs is measured in millions of cycles per second, or megahertz. Thus at the Cheetah speed setting *SimCity 2000* will run approximately 50–80 percent faster on a 66 MHz 486 than on a 33 MHz 486. The clock speed also determines the speed of Macintoshes; a fast Motorola 68040 CPU running at 40 MHz, as found in a Quadra

840AV, will run many times faster than an older 20 MHz Motorola 68030 CPU in a Mac IIsi.[1]

If you have an older 386 PC or Macintosh II, *SimCity*'s performance may be too slow for you, even at the Cheetah setting. To address this issue, you can resize your City window so that it occupies less "real estate" or screen space. By reducing the graphic workload on your computer, you can speed up *SimCity* by as much as 55 percent! The next section describes how to do this.

How to Speed Up the Simulation Even More

Unfortunately, turning off the sound effects and music has only a marginal effect on improving speed for both the Macintosh and PC. In tests I conducted, there was no visible improvement in speed with the sound off. This is surprising since there theoretically should be some CPU overhead involved in processing the sound. At any rate, don't turn off the sound or music to try to speed up the simulation; it doesn't really help.

You can speed up the simulation by about 55 percent by performing the following tasks:

1. Select **Cheetah** as your speed from the **Speed** menu.
2. Turn on **Auto-Budget** from the **Options** menu.
3. Select **No Disasters** from the **Disasters** menu.
4. Turn off all newspaper delivery options by toggling off the **Extra** and **Subscription** menu options from the **Newspaper** menu.
5. Close all maps and graphs.
6. Center your City window view on empty land that is devoid of nearby developments.
7. Minimize your City window by dragging the Resize box at the lower-right corner of your City window diagonally upwards toward the left. Size the window as small as possible, as is illustrated in Figure 6-1.

Table 6-1 shows the results of running the DOS and Windows versions of *SimCity 2000* on a 486 local bus, 66 MHz–based PC and the Macintosh versionof *SimCity 2000* on a Mac IIsi. This speed comparison is not really a fair contest between the Mac and the PC, because the Mac IIsi has a 68030

---

[1]Maxis reports that early prototypes of the PowerPC, which is Apple's new line of Macintoshes based on the Power PC RISC (Reduced Instruction Set Computing) CPU, ran *SimCity* blazingly fast. In fact, you might even need to run it at the Turtle speed setting!

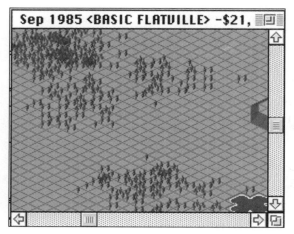

Figure 6-1
Speeding up the simulation by minimizing your City window. This frees up your CPU from unnecessary graphics drawing.

microprocessor, which is the equivalent of a 386. There are two speed comparisons for each computer: the first listing shows the speed of the computer using a City window that is maximized, while the second listing shows the speed of the computer with the City window minimized. The speeds shown are listed in terms of the number of city months that pass for each minute of your time. In other words, if the speed shown is 12, then 12 months would pass in *SimCity 2000* for each minute that you sit in front of your computer.

Notice that in the speed comparison table, *there is no speed improvement when minimizing your window while using the Turtle and Llama speed settings!* But you will get a whopping speed boost of up to 55 percent (or more!) by minimizing the window under the Cheetah setting. For example, running the DOS 1.1 version of SimCity on a fast (66 MHz) 486 PC at the Cheetah speed, you can have up to 345 years per hour pass by with the City window maximized, or up to 560 years pass by with the City window minimized. This is a performance boost of over 62 percent!

Note that Table 6.1 shows that the Windows version of *SimCity 2000* is ten times slower than the DOS version when running at the Cheetah speed.

Tip: The larger your City window is, the slower your computer will run *SimCity 2000*. If your computer seems to run too slowly, try resizing the City window smaller.

CHOOSING YOUR BUDGET OPTIONS

When you toggle on **Auto-Budget** under the **Options** menu the Budget window will not automatically open up each January. Instead, whatever budgeting decisions you made for the last year will be held over and applied to the new budget year.

```
Options
Auto-Budget
✓Auto-Goto
Sound Effects
Music
```

The only thing that may be different is that sometimes your city advisors take it upon themselves to enact city ordinances without your permission. You can always override these decisions by opening the Ordinances window and toggling on or off the ordinance in question.

GOING TO DISASTERS QUICKLY

With **Auto-Goto** toggled on under the **Options** menu, *SimCity* will move you to the scene of a disaster or other major catastrophe so that you can see its epicenter — and you will be interrupted if you were busy doing something elsewhere in your city. Should you decide to leave Auto-Goto off, you will still see

Table 6-1 *SimCity* Speed Comparison

SimCity Version	Type of Computer	Turtle Speed	Llama Speed	Cheetah Speed
DOS 1.1	486, 66 MHz local bus PC with SVGA local bus video acc. card	4 months/min. (20 city years/hr.)	12 months/min. (60 city years/hr.)	69 months/min. (345 city years/hr.)
DPS 1.1	Same 486 system as above, City window minimized for max. speed	4 months/min. (20 city years/hr.)	12 months/min. (60 city years/hr.)	112 months/min. (560 city years/hr.)
Mac 1.1	Mac IIsi (Motorola 68030, 20 MHz)	3 months/min. (15 city years/hr.)	7 months/min. (35 city years/hr.)	8.5 months/min. (42.5 cityyears/hr.)
Mac 1.1	Same Mac system as above, City window minimized for max. speed	3 months/min. (15 city years/hr.)	7 months/min. (35 city years/hr.)	12 months/min. (60 city years/hr.)
Windows 1.0	486, 66 MHz local bus PC with SVGA local bus video acc. card	3 months/min. (15 city years/hr.)	6 months/min. (30 city years/hr.)	6 months/min. (30 city years/hr.)
Windows 1.0	Same 486 system as above, City window minimized for max. speed	3 months/min. (15 city years/hr.)	6 months/min. (30 city years/hr.)	1 months/min. (55 city years/hr.)

the Emergency icon activate itself and the Status window warn you of the type of disaster, but you won't automatically leave the area you are currently in.

ENJOYING THE SOUND EFFECTS AND MUSIC

To turn off sound effects, such as helicopter traffic reports, honking cars, sirens, etc., pull down the **Options** menu and select the **Sound Effects** toggle option so that the check mark next to the name disappears. When you pull down the Options menu, anytime you see the check mark next to Sound Effects, it means that the sounds are enabled.

Music can also be separately switched off or on by using the **Music** toggle under the **Options** menu. To turn off the music, simply select the **Music** option and make sure that the check mark next to its name disappears. Anytime you see the check mark next to Music, it means that the music is turned on.

Since there is no inherent speed advantage to turning off sound and music, you might as well leave it on—that is, unless you intend to play *Sim-City* at the office and want to avoid being detected by the boss!

Taking Advantage of *SimCity*'s New MIDI Sound Support

SimCity 2000 is one of a new class of games that includes General MIDI (Musical Instrument Digital Interface) support. If you have a MIDI wave table synthesis sound card and you installed *SimCity* to take advantage of it, you can enjoy the superior sound capabilities that MIDI cards have to offer. These cards take actual sound wave samples of real instruments and store them digitally inside the card. Each card can store hundreds of samples, which means that you can have the entire range of symphonic sounds and percussion effects inside your computer! With up to 32 voice polyphony (meaning you can have 32 instruments playing simultaneously), you can play full symphonies or have any piece of music orchestrated with any instrument you wish. For example, you could play Beethoven's Fifth Symphony using glass harmonicas to substitute for the violins, or steel drums to fill in for the basses. As a professional musician myself, believe me—once you hear a MIDI card, you'll never want to go back to ordinary Sound Blaster-type organ music. General MIDI is the wave of the future for sound cards.

You can buy a Sound Blaster-type card and a MIDI card for use simultaneously in your computer, using the Sound Blaster card for sound effects and the MIDI card for music. Some cards combine the functions of the two: for example, you can buy a Sound Blaster with Wave Blaster attached to it. This gives you both types of sound in one card that takes up only one expansion slot in your computer. Before buying a MIDI sound card, check with your dealer or computer supplier to ensure that the card works with the sound card you have, or that it comes with a built-in Sound Blaster emulation. Many MIDI cards come with Sound Blaster capabilities already built-in, so you don't need to have a separate sound card for sound effects.

SimCity's music also treads new ground in sophistication. No longer do you have to listen to trite melodies played over and over that, if allowed to continue, will send you to the nuthouse. In *SimCity*, the music is only triggered by certain events or actions that you take; when you do nothing you get peace and quiet. This is a refreshing change from most other computer games that blare out inane music that grates on your nerves. What's more, there's a variety of music to evoke different moods: when things are going badly, you get somber music; when you get good news, the music is upbeat.

Later, in Chapte 10, you'll learn how to change the MIDI sound files for the Windows version of *SimCity 2000* to your own MIDI files. You can then play any kind of music in lieu of what is shipped with the game.

PART

II

Politics—SimCitizens, City Councils, and Hidden Agendas

C H A P T E R
7

Sims, Their Neighbors,
and SimNation

SimCity 2000 is populated by Sims: determined, vocal electronic life forms. They are very much like humans in their wants and needs. But they are a lot smaller, and they live a lot faster. They can live to about 90 simulated years, which can range, in our time, from minutes to hours, depending on the power of our computer and the size of the city.

Sims are divided into and tracked by age groups. Each of these groups is five years in length, and is represented by a bar in the Population window:

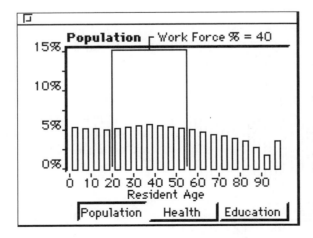

While they are divided into 20 groups for graphing and simulation purposes, they go through five main stages of life:

- From birth to age five, young Sims live at home. They learn about life and the world from their parents and play computer games.
- Children from five to 15 go to a combined elementary, middle, and high school, where they continue to learn. After school, they do their homework and play computer games.
- If there are colleges, Sims from 15 to 20 attend classes. If there is no college, they laze around the house, drive their parents crazy, and play computer games all day.
- Sims between the ages of 20 and 55 are the work force. The jobs they get depend on their level of education and the types of industry that exist in their city. These Sims are the taxpayers and are very serious. They read newspapers, watch you closely, and complain about taxes and anything and everything else that displeases them. This is also the Sims' reproductive age, where they beget their beloved but bratty Simlings. Working Sims are far too busy and serious to play computer games.
- Above 55, Sims retire, read the newspaper, complain—but only recreationally—about the mayor, and play computer games.

The health and education levels of your Sims are major factors in the growth of your city, and maintaining and improving these levels is your responsibility.

SimHEALTH

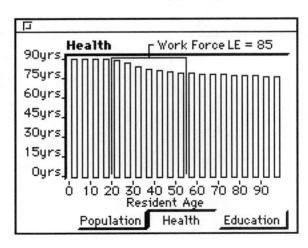

Your Sims' health is measured in life expectancy (LE). If you don't keep your Sims healthy, they'll die young, which is bad from the SimHumanistic point of view, as well as the practical one. If your population is dying young, then a high percentage of the population you have is young, which means that you'll need more schools per capita, which cost more and fill the place with all those noisy SimBrats. And the SimGrandparents all die young, so there're no convenient babysitters around.

Building up a long life expectancy is a slow, multigenerational process. Children are assigned their life expectancy at birth. A good supply of fully funded hospitals is the primary way to increase the life expectancy of newborn babies. The passage of city Free Clinic, Public Smoking Ban, or Pollution Control ordinances also has a small but noticeable effect on infant LE.

As Sims age and move up through all the five-year age groups, their life expectancy declines a little, depending on the amount of pollution in the city. The more pollution, the more their LE declines.

SimEDUCATION

The EQ, or education quotient, of your Sims has a direct effect on which industries your city can support. If you want those high-tech, high-paying, low-polluting jobs that won't become obsolete and leave your industrial base a hollow shell of people looking for Roger, then build up your Sims' EQ.

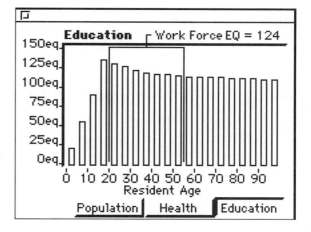

An EQ of 85 is the equivalent of a high school education. An EQ of 100 is the equivalent of the current United States average. The maximum EQ in *SimCity 2000* is 150.

Children in the zero-to-five-year range get their start on the road to educational enlightenment by hanging out with their parents, watching and imitating, and a little bit of home schooling. When they reach age five, they enter school with an EQ that is one-fifth of their parents'. (Their parents' EQ is the average EQ of all working-age Sims.)

During the next 10 years of schooling, young Sims study and learn and increase their EQ by as much as 70 points—if there are enough well-funded schools. (Schools serve an average total population of 15,000, and up to 1,500 students.)

If you have colleges ready and funded when the Sims hit college age, then the Sims will attend and raise their EQ by an additional 50 percent. (Colleges serve an average total population of 50,000, and up to 5,000 students.)

After college, or after high school if there are no colleges, Sims start to forget. Their EQs begin to decay and they continue to sink as they get older. The presence of libraries and museums will stop this erosion of knowledge, as will enacting the city Pro-Reading Campaign ordinance. (Libraries serve a total population of 20,000 and museums serve 40,000.)

HEALTH, EDUCATION, AND JOBS

SimCity 2000 leans very heavily in favor of high-tech industries, and this bias relates closely with both health and education. High-tech industries pollute less (on the average—at least in *SimCity 2000*), and this fact has a direct effect on life expectancy (pollution erodes LE).

High-tech industries will grow faster if your city's average EQ for working-age Sims is above 100. (You can maintain this level with schools for the whole population and colleges for about half the population.)

In addition, aerospace and electronics are very high-tech industries that are very demanding of a high EQ, above and beyond the others. Like other high-tech industries, they receive a growth boost at an EQ of 100. They get another boost if your EQ is above 130—and sink like a rock if your EQ is below 80.

SimMIGRATION

When a city is first created and Sims move in from other places, every Sim is an immigrant. Simmigrants are mostly in the working-age range (20 to 55). Some bring their parents along, some bring their kids. But most are there either because they really need the work or because they foresee wonderful opportunity for growth and advancement in a new town, and they travel light.

The working-age Simmigrants come into town with a life expectancy (LE) of 59 and an educational quotient (EQ) of 85. The few parents and children that come along are, on the average, slightly lower in EQ.

Neither of these levels is anything to be proud of, so get those hospitals and schools in early. Improvement in health and education begins with the first generation to be born in your city.

YOUR NEIGHBORS

The cities you build don't exist in a vacuum. You have either three or four neighbors, depending on whether or not you have a coastline along one edge of your city.

You can't get your neighbors' statistics, other than population. They exist as trade partners and as competitors for people and industry, but they are really a minor factor in the growth and development of your city. As far as the simulator is concerned, your trade and immigration are generated from the nation at large, not just from your three or four neighbors.

On the other hand, you can have a definite effect on your neighbors' rates of growth. The more direct the lines of trade you run to neighboring cities, the faster those cities will grow. So where you put your commercial (roads off the edge) and industrial (highways and rails off the edge) carrying capacity affects neighbors more than it does you.

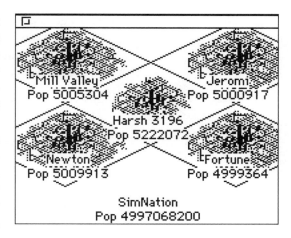

The main offshoot of this is that you can decide to boycott a particular neighbor and not trade with them. It'll hurt them more than it will hurt you. Other than that, and the possibility that some of your Sims may want to vacation in a neighboring city or easily visit relatives there, neighbors have no effect on your city and its growth.

The names of the neighboring cities are picked at random from this list of 36 names when you create your city:

Oak Creek	Denmont	Fort Verdegris	Schwinton
Mill Valley	Petaluma	PortVille	Ashland
Eubanks	Aurac	Tent Pegs	Cherryton
Blake	Pioneers	Fortune	Phippsville
Jeromi	Harpersville	Washers Grove	Stars County
Villa	Serviland	Newton	Avon
Dexter	Sinistrel	Jenna	Yestonia
New Boots	Hoek Creek	Stimpleton	Little Rouge
Krighton	Cats Corner	Rimmer	Lister

Neighbors develop and decline roughly in step with your city, following the SimNation model.

SimNATION

SimNation is a simple national model that grows roughly at the same rate as your city. Its main functions are:

- To generate an overall national population that becomes a source of immigration

- To provide a source of raw materials for import and customers for export

- To generate demand for the output of various industries, depending on the year, available technology, and industry in your city
- To cycle through economic trends (depression, recession, steady, and boom) that control interest rates

CHAPTER
8
Newspapers

The main function of the newspapers in *SimCity 2000* is the same function that real newspapers serve: to keep you informed of what's happening in the city (both good and bad), in the region, and in the world.

Newspapers bring three important things to *SimCity 2000*: realism, fuzziness, and fun. Realism, because real mayors don't have evaluation windows giving them absolutely accurate information, and they definitely don't have pop-up messages that notify them of important events around the world. Fuzziness, because the information you need from newspapers isn't always totally correct, isn't exactly what you need, and is usually buried in among a thousand other things you don't need or care about. Fun, because, heck, it *is* a game.

The most important information for successful mayors to glean from the papers consists of:

- Commentary on issues your Sims are concerned about
- Feedback on your approval rating and public opinion
- Disaster notices
- News of inventions that give you access to new technology in your city
- Warnings of impending power plant breakdowns
- Promotions and announcements of city size

As in a real newspaper, the most important information is found in the story's title and the first couple of sentences. The rest is filler.

COMMENTARY AND FEEDBACK

The commentary section picks and discusses the major problem, as chosen by an informal poll of your Sims. It tells you what the Sims think is the major problem—be careful here, this is what the Sims *think* is the major problem, from *their* perspective. What concerns them may not be the most important thing for the city or for your survival as mayor. If you always jump to do the bidding of the commentator, you could be missing something more important in the long run.

Not every paper has a commentary section; only two out of the six do, including the first paper you get. Two of the other papers will have the mayor's approval rating.

HOW THE NEWSPAPERS WORK

There are up to six papers, depending on the size of your city. Each paper will have different stories, so it is important to look through as many papers as you can. Simulator time stops when a paper is open, so don't worry about losing a month or two while you read.

New papers are generated every month, so if you're a real newshound, not only will you get the full subscription for delivery twice a year (select **Subscription** in the **Newspaper** menu), you'll actively seek and read more papers. If, on the other hand, you only want to know about special events, then just subscribe to extra additions (select **Extra!!!** in the **Newspaper** menu). If, on the third hand (assuming you have three), you just don't want to know (the mayor-as-ostrich approach), then don't subscribe to anything—but you'll still receive papers announcing disasters.

Stories are triggered by events in the simulator, in your city, and around SimNation. When the stories are gathered to generate the papers, they are each weighted according to how important they are and how long the information will be useful. The stories with the highest ratings are printed; the rest wait until a slow news month lets them through or until they expire. If there isn't enough hard news to fill a paper, then silly or human interest stories are inserted as filler.

On occasion, you may see conflicting stories. Since traffic can be good in one neighborhood and bad in another, both good and bad traffic stories may be found in the same paper.

The goal in creating the papers was to put enough different possibilities and randomness in the stories to keep them changing and interesting, but to keep them tight enough to make sense—most of the time. To keep the papers from getting too tiring too quickly, the stories were written with replaceable variables—words and phrases—in them. As the stories are chosen and generated, different people, places, things, and such are inserted in a way that usually makes sense. When appropriate, stories also take information from the simulation, such as the prime rate or approval statistics for the mayor.

All in all, the amount of text for all the stories with all the variables fills a 200K text file. There are 300 different stories in more than 60 different story categories, including:

- Stories about the city's founding, city growth, inventions, and innovations
- National news stories about wars, the national market, sports, and fluctuations in the federal interest rate
- Local news about politics, diplomacy, and disasters, as well as medical news and the good old upbeat story
- Stories that complain about high crime, high traffic congestion, high pollution, poor education, poor health, and poor employment levels
- Stories that brag about low crime, low traffic congestion, low pollution, good education, good health care, and good employment statistics
- Disaster reports about fires, floods, plane crashes, helicopter crashes, tornadoes, earthquakes, monsters, meltdowns, microwave power plant accidents, volcanoes, serious pollution disasters (as opposed to general complaints about pollution), chemical spills, hurricanes, and riots
- Warnings about aging power plants, overcrowded prisons, complaining teachers, bridges down, citizens upset about bulldozing of trees, and city council actions
- Stories that demand more or improved power, transit systems, police coverage, fire protection, water systems, hospitals, schools, seaports, airports, zoos, stadiums, marinas, parks, and connections to neighboring cities
- Weather reports
- The good, old-fashioned human interest junk story.

FUN WITH NEWSPAPERS

When stories are packed with random variables to keep them interesting, sometimes they don't make perfect sense. Actually, the stories that don't are the most fun to read. Look for them at a newsstand near you—both in and out of *SimCity 2000*.

And sometimes stories are generated that make sense but mock reality, like the human interest story about the guppy who walked 5,000 miles home, wagging his uvula behind him.

Among the silly and useless statements that appear in various stories are the political quotes, which are assembled from three parts: one from column A, one from column B, and one from column C, to form a completely meaningless quote about some important political topic. Keep an eye out for them.

We won't spoil your fun by listing all the funny variables in the newspapers, but we will tell you that there are nearly 1,400 different words and short phrases that can be inserted into the stories, including:

- 24 countries
- 14 different types of criminals
- 14 different crimes, including expectoration and defenestration (look them up)
- Many diseases and maladies
- 18 feelings
- Uncountable names, first, last, male, female, and international
- 20 junk inventions, including a simulated city
- 17 exclamations, from "Gee whilickers" to "Well, buy me a Cadillac and call me Elvis"
- 11 different types of llamas, ranging from the Grand Llama to Joey the Wonder Llama

And for those of you who don't want to sit and wait for other people to entertain you, you can make your own fun with *SimCity 2000* newspapers. Don't forget that stories use both your name (as you input it during installation or first startup) and the name of the city, so when naming yourself or your city, you can be creative and come up with some serious silliosity.

For city names, nouns—the sillier, the better—work the best (dig out those dictionaries). Nouns such as body parts (*Nose, Ear, Gluteus Maximus, Kneecap, Cheeks, Skin, Eustachian Tube*), bodily functions related to digestion and indigestion, and articles of clothing (*Shirt, Socks,* and various undergarments) work well as city names[1]. Adding the word *My* or other modifiers such as *Big, Tiny, Oblong, Broken,* or *Wounded* before any of these words adds a personal touch.

---

[1] We could have come up with other, less couth examples, but this is a family book.

Here are just a few samples of the statements to play with to test out city names:

- "It was the official first day in (city name) history."
- "Let all gathered here today always remember the purity and innocence of (city name) as she stands before us today. . . ."
- "The mayor of this city is confident that (city name) will rise to its citizens' lofty expectations."
- "But if traffic congestion in (city name) isn't alleviated, I'm sure things will get worse."
- "You need only look out your window to realize that (city name) is filling the air with carcinogens. . . ."
- "The power source that kept (city name) humming a year ago is turning the city mute."

For names of mayors, almost any silly word or name can generate a chuckle. But seeing your own name in a newspaper (especially if it's spelled correctly) is a good cheap thrill, too.

CHAPTER
9

The City Council and Ordinances

No mayor ever rules entirely on his or her own, but in *SimCity 2000* you're just about as close as you can get. There is a City Council made of nameless, faceless Sims, but for the most part they blindly follow your directions.

On occasion they will pass an ordinance on their own initiative, but you can always veto it. If you want to keep them from stepping out of line, just select **No Disasters** in the **Disasters** menu and they'll never pass an ordinance without your specific instructions.

So don't worry about the patsies on the City Council. Rule as you will. But knowing about all the different ordinances is useful. There are five areas of city management covered by ordinances:

- Finance ordinances are ways to bring in money above and beyond taxes.
- Education ordinances provide for small but effective campaigns and classes to improve city life.
- Safety & Health ordinances work toward minimizing disaster damage and increasing your citizens' life expectancy.
- Promotional ordinances are aimed at bringing in new immigrants, new businesses, and tourists.
- Other ordinances cover whatever won't fit into any of the other areas.

Here are the details on all the ordinances:

The actual fiscal impacts of some of the ordinances are based on factors that are hard to find or impossible to know from the player's point of view. The calculations shown here are approximate but based on information that you can easily find and that is close enough for planning purposes.

Finance				Safety & Health		
1% Sales Tax	✓	5998		Volunteer Fire Dept.	✓	-4010
1% Income Tax	✓	12k		Public Smoking Ban	✓	-999
Legalized Gambling	✓	11k		Free Clinics	✓	-6015
Parking Fines	✓	6015		Junior Sports	✓	-3007

Education				Promotional		
Pro-Reading Campaign	✓	-2005		Tourist Advertising	✓	-5998
Anti-Drug Campaign	✓	-2406		Business Advertising	✓	-5962
CPR Training	✓	-2005		City Beautification	✓	-3007
Neighborhood Watch	✓	-4010		Annual Carnival	✓	-1999

Other				Estimated Annual Cost	
				Finance	36k
Energy Conservation	✓	-69k		Safety & Health	-14k
Nuclear Free Zone	✓	0		Education	-10k
Homeless Shelters	✓	-6015		Promotional	-16k
Pollution Controls	✓	-5962		Other	-81k

Done	YTD Total$	-22k	EST Total$	-72k

1 Percent Sales Tax

- Type: Finance.
- Yearly fiscal impact: The city treasury receives approximately $1 for every 75 Sims in the commercial population.
- Pros: Brings in money.
- Cons: Slight negative effect on commerce.
- Comments: This one's a close call. It brings in enough money to be useful, but not enough to make it a definite choice every time. Could be used for short terms to finance a bridge or highway, then repealed.

1 Percent Income Tax

- Type: Finance.
- Yearly fiscal impact: The city treasury receives approximately $1 for every 75 Sims in the residential population.
- Pros: Brings in money.
- Cons: Moderate negative effect on residential growth.
- Comments: This is the biggest money maker of all the ordinances. Financially, it's worth enacting—especially if you build a zoo or

enact another ordinance that will counteract the negative effect on residential growth. As far as benevolence and caring about your citizens goes, it's a personal call. Rumor has it that an early beta version of *SimCity 2000* let you adjust the income tax rate, but when a tester cranked it up to 50 percent, a bunch of Sims came out of his computer and strangled him—so for safety's sake, 1 percent is the limit.

Legalized Gambling

- Type: Finance.
- Yearly fiscal impact: The city treasury receives approximately $1 for every 38 Sims in the commercial population.
- Pros: Brings in money.
- Cons: Increases crime in the city.
- Comments: Good money here—for a while—even if it is tainted. But soon the crime will get out of hand and become more of a liability than it's worth. Proper funding (payoffs?) for police can help, but the police funding and the loss to land value-based taxes cost more than the gambling brings in. Allowing gambling is a judgment call: it's either a declaration of a wild and crazy (and dangerous) city or an act of desperation by a broke city.

Parking Fines

- Type: Finance.
- Yearly fiscal impact: The city treasury receives approximately $1 for every 150 Sims in the residential population.
- Pros: Brings in money.
- Cons: Very slight negative effect on commerce.
- Comments: Unless you really need a quick couple hundred bucks, don't bother. Why hassle your Sims if there's no big payoff?

Pro-Reading Campaign

- Type: Education.
- Yearly fiscal impact: The city treasury is charged approximately $1 for every 450 Sims in the residential population.

- Pros: Reduces education quotient in Sims after they leave school.
- Cons: Just the cost.
- Comments: It's a small price to pay to keep your education level up and make your city eligible for those all-important high-tech industries.

Anti-Drug Campaign

- Type: Education.
- Yearly fiscal impact: The city treasury is charged approximately $1 for every 850 Sims in the Total Population.
- Pros: Reduces crime.
- Cons: Just the cost.
- Comments: A very small price to pay for crime reduction. An absolute must if you legalize gambling.

CPR Training

- Type: Education.
- Yearly fiscal impact: The city treasury is charged approximately $1 for every 1,000 Sims in the Total Population.
- Pros: Improves overall health of citizens.
- Cons: Just the cost.
- Comments: CPR is a good thing to know—for Sims and humans alike. Pay it. And take a class yourself!

Neighborhood Watch

- Type: Education.
- Yearly fiscal impact: The city treasury is charged approximately $1 for every 230 Sims in the residential population.
- Pros: Reduces crime in residential areas.
- Cons: Just the cost.
- Comments: Since crime is probably the biggest problem facing cities today (SimCities and otherwise), anything you can do to fight it is worthwhile.

Volunteer Fire Department

- Type: Safety & Health.
- Yearly fiscal impact: The city treasury is charged approximately $1 for every 230 Sims in the residential population.
- Pros: Effective at preventing and putting out fires in a small city, especially when teamed with adequately funded professionals, but less effective in a huge city.
- Cons: Just the cost.
- Comments: Good investment in smaller towns and cities, but once the city reaches a population size for which it's cheaper to maintain a professional staff than the volunteers, dump it. You can't deploy volunteer fire departments in emergencies.

Public Smoking Ban

- Type: Safety & Health.
- Yearly fiscal impact: The city treasury is charged approximately $1 for every 500 Sims in the commercial population.
- Pros: Increases the overall health level in the city.
- Cons: Slight negative effect on commercial growth, because all the SimSmokers are walking out of the office for a cigarette every five milliseconds.
- Comments: This ordinance is neither so good nor so bad that one can call it either way. Let your personal lifestyle be your guide here.

Free Clinics

- Type: Safety & Health.
- Yearly fiscal impact: The city treasury is charged approximately $1 for every 150 Sims in the residential population.
- Pros: Increases the overall health level of the citizens, especially by providing prenatal care so that newborns are assigned a higher life expectancy at birth.
- Cons: Just the cost.
- Comments: Do it. For the children.

Junior Sports

- Type: Safety & Health.
- Yearly fiscal impact: The city treasury is charged approximately $1 for every 300 Sims in the residential population.
- Pros: Increases the health level of the youth of your city and reduces crime.
- Cons: Just the cost.
- Comments: What the heck, it keeps them off the streets.

Tourist Advertising

- Type: Promotional.
- Yearly fiscal impact: The city treasury is charged approximately $1 for every 75 Sims in the commercial population.
- Pros: Can increase business in the tourism industry.
- Cons: Cost and possible uselessness.
- Comments: If you advertise for tourists, be sure you have something worth coming to see: parks, stadiums, rivers, coastline, zoos, marinas. . .

Business Advertising

- Type: Promotional.
- Yearly fiscal impact: The city treasury is charged approximately $1 for every 75 Sims in the Industrial Population.
- Pros: Can increase industrial growth.
- Cons: Cost of the program and of the infrastructure to support the new business.
- Comments: Build new infrastructure (transportation, power, and water) and prepare your city before enacting this one.

City Beautification

- Type: Promotional.
- Yearly fiscal impact: The city treasury is charged approximately $1 for every 300 Sims in the residential population.
- Pros: Increases residential growth and land value.

- Cons: Just the cost and those flashback images of Lady Bird Johnson.
- Comments: A cheap way to clean up your act.

Annual Carnival

- Type: Promotional.
- Yearly fiscal impact: The city treasury is charged approximately $1 for every 230 Sims in the commercial population.
- Pros: Boost the tourism industry and commerce.
- Cons: Just the cost.
- Comments: Carnivals aren't effective at all in small towns, and they're no big deal in large cities either. Wait until you have a population of at least 10,000 and a bit of tourism in your city, and even then figure you're doing more to boost local morale than to increase commerce or tourism. The fiscal impact of this one is very approximate, especially for larger populations.

Energy Conservation

- Type: Other.
- Yearly fiscal impact: The city treasury is charged approximately $1 for every 75 Sims in the Total Population.
- Pros: Can save you the cost of building new power plants, may lessen power plant pollution, and is ecologically trendy.
- Cons: Just the cost.
- Comments: This ordinance simulates an educational campaign that teaches Sims in all zone types to save energy, so it takes a few years for everyone to learn and incorporate the knowledge into their behavior. Once you have the money to buy one of the more expensive high-output, non-polluting power plants (microwave or fusion), this ordinance isn't as necessary, but it's still a good idea to help keep your Sims thinking about conservation.

Nuclear-Free Zone

- Type: Other.
- Yearly fiscal impact: N/A.
- Pros: Small boost for residential growth.

- Cons: Small impediment to industry.
- Comments: Since it costs nothing and the pros and cons balance out, this ordinance is more of a personal statement than a financial or political tool. If you enact a nuclear-free zone, you can't build nuclear power plants. If you have a nuclear power plant in your city at the time you enact a nuclear-free zone, then when its life span runs out, it won't be automatically replaced, even with No Disasters turned on in the Disasters menu. If you allow a military base in your city, the military can bring in missile silos if they want—nuclear-free zone or not!

Homeless Shelters

- Type: Other.
- Yearly fiscal impact: The city treasury is charged approximately $1 for every 150 Sims in the residential population.
- Pros: Helps move unemployed into the labor force and gives a slight boost to land value.
- Cons: Just the cost.
- Comments: The homeless in *SimCity* are easy to ignore, but how you treat them says a lot about you as a person and as a leader among Sims.

Pollution Controls

- Type: Other.
- Yearly fiscal impact: The city treasury is charged approximately $1 for every 75 Sims in the Industrial Population.
- Pros: Reduces the overall pollution from industry and automobile emissions.
- Cons: Has a slight negative effect on industrial growth.
- Comments: Since pollution is tied directly to your Sims' health level and life expectancy, anything you can do to cut it down is worthwhile. You can overcome the negative effect on industry by promoting non-polluting industries and increasing your Sims' education quotients.

CHAPTER
10
Tips and Tricks

This chapter contains a wealth of useful background information that will aid you in your city-planning decisions. You'll discover all the Easter Eggs,[1] learn how to embezzle funds and hex-edit your city files, and also learn how to create your own scenarios. The chapter concludes with advice on how to obtain *SimCity* help online, and how to exchange cities electronically.

CREATING EXTERNAL MARKETS FOR INDUSTRY

External markets are the markets outside *SimCity* to which you export your industrial output. You don't have any control over the economic conditions outside your city, and occasional external recessions are possible. In the *SimCity* model, external markets must be developed *before* internal markets. Since industrial zones enable external markets to grow, you should build more industrial zones than commercial zones to allow this to happen.

---

[1]In computer programs, the term *Easter Eggs* refers to hidden or undocumented features that are inserted by programmers for their own enjoyment. In most cases, nobody knows about them, and they remain secret and undiscovered. For example, one classic Easter Egg in Microsoft Windows 3.1 is found under the **Help** menu in the Program Manager. Select **About Program Manager** and then, while holding down Ctrl and Shift, double-click on the Windows 3.1 icon. Close the dialog box, then open it up again and double-click again on the icon; you'll see an interesting animation sequence. If you repeat this trick, you'll see something even more interesting.

CREATING INTERNAL MARKETS FOR COMMERCE

Internal markets represent the consumption, within your city, of goods and services that are produced there. Only after your industrial base has been established will your internal markets begin to grow. The goods that were formerly exported to external markets will then be consumed within your city. As your population grows, it will demand more and more of these internally produced services and goods. This is where your commercial zones come into play. They provide the means to service the internal market, and are essential to further growth.

The goal you should aim for is to bring your city through the transition from an external-market economy to an internal-market economy. This transition is marked by a shift away from industry to commerce, at which point your city will really boom. The proper industry-to-commerce ratios are given in Chapter 2. Armed with this knowledge, you'll be better able to manage the proper mix of industrial zones and commercial zones.

USING THE PAUSE FUNCTION

Using Pause allows you to build and bulldoze while the simulator is stopped. This is helpful for some scenarios or cities, because you can freeze development while you take care of any problems, then speed up the simulator to collect your taxes the following January. You make better use of your time because you are not constantly distracted by other events. You should use the Pause function frequently.

RUNNING SIMCITY UNATTENDED

One of *SimCity*'s best aspects is its ability to function unsupervised. You can leave the simulator running overnight on your computer, and wake up in the morning to find out how your city has evolved or changed. If you do this, though, you should turn off your monitor or turn on a screen saver.

The Auto-Budget command must be toggled on for the simulation to run unattended without pausing. This is so that *SimCity* won't pause each January for a proposed budget. Also, be sure to disable all disasters, or else you may find by morning that your city has burned to the ground while you were asleep at the switch!

Another important consideration when you run *SimCity* unattended is that you need to have enough money in your treasury to "auto-replace" power plants every 50 years. If you don't have enough money to build a new plant, the old one will explode and won't be rebuilt automatically, whereas if you have enough money, the plant will be rebuilt automatically (or be "auto-replaced").

DEALING WITH TRANSPORTATION

No Sim can travel to a different zone without using some form of transportation.[2] Furthermore, Sims can travel a maximum of only three blocks through a zone to reach transportation, such as roads, rail depots, and subway stations. Rail lines and subways are accessible only through rail depots and subway stations. An intermodal transfer between a rail depot and a subway station is possible, but only if a road connects the two stations.

Each road has a limited capacity for traffic; when this level (about 70 to 80 cars per minute) is exceeded, traffic jams form that drastically lower the capacity of the road. As a result, more drivers will be frustrated and return to their zones of origin. This process will eventually cause those zones to decay.

The Trip Generator

SimCity simulates traffic flow by a method known as *trip generation*. Each zone attempts to generate a number of trips, according to its population, that terminate in a different zone type. A trip is considered successful if it progresses down a road, rail, or subway and reaches its destination zone. The SimCitizen from the zone of origin is given 100 steps to make a one-way trip to another zone type. Depending on the mode of travel, the trip can be short or long. As you can see from Table 10-1, a residential zone attempts to make a 100-step trip to both an industrial zone *and* a 100-step trip to a commercial zone. Similarly, the commercial zone tries to make a 100-step trip to a industrial zone *and* a 100-step trip to a residential zone. Likewise, the industrial zone tries to make 100-step trips to both a residential zone and a commercial one. Unsuccessful trips cause the zone of origin to cease developing and eventually to decay.

Roads, rails, and subways allow your Sims to travel from zone to zone; they allow travel over greater distances than those that are possible on foot. If no transportation links exist between the origin and destination zones, the trip will be considered a failure. As you can see from Table 10-2, cars take three steps per tile of road traveled, whereas buses take two steps. Theoretically, for cars traveling on roads, this means the maximum range is 33

---

[2]This is an exception to the usual rules: If a road, rail depot, or subway station is within three blocks of a zone boundary, the Sims can travel between the zones.

Table 10-1 Origins and Destinations for Trip Generation

Origin Zone	Destination Zone
Residential	Commercial or industrial
Commercial	Residential or industrial
Industrial	Residential or commercial

Table 10-2 Steps Taken for Each Travel Mode Taken

Travel Mode	Number of Steps Taken	Travel Mode	Number of Steps Taken
Car on road	3	Bus on road	2
Car on highway	1	Bus on highway	1
Subway	1	Subway station	4
Train	1	Train Depot (Station)	4

Note: At present, there are bugs in the *SimCity 2000* program that cause the trip generator to miscount the number of steps taken for each mode of transit. For example, you should be able to travel farther on highways than on roads, but this is not the case in the current version of *SimCity 2000*.

blocks; for buses, 50 blocks. In practice, however, the maximum range is about 24 blocks for both buses and cars, owing to other factors that subtract steps from the 100 that are allowed. Trains and subways take one step for each tile traveled, and train depots and subway stations consume four steps as Sims enter or leave.

Off-Screen Neighbor Connections

Roads to off-screen neighbors serve commerce. They function like airports to give commerce a boost. You need to build only one road off-screen, but if you want to build more than one, be sure to build only one per side. Each neighbor city's economy gets a little boost from the addition of the road.[3]

---

[3]Unfortunately, there are some bugs in the program that reduce the boost that off-map road connections give to commerce.

Highways and rails to off-screen neighbors serve industry. They function like seaports in boosting industry. You need to build only one highway or rail line off-screen. If you want to build more than one connection, be sure to build only one per side. Each neighbor city's economy gets a little boost from the addition of the highway or rail connection.[4]

The *SimCity* internal model favors the development of industry first, then that of commerce. This fact means that early in your city's growth process, you should build highway or rail connections but not roads, since roads help only commerce. Later on, when commerce begins to take off, you can build the road connections.

Trains, Planes, and Cars Freezing On-Screen

Sometimes trains, planes, and cars freeze on-screen. They appear to get stuck or, in the case of trains and cars, sometimes fail to connect with adjacent tracks or roads. Don't worry about this visual anomaly—the Sims are still able to commute from place to place.

DEALING WITH OTHER *SIMCITY* CONCERNS

This section rounds up tips for making the best use of a variety of *SimCity* program entities.

Police and Fire Stations

Check the efficiency of your police stations by using the Query tool to find out the arrests/crimes ratio. If you have many more crimes than arrests, you should build more police departments and check to make sure that your funding is at 100 percent. (The level of funding determines the effective radius of a police or fire department. Lack of power will also reduce the coverage area.) If necessary, you can improve the performance of the police departments by building a prison.

Avoid placing police and fire stations on waterfronts or on the edges of maps, because most of their coverage is then wasted on uninhabited areas. Use the Map window to see areas of police/fire coverage and to strategically plot the most efficient placement for each new station.

---

[4]Alas, there are bugs in this part of the model as well. Highway and rail connections to neighboring cities do not have as great an impact on industry as they should.

SimCity 2000 can handle up to 33 fire, police, or military units dispatched to the scene of a disaster, but if you send any more than these, they will not appear and will not help.

Crime

Crime is generated by power plants and dense industrialized areas, and to a lesser extent by light industry such as electronics, media, and finance. Crime also appears in dense commercial and residential zones, but is generally not as bad as that in industrial zones. Crime is related to population density: The higher the population per unit area, the higher the crime rate. High pollution also fosters high crime rates.

One cheap answer to the problem of crime is to build parks near industry and other high-crime areas. High crime is usually accompanied by low land values, so if you raise the land values through the addition of parks, you can reduce crime. Another way to reduce crime is to zone dense industry near water, forests, and higher-elevation land. Crime will be minimized, because higher land values drive crime rates down.

Residential Zones

These are the zones where your Sims live. They build houses, apartments, condominiums, and churches in residential zones. There are two densities: low and high. Low density restricts housing to 1×1–tile single-family dwellings, with high land values. High-density zones allow 1×1-, 2×2-, and 3×3-tile buildings with lower land values.[5]

Try to build residential zones near water or near slopes. The water and sloping land tiles will create higher land values and thereby increase your tax revenues. Land values rise with proximity to sloping land, but they do not rise with elevation alone. Thus, for example, a stair-stepped landscape will have high land value, whereas a large, flat mountaintop will have the same land value as the valley, except for the very edges of the mountain top or the portion of the valley closest to the base of the mountain.

In general, the total area of residential zones should be equal to the combined total area of industrial and commercial zones ($R = I + C$).

---

[5]You can raise the land values for high-density zones by building plenty of police stations to help suppress crime. Thus, if you build a city with plenty of police protection, the land values throughout will have essentially the same value whether the land is zoned high- or low-density. This rule also holds for commercial and industrial zones.

The lost arcology

CRYSTAL CITY

The Sydney Opera House
(replaces the Llama Dome
in the Australian version of
SimCity 2000)

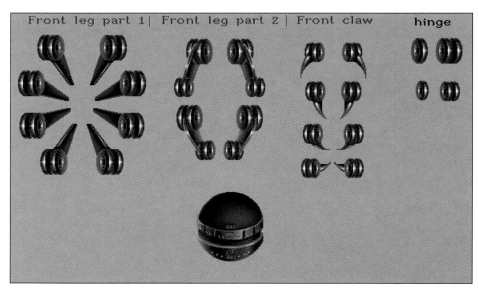

Pieces of the monster — front legs only

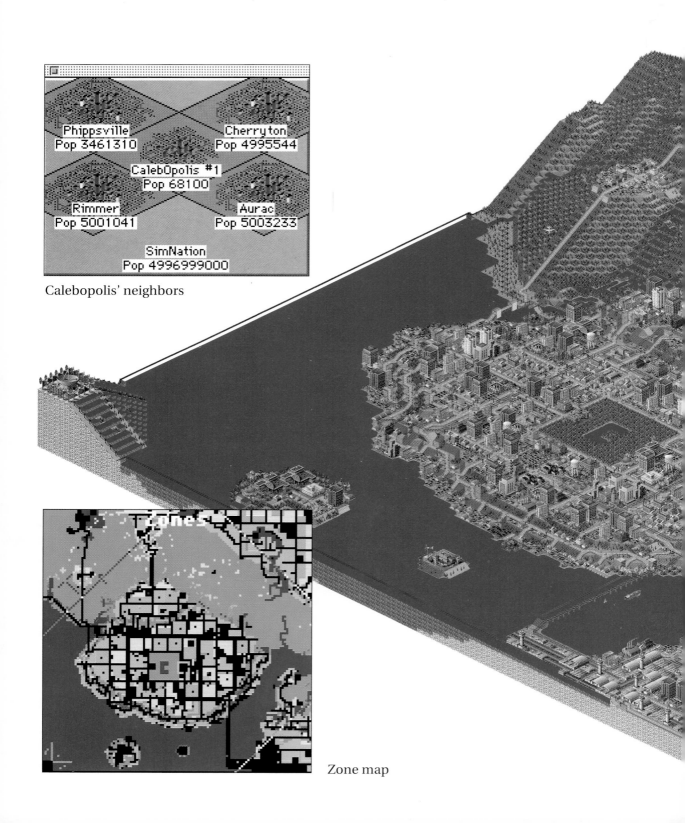

Phippsville
Pop 3461310

Cherryton
Pop 4995544

CalebOpolis #1
Pop 68100

Rimmer
Pop 5001041

Aurac
Pop 5003233

SimNation
Pop 4996999000

Calebopolis' neighbors

Zone map

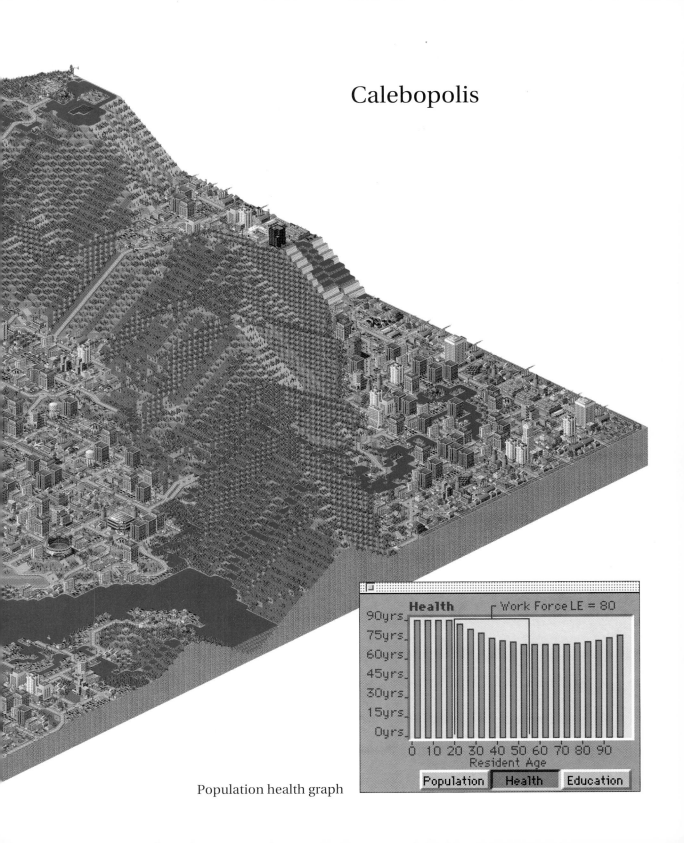

Calebopolis

Population health graph

Mattropolis

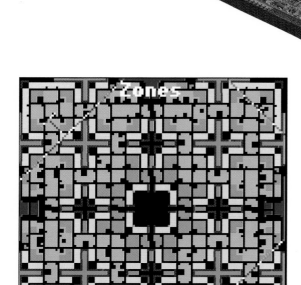

Mattropolis' neighbors

Jeromi	Fortune
Pop 104487	Pop 9234
Mattropolis II	
Pop 214060	
Mill Valley	Newton
Pop 2098	Pop 7061
SimNation	
Pop 350103000	

Zone map

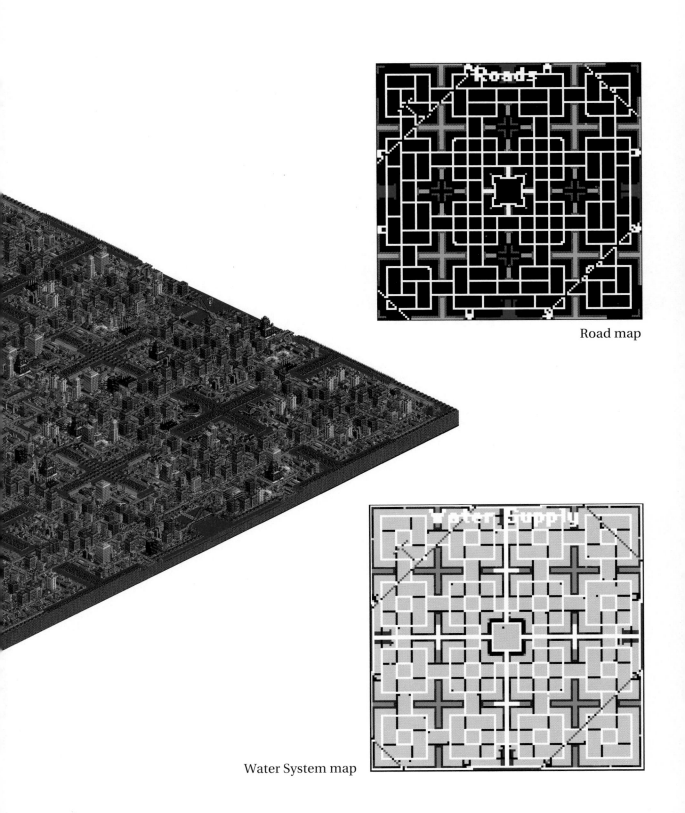

Road map

Water System map

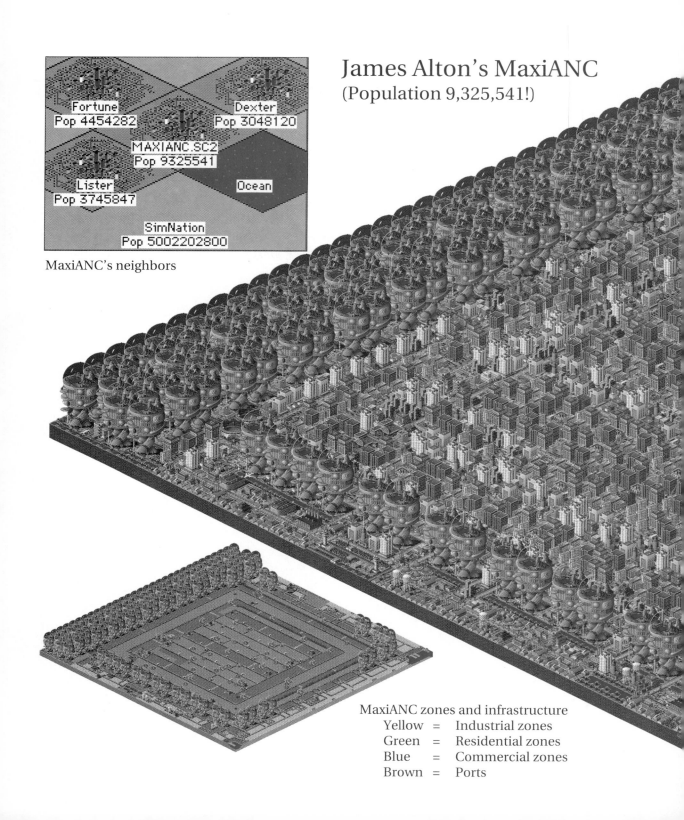

James Alton's MaxiANC
(Population 9,325,541!)

Fortune
Pop 4454282

Dexter
Pop 3048120

MAXIANC.SC2
Pop 9325541

Lister
Pop 3745847

Ocean

SimNation
Pop 5002202800

MaxiANC's neighbors

MaxiANC zones and infrastructure
Yellow	=	Industrial zones
Green	=	Residential zones
Blue	=	Commercial zones
Brown	=	Ports

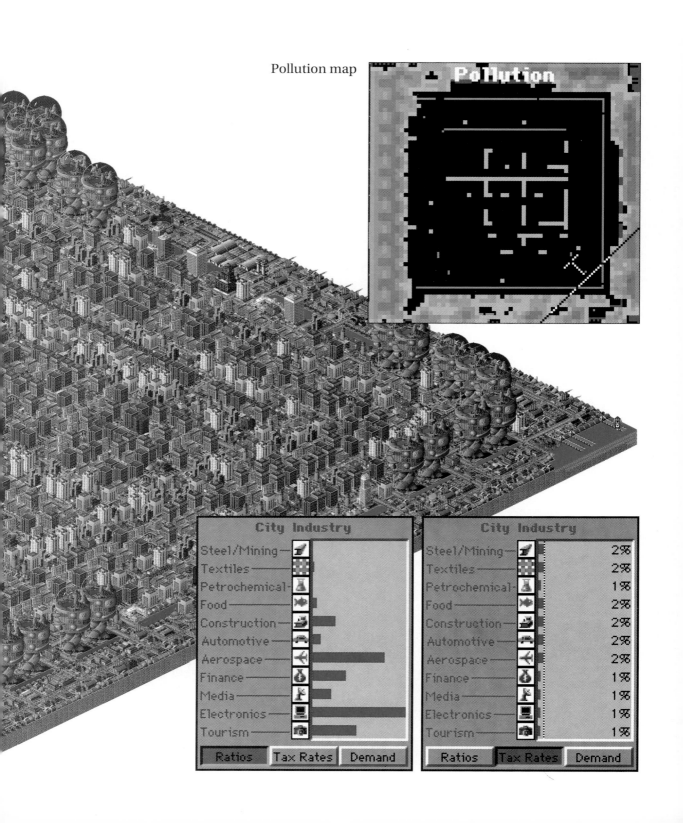

Pollution map

Pollution

City Industry				City Industry		
Steel/Mining				Steel/Mining		2%
Textiles				Textiles		2%
Petrochemical				Petrochemical		1%
Food				Food		2%
Construction				Construction		2%
Automotive				Automotive		2%
Aerospace				Aerospace		2%
Finance				Finance		1%
Media				Media		1%
Electronics				Electronics		1%
Tourism				Tourism		1%
Ratios	Tax Rates	Demand		Ratios	Tax Rates	Demand

James Moore's Rubigger
(Population 9,325,128)

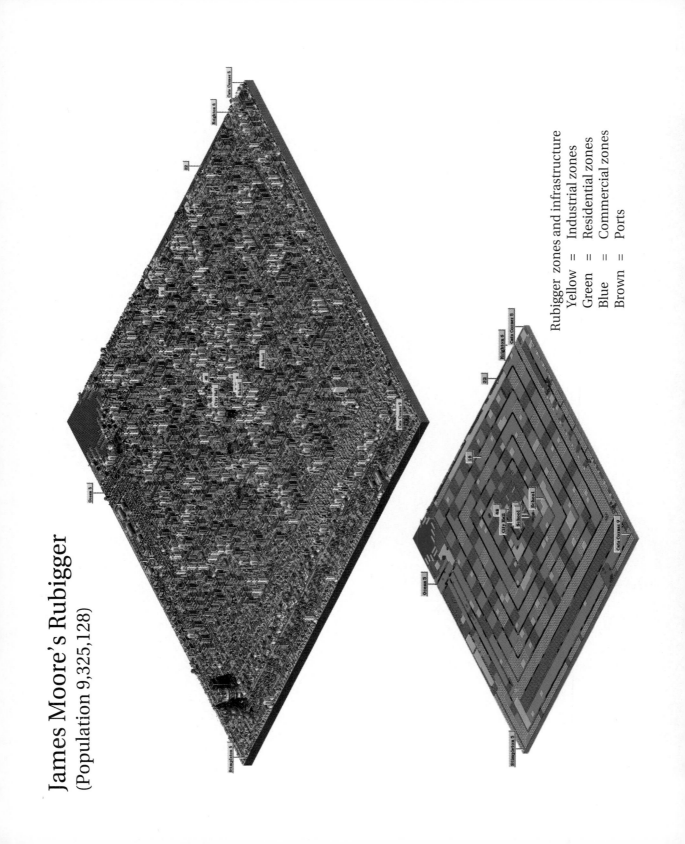

Rubigger zones and infrastructure
Yellow = Industrial zones
Green = Residential zones
Blue = Commercial zones
Brown = Ports

Commercial Zones

In commercial zones, the Sims will build retail stores, shops, and offices. Commercial areas are mainly dedicated to producing goods and services used within your city, so they're not much needed in its early development. In essence, commercial zones produce goods for the internal market, which develops only after the external market has been tapped. Therefore, when your population reaches a threshold level of 100,000 or so, the ratio of commercial to industrial zones should change in favor of commercial zones ($C >$ I for cities greater than 100,000).

Commercial zones develop faster if they're placed near the city center. Airports and road connections off-map help boost commerce. There are two zone densities: low and high. Low density restricts commercial development to 1×1-tile buildings with high land values. High density allows 1×1-, 2×2-, and 3×3-tile buildings with lower land values.

Industrial Zones

Industrial zones contain warehouses, factories, chemical plants, and other industries that provide jobs for your city. Industrial zones furnish products for the external market and are much needed in the early development of your city, more than commercial zones. Below a population level of 100,000, the ratio of industrial to commercial zones should favor industrial zones ($I >$ C for cities less than 100,000).

Industrial zones emit pollution, so they can have a negative impact on surrounding zones. There are two zone densities: low and high. Low density restricts zone development to 1×1-tile buildings with high land values and low pollution values. High-density zones allow 1×1-, 2×2-, and 3×3-tile buildings with lower land values but higher population densities, and these buildings emit much more pollution.[6]

If you build industrial zones on the edge of the map, much of the pollution will be dispersed over uninhabited areas. You can also mitigate pollution emissions by adding lots of parks to buffer your other nearby zones. There is a "dead zone" with a radius of 3 to 5 tiles around an industrial zone, where pollution drives people off. Keep residential and commercial zones out of this area, or they will develop poorly and the residents will complain to City Hall about pollution.

Seaports and off-map highway and rail connections help boost industrial growth.

---

[6]See Chapter 2 for a table of pollution levels for each zone density.

Pollution

Seaports, airports, industrial zones, fossil-fuel power plants, and traffic are the main sources of pollution in *SimCity 2000*. However, dense industrial zones are the primary sources of most pollution, so you'll want to avoid locating them too near residential zones. You should also avoid putting heavily congested roads next to residential zones, because the traffic will produce pollution and drive away the Sims who live in the vicinity.

Airports and Seaports

Only one airport and one seaport are needed per city. Both port types need room to grow, to expand with the needs of the city. Check periodically to see if all available land in the port zone is occupied, then expand the port as necessary. Heavy pollution emanates from both the seaport and the airport, so avoid placing them near residential zones.

Airports need space to build their runways. A suggested minimum size for a budding airport would be 2 tiles wide by 6 tiles long. Also, to avoid air crashes, don't build an airport near tall buildings. Be sure to supply adequate power to the airport; in some difficult cases, it may be necessary to cover the entire airport zone with power lines in order to get the airport to develop.

Airports are best located in corners of the map, on islands, peninsulas, and other areas with water nearby. Air crashes can be avoided through judicious planning of the nearby zone types and roads. Avoid placing heavily congested traffic areas around airports, because the traffic attracts helicopters, which may hang around and crash into airplanes. Also, don't allow high-density zones directly in front of or behind the runways, because if high-rises are built, airplanes may crash into them. You can, however, allow these high-density zones on the sides of the runway, where the risk of air crashes is smaller. To minimize the destruction caused by air-crash fires, each airportshould be within the radius of coverage of a fire station.

In the early stages of your city's growth, emphasize industrial development and build a seaport. Later, when moving to an internal economy based on commerce, you can build an airport to accelerate commercial growth. When your population reaches 10,000, it's time to build a seaport. When it reaches 15,000, you should build an airport.

If you are running *SimCity* unattended for a long time, you should either choose **No Disasters** from the **Disaster** menu or unplug the airport from the power grid to prevent crashes from burning your city down while you slumber or attend to other matters. To disconnect the airport, bulldoze the power line leading to the power plant.

Power Plants

Coal power plants and other dirty or dangerous power sources should be situated on the corners and edges of the city map. This placement will minimize the negative effects of pollution, since half the pollution will blow off the map (and into somebody else's backyard). Nuclear fission power plants should be placed in the corners of your city map. This placement cancels three-quarters of the risk of a meltdown, since even if the plant blows up, three-quarters of the radiation will be shunted off the map.

Hydroelectric power plants can be created even where there is no waterfall or slope. If there's no slope for the hydro plant, use the bulldozer to raise land elevations. If there's no water cascading down the slope, use the Landscape Water tool to add waterfalls. After artificially creating the right conditions, build the hydroelectric power plant. Using this technique, you can build as many hydro power plants as you wish, even terracing them up hills to create massive power-generation facilities.

More electricity is generated when the wind generators are built on higher-elevation land. Even so, the power output will fluctuate depending on weather conditions.

Churches, Hospitals, and Educational Institutions

Unlike the original *SimCity Classic*, *SimCity 2000* allows you to bulldoze nuisance churches that steal valuable residential land. The land underneath a church, unfortunately, is dezoned, so if you bulldoze it, you'll have to spend additional money to rezone it. Other than that, there is no "divine retribution" for destroying churches as there was in *SimCity Classic* (for example, tornadoes would strike your city). It's still probably best to leave churches alone, because they'll pop right back up somewhere else the minute you bulldoze them.

Check your grades for your hospital and educational facilities by using the Query tool. If your grades are low, it is time to increase the number of schools or hospitals or raise funding levels.

Stadiums, Marinas, and Zoos

Stadiums, marinas, and zoos help build up your residential zones and boost the tourism industry. The simulation only checks to see whether there is a stadium, marina, or zoo, not where it is located. This means you can place them anywhere on the map, since they don't have any local effects.

Arcologies

The number of arcologies (also called *arcos*) and the maximum population are determined by which version of *SimCity 2000* you have! I know it sounds crazy, but if you bought Version 1.00 of *SimCity* for either a DOS machine or a Macintosh, then you have a bug in the program that limits the maximum number of arcos to 140. If you build more than this number, the simulation won't recognize the additional population. With Version 1.00, the maximum arco population is 9,100,000 people, since 140 arcos × 65,000 people per Launch Arco = 9,100,000. Also, if you build more than 139 arcos in Version 1.00, the Analysis button in the City Hall Query window will be disabled. It will not become active again unless you reduce the number of Arcos *and* destroy and rebuild the city hall.

The Macintosh Version 1.1 and the Windows Version of *SimCity 2000* fix the arcology bug and remove the population ceiling of 9,100,000 for arcos. Note that the 140-arco limitation still exists for the DOS Version 1.1, but before downloading the 1.1 patch, see the comments later in this chapter advising against it.

"Newspaper Strikes"

In the Macintosh version of *SimCity*, sometimes the newspapers won't be able to load if you don't have enough memory. In some circles, these events are called "newspaper strikes." You can get the newspapers to work again by freeing up more memory. To do that, quit other open applications or remove extensions from your System Folder, then restart your Macintosh.

Taxation and Finance

One way you can save money for safety services in *SimCity 2000* is by disabling disasters, After all, if there are no disasters, you don't need to fund your fire department!

Thanks to *SimCity* veteran Kevin Endo, who discovered this simple relationship, you can approximate the tax revenues you collect by using the following formula:[7]

$$\textit{Property Tax Revenue } = \textit{Population x Tax Rate} \times 1.29$$

---

[7]This revenue formula well approximates the revenues from a city with no arcos. However, when you have a lot of arcos in your city, the formula will deviate drastically from the actual revenue results.

This formula doesn't take into account the land value, which is a part of the tax revenue formula, but as a rough approximation it serves as a pretty good guide.

Land Values

You can artificially boost land values by planting trees, building parks, terracing hillside slopes, or adding water.

Proximity to water raises land values. Therefore, build commercial and residential zones near water before building elsewhere. Don't squander precious shoreline by building industrial zones on waterfronts. This destroys land values by producing pollution. Also, don't bulldoze forests indiscriminately, since they always raise land values nearby.

SimCity also bases land value on proximity to "downtown," the geographical center of your population mass. The closer the land is to your "downtown," the higher the land values.

Land values are negatively influenced by pollution, crime, and the distances Sims must travel to get to work. Long trip ranges between origin and destination zones cause the origin zone to decrease in value. High land values help improve the quality of life; more important, they increase your tax revenues.

Disasters

Once a disaster starts, all time freezes. Although you can zone and build, your newly built zones and structures will not have any effect on the model until the emergency is over. This means that if there is a fire and you decide to build a fire station, too bad—the fire trucks will not be available for dispatch until after the emergency.

Nuclear accidents contaminate nearby land, making it unusable and highly toxic. You can spot the tiles that are spoiled because they are marked with a radioactive symbol that appears in each block. Unfortunately, there is no way to remove these contaminated tiles, even using the Magic Eraser tool. You'll just have to wait an eternity for the radiation levels to decay to tolerable levels.

Fires cannot be bulldozed directly. To extinguish fires manually, you can bulldoze fire breaks and let the fires burn out, or you can send firefighting units and police. You can also use the Landscape Water tool to surround the fire with water. This will contain the blaze, since fires cannot cross water.

You can also precipitate a helicopter crash; to do this, click on the helicopter using the Centering tool. The helicopter likes to hang around heavy traffic, and, as we have mentioned, allowing it to linger around the approaches to the airport will increase the likelihood of an air crash. The moral here is: Don't build lots of roads around airports!

The Trick to Clearing Rubble from Disasters

James Alton, a veteran *SimCity* mayor, has discovered a fast and easy way to clear rubble from disasters. If you want to clear large tracts, instead of bull-dozing one square at a time with the Demolish/Clear Bulldozer tool, use the Dezone Bulldozer tool. This will clear rubble over all zoned areas. If an area is not zoned, you can zone it low-density to save money and then use the Dezone Bulldozer to mop up the rubble. Clearing rubble is an important way to help keep fires from spreading.

Strange Noises

During play, you may hear strange noises, such as explosions or animal roars. The explosions are most likely those of airplanes crashing into tall buildings in the flight path of your airport. If you have **No Disasters** selected from the **Disasters** menu, the planes will still crash and blow up, but there will be no resulting damage or fire. The animal noises may be from the zoo, or they could be from Nessie, the friendly Loch Ness monster. Nessie, by the way, likes to hang out around marinas and lunch on sailboats.

The buzzing sound you hear when you build power lines is really game designer Will Wright's recording of his own vocal imitation of arcing electricity. Originally, Maxis intended to replace the sound with the real sound of a Tesla coil discharge, but so many people loved Will's sound that the makers left it in.

POPULATION RECORDS

The world record for city population (with the 140-arco limitation), previously held by James Alton's MaxiANC with a population of 9,326,461, was recently shattered by Jerry Moore's RUBIGGER, with a population of 9,395,128. However, to be fair, it should be said that Moore's RUBIGGER was built with the aid of the Magic Eraser (discussed later in this chapter), whereas Alton's city was built without any cheats. You can see a color picture of Alton's city and Moore's city in the color insert of this book.

In Version 1.00 of *SimCity 2000*, both for the Macintosh and for DOS machines, it's theoretically possible to build a city of 9,665,760 people, including a maximum of 140 Launch Arcos with a population of 65,000 each (for a total of 9,100,000 people) and a surface population of 565,760 people in high-density zones. Realistically, you won't be able to achieve this population, since some of your land will have to be devoted to transportation and utility purposes. Version 1.1 of *SimCity 2000* for the Mac and Version 1.0 for Windows (but not Version 1.1 for DOS) remove the arco population limit, so reaching a population of 66,560,000 people (1,024 arcos × 65,000 people = 66,560,000 people) is conceivable—although, again, you probably can't actually reach this level, because some land must be devoted to other purposes.

Thus, if you are running a DOS version of *SimCity 2000*, you can't build more than 140 arcos, and your population is effectively limited to just over 9 million people. Many people were disappointed by the fact that the 1.1 upgrade for DOS didn't allow them more than 140 arcos. Later in this chapter, you can read Maxis's explanation about why this arco limit was not changed.

In MaxiANC, James Alton's city, you can see a very compact city design that uses mostly high-density zones. Most of the heavily polluting industrial zones are located on the periphery of the map, and most of the residential and commercial zones have been placed in the center of the city. The city was designed using a unique "layered" effect that works to separate industry from commercial and residential zones in order to avoid the harmful effects of crime and pollution. To this end, a buffer zone of water and parks between industrial and residential or commercial zones helps create a protective barrier from these harmful effects.

The arcologies in MaxiANC, which produce very high crime rates, have many police departments distributed among them to help keep crime in check. James Alton also cleverly puts some industry near the center of the city so that interzonal development and cross-pollination will occur, but only a very few industrial zones are placed, to "seed" the area. These small, low-density 1×1 industrial "strips" are strategically located so that all the residential and commercial zones in the center of the city have access to them. If you look at the Map Mode View of MaxiANC in the color insert of this book, you'll see these industrial zones colored yellow-green. *SimCity 2000*'s trip generator checks only to see if there are industrial, residential, and commercial zones that are within trip range of one another; it doesn't check to see how many zones are being reused as bases for other zones. Thus, one industrial zone in the center of the city could theoretically provide all the trips necessary for thousands of nearby residential and commercial zones. This is, in fact, what happens in Alton's city. Furthermore, since each of the 1×1 industrial-zone strips is of the low-density type, pollution is minimized and the center of the city is not harmed by their presence.

The seaports and airports, which are also heavy polluters, are located near the edge of the map to minimize the effects of pollution on the residents. Half the pollution from the ports is blown off the edge of the map, and therefore doesn't bother the Sims.

Moore's city, RUBIGGER, has a cleverly designed road that spirals out from the center of the city like a whirlpool. This minimizes traffic congestion, since there are no traffic intersections. Thanks to judicious use of the Magic Eraser, this city is not overrun with arcos; there are only four of them, one of each type. But the population from the "erased" arcos remain, even though the people are not visible. The land that these arcos formerly occupied has been converted to other uses, thus enabling a greater population to exist. The citizens of RUBIGGER are healthy (H=83) and highly educated (EQ=121), but disproportionately old. There is a huge population of senior citizens, with an average age of 90, and only 31% of them are active members of the workforce.

COMMITTING EMBEZZLEMENT

The maximum amount of money you can have is just over $2 billion ($2,139,029,504, to be exact). There are some nefarious ways of surreptitiously increasing your funds. On the Macintosh, there's a good keyboard cheat that brings you in $500,000 at a time, and in the DOS version there's a negative-interest bond fund trick, which will net you $1,548,199 per year. The Windows version has a special programmer's "back door" that allows you to open a Debug menu, under which you'll find an option for adding $500,000 at a time. The next section details the way to embezzle money for each version.

Macintosh Embezzlement

In Version 1.00 of *SimCity 2000* for the Macintosh, you can embezzle up to $500,000 at a time by typing **porntipsguzzardo**. You can also type **cass** to obtain $250 at a time, but if you do this too many times, a disaster will strike your city.

In Version 1.1 for the Macintosh, the programmers have changed the embezzlement codes. In addition to typing in the new words, you must first click on the Map window and then on the Status window. To embezzle $500,000 using this cheat, follow these steps:

1. Open the Map window to its smallest size.
2. Click the mouse pointer anywhere inside the Map window.
3. Type **pirn**.
4. Click the mouse pointer inside the Status window.

5. Type **topsguzzardo**.

You should notice that you now have $500,000 more than you had before. If you want more money, simply type **ardo** once more.

Typing **cass** in Version 1.1 for the Macintosh will bring in $250 at a time, but if you use this more than three times, you risk having a disaster strike your city.

SimCity 2000 DOS 1.0 and DOS 1.1 Embezzlement

In this section, you'll learn all about the various methods of coaxing free money out of the DOS versions of the simulation.

The DOS Mega-Cheat: The Double-Fund Trick

While we were writing the preceding edition of this book, we were told that there was a secret *Mega-Cheat*, which would allow DOS users of *SimCity 2000* to embezzle lots of money. But the programmers wouldn't tell us what the cheat actually was. Since that time, someone discovered on the Internet that there was a bug in the Easter Egg "fund" trick that would allow you to collect negative interest on your bonds (but only with brand-new cities that had not been built up), to the tune of $1,548,199 per year! Instead of having positive interest applied to your bonds, which would normally be the case when you took out a 25% bond with the Fund trick, the Double-Fund trick would create negative interest on your bonds that would be credited to your account as income. We don't know whether this is the Mega-Cheat or whether it's just a bug, but we suspect that it's the latter.

Here is how the Double-Fund Trick works:

1. Type **fund** twice; each time, accept the 25% bond that is offered. In effect, you're taking out two 25% bonds.
2. Open the Budget window, then open the Bonds window.
3. In the Bonds window, issue a new bond.
4. Now pay off the first two bonds.

After doing this, you'll see some negative interest rates show up in the Bonds window. When you return to the simulation, wait until the next budget year begins. In January, you'll find that you're now collecting $1,548,199 per year (the first year it's prorated by the month).

Note that the Double-Fund Trick works only with brand-new cities, before you have built anything.

In the Windows version of *SimCity 2000*, Maxis has fixed the negative-interest-rate bug, so this cheat no longer works.

Using the SC2KCHT2.ZIP Shareware Cheat Utility

Thanks to the efforts of Ron Mendoza, there is a shareware cheat utility, called SC2KCHT2.ZIP, that allows you to add up to $2 billion in both the Windows and DOS versions of *SimCity 2000*. At present, only the earlier version of this utility, SC2CHT.ZIP (not SC2KCHT2.ZIP) is available in the CompuServe Gamers Forum in the Strategy Library, and it doesn't work with Windows *SimCity 2000* files. By the time you read this, however, the updated SC2CHT2.ZIP should be available online.

    Be careful when you use this utility, because it can corrupt some city files. Therefore, as a precaution, before using SC2CHT2 you should make a backup copy of your city file.

Hex-Editing Your PC City Files for More Money

You can also hex-edit your DOS and Windows city files for *SimCity 2000* to add more than $2 billion to your coffers. All you need is a binary file disk editor, such as the Norton Utilities DiskEdit or PC Tools. A text editor or word processor won't work, because they can handle only ASCII characters (the letters and other characters you see on your keyboard). Data files on both the PC and the Macintosh are represented in a hexadecimal notation system, where the characters **0** through **9** and **A** through **F** represent the integers 0 through 15. An individual byte is represented by two hexadecimal characters, such as **1F** or **04**, and this byte can hold any decimal number from 0 to 255. (Including the zero, this comes to 256 possible numbers.)

    In *SimCity 2000*, your money is stored in a special hexadecimal data structure that looks like this:

00	02	4E	20
This byte is where you store more than $2 billion in hexadecimal format. Each hexadecimal increment of 1 (such as **01** hex to **02** hex, or **7E** hex to **7F** hex) represents an increase of $16,842,752. This byte can range from **01** hex ($16,842,252) all the way up to **7F** hex ($2,139,029,504). Past **7F** hex you'll get negative numbers, owing to the way decimal numbers are stored in hex format.	This byte is the tag marker for the money data structure. The **02** pointer lets the *SimCity* program know that it is reading a new data structure. Don't mess with this byte, or else you'll screw up your city file!	This byte is where you store increments of $256 in hexadecimal format. Each hexadecimal increment of 1 (such as **01** to **02**, or **0E** to **0F**) represents an increase of $256.	This byte is where you store up to $256. Each hexadecimal increment of 1 (such as **01** to **02**, or **0E** to **0F**) represents an increase of $1.

The *only* bytes that are used for your money are the **00**, **4E**, and **20** bytes. The **02** byte *is not used to store money; instead, it acts as a tag marker to let the SimCity program know where the money data structure is located.* For example, in the byte string above, the **00** means that you have no money in the $16,842,752 place holder, the **02** is the file marker for the money data structure, and **4E 20** is the hexadecimal equivalent of $20,000.

Your city's money is located in the first 50 bytes or so of your city file. Its exact location changes from city to city, so you'll need to inspect your city file visually to see where the money is stored. To find your money location, just count from the beginning of your file to the fourth **00 02** hex pattern that you find. That's the location of your money data structure. Be sure to look for the pattern **00 02** and not just **02**, because sometimes you'll see an intervening **02** that's *not* a marker, but is just part of another data structure, such as the city's date. This may fool you into miscounting the correct location of the money data structure. (If the city you're hex-editing *already* has more than $16,842,752, you should just count to the fourth **02** marker, noting that there should be at least six intervening bytes between each **02** marker and the next.)

Next, you change the **00** (located before the fourth **02** hex marker in your city file) to a **7F**. This adds $2,139,029,504 to your city's coffers! The new byte string will look like this, assuming that you have $20,000 (hex **4E 20**) to begin with:

7F   02   4E   20
|
Change this byte from **00** to **7F**.

The hex-editing procedures outlined below are to be used only on saved cities with the file extension .SC2 that you have previously created on an IBM PC or compatible. *You can't use this technique on the scenario files.* (Scenarios have the file extension .SCN; they're all found in the SCENARIOS subdirectory of your SC2000 directory.)

Always make copies of your city files and do your hex-editing on these copies. *Never hex-edit your original city files, the scenario files, or the SC2000.EXE program*.

Also, never hex-edit compressed files on a DoubleSpaced disk under DOS 6.2. In fact, we recommend that you not hex-edit on compressed hard disks at all. This is because when you make direct changes to individual sectors of your disk, these sectors may not be the same locations where your file is actually stored on! It would be better to copy your file to a floppy disk and hex-edit it while it's on the floppy.

Follow these steps to hex-edit your *SimCity 2000* city file:

1. Make a copy of your city that you can edit, so that if you make a mistake, you won't lose your original city.

2. Using the Norton Utilities DiskEdit program, open the newly made copy of your city.

3. Your city's funds are stored in hexadecimal format in the first 50 bytes or so of the program. Counting from the beginning of the file, look for the fourth 00 02 hex pattern. (Of course, if you have more than $16,842,752 to begin with, you won't see the 00 before the 02; there will be some other hex number in its place.) When you find it, the bytes immediately to the left and right of the 02 value are where your city's money is stored. If you have $20,000 in your city funds, look for the sequence of bytes that looks like this (the last two bytes, 4E 20, are the hexadecimal representation of $20,000):

$$00 \qquad 02 \qquad 4E \qquad 20$$

4. If the amount of money you have is different from $20,000 to begin with, the last two bytes, **4E 20**, will be different. If you have a hexadecimal-to-decimal conversion calculator, you can easily figure out what the last two bytes should be. (There is such a calculator in the Norton Utilities DiskEdit program; just select the Hex Converter option under the Tools menu and then type the amount of money you have into the decimal-text box. The hexadecimal equivalent will immediately appear in the hex-text box above it.)

5. Once you've located the money data structure, change the **00** (located to the left of the **02** tag marker) to a **7F** by clicking on the hexadecimal number **00** and then typing over it.

6. Pull down the Edit menu in the DiskEdit program and select Write Changes.

7. A dialog box will pop up, asking you to confirm the changes. Click on the Write button to make the change permanent in your city file.

8. Exit the DiskEdit program and start up *SimCity 2000*. Your hex-edited city will now have over $2 billion!

Windows Embezzlement: The Debug Menu Cheat

The Windows programmers of *SimCity 2000* created the granddaddy of all Easter Eggs with the secret Debug Menu Cheat. The programmers added this secret "back-door" entrance so that they could conveniently test the program for bugs during its development. Each time you use the Add Money menu

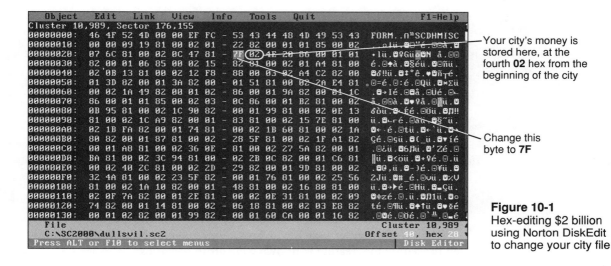

Your city's money is stored here, at the fourth **02** hex from the beginning of the city

Change this byte to **7F**

Figure 10-1
Hex-editing $2 billion using Norton DiskEdit to change your city file

option under the Debug menu, you can add $500,000 to your city coffers. To open the Debug menu and embezzle some money, follow these steps:

1. Click on the Toolbar so that it becomes active and highlighted.

2. Type in the characters **oivaizmir** and you'll see a Debug menu appear on the right side of the menu bar.

3. Open the Debug menu and select Add Money.

4. After the end of the month, you'll see that your city has $500,000 more cash than it had before!

You can also type in the word **cass** to add $250 at a time, but this trick doesn't always work, nor is it without risks. If you get too greedy and use the cass cheat one time too many, your city may be hit by a disaster.

The Debug Menu Cheat also lets you add all inventions, rewards, and gifts, and show version information. You can also experience new disasters, such as Nuclear Meltdown, Microwave, Volcano, Firestorm, Mass Riots, Major Flood, and Toxic Spills.

CREATING YOUR OWN SCENARIOS ON THE MACINTOSH

If you have a copy of ResEdit, you can create your own scenarios, complete with your own customized win conditions, disaster, and map. If you don't have a copy of ResEdit, you can download it from the Internet at ftp.apple.com by using this FTP (File Transfer Protocol) address:

ftp.info.apple.com

The ResEdit file itself is found in the Apple.Support.Area/Apple.
Software.Updates/Macintosh/Utilities.Software/directory. If you have access
to the World Wide Web, you can find *ResEdit* at http://www.info.apple.com
if you look in the Software Updates section of the Web page.

Macintosh files are organized differently from PC files, in that they have
special self-contained data structures called *resources*. All ResEdit allows you
to do is to view, copy, or edit these resources, whether they are sounds, pictures, text, icons, or anything else. Every one of these resources can be copied
to other Macintosh files, and this is how you'll create your own scenario files.
Essentially, you'll take a scenario's resources, copy them, and then paste
them into your city file. There you'll be able to edit them in *ResEdit* and
thereby customize your scenario. After finishing this task, you change the
type of the city file from CITY to SCEN and then save the file.

Thanks to Internet user Kevin Endo, we're able to publish this step-by-
step procedure for creating your own Macintosh scenarios:

1. While in *SimCity 2000*, create a city that you want to use for your
   scenario.
2. Make a copy of your city and save the file.
3. Start up *ResEdit*, then open one of your scenario files, such as Dullsville
   or Charleston.
4. While still in ResEdit, open the copy of your city.
5. Select the Scenario file window in *ResEdit*.
6. Select each resource from the scenario file for your city and then, using
   the Edit menu, copy and paste each resource from your scenario file to
   your city file, as shown in Figure 10-2. There should be four resources
   that you copy: PICT, SCEN, TEXT, and TMPL.

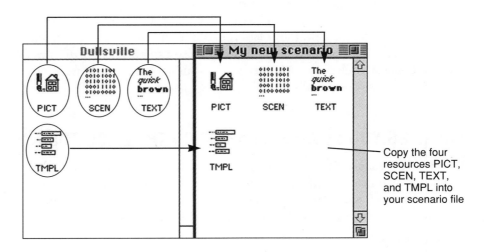

Figure 10-2
Using ResEdit to
create your own
scenario.

7. Now that you have these four new resources in your city file, you can edit each of them. A description of each resource follows:

- **PICT:** This is the picture that goes with the Scenario selection window. If you want, you can delete the old picture and create a new one using a graphics program. The PICT should have an ID of 128.

- **TMPL:** Leave this resource alone.

- **TEXT:** There are two TEXT IDs in this resource, which are listed as follows:

    - 128 describes the scenario on the Scenario selection screen.
    - 129 is used for the extended description that pops up just before the city begins.

- **SCEN:** This resource has all of the goal details, including Disaster Type, Disaster Xloc, Disaster Yloc, Time Limit, City Size, Ind Goal, Res Goal, Com Goal, Cash Fund–Bonds, Land Value, Pollution, Crime, Traffic Limit, and four other goals:

    Disaster Type: There are 16 different disasters. The value 0 means no disaster, 1 means fire, and so forth. All you need to do is type in the number for the disaster you want, as listed in Table 10-3.

    Disaster Xloc, Yloc: These are the origin coordinates for the disaster. The location is probably based on the 128-vertical-by-128-horizontal-tile size of the map. A location of 64, 64, therefore, would be somewhere in the center of the map.

    Time Limit (months): You must reach the scenario's goal before this number of months have elapsed. A period of 10 years would be 120 months; 20 years would be 240 months.

    City Size: Your total combined residential, industrial, and commercial zone populations must reach this level.

    Ind Goal: You must build your industrial zone population to this size.

    Res Goal: You must build your residential zone population to this size.

    Com Goal: You must build your commercial zone population to this size.

    Cash Funds–Bonds: This is how much money you must have on hand, minus the amount you owe on your bonds, when the time limit expires.

    Land Value Goal: Your average land value must increase to this level.

Table 10-3 Disaster Types for the Macintosh Scenarios

Disaster Number	Disaster	Disaster Number	Disaster
1	Fire	9	Meltdown
2	Flood	10	Microwave
3	Riots	11	Volcano
4	Pollution	12	Firestorm
5	Air crash	13	Mass riots
6	Earthquake	14	Major floods
7	Tornado	15	Chemical spills
8	Monster	16	Hurricane

Pollution: Pollution must not exceed this level.

Crime: Crime must not exceed this level.

Traffic Limit: Traffic must not exceed this level.

Build Item 1: This object or zone must be built.

Build Item 2: This object or zone must be built.

Item 1 Tiles: This number of tiles, or acres, of Item 1 need to be built.

Item 2 Tiles: This number of tiles, or acres, of Item 2 need to be built.

8. Once you've edited the SCEN resource and have finished your other changes, you'll need to change the file type from CITY to SCEN. (This type name tells *SimCity* that the file is actually a scenario file, as opposed to a city file.) To do this, while still in *ResEdit,* select the Get Info command from the File menu and then, when the Get Info dialog box opens, delete the CITY file type and replace it with SCEN, as shown in Figure 10-3.

9. Exit ResEdit, being sure to save your changes to the city file.

10. Make sure that the city is in the same folder as the *SimCity 2000* program and go play! You may have to play with the PICT to make it fit right. Also, expect to spend some time experimenting with the goals to make your scenarios challenging yet reachable.

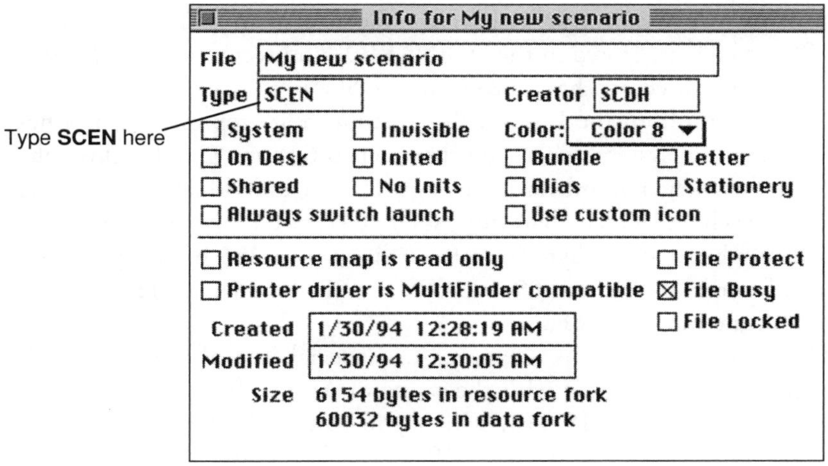

```
▓▓▓▓▓▓▓▓▓▓ Info for My new scenario ▓▓▓▓▓▓▓▓▓▓
```

File | My new scenario |

Type | SCEN | Creator | SCDH |

☐ System   ☐ Invisible   Color: | Color 8 ▼ |
☐ On Desk   ☐ Inited   ☐ Bundle   ☐ Letter
☐ Shared   ☐ No Inits   ☐ Alias   ☐ Stationery
☐ Always switch launch   ☐ Use custom icon

───
☐ Resource map is read only   ☐ File Protect
☐ Printer driver is MultiFinder compatible ☒ File Busy
                                          ☐ File Locked
Created | 1/30/94 12:28:19 AM |
Modified | 1/30/94 12:30:05 AM |
    Size   6154 bytes in resource fork
           60032 bytes in data fork

Type **SCEN** here

Figure 10-3
Select the **Get Info** command from the **File** menu, and then, when the Get Info dialog box opens, delete the CITY file type and replace it with SCEN. Before exiting ResEdit, save the changes to your new scenario file.

CREATING YOUR OWN SCENARIOS ON THE PC

You can create your own scenarios for the DOS and Windows versions of *SimCity 2000*, but, unfortunately, it's too difficult to create your own map. Instead, you'll have to base your newly created scenario on one of the existing scenario maps. You'll need a disk editor such as the Norton Utilities DiskEdit, PC Tools, or some other binary file editor. A text editor or word processor won't work, because it can only handle ASCII characters (the letters and other characters you see on your keyboard). In addition, it's helpful to have a hexadecimal-to-decimal conversion calculator, because the binary codes in your *SimCity* files are stored in hexadecimal form and need to be converted into a base-10 integer form that you can understand.

Always make copies of your scenario files and do your hex-editing on these copies. *Never hex-edit your original scenario files or the SimCity .EXE program.*

   Also, never hex-edit compressed files on a DoubleSpaced disk under MS-DOS 6.2. In fact, we recommend that you not hex-edit on compressed hard disks at all, because, when you make direct changes to individual sectors of your disk, these sectors may not be the same locations where your file is actually stored in! It would be better to copy your scenario file to a floppy disk and hex-edit it there.

Note that your *SimCity* files have the file extension .SC2, but your scenario files, which are stored in the SCENARIO subdirectory of your SC2000 or SC2K4WIN directory, have the extension .SCN.

Data files on both the PC and the Macintosh are represented in a hexadecimal notation system, where the characters 0 through 9 and A through F represent the integer numbers 0 through 15. An individual byte is represented by *two* hexadecimal characters, such as 1F or 04. Using this notation, you can number a single byte from 0 all the way to 255 by using the hexadecimal format: **00, 01** . . . , **09, 0A, 0B** . . . , **0F, 10, 11** . . . , **1F**, and so on from **20** all the way up to **FF**.

The scenario conditions are stored in a special part of the scenario file that is preceded and tagged with the string of ASCII characters SCEN (or, in hexadecimal, **53 43 45 4E**), which you can find using your editor's search function, as shown in Figure 10-4. Ten bytes after the N in SCEN, the data structure for the scenario actually begins. Table 10-4 shows how the data structure is organized; Table 10-5 shows the numbering scheme for each disaster type. For a description of each record in the data structure, see the listing of data types in the preceding section about scenario creation on the Macintosh.

As a practical example of this kind of manipulation, to create a volcano disaster in your scenario, all you do is replace the disaster record's bytes with **0B**—which, as shown in Table 10-5, represents Disaster 11, the volcano disaster. The X Location and Y Location records tell the simulator where the disaster originates, so you need to enter some value between 0 (hex **00**) and

Type **SCEN** here

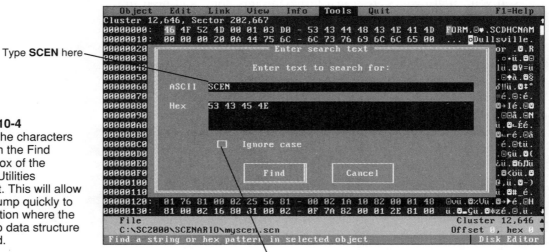

Figure 10-4
Typing the characters SCEN in the Find dialog box of the Norton Utilities DiskEdit. This will allow you to jump quickly to the location where the scenario data structure is stored.

Toggle this checkbox off

Table 10-4 The Scenario Data Structure

Data Structure Record	Number of Bytes in Record	Relative Location within Data Structure
Disaster	1	1st byte
Disaster X Location	1	2nd byte
Disaster Y Location	1	3rd byte
Time Limit (in months)	2	4th and 5th bytes
City Size Goal	4	6th, 7th, 8th, and 9th bytes
Residential Goal	4	10th, 11th, 12th, and 13th bytes
Commercial Goal	4	14th, 15th, 16th, and 17th bytes
Industrial Goal	4	18th, 19th, 20th, and 21st bytes
Cash Goal-Bonds	4	22nd, 23rd, 24th, and 25th bytes
Land Value	4	26th, 27th, 28th, and 29th bytes
Pollution Limit	4	30th, 31st, 32nd, and 33rd bytes
Crime Limit	4	34th, 35th, 36th, and 37th bytes
Traffic Limit	4	38th, 39th, 40th, and 41st bytes
Build item 1	1	42nd byte
Build item 2	1	43rd byte
Item 1 tiles	2	44th and 45th bytes
Item 2 tiles	2	46th and 47th bytes

128 (hex 80) for each of these bytes (since the coordinate system for the map is based on a 128×128 coordinate grid).[8] The rest of the data records in the Scenario data structure are self-explanatory. All you have to do is plug in the goal condition numbers, in hexadecimal form, that you want for your scenario. For example, if you want to change the win condition for Dullsville so that you need to have only 10,000 people (instead of 20,000 people), change the bytes in the City Size Goal record from 20,000 (hex **4E 20**) to 5,000 (hex **13 88**). Figure 10-5 shows what the data structure looks like for Dullsville.

---

[8]For the middle of the map, you might try an X location of 64 (hex **40**) and a Y location of 64 (hex **40**).

Table 10-5 Disaster Types for the PC Version of *SimCity 2000*

Disaster	Disaster Number (Integer Form)	Disaster Number (Hexadecimal Form)
None	0	00
Fire	1	01
Flood	2	02
Riots	3	03
Pollution	4	04
Air crash	5	05
Earthquake	6	06
Tornado	7	07
Monster	8	08
Meltdown	9	09
Microwave	10	0A
Volcano	11	0B
Firestorm	12	0C
Mass riots	13	0D
Major floods	14	0E
Chemical spills	15	0F
Hurricane	16	10

Here's a step-by-step procedure for creating your own scenario using the Norton Utilities DiskEdit and the Dullsville scenario:

1. While in your SCENARIOS subdirectory, copy your DULLSVIL.SCN scenario file to a new file with a different name. Make sure that the new file has the extension .SCN. For this example, we'll use MYSCEN.SCN.

2. Start the DiskEdit program.

3. Open MYSCEN.SCN inside DiskEdit.

4. Once the file is open, pull down the Tools menu and select the Find command.

5. In the Find dialog box that opens next, click the Ignore Case check box off and then click the mouse in the ASCII text box. Next, hold down

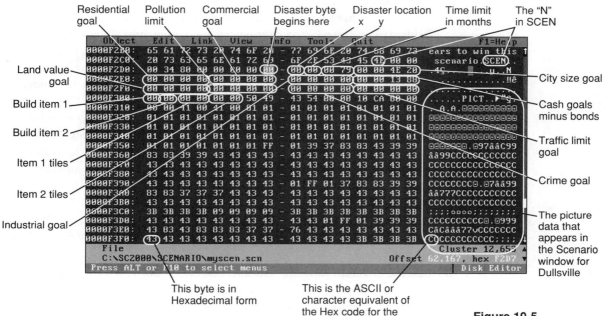

Labels around figure:

Residential goal · Pollution limit · Commercial goal · Disaster byte begins here · Disaster location x y · Time limit in months · The "N" in SCEN

Land value goal · Build item 1 · Build item 2 · Item 1 tiles · Item 2 tiles · Industrial goal

City size goal · Cash goals minus bonds · Traffic limit goal · Crime goal · The picture data that appears in the Scenario window for Dullsville

This byte is in Hexadecimal form

This is the ASCII or character equivalent of the Hex code for the byte located at the left

Figure 10-5
The Scenario data structure for Dullsville as viewed from within Norton Utilities DiskEdit. The relevant part is 10 bytes after the character *N* in SCEN, where you would type in the Disaster type in hexadecimal form. The other records follow byte after byte, according to how long each record is.

Shift and type the characters **SCEN**, as shown in Figure 10-4. Finally, click on the Find button to scroll your file view quickly to the location where the data structure is stored.

6. You'll see the data structure, as shown in Figure 10-5, for the Dullsville scenario. Change the disaster or scenario goal by moving the cursor to the data record and typing in the hexadecimal number equivalent to your decimal goal. If you don't know the correct hex number to put in, use the Hex Converter option under the Tools menu of DiskEdit to convert the decimal number to hex. You must count the position of each record by the number of bytes from the starting Disaster byte, which itself is always the 10th byte after the N in SCEN. Relative to the Disaster byte, always count your position starting with "1st byte" for the Disaster byte, "2nd byte" for X location, and so on, reading from left to right in the disk file. Thus, to create a volcano disaster, simply type in **0B** at the 10th byte after the N in the SCEN that precedes it. If you want to create a time limit of 36 months to win your scenario, look up the position of the Time Limit data structure in Table 10-4. You'll see that it occupies the 4th and 5th bytes from the Disaster byte (counting the Disaster byte as the "1st byte"), so all you need to do is count four bytes beginning with

the Disaster byte and type in **00 24** at the 4th- and 5th-byte locations. If you want to change the total city population goal (that is, combined residential, industrial, and commercial zone populations), look up the position of the City Size Goal record in Table 10-4. You'll see that it's located at the 6th, 7th, 8th, and 9th bytes from the 1st Disaster byte; therefore, to enter a population goal of 100,000 people, you would enter the hex values **00 01 86 A0** into these successive byte locations. By extending this procedure to the other scenario goals, you can customize your own scenario. You can also change the MYSCEN.SCN text description by scrolling the screen back up a page or two and then typing over the short and extended descriptions for Dullsville. Make sure you don't type over anything other than the text that is there, and don't create a longer description.

7. Pull down the Edit menu and select the Write Changes command. When the dialog box asks you to confirm the changes, click on the Write button.

8. Exit the DiskEdit program and start *SimCity 2000*. You'll see your new scenario listed in the Scenarios selection window. Unless you've changed the text description for the scenario, it will look exactly the same as your real Dullsville scenario listing. The only way to determine which scenario is your newly created one is to open it and play it. If you've created a disaster, the disaster should occur right away.

When you start the scenario, your new scenario goals and disasters will take effect. You can extend this method of designing your own scenario to include the maps of any of the other scenarios that come with *SimCity 2000*. Just make a copy of the chosen scenario and edit it as you would the Dullsville scenario.

LISTENING TO YOUR OWN MIDI MUSIC AND SOUNDS IN *SIMCITY 2000 FOR WINDOWS*

All the MIDI music and sounds used in *SimCity 2000 for Windows* are stored in the SC2K4WIN\SOUNDS subdirectory of your hard disk. The MIDI files have the three-character file extension .MID; the Wave sounds have the file extension .WAV. If you would like to change the music and sounds that are used in the program to your own MIDI and sound files, follow these steps:

1. Open the Windows File Manager and create a new subdirectory within your SC2K4WIN\SOUNDS subdirectory, called OLD.

2. Copy all the .MID and .WAV files to the newly created SC2K4WIN\SOUNDS\OLD directory. This will enable you to restore the *SimCity* music and sound files if you later decide to go back to the original files.

3. Copy all of your new .MID and .WAV files that you want to use in place of the *SimCity* sounds to the SC2K4WIN\SOUNDS directory.

4. Rename each of your new .MID files to match the existing *SimCity* MIDI files 10001.MID, 10002.MID, 10003.MID, and so on. For example, if you have a MOZART.MID you want to use, you would rename it 10001.MID.

5. Rename each of your new .WAV files to match the existing *SimCity* .WAV files: 501.WAV, 502.WAV, 503.WAV, and so on. For example, if you want to substitute the chimes sound file (stored in your Windows directory) for the error beep, you would rename CHIMES.WAV to 501.WAV.

We prefer to listen to classical music, so we've substituted classical music MIDI files for those that came with *SimCity*. So now, when we open up *SimCity*, we're greeted with Bach, Beethoven, and Brahms!

Where to Download Free Classical Music MIDI Files For Use in *SimCity 2000* for Windows

If you'd like to download some free MIDI music, you can find it at the Archives of Classical Music Sequences World Wide Web site at the following address:

http://www.hk.net/~prs/midi.html

For a list of other Web sites with MIDI music, consult Stanford University's Yahoo Web Site at

http://akebono.stanford.edu/yahoo/Computers/Music/MIDI

HOW TO EXPORT *SIMCITY 2000* FILES FROM THE MACINTOSH TO THE PC

It's easy to export Macintosh *SimCity 2000* city files to the PC. In order to do this, though, you need a transfer utility on your Macintosh that allows you to read MS-DOS disks, and you need a 3½" floppy drive on your PC. To transfer the city file from the Macintosh to the PC, follow these steps:

1. Copy the file to a DOS disk using the Apple File Exchange Utility or some other DOS file exchange program that allows you to read MS-DOS 3½" disks on your Macintosh.

2. Rename the file. The new name can include up to eight characters followed by a period and the characters SC2. (For example, to change the name of a city you have named My City on the Mac, you can give it a name such as MYCITY.SC2, with no spaces between characters.)

3. Once you have MYCITY.SC2 on the diskette and properly named, simply walk it over to your PC, insert the diskette, and copy the file to your SC2000 directory.

4. When you next play *SimCity*, select the Load City command and then, in the File Selection box, choose the MYCITY.SC2 file.

HOW TO EXPORT *SIMCITY 2000* FILES FROM THE PC TO THE MACINTOSH

Exporting city files from the PC to the Macintosh is a little trickier than the other way around. In order to do this, you must have the ResEdit resource utility (which you can get from Apple); you must have a DOS disk reader on your Macintosh, such as the Apple File Exchange Utility, DOS Mounter, or some other transfer utility; and you must have a 3½" disk drive on your PC.

Follow these steps to copy the file from the PC to the Macintosh:

1. Save your city in *SimCity 2000* for the PC. We'll call it MyCity for this example.

2. Copy the city file to a 3½" diskette.

3. Eject the diskette.

4. Start up the Apple File Exchange or whatever MS-DOS transfer utility you have installed on the Macintosh.

5. Insert the diskette containing your city file.

6. Copy or transfer the file to your *SimCity* folder.

7. Start the ResEdit program on your Macintosh.

8. Pull down the File menu in ResEdit and select the Open command.

9. Open your newly transferred city file by double-clicking on its name (MyCity.SC2) in the Open File dialog box.

10. Next you'll get a message that asks, "The file 'MyCity.SC2' has no resource fork. Opening it will add one. Do you wish to open it?" Click on the OK button. (Macintosh files, unlike PC files, are divided into data forks and resource forks, so you need to add a resource fork to the city file in order to make it work on the Macintosh.)

```
┌─────────────────────────────────────────────────┐
│ ▣▓▓▓▓▓▓▓▓▓▓  Info for MYPANTS.SC2 ▓▓▓▓▓▓▓▓▓▓▓     │
├─────────────────────────────────────────────────┤
│ File │ MYPANTS.SC2                          │     │
│                                                   │
│ Type │ CITY        │    Creator │ SCDH      │     │
│  ☐ System       ☐ Invisible   Color: │ Color 8 ▼ │
│  ☐ On Desk      ☒ Inited      ☐ Bundle   ☐ Letter│
│  ☐ Shared       ☐ No Inits    ☐ Alias    ☐ Stationery│
│  ☐ Always switch launch       ☐ Use custom icon  │
│ ─────────────────────────────────────────────── │
│  ☐ Resource map is read only        ☐ File Protect│
│  ☐ Printer driver is MultiFinder compatible ☒ File Busy│
│  Created │ 11/4/93 5:36:34 PM │      ☐ File Locked│
│  Modified │ 1/30/94 12:43:40 AM │               │
│     Size   286 bytes in resource fork            │
│            111899 bytes in data fork             │
└─────────────────────────────────────────────────┘
```

Figure 10-6
Using ResEdit to add a Creator and File Type Resource to your PC file so that the Macintosh version can read it.

11. Pull down the File menu and select Get Info for MyCity.SC2.

12. In the Get Info dialog box that next appears, type in **CITY** for the Type and **SCDH** for the Creator, as shown in Figure 10-6.

13. Pull down the File menu once again and select Close.

14. The next dialog box to appear will ask "Save MyCity.SC2 before closing?" Click on the Yes button.

15. Exit ResEdit.

16. Start *SimCity 2000* for the Macintosh and select the Load City option.

17. Double-click on the MyCity.SC2 file; it will open for game play.

HOW TO IMPORT *SIMCITY CLASSIC* FILES

To import a *SimCity Classic* file, first make a backup of the city file (in case something goes wrong) then rename the file with the extension .SC2. Next,open the file from within *SimCity 2000*. You'll be asked whether you're sure you want to convert the file to *SimCity 2000* format. Just click on Yes to convert the file and make it playable in *SimCity 2000*. Thereafter, the file will be stored as a *SimCity 2000* file and you won't be able to restore it to the original *SimCity* Classic format.

   In *SimCity Classic*, it was possible to overlap zones and buildings by using the Bulldozer to carve out sections and then rezoning or rebuilding the gouged-out hole. When you import a city that has this overlapping of zones into *SimCity 2000*, the resulting structures may look like brown rectangles. The brown rectangles will not harm your city, but they resemble urban blight, so you may want to get rid of them. To erase these brown spots, you'll need to bulldoze the area and then rezone over it. Another point to remember when importing *SimCity Classic* files is that rail lines will no longer work without rail depots. Cities that are based entirely on rail lines without such depots will fail.

MISCELLANEOUS TIPS AND TRICKS

This section lists some tips and tricks that you may find useful in your quest to master *SimCity 2000*.

Bulldozing Underground Pipes and Subways

There's really no secret to bulldozing underground structures. Simply select the Underground view of your city (click on the Underground button), then click on the Demolish/Clear Bulldozer. While you're in the Underground view on the PC, you can also demolish underground pipes and subways by holding down   and clicking the left mouse button on the objects in question.

Doubling the Capacity of a Water Pump

By surrounding more sides of a water pump with water, you can increase the pumping capacity of the pump. If you put the pump out on an island, surrounding it with water on all four sides, you can dramatically increase its pumping capacity—by as much as a factor of four. Water pumps will always pump more water when nearer to fresh water.

Phantom Water Pump Trick

Jerry Moore, creator of the RUBIGGER.SC2 city described earlier, informs us of a new cheat, which he coins the "Phantom Water Pump Trick." This trick fools all versions of *SimCity 2000* into thinking that your city always has a water surplus (even though the pipes may not actually pulsate with flowing water). The trick will only work if you start out with no water pumps. If you have pre-existing water pumps or desalinization plants, you'll need to bulldoze them before the trick will work. Before you add any new water pumps to your city, do the following:

1. Pick an area on the outskirts of your city and dezone a 3×3 grid.
2. Place a single water pump in the center of this grid.

3. Connect the water pump to power.

4. *Do not* connect any pipes to this pump. Now go back to building your city. Pretty soon you'll see the water shortage messages go away, and if you open your graph window and select the water icon button, you'll see that the water-surplus graph line has shot up to maximum capacity!

The Magic Eraser: Using the Landscape Tree Tool

It's possible to overlap some kinds of buildings and erase corners just as in *SimCity Classic!* Here's how to do this:

1. Select the Landscape Tree tool.

2. Click the tool on the map and hold down the mouse button. You'll see a tree or two plop down—but don't worry, that's OK.

3. While holding down [Shift] and the mouse button, move the cursor over any zone, building, or object, and you'll "erase" it as if you had a magic eraser!

Using this technique, you can get rid of polluting buildings but still keep them functioning. For example, you can build a coal power plant and then erase it down to one tile. Pollution will be reduced, yet the power plant will still generate electricity. Unfortunately, the more of the power plant you erase, the less power it will be able to produce, since the power output seems to be related to the area covered by the plant. The Magic Eraser works best for erasing arcologies, since the population of the arcology remains even after it has been erased completely.

The Magic Eraser works in all versions of *SimCity 2000*.

FINDING EASTER EGGS

This section details all the Easter Eggs that can be found in the DOS and Macintosh versions of *SimCity 2000* Version 1.00 and Version 1.1, as well as the Windows 1.0 version. Note that any future versions of *SimCity 2000* may alter or replace these Easter Eggs.

Macintosh-Specific Easter Eggs

The words shown below, when typed in the Macintosh Version 1.00 of *SimCity 2000*, do special things. Table 10-6 describes what they do. The footnote below the table tells you how the Embezzlement Cheat has been changed for Version 1.1.

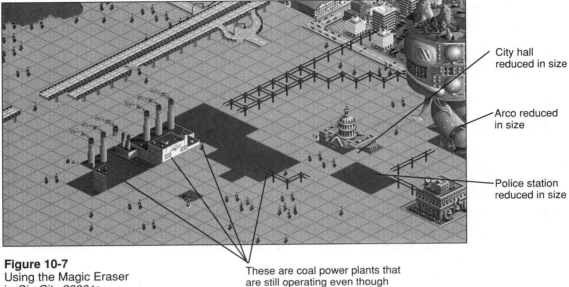

City hall
reduced in size

Arco reduced
in size

Police station
reduced in size

Figure 10-7
Using the Magic Eraser
in *SimCity 2000* to
overlap buildings.
Using this tool, you can
eliminate the pollution
from a power plant and
yet still maintain some
of its power-generation
capacity.

These are coal power plants that
are still operating even though
they have been reduced in size.

DOS/Windows-Specific Easter Eggs

Table 10-7 lists words that, when typed in the DOS Version 1.00 and 1.1 of
SimCity 2000, do special things. Note that the "Porn" Easter Egg has been
removed from Version 1.1.

Table 10-8 lists words that, when typed in the Windows version of *Sim-*

Table 10-6 Easter Eggs for the Macintosh (Version 1.00 and 1.1 Only)	
Easter Egg Word You Type	**Description**
Joke	Self-explanatory
Vers	Yields the version number of your software
Fund	Gives you a $10,000 bond at 25 percent interest
porntipsguzzardo[a]	Gives you $500,000 and all the rewards become available
Cass	Gives you $250, but after three to five times, your city is stricken with a disaster

[a]This Easter Egg for Version 1.1 has changed. To get it to work, open the **Map** window, click
inside it, type **pirn**, and then click inside the Status window. Next, type in **topsguzzardo**.

Table 10-7 Easter Eggs for the PC (Version 1.00)

Easter Egg Word You Type	Description
heck	See for yourself
vers	Gives the version number of your software
fund[a]	Gives you a $10,000 bond at 25 percent interest
porn[b]	If you have a sound card, you hear one of the programmers moaning, "I can't get enough"
memy	Memory check
test	Doesn't do anything
damn	See for yourself
darn	See for yourself
cass	Gives you $250, but after you use it three to five times, your city is stricken by a disaster

[a]If you type **fund** twice and accept two 25% bonds, then issue a new bond and pay off the original two bonds, you can get $1.5 million a year!

[b]This no longer works in Version 1.1.

Table 10-8 Easter Eggs for Windows Version 1.0

Easter Egg Word You Type	Description
cass	Gives you $250
noah	Causes major floods
mrsoleary	Causes major fires
gilmartin	Builds military base
buddamus	Give you $500,000 and access to all the inventions and rewards, no matter what year
joke	See for yourself
oivaizmir	Programmer's "back-door" Debug menu. Displays Debug menu, so that you can add $500,000 at a time, show version information, add all gifts, and add all inventions. You can also experience new disasters, such as Nuclear Meltdown, Microwave, Volcano, Fire Storm, Mass Riots, Major Flood, and Toxic Spills.

City 2000, do special things. Note that these Easter Eggs only work if the Toolbar is highlighted, and you may have to click and drag the Toolbar first before getting them to work.

Launch Arcos Do Launch! (Mac 1.1, DOS 1.1, and Windows)

In Version 1.0 of the Macintosh and DOS versions of *SimCity 2000*, many people were disappointed that the Launch Arcos didn't actually launch themselves into space. So to satisfy the public's desires, Maxis decided to make the Launch Arcos actually launch in the Macintosh and DOS Versions 1.1, as well as in the Windows Version 1.0. After a certain number of Launch Arcos have been built, you'll see the message, "The Exodus has begun." Then, one by one, your arcos will start to blow up. After all the arcos are gone, you'll see the message, "Your Launch Arcos have departed into Space to found new worlds. You have been compensated for the construction." Even though your arco population is gone, you won't notice a change in the population until January of the following year.

The Helicopter (Both Mac and PC)

If you click on the helicopter with the Centering tool, you can make it crash. You can also listen with glee as the poor pilot radios his last message.

Clicking on the Mayor's Mansion (Both Mac and PC)

If you have a sound card and your approval rating is positive, you'll hear a rousing cheer when you click on the Mayor's mansion. If, however, your approval rating is in the dumps, you'll hear catcalls and boos.

Figure 10-8
Land Analysis tool

LAND USE		ACRES		% of CITY
Transportation	–	491	–	%40
Power	–	95	–	%7
Water	–	15	–	%1
Residential	–	196	–	%16
Commercial	–	98	–	%8
Industrial	–	202	–	%16
Ports/Airports	–	0	–	%0
Education	–	34	–	%2
Health/Safety	–	61	–	%4
Recreation	–	16	–	%1
Arcologies	–	16	–	%1

Land Analysis Tool in City Hall (Both Mac and PC)

This nifty tool becomes available only after you've been rewarded with a City Hall. After you've built the City Hall, if you click on it using the Query tool, you'll see an Analysis button inside the Query dialog box. If you click on this button, you'll see a text box that shows how your land is being used. For each land-use category, as illustrated in Figure 10-8, you can see how many tiles, or acres of land, are being used for this purpose and, in the far-right column, what percentage of your total land holdings this category takes up. Find out, for example, how much of your city is devoted to transportation purposes, or whether your industrial-to-commercial-zone ratio is correct for the kind of economy you have.

Neil Gaiman Quotations in the Library (Both Mac and PC)

In the Macintosh and DOS Versions 1.1 and the Windows Version 1.0 of *SimCity 2000*, there is a new Ruminate button in the Library that, when clicked, causes quotations from the author, Neil Gaiman, to appear onscreen.

Bulldozing Trees Causes Bull Moose Roar (DOS Versions 1.0 and 1.1 Only)

If you bulldoze enough trees in the PC version of *SimCity 2000* and ignore the complaints of the citizens, you'll get a warning message about destroying the habitat of the Bull Moose. Thereafter, if you persist in your deforestation efforts, a text box will pop up asking you if you want to hear the endangered Bull Moose roar at you (if you have a sound card on the PC).

Trees Grow Spontaneously

Trees will grow by themselves on empty land, and—like real trees—take decades to mature. You probably won't notice this unless you stare at a given piece of land, eyes glazed over, for a very, very long time. As you perform this activity, it helps to have a beer on hand.

MaxisMan!

Faster than a speeding bullet, faster than a speeding locomotive—yes, it's MaxisMan! Believe it or not, there *is* a MaxisMan (sometimes he is referred to as "SuperSim"), who will appear *if* you don't have a military base to help you fend off disasters. He will dispatch the monster or blow away the chemical clouds, helping to rescue your city. Don't count on him, though; most of the time he never appears.

The Green Little Beastie: Nessie, the Loch Ness Monster

From time to time, you may notice a low-pitched roar (if you have a Mac or a PC with a sound card). If you look around in your lakes, you may see

Nessie, the Loch Ness Monster, surface from the water for a brief cameo appearance. She's very nice and a vegetarian, so you don't have to worry!

Watching the Movie at the Drive-In Theater

Watch the movie at the drive-in theater closely. We think you'll recognize the principal character; he has star billing in one of Maxis's other products.

GETTING HELP ONLINE AND EXCHANGING CITIES

There are many online services where expert players congregate who can help when you get stuck on a particular problem. Help is available on the Internet, Prodigy, CompuServe, America Online, and many local BBS (bulletin board system) services. Also, if you have a bug report or a specific complaint, problem, or request that you wish to address to Maxis, you can do so directly through e-mail (electronic mail). Maxis has online representatives on CompuServe (in the Game Publishers B Forum under the Maxis topic), on America Online (keyword is Maxis), and on the Internet. You can address e-mail to the Maxis representative on the Internet at support@maxis.com, and on CompuServe to the Maxis representative at address 71333,1470 (from the Internet, you would address mail to the CompuServe network like this: 71333.1470@compuserve.com). Thus, if you are on Prodigy, you can send Internet mail to either of the two addresses, using either 71333.1470@compuserve.com or support@maxis.com.). On America Online, you can send email to Maxis by typing in the email address Maxis in the Compose Mail dialog box's Address Field.

Since most services, with the exception of the Internet, stick you with an hourly connect charge, your best bet for seeking advice at the lowest cost is on the Internet. To join any of these online services, you must have a modem and special telecommunications software.

Learning More about *SimCity 2000* Online

You can learn more about *SimCity 2000* by joining one of the special interest groups that exist on Prodigy, CompuServe, America Online, and the Internet.

Prodigy, CompuServe, and America Online

Prodigy and CompuServe are the two largest commercial online networks; America Online is a very close third. Over two million people subscribe to

Prodigy; over 1.5 million are members of CompuServe. The Internet, which is a public network that is available to all for a nominal access charge through various private service providers, has *over 20 million people* on it! Commercial online services such as Prodigy, CompuServe, and America Online offer a much friendlier and easier interface to their information, but they don't share information with one another (although you can send e-mail). In other words, if you're a Prodigy subscriber, you can see the game bulletin boards on Prodigy, but you can't see the entertainment forums on CompuServe, and vice versa. Users can, however, exchange e-mail among all of these services: Prodigy, CompuServe, America Online, and the Internet.

Learning about *SimCity 2000* on the Prodigy Games BBS

Once you're logged onto the Prodigy service, you can correspond with other *SimCity* addicts by jumping to the games bulletin board. You do this by selecting the Jump command and typing in **Games BBS**. In the next window, you'll need to choose a topic to read about. Click on the Choose a Topic button and select the Other Games category (some *SimCity* postings are also found under the War/Strategy Games topic). After choosing the topic, click on the Begin Reading Notes button; you'll see a list of subjects pop up onscreen for the topic. Each subject contains notes and replies to the notes from other Prodigy subscribers. To find the *SimCity* subjects, just scroll down through the alphabetical list of subjects, stopping at those that interest you. When you find a subject of interest, click on its button name and you'll see the first note or message. To read the replies to a note, click the Replies button.

Learning about *SimCity 2000* on CompuServe

Once you're logged onto CompuServe, you can go directly to these forums, which contain *SimCity*-related stuff:

- Game Publishers B Forum under Maxis section
- Macintosh Entertainment Forum
- Gamers Forum

Learning about *SimCity 2000* on America Online

To go to the Maxis forum on America Online, select the Go To menu, then choose the Keyword menu option. In the dialog box that opens, type in the keyword **Maxis**, and the Maxis forum will immediately open up. Once you're there, you can look at messages, download cities and other files, and find about Maxis's latest product announcements.

Exchanging Cities via E-mail on Prodigy, CompuServe, and America Online

One of the most exciting things about *SimCity 2000* is that you can trade and share your cities with others. Before sending your cities, you should compress them using PKZIP, WinZip,[9] or some other compression utility. By doing so, you'll reduce their size by 50 to 70 percent, thus saving you time and money on your telephone bill and your online connect charges. For example, a city file of 114,000 bytes would, when compressed by WinZip, be about 49,000 bytes in size, a reduction of 57 percent. A city file of 67,000 bytes would compress to 20,000 bytes, a reduction of 70 percent. You can now e-mail your cities directly to anyone else on all three online services.

The Internet

The Internet has a wonderful bulletin board called USENET. This information resource is filled with over 10,000 topics (called *newsgroups*); new topics are added or deleted every day as people join in or drop out. Each topic can have thousands of individual messages on all kinds of subjects that are subsets of that topic. For example, the comp.sys.mac.games topic covers almost all the games that have to do with the Macintosh (including the Macintosh version of *SimCity*). The comp.sys.ibm.pc.games.strategic topic covers games on the PC (including the DOS version of *SimCity*). You can now access all 10,000 USENET newsgroups via CompuServe, Prodigy, or America Online.

All three of these online services plan on offering Web browsers for surfing the World Wide Web in 1995. These Web browsers make it easy to find anything you want on the Internet. They also allow you to read the USENET newsgroups and to download files directly to your computer. However, since all three services charge an hourly connect fee for the use of the Web browser, it may be more economical to sign up with a local Internet service provider in your area.[10]

---

[9]WinZip is a Windows version of PKZIP; you can obtain it for free evaluation from almost any BBS or online service. If you like the program and plan to use it regularly, the author (Nico Mak Computing) requests that you register the program and pay a small registration fee. It's available on the world wide web at http://www.winzip.com.

[10]There are hundreds of local Internet providers all over the world. For a small monthly fee, or perhaps a small hourly connect charge, you are given a private account on the Internet that allows you to send and receive e-mail and transfer files between your machine and any other machine on the Internet. This program is called FTP (the file transfer protocol).

Getting Help From Maxis

You can e-mail Maxis for technical support at the following address: support@maxis.com.

Exchanging Cities Via E-Mail on the Internet

If you have an account on the Internet, you can send your cities anywhere in the world via e-mail (but not yet from CompuServe, America Online, or Prodigy.) You must convert your city file to a text-only version so that the Internet's e-mail facilities can handle it. This encoding and decoding can be done automatically for you if you have an e-mail program such as Eudora, which is available from ftp://ftp.qualcomm.com. Eudora is available for both the Macintosh and Windows.

Searching the Internet for Interesting *SimCity* Files

With all these incredible resources at hand on the Internet, you might wonder, *How do I find out what's there?* Well, that's a really good question, because with all the thousands of machines networked together on the Internet, it would be impossible for you to browse through each and every one. The answer to your question is to use Stanford University's Yahoo World Wide Web Search program.

To get to this site, you'll need to have a Web browser and then type in the following address:

http://akebono.stanford.edu/yahoo/

Once you're there, you can click on the Search icon, then type in *SimCity* to get a listing of all sites with *SimCity*-related stuff (as this book went to press, Maxis was not listed on the Yahoo site, but this should change soon).

SimCity Discussion Group

There's a unique *SimCity 2000* discussion list that's distributed daily to anyone who wishes to subscribe and who has an e-mail account on the Internet, Prodigy, America Online, or CompuServe. To join this list and have the messages automatically sent to your mailbox, you need to send an e-mail message to majordomo@cisco.com that consists of the following line:

subscribe simlist-digest

Questions about the list should be sent to this address:

simlist-owner@cisco.com

If you want to send a *SimCity*-related article to be included in the SimList, you send an e-mail message containing the text to the following address:

    simlist@cisco.com

Each day, a new *SimCity 2000* digest is generated automatically at midnight PST, after which it is distributed worldwide to everyone who has subscribed to the list.

The SC2000 FAQ

The SC2000 FAQ is a list of frequently asked questions (FAQ) about *SimCity 2000* that is available at the Maxis World Wide Web site, which is temporarily at

    ftp://ftp.netcom.com/pub/ma/maxis/http/faq/sc2k/sc2k.html

Since Maxis may be changing its Web site to a full-fledged http server in the near future, you may encounter difficulties with the above address. If you do, you should try the general Maxis Web page at

    ftp://ftp.netcom.com/pub/ma/maxis/http/maxis.html

If you don't have a Web browser, but do have FTP (File Transfer Protocol) access, you can download the sc2k.faq by logging on as **anonymous** to ftp.netcom.com and then changing directories to the

    /pub/ma/maxis/http/faq/sc2k

directory. Once you're there, you can download the sc2k.faq file, which is an ASCII text file of about 100K.

You can then use any word processor or text editor, such as Windows's WRITE.EXE, to view the FAQ.

Calling the Maxis Bulletin Board

If you don't mind paying a fortune in long-distance telephone charges, you can call direct to the Maxis BBS line in Orinda, California. This bulletin board has the latest patches, upgrades, drivers, and other paraphernalia related to *SimCity 2000*. You must set your modem to the following telecommunications protocol: no parity, 8 data bits, 1 stop bit, and full duplex at speeds of up to 14,400 bps. The number to call is 510-254-3869.

SIMCITY 2000 MACINTOSH VERSION 1.1 CHANGES

SimCity 2000 Version 1.1 for the Macintosh fixes many bugs and problems that existed in Version 1.0, but—unfortunately—also changes some of the cheats and Easter Eggs. The following is a brief list of some of the changes:

- The Budget should work properly now; transit figures should be correct.

- The Bulldozer tool should always default to Bulldoze instead of to whatever Bulldozer tool was last used. This change should prevent the accidental mass destruction that was formerly caused by forgetting that the last Bulldozer tool used had been Raise Terrain, Lower Terrain, or Level Terrain.

- Airports should be built with the correct ratio of towers to runways.

- Several problems that show up when you have more than seven stadiums or teams should be gone.

- Figures in the Analysis window (from the City Hall Query window) should give correct numbers now.

- Formerly, destroying bridges sometimes left an unusable shoreline tile. This problem is now fixed.

- You'll find a new button when you use the Query tool on a library.

- Querying on certain tiles of the Forest Arcology in certain situations formerly returned a report of bare land; this should not happen now.

- You can build more than 140 arcologies now, and the population will be affected. The new version allows the population to exceed 9.6 million people, whereas in Version 1.00, no more than 140 arcos were counted toward the population.

- The charges for placing highways and reinforced bridges have been corrected.

- Schools should now work properly at population levels exceeding 60,000.

- The date should now display properly beyond the year 9999.

- The power graph should be more accurate.

- Launch Arcos now launch into space.

In Version 1.1, cities that were created with Macintosh Version 1.0 will continue to have the same bugs they had before. Only new cities that are created with the updated Version 1.1 will be bug-free.

SIMCITY 2000 DOS VERSION 1.1 CHANGES

In the preceding edition of this book, we assumed that the DOS Version 1.1 update would be identical to the Macintosh Version 1.1 patch, but this was not the case. It wasn't until October 26, 1994, long after the Macintosh Version 1.1 update was available, that Maxis released the DOS Version 1.1

patch. Many people, ourselves included, were sorely disappointed to discover that many bugs in the model still existed, including the 140-arco limit. Not only that, but some people found that after they installed the upgrade, the program would no longer run! Maxis has since recommended that you *not install the DOS 1.1 patch unless you're having trouble getting SimCity 2000 to run on your computer.*

Here's what Maxis advises regarding the DOS 1.1 Patch:

WARNING! We STRONGLY suggest that you NOT download this file unless you are having problems with SimCity 2000. The code is sizably larger than the original (perhaps 100 KB) and WILL NOT ALWAYS WORK on 4 MB systems! Specifically, you may need to disable some or all BIOS shadow RAM if you have 3712 KB of RAM after shadowing. You need 3840 KB or more to run SC2000 properly. It may start on those systems with 384 KB BIOS shadowing, but can crash with weird error messages. Please verify that you have MORE than 3072 KB extended memory before contacting us with difficulties.

When he was asked if the DOS version of *SimCity 2000* would ever be updated to fix the model's bugs, Chris Weiss, the support representative for Maxis, stated:

The SC2K (SimCity 2000) DOS patch? Well, that's a tough one. The three main things holding it up are: First, the original programmer is no longer with us (he's working for Microsoft now) and the code is . . . well . . . few people have touched it and lived. Second, the program is huge. On a 4-meg machine running a large city, SC2K has under 100K of headroom for DOS and mouse drivers (that's including high memory). There just isn't much space to add anything, which is why you have to change the tilesets from SCURK (SimCity Urban Renewal Kit); there just wasn't enough space to add that code to SC2K. Third, the Windows version is available, which works on most machines that the DOS version does not work on.

About the microsimulator limit—it would take a major code rewrite and a lot more memory to remove this limit. That's just the way it is. Lack of foresight on our part, I guess.

It turns out that the DOS 1.1 update was primarily designed to solve hardware incompatibilities, although some changes were made to the model, such as allowing Launch Arcos to launch and fixing the Bulldozer tool. But the patch doesn't help you build record-breaking populations, and in fact is actually a hindrance, since you have to get your arcos fully populated before they launch.

SIMCITY 2000 WINDOWS 1.0 CHANGES

SimCity 2000 for Windows has a number of changes, additions, and Windows-specific features that are different from those in the Macintosh and DOS versions. The following listing details these new features:

- All the standard Windows conventions are present, including opening and saving files, opening and closing menus, and opening, closing, maximizing, and minimizing windows.

- Built-in onscreen Windows help is available. You can access help through the Help menu, or by pressing ⚠. While you're inside any window, if you press ⚠, it will bring up context-sensitive help.

- Clicking on the window buttons on the City toolbar opens a floating window that does not vaporize once you let go of the mouse button. You don't need to click and drag the window button to open windows.

- The Status box in the DOS and Macintosh version of *SimCity 2000* has been moved to the Status Bar at the bottom of the screen. Weather conditions are now spelled out instead of being depicted by an icon image.

- You can give your city two names: one is an eight-character DOS file name, and the other a full name of up to 30 characters, including letters, numbers, spaces, and symbols.

- Shift-clicking, previously used for getting help and opening Query windows, does not work in this Windows version.

- A new close-up fourth zoom level is now available. The three existing zoom levels remain, but this new one has been added to help you discern small details when you're running *SimCity 2000* on large high-resolution monitors, such as 1024 × 768 pixels (horizontal x vertical picture elements) on a 14-inch monitor or 1280 × 1024 pixels on a 17-inch monitor. Each of the three existing zoom levels retains its individual artwork, but the fourth zoom level magnifies the third zoom level's artwork even more. This new zoom level was needed because when the simulation is running at high resolutions, everything looks much smaller, and the old zoom rendered details such as power lines invisible.

- The 140-arco limit has been removed, and Launch Arcos launch. Furthermore, most of the Macintosh Version 1.1 changes to the model have been incorporated.

- The Easter Eggs and cheats differ from those in both the DOS and Macintosh versions of *SimCity 2000*. In particular, the negative-interest-rate double-bond fund trick no longer works, and the keyboard cheats have been changed.

- The Windows .SC2 city file structure has been changed slightly from that of the DOS .SC2 city file, so if you were using DOS Debug to hex-edit your city files, it may no longer work. You can still use the Norton Utilities DiskEdit program or any other disk-editing utility to hex-edit your .SC2 city files, but you'll have to visually spot where the hexadecimal bytes are located.

- Sounds are now stored as .WAV files, and music is stored as MIDI files (.MID) in the SC2K4WIN\SOUND directory. You can now change the MIDI music to classical music (which you can download free from the Internet), or change the WAV sounds to something you've recorded, by simply substituting your .MID and .WAV files with the names in the SOUND directory. Be sure to copy and back up the existing *SimCity 2000* sound files to another directory, in case you later change your mind and want to reuse the old files.

- Although the city (.SC2) files are interchangeable with those from the DOS and Macintosh versions of *SimCity 2000*, the tile sets are not. Therefore, *SCURK* (*SimCity* Urban Renewal Kit) for DOS will not work with the Windows version of *SimCity 2000*. Maxis expects to release *SCURK* for Windows in the spring of 1995.

- *SimCity 2000* for Windows requires that you use a 256- color video driver. At present, you can't run the program with color resolutions greater than this. Windows Version 1.1, expected in the spring of 1995, should allow you to use more than 256 colors.

- The Windows version of *SimCity 2000* runs much more slowly than the DOS version, since the program has to share processor time with other applications, including the Program Manager. *SimCity 2000* makes use of Microsoft's new WinG (Windows Game Application) drivers, which enable *SimCity 2000* to be playable in Windows. Without these special drivers, the screen redraws would be four times slower! You'll notice that the WIN.INI file for your Windows initialization has been updated to include a special WinG section. These new WinG drivers were installed to your Windows directory by the *SimCity* installation program.

- In order to run the Windows version of *SimCity 2000*, you'll need to be running Windows in 386 Enhanced Mode (not Standard Mode), and you'll need a Virtual Memory Swap File of at least 10 MB. You'll also need to check your Program Manager's available free memory. (Under the Help Menu in the Program Manager, select About Program Manager). You'll need at least 7 MB and 30% System Resources free.

OBTAINING UPGRADES

All the update/upgrade files require that you have previously installed *SimCity 2000*. You can obtain update/upgrade files by contacting Maxis (voice 510-254-9700), or you can download them from CompuServe, America Online, Prodigy (using Prodigy's World Wide Web Browser), the Maxis telephone BBS, or the Internet.

The DOS 1.1 update file is named SC211UPD.ZIP, and needs to be decompressed into your SC2000 DOS directory. Maxis strongly advises you *not to update your DOS Version 1.0 to Version 1.1 unless SimCity 2000 crashes on your computer.* The DOS Version 1.1 only fixes operational bugs in the program; it does not change the *SimCity* model (except for making Launch Arcos able to launch), nor does it lift the 140-arco limit. In fact, many people have reported that the DOS Version 1.0 of *SimCity 2000* works better than Version 1.1!

The Macintosh 1.1 update file is called *SimCity*2001.1update.sea.hqx, and you'll need to use the latest version of Compacter Pro or Stuff-It to de-binhex the file before you can create a self-extracting version of the program. Table 10.9 shows where you can find these files.

Table 10-9 Where to Obtain Update/Upgrade Files for *SimCity 2000*

Location	Procedure
CompuServe	Go to Game Publishers Forum B and look in the Maxis Library for the SimCity 2000 Version 1.1 Update file (both Macintosh and PC have separate listings)
America Online	Using the GOTO menu, select Keyword. In the dialog box, type **Maxis**. If you click on the Software Library listing, you'll open a screen that gives you the option of opening Mac Software Files or PC Software Files. Note that the DOS Version 1.1 update file is not available on America Online.
Prodigy	Use the Prodigy World Wide Web Browser (only available at present for Windows) by using the command Jump and then typing in the word **WWW**. In the Web browser's URL address field, type in **ftp://ftp.netcom.com/pub/ma/maxis/http/maxis.html** (all on one line, with no breaks). You'll open up Maxis's Web page, and there you can just click on the Software Library icon to get a listing of files you can directly download using your Web browser. (Note that this URL address will change when Maxis moves to an official http Web server.)
Internet	Using the World Wide Web, type in the URL address **ftp://ftp.netcom.com/pub/ma/maxis/http/maxis.html** Maxis's Web page will open, and you can click on the Software Library icon to get a listing of files you can download. (Note that this address will change when Maxis moves to an official http Web server.) Using FTP (File Transfer Protocol), you can transfer the files by logging in as **anonymous** to the ftp.netcom.com address, then CD (change directory) to the Maxis directory at /pub/ma/maxis/http/softlib/upgrades/mac for Macintosh files, or /pub/ma/maxis/http/softlib/upgrades/pc for PC files.
Maxis BBS Telephone Line	The telephone number for the Maxis bulletin board is 510-254-3869. Use 8 data bits, no parity, and 1 stop bit for your modem logon settings.

PART
III

Planning—City Design and Scenario Solutions

CHAPTER
11

A Survey of Cities

Here is a survey of four very different cities designed by four very different people.

- The first city, Tari's Kingdom, is the least planned, least organized, and most realistic. It grew, changed, and sprawled. Areas were redeveloped. Projects were started and stopped. There are parts of the city that are in great shape, and there are other parts that you wouldn't want to visit late at night without an armed escort.

- The second city, Harsh, was a concerted effort to maximize population through an efficient grid system. This city was built by brute force, always with the goal of growth in mind. Issues such as education, pollution, and crime were dealt with as needed, almost as side issues.

- The third city, Mattropolis, was designed from the beginning with nothing less than perfection in mind. Instead of courting growth or high population, the ultimate goals were symmetry, efficiency, a smooth-running infrastructure, and a high quality of life.

- The fourth city, Calebopolis, is the ultimate fantasy city. A city of beauty and natural wonders, it exists only for the convenience, pleasure, and worship of the city's creator.

TARI'S KINGDOM

Tari's Kingdom was created by Tari Kobylanski, a young grandmother who lives in Concord, California. Incidentally, her face was used to represent the Health and Welfare adviser in the SimCity 2000 *budget window.*

Your city is humbly called Tari's Kingdom. What was your goal when you started it?

Well, this is the very first city that I built. My first major goal was to get one of those cool-looking arcologies. Then I wanted to see how many people I could get in there, and how much money I could make. And keep my residents happy.

So, what was your goal, really?

Lots of money. Lots of power.

The true Tari emerges.

I wanted it to look neat, too.

As far as meeting your goals, how did you do?

I think I did great. I'm pleased with it.

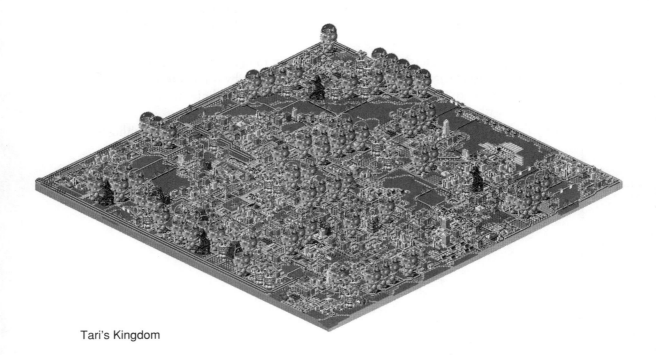

Tari's Kingdom

Your population is almost 6,000,000—far outstripping your neighbors.

I don't think I had enough connections to my neighbors. . . . I didn't know about that until recently.

Were there any problems that cropped up along the way?

Well, I was learning as I was going, and I didn't think about highways until was no room left to put them. And I didn't leave enough room for all the arcologies I wanted. So I had to do a lot of demolition to make some space. And I was taken by surprise at how many extra police you need with arcologies around.

And I tried legalizing gambling, but that didn't work. It was great at first—I made a lot of money—but after a while it started attracting a rowdy crowd and my population started getting a little angry. So I took it out.

What about the landform?

This landform was random. All I did was take out some of the hills. I have a hard time building on hills. If I want some hills later, I'll put them in.

What are you most proud of in your city?

Well, I managed to trap an airplane between some arcologies . . .

Neighbors window

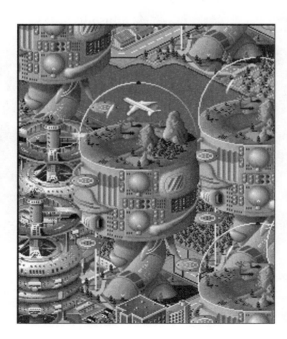

The trapped airplane

What are the neatest features you put in your city?

I put roads and highways around the edges.

This highway in the middle here that goes nowhere was the 880[1], but now it's the Santa Monica Freeway[2]. It just kinda stops there. This is the old downtown section, which has gone into decline, but they put in an arcology and started to put in the freeway, and that's as far as it's gone so far.

And these bridges meet like this because sometimes I just try things to see what happens when you try to connect things at perilous points. That would make a very exciting intersection to drive through, as you're coming down the hill off that bridge.

I tried to keep a lot of open space and greenery in one section, to keep down the pollution a bit. And I use a lot of public transportation. A lot of bus stations and subway stations.

I ran a subway tunnel right under the prison and put the station right next door. There's a lot of activity there . . . I don't know if it's the workers commuting or the prisoners escaping.

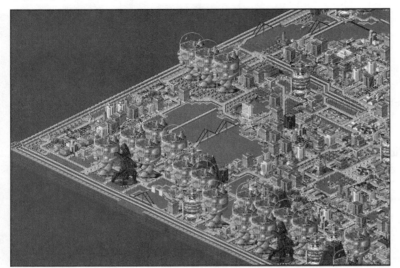

Highways at the edges

The highway to nowhere

The dangerous bridge crossing

---

[1]Part of Interstate 880 in Oakland broke in the Loma Prieta earthquake of 1989.
[2]The Santa Monica Freeway broke in the 1994 Northridge earthquake.

Green space

What would you do differently now?

I'd design the whole thing neater, with a better grid system for transport. I'd place my water pumps better. And I'd do things like put the library next to the school. It won't make a difference in the game, but that's where it should be, to be best used.

Where is this city?

This city is probably somewhere in the Midwest, because it's very flat. Maybe Iowa. A techno-center in Iowa that nobody knows about. It's a flat area, and someone came in with lots of money and lots of ideas and decided to build the ideal city, totally self-contained, and it never snows. Maybe this whole city itself is in one big arcology?

What about the people who live there?

I'd say the majority of them are typical—yuppies. And the more technical people and the younger people would be living in the arcologies, environmentalists and others like that. The rest of the town has a lot of industry, so you'd have a lot of blue-collar workers down there, too.

The year in the game is 3107. . . .

It actually reached 9999 and rolled over to 0000 and made it back to 3107.

So what year do you see this city actually existing?

The thing of it is, there are some things that are so old fashioned, like coal power plants, and some things that are so far fetched, or in the future, like the arcologies. I would like to see it in my lifetime, so I'll say the year 2000.

Would this be a fun place to live? What did you put in for recreation?

I've got lots of marinas. I lined up a lot of marinas together like they have them in the [San Francisco] Bay, or the [Sacramento] Delta area. Lots of parks.

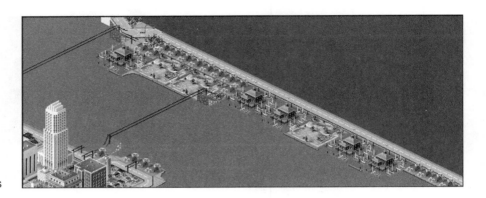

Water sports

Would you move to this city?

Sure. I'd live in one of the arcologies. Just because I think it's something I should do.

HARSH

Harsh was created by Ocean Quigley, an artist living in Oakland, California.

What was your goal in building this city?

I built this city solely for the purposes of money and population.

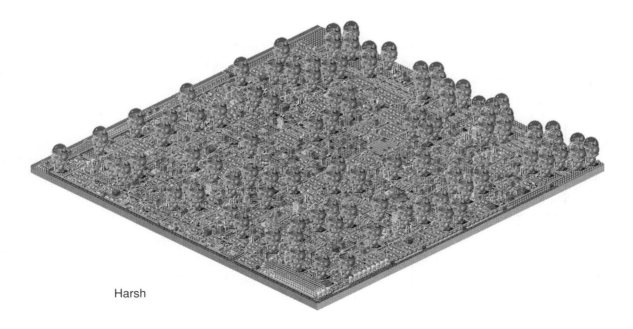

Harsh

We see you have $20,000,000, and about 5,000,000 Sims, the highest of all your neighbors. Looks like you succeeded.

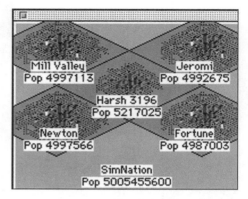

Harsh neighbors' window

What problems did you run into?

Well, water was the biggie. With that many people, you need a lot of water. In fact, I had this area all honeycombed with water pumps, but I had to put in marinas because my population demanded it. Seaports as well.

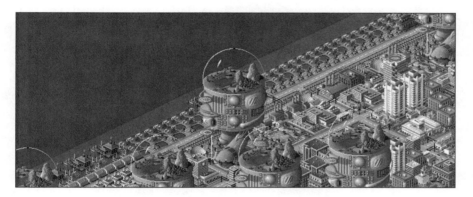

Water pumps on parade

Did you build this from a custom landscape?

I started with it flat and added everything.

Industry on the edge

Take us on a tour of Harsh. What are the different areas of the city?

Well, actually, I decided that I'd put heavy industry around the corners, to alleviate some of the pollution, because a lot of it goes off screen.

I don't believe in suburban sprawl. Every grid is 6 by 13 tiles, but symmetry was destroyed by the air force base. I decided to accept a military base, because maybe it would increase my population, maybe increase my economy, you

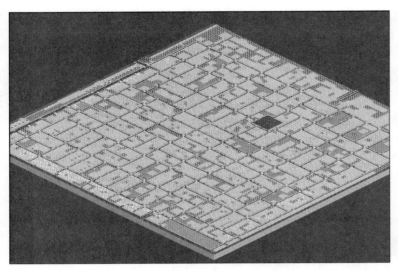

Grid system marred by
military base

know, all the reasons why cities want military bases.

But I wasn't really after symmetry, it was just convenient and efficient. I figured it was the easiest way to get a huge population and still have adequate transportation.

Everything was zoned high density, except when I put industry in the city center, I made it low density, to limit pollution. As the game continued, I found that I had to put in more and more things. I had to put in schools to support the arcologies. My school grade plummeted from A to F over a 60 or 70 year period again and again and again as my population climbed quickly.

I tried to make sure that each arcology was surrounded by parks to reduce the crime. I also put police stations fairly close to every arcology.

Arcology with
parks and police

Any specific problems you had to overcome?

I hit a prolonged recession in the early 21st century. I think it was because I didn't have enough airports.

And there was a definite problem meeting the power needs of the city until I had access to the advanced technology plants. I went from coal to solar, because I could put solar in the middle of the city and not cause pollution. And then from solar to fusion.

One thing that was annoying was, when I built highways to neighboring towns that had less than a million people, within five or ten game years they'd climb past me in population. They'd stay low until I built the highway to them. Once we were hooked up, they became serious competition. I don't know for sure if their growth was slowing mine down, but that was my perception . . . it felt like they were causing problems, so a couple times I bulldozed the highway links and then put them back later.

What about finance along the way?

I only had to issue one bond. There was a plant that was about to go. I cleared the area for it but didn't have enough to replace the power plant. So I had to issue a bond to pay for it.

I kept taxes very, very low, going for population over cash. And I used the Matt[3] maneuver, where you turn all taxes down to almost zero for the first 20 years or so of the game. That way, a lot of people move in, but since the city is still small, you don't lose very much money.

Water mains run under the streets

Any special features?

I used underground transportation a lot. But I found that subways had a minimal effect on traffic. Then I put buses in and that worked great.

And water . . . I ran the water mains under the streets. But even with all those water pumps and all the water towers, I still get shortages during the dry season.

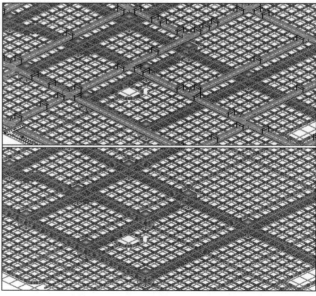

How much time did you put into Harsh?

Twenty-five or thirty hours.

---

[3]Matt Kim, builder of Mattropolis, described later in this chapter.

Water towers
and treatment

Where is this city?

This is in Euclidia, you know, like a plane . . . it's on a lake somewhere in the Midwest.

Would you live there?

No way. Never.

You didn't build this to be your dream city . . . .

No. This is a very pragmatic city. A study in how to put all the systems through horrible overcrowding and pollution.

What year do you see this city being real?

Maybe 2050, 2060. I think that by the year 3000 technology will have changed so greatly that *SimCity* will no longer be an accurate simulator. The paradigms will be so different that we won't even recognize cities as cities in the sense that we know them. If you have some exotic manufacturing technology, it might not require the equivalent land area. And if the whole distribution system changes, you'll need a different commercial space.

MATTROPOLIS

Mattropolis was created by Matt Kim, a freelance page-layout artist living in Oakland, California. Matt is a very methodical person, as reflected in his city.

What was your goal in building Mattropolis?

When I started, I didn't have a real design goal. It sorta became who I am. I

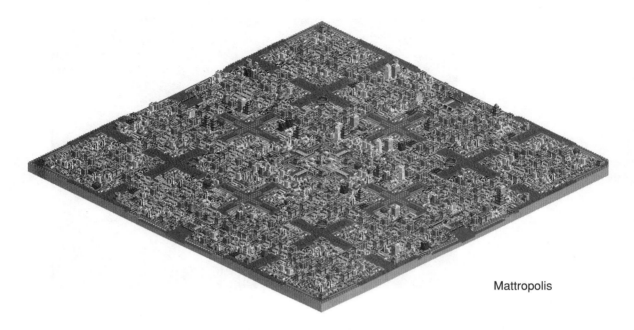

Mattropolis

think the city is a reflection of the player. I just kept trying to make my city better.

Did you use a custom landscape?

I did extensive terraforming. Coming up with it was a long, involved process. I spent probably two or three weeks before I came up with the final landform.

How did you go about building this city?

A symmetrical grid

Well, before I built it, I watched other people play for a long time, then I sat and read the manual cover to cover twice[4], then I mapped it all out on graph paper. I counted the tiles and figured out how to divide it exactly into 16 identical, symmetrical sections. Then I built it on the computer.

I spent a lot of time working on the symmetry of the thing, so that all sections are symmetrical. And even after the city was finished, I spent an extra day making sure

---

[4]You gotta love this guy. —MB

272   PART III: PLANNING—CITY DESIGN AND SCENARIO SOLUTIONS

One community

all the power lines were perfectly symmetrical, too. And if you zoom back to see the whole city, then rotate it, it looks exactly the same from every angle.

Basically, each of the 16 sections is a complete, self-contained community, with all the zones and all the niceties.

The idea was to put the industrial zones around the outer edge of each community, to minimize pollution in the middle. I separated the different sections with water and trees to control the pollution crossover from one community to another. And I put the infrastructure buildings—police, museums, stadiums—in the corners, because it seemed like the corners produced more pollution. And then I used the 6 by 13 grid to fill out each section.

What about the middle of the city?

I put the airport in the middle, serving the whole city. And I put the Llama Dome in the exact center, for aesthetics.

Where did you put city hall?

There's no city hall. I don't need it.

But the city hall gives you statistics. . . .

I don't need them. My city's already excellent.

You really like symmetry. . . .

You can see the symmetry in the Map window. See, here are the zones and roads.

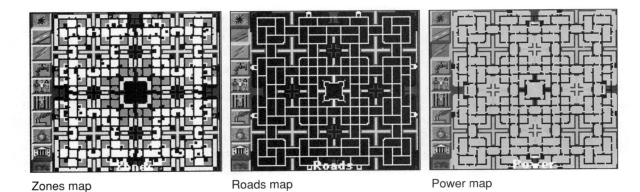

Zones map   Roads map   Power map

And a by-product of making everything symmetrical is that some of the things that you don't have control over come out symmetrical, too. Population density is symmetrical. Crime rate is close. Police power is symmetrical. Pollution is close. I was real happy about the way the land value worked out. The schools and colleges are in patterns, too.

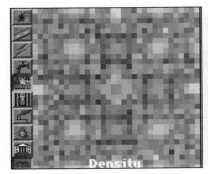

Population density map

Crime rate map

Police power map

Polution map

Land value map

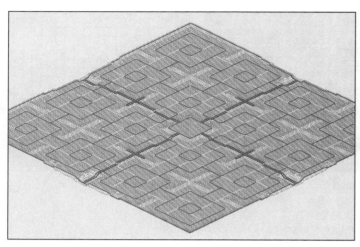

Mattropolis water
system

My water supply is kinda pretty, too. I ran some of the mains under the roads. I went back and redesigned it so it became a pattern, and it works, too.

How much time do you have invested in this city?

Including planning and three or four attempts that I destroyed before I got it right, about 100 hours.

Where does this city exist?

It doesn't exist anywhere. It's an ideal city.

If you could build it, if somebody said, "I like your design, here's a billion dollars, go to it," where would you put it?

I don't know. I'd put it in a good climate area, with no disasters.

That rules out California.

All these earthquakes, fires, and riots are too disturbing to me. I made the city with no fire stations and ran with no disasters.

Would you live in this city?

Oh, yeah! And I'd just drive around admiring the beauty of its layout.

Where would you live?

I don't know.

If you were to build yourself a nice home or mansion, where would you put it?

I'm a man of the people. I'd live with the people, and not separate myself off with a mansion. There's no mayor's house, no statue.

Whom do you picture living in this city?

It's a people's city. Everybody lives the same, because it's all symmetrical. Everybody is equal.

Any final comments?

I can't think of a city more beautiful than mine.

CALEBOPOLIS

Calebopolis was created by Caleb John Clark, a freelance writer living in Oakland, California.

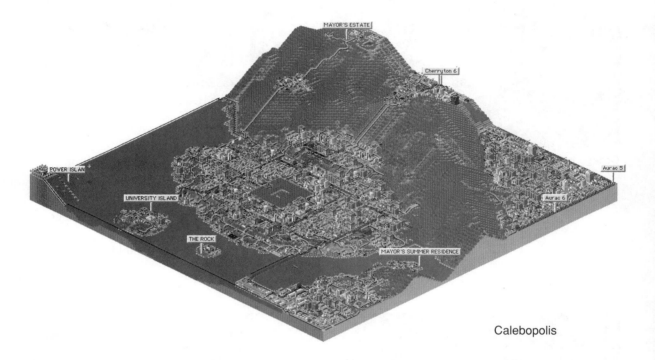

Calebopolis

What was your goal in building Calebopolis?

To create my fantasy city, the place where I want to live.

Power Island

Take us on a tour.

OK. I like water, because I grew up in a small town. So I put in a lot of coastline. This is Power Island. I kept it separate because power generators are so noisy. Even the wind ones. And I ran the power lines off the edge, because I don't like the way that they look.

I'm a strong believer in higher education—and serious partying—so I built an island dedicated to higher education. It has a museum and

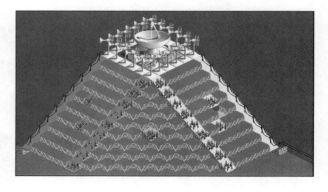

The Rock

College Island

library and everything. It has its own self-sufficient power source, and the only way to get there is by sailboat.

I made Alcatraz, because I moved to the Bay Area, and I think it's a good idea.

I'm big on coastline. My favorite part of *SimCity* is building extremely high-value real estate.

High land-value coastline

We notice that your terraces give good protection from floods.

I did a lot of custom terraforming.

Here's the airport over here.

And I love these small towns, too. Little neighborhoods. My summer house is over here, with my private marina. With a little residential and commercial [property], it's a complete community.

Here's the central part of the city, with the park. The *C* is for Calebopolis. This is as bad as it gets. Right here.

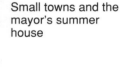

The airport

Small towns and the mayor's summer house

City center and the park

The statue of the
mayor

Bad in what way?

The thickest city part. Lots of people.
This is a statue of me.

Here's a tunnel that leads
through the mountain to the hidden
city of Calebopolis.

Tunnel to the hidden city

And here's a complete other hidden city, with its own water and power
sources.

The hidden city

What goes on in this other city?

This is more of a yuppie kind of city, but it has some industrial areas. You can't get away from industry in this game. It's a higher-class city than the major section, which is more of a standard San Francisco type of city.

How would you describe Calebopolis as a whole?

Utopia.

A self-aggrandizing utopia?

In this city, I'm as close to God as I can get. With *SimCity*, you're really more than a mayor, you can bulldoze houses with no repercussions. You can blow schools up and nothing happens. You can even bulldoze churches. With all this power, I created what I would create if corrupted by power.

The mayor's house and shopping area

Here's my house. It's got a great view of the city. I have my own personal shopping area so I don't have to drive all the way down the mountain to go shopping for food. I also have my own personal zoo, my own personal park, my own personal marina, and my own power source. I like to camp, that's why there's so much wilderness area.

About how many hours do you have invested in this city?

About a 40-hour week.

Any other utopian design ideas?

If I built another one, I'd build lots of little meandering streams and waterfalls and islands . . . islands that were connected by subways, with only one stop on each island. Like Bermuda or the Bahamas, except you have an incredible subway system you can just cruise to another island.

And I'd use all low-density. The instinct when you play *SimCity* is to use high-density and get the cool, big buildings, and go for population and money, but you lose track of your goal, of quality of life.

CHAPTER
12
Disasters for Fun and Profit

One of the most-loved—and most-hated—features in *SimCity* and *SimCity 2000* is the presence of disasters. Nothing quite matches that feeling of power that you get when, with the flick of a finger, you rain devastation and destruction upon those complaining little ingrates. Nothing, that is, except the feeling of power that surges through your veins when you reload the doomed city from disk (saved, of course, just before you set loose the disasters) and bring the city and its people back to life. And nothing inspires such a feeling of nauseous despair as when, at the whim of a random number in the simulator, your pride, your joy, your creation, your city is ravaged by the forces of simulated nature.

All disasters, including those that are set off as part of a scenario, stop time. This feature keeps fires from burning for months or years, as they did in *SimCity Classic*. It also takes away your ability to add police and fire stations quickly for more emergency help after the disaster has started. You can always add the stations, but the simulation won't acknowledge them until the disaster is over and time starts again.

The prime rules of disaster recovery are:

1. Put out fires now, *first*, RIGHT AWAY.
2. Restore utilities and infrastructure.
3. Remove the rubble.
4. Rezone when necessary.

A trick to disaster damage control and speedy recovery is to use the bulldozer in De-zone mode. This works with any disaster that involves fires. Fires burn anything, including rubble. De-zoning removes rubble, starving fires so that they go out faster, but it works only on zoned areas, not on infrastructure. If fires are ravaging unzoned areas, you can first zone whatever rubble there may be and then de-zone it.

Dispatching the police and fire departments with the Emergency tool can help in some disasters, and if you have a military base, the military sometimes helps out. But if you make the decision to turn down the offer of a military base after your city has reached the population level of 60,000, then, in one disaster out of four, Captain Hero will appear and put out fires, stave off flood waters, tackle tornadoes, and fight the monster. See Chapter 2 for complete instructions on using the Emergency tool to fight disasters.

THE DISASTERS

Here are all the disasters, with their complete personal statistics.

Fire and Firestorm

- Triggers: Menu, random event modified by simulation conditions, scenario.
- Nuisance value: Serious, bad, rotten.
- Conditions: The likelihood of a fire occurring goes up during the dry

season, especially when the temperature is high. Fires occur less often when you have good fire coverage. The Volunteer Fire Department Ordinance can help prevent and put out fires in smaller towns.

- Related disasters: Can be caused by earthquakes, air crashes, riots, monsters, and tornadoes.
- Effect: Fires burn anything but bare land and water, and they spread fast. Firestorms are huge fires.
- Countermeasures: Fight fires by dispatching fire fighters or military help through the Emergency tool. Control fires by creating firebreaks either by bulldozing (be sure to remove *all* rubble—it burns) or by placing water to block their path. You can also use the bulldozer in De-zone mode to clear rubble and starve the fire. Another way to make firebreaks is by using the bulldozer in the raise- or lower-terrain mode. This technique is very effective, since it affects a number of tiles at once and clears them all in one step, but it is expensive and can be very destructive to any innocently bystanding tiles.
- Comments: Fires in *SimCity 2000* are really mean. Part of the final tuning of the game was to make the Oakland scenario a real challenge, and so fires had to be allowed to spread very fast. One wonders if Will's house in Oakland burning down had anything to do with this. In any disaster where there is a fire, *stop the fire first.* Ignore everything else until the fire is out. Don't wait and think about it. *Stop the fire* or you may have to rename your city Ashland.

Flood

- Triggers: Menu, random event modified by simulation conditions, scenario.
- Nuisance value: Mild to moderate.
- Conditions: Most likely in the wet season.
- Related disasters: Can be caused by hurricanes.
- Effect: Water rises from the shoreline and floods the sea level (lowest land elevation) tiles, turning buildings and infrastructure to rubble.
- Countermeasures: Preparation is the best countermeasure. Build one-tile-high dikes near the ocean or rivers for protection. Don't build too close to the water. Once a

flood starts, you can block its path by deploying police, fire, and the military with the Emergency tool to protect small strategic spots. But mostly you wait until it stops and then go in and clean up.

- Comments: Floods usually occur on the coastline, but rivers will flood sometimes, too. Major floods also occur, but they can be triggered only by scenarios. Major floods can wash away tiles as many as two levels of altitude above sea level.

Tornado

- Triggers: Menu, random event modified by simulation conditions, scenario.
- Nuisance value: Mild to moderate.
- Conditions: High winds.
- Related disasters: Can cause explosions and sometimes fires.
- Effect: Tornadoes travel quickly and leave a narrow path of destruction in their wake.
- Countermeasures: Keep an eye on the papers for high wind warnings and be prepared to boost your fire coverage. Once a tornado strikes, follow it and put out fires (if any) along its path. Restore utilities and power as quickly as you can.
- Comments: The damage that a tornado causes can vary greatly, from almost nothing to moderately extensive. A lot depends on luck and what's in the tornado's path.

Plane Crash

- Triggers: Menu, random event modified by simulation conditions, scenario.
- Nuisance value: Mild.
- Conditions: Presence of airport.
- Related disasters: Causes explosions and fires.
- Effect: Planes spiral to the ground and crash, causing an explosion and starting a fire.
- Countermeasures: If you have an airport, expect a plane crash. Once it crashes, control the fire. Most random crashes happen near the airport, so place them away from population centers.
- Comments: The damage that a plane crash causes is so small (if you control the fires right away) that it shouldn't deter you from building an airport if you want one.

Helicopter Crash

- Triggers: Menu, random event modified by simulation conditions, scenario, user.
- Nuisance value: Mild.
- Conditions: Presence of airport.
- Related disasters: Causes explosions and fires.
- Effect: Helicopters spiral to the ground and crash, causing an explosion and starting a fire.
- Countermeasures: If you have an airport, expect an occasional copter crash. Once it crashes, control the fire. Most random crashes happen near the airport, so place them away from population centers.
- Comments: After the annoying noise that the traffic helicopter made in the original *SimCity*, most people are glad that the helicopter crashes. Clicking on a flying helicopter with the Centering tool shoots

it down. (This was possibly the most-requested feature that was added to *SimCity 2000*.)

Earthquake

- Triggers: Menu, random event, scenario.
- Nuisance value: Serious to ruinous.
- Conditions: No particular conditions, no warning.
- Related disasters: Earthquakes themselves damage buildings and infrastructure, but the real damage is caused by explosions and fires, as well as the subsequent looting and riots.
- Effect: The city shakes, buildings crumble, the infrastructure falls apart, and fires start.
- Countermeasures: There's nothing to be done about an earthquake. All you can do is clean up afterwards. Control the fires first, quell the riots, and then rebuild the infrastructure and clear the rubble.

- Comments: A civic lesson for us all: In the last dozen or so years, including yesterday morning (January 17, 1994), there have been three major earthquakes in California. All three have been true tragedies, causing death, injury, and human suffering. But earthquakes that have happened during the same period in other parts of the world—where there are no building codes, or they aren't enforced—have caused so much more death and destruction. Maybe in the next version of *SimCity*, there will be an ordinance to shore up freeways and enforce building codes.

Monster

- Triggers: Menu, random event, scenario.
- Nuisance value: Mild to serious.
- Conditions: No conditions, no warning.
- Related disasters: Monsters can cause fires.
- Effect: When the monster shows up, it will blow up buildings and

then replace them with fire, water, or
trees in the Mac version, but always
with fire in the DOS version.

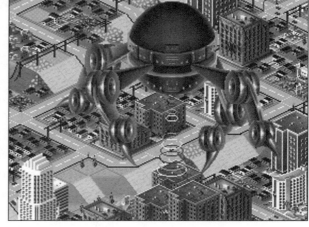

- Countermeasures: All you can do is
  hope for a benevolent alien that plants
  trees or water instead of one that plants
  fires. (DOS people, you're out of luck
  here.) In any event, hope it goes away
  soon. While the monster is causing
  problems, follow it and put out the fires
  (if any). Once it's gone, clear the rubble,
  restore the utilities and infrastructure,
  and rebuild. If you're lucky, Captain
  Hero will come to your rescue.

- Comments: Depending on your
  personal preference, the monster is either a real alien or a movie
  monster out of control. Either way, it's a real pain.

Hurricane

- Triggers: Menu, random event modified
  by simulation conditions, scenario.
- Nuisance value: Serious.
- Conditions: High winds and the
  presence of a coastline.
- Related disasters: Hurricanes generate
  winds that are high enough to damage
  buildings and whip up the ocean enough
  to cause flooding.

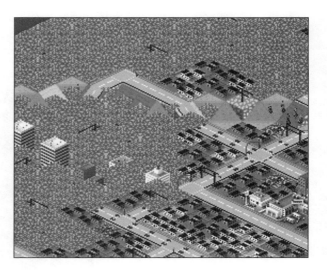

- Effect: Buildings crumble and
  occasionally explode; the water rises and
  floods along the entire coastline.
- Countermeasures: There's nothing to do
  for the winds, but as far as the rising
  water goes, treat it as you would a flood:
  build dikes, keep important structures away from the water, and
  deploy all your emergency staffs to protect important or strategic
  spots along the coastline. Then it's a matter of cleaning up and
  rebuilding.
- Comments: You don't actually see hurricanes, just the destruction

they cause. If you don't have a coastline, you won't get a random hurricane. If you set off a hurricane in a city with no coastline, one edge of the city will flood.

Riots

- Triggers: Menu, random event modified by simulation conditions, scenario.
- Nuisance value: Mild, as long as you tend to them right away.
- Conditions: High heat, high crime, and high unemployment.
- Related disasters: Rioters light fires.
- Effect: Rioters start as a small group of protesters carrying signs, then things get ugly. Rioters split up and multiply. They stay on roads, then start lighting fires after a while. If you stop them right away, they're a minor disturbance. If you don't, they'll burn down the whole city.
- Countermeasures: Surround the rioters with police to control them, and deploy fire fighters to quench the flames.
- Comments: Riots were added to the **Disasters** menu at the very last minute and aren't listed in the manual. Riots are cellular automata (see Chapter 16) and rioters are both repelled and quelled by police. They can be blocked by fire departments and will eventually disperse.

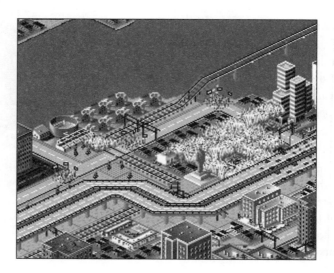

Mass Riots

- Triggers: Random event modified by simulation conditions, scenario.
- Nuisance value: Moderate to serious.
- Conditions: High heat, high crime, and high unemployment.
- Related disasters: Fires.
- Effect: Same as regular riots, but more groups of rioters to begin with. The number of rioter starting groups increases with the size of your city.
- Countermeasures: Surround and disperse rioters with police. Deploy your fire departments to keep the fires under control.
- Comments: Rioters are both repelled and quelled by police. They can be blocked by fire departments and will eventually disperse.

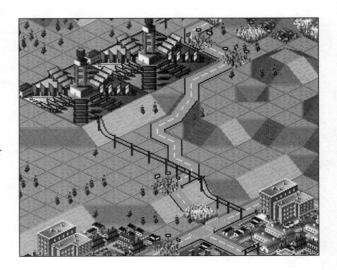

Volcanoes

- Triggers: Scenario only.
- Nuisance value: Mean, ugly, rotten.
- Conditions: N/A.
- Related disasters: Volcanoes cause fires and spew toxic gas.
- Effect: A huge mountain rises out of the earth, destroying everything above and around it, spreading fires, and spewing smoke and toxic gas.
- Countermeasures: There really aren't any. Once a volcano erupts, you're locked out until it has run its course— and by then fires have spread beyond control. All you can do is be ready to stop simulation time as soon as you can,

and then bulldoze firebreaks around the whole burning area. You'll have to be brutal with that 'dozer—don't let a single spark spread.

And be sure to clear the rubble when you bulldoze. You'll have to sacrifice a lot of homes and infrastructure to save the rest. Once the fires are under control, use your emergency fire, police, and military forces to contain the toxic clouds, if they haven't already dissipated.

- Comments: The volcano is so mean and destructive that it would have been cruel and unusual punishment to have it ever happen randomly. Unless the volcano erupts in a barren desert, or near a coastline or wide waterway that will block at least part of the fire, you can plan on losing between one-fifth and one-twelfth of your total landform. Volcanoes are big enough that the cost of leveling them is as much as that of buying a new arcology.

Pollution Disaster

- Triggers: Random event modified by simulation conditions, scenario.
- Nuisance value: Mild.
- Conditions: Presence of a lot of polluting industries.
- Related disasters: N/A.
- Effect: A toxic cloud moves through the city, flowing downhill when it can and wandering aimlessly on the flatlands. Whenever it touches a building, the Sims run for cover and abandon the building.
- Countermeasures: Pollution disasters can be prevented, or at least the odds of their happening can be kept to a minimum, by keeping polluting industries out of town. Once they happen, surround the clouds with police and the military if you have them.

- Comments: This is a full-fledged disaster, above and beyond the general pollution in a city. Police and military won't stop the pollution cloud, but they can contain it until it dissipates.

Chemical Spill

- Triggers: Random event modified by simulation conditions, scenario.
- Nuisance value: Mild to medium.
- Conditions: Presence of a lot of polluting industries.
- Related disasters: N/A.
- Effect: A group of toxic clouds moves through the city, flowing downhill when they can and wandering aimlessly on the flatlands. Whenever they touch a building, the Sims run for cover and abandon the building.
- Countermeasures: Same as for pollution disaster, except more so. Try to prevent them by eliminating those industries that pollute the most, and surround the cloud with police and the military if you have them.
- Comments: The number of toxic clouds that appears depends on the size of the city: the bigger the city, the worse the disaster.

Nuclear Meltdown

- Triggers: Random event modified by simulation conditions, scenario.
- Nuisance value: Serious bummer.
- Conditions: Presence of a nuclear power plant and a roll of the dice.
- Related disasters: Nuclear meltdowns cause fires, spew toxic gas, and spread radiation.
- Effect: The plant blows up, sets fires, and spreads radioactive fallout and toxic gas.
- Countermeasures: The only way to avoid a nuclear meltdown (without wimping out and turning on the No Disasters setting) is to ban nuclear

power plants from your city. If you want nuclear power plants, place them away from population centers or other power plants, so that if and when they blow they do as little damage as possible. There's nothing you can do about the radiation—just wait a few hundred years. Put out the fires, try to control the smoke, and declare the site fit only for filming post-holocaust films like *Mad Maxis*.

- Comments: These are the "regular" nuclear power plants—the fission plants. Fusion plants do not have meltdowns.

Microwave Power Beam Disaster

- Triggers: Random event modified by simulation conditions, scenario.
- Nuisance value: Moderate.
- Conditions: Presence of a microwave power plant.
- Related disasters: Fires.
- Effect: The power beam loses its tracking signal and misses the collector dish. It tries to correct but goes the wrong way, scorching the land (and burning anything on it) with a powerful beam of microwave energy. The scorching is usually in a narrow, straight line.
- Countermeasures: If you have microwave power plants, you run the risk. It's small, but worth thinking about. If you use microwave power plants, locate them in the corners of the city, away from population centers or other power plants. Once the beam loses its tracking, follow it, control the fires, clean up, and rebuild.
- Comments: That's the price we pay for progress. . . .

THE NON-DISASTER

When power plants blow up at the end of their 50-year life span, it's a minor nuisance, not a disaster. They may make a noise, but really they just crumble. Nuclear plants don't leak radiation when they go boom from old age.

CHAPTER
13

Beating the Scenarios

Like the original *SimCity*, *SimCity 2000* has scenarios—each one a game in itself. Each scenario has a city, either in bad shape or poised on the brink of disaster. You are given a time limit and a win condition. Win conditions are either population or financial goals (or both) that must be met within the time limit.

In addition to the five scenarios that come with *SimCity 2000*, this chapter also solves the 10 scenarios that come with *SimCity 2000 Scenarios Volume 1: Great Disasters* and the additional Great City Scenarios that come on the *SimCity 2000* CD Collection.

The solutions for the five originals will be very detailed. The other solutions will be a little less detailed, but they'll guide you to scenario success.

And don't forget that you can make your own scenarios, or at least modify the existing ones, by following the instructions in Chapter 10.

BASIC SCENARIO STRATEGIES

First, for the most fun (and confusion) just jump right in. Start the scenario, set the speed to Cheetah, watch what happens and try your best to figure out what to do. If you can win any of the scenarios on this first dry run, then you should seriously think about a career in politics. Or better yet, since you obviously have the ability to work under pressure and make tough decisions when lives are in the balance, you might apply for a job as either an oil well firefighter or a spy; then again, you may think about a career as a computer game designer (the pay isn't as good, but it's safer).

Once you've given it a once through in panic mode, try it again. This time, don't worry about winning. Set the speed to Slow and watch. Think and plan for the next time.

You may even want to pause the simulation and take a detailed, leisurely tour of the city. Find the problem spots. Find the high-population areas that need protection. Locate the utilities (water and power) so you can either protect them or be ready to replace them as soon as possible. Keep in mind the tips in Chapter 12.

Oh, and the first thing you should always do when starting a scenario is select No Disasters from the Disasters menu. It won't stop the disaster (if any) that is part of the scenario, but it will stop any others from randomly stumbling in. There's nothing more frustrating than cleaning up after a messy hurricane, only to be struck by fires, riots, and tornadoes just as you're about to win.

As with all disasters, when the scenario disasters occur, time in the simulation stops. This keeps fires from burning for months or years, as they did in *SimCity Classic*. It also takes away your ability to add police and fire stations quickly for more emergency help once the disaster has started. You can always add the stations, but the simulation won't acknowledge them until the disaster is over and time starts up again.

WINNING A SCENARIO

To win a scenario, you have to meet the win condition(s) within a certain amount of time. As soon as you meet the win condition(s) you will be declared a winner. You won't have to wait until the end of the time limit to receive your reward, which is a hearty congratulations and a city to run and rule (see the announcement at left). If you don't make it, you're kicked out of town.

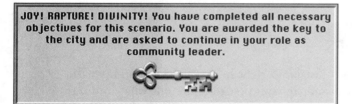

There are a number of different ways to win each of the scenarios. Use the one (or two) that are shown here to give you some ideas, then blaze your own trail to success with the scenarios.

DULLSVILLE

The lone surviving scenario from *SimCity Classic*, Dullsville is no more than a small "starter city," waiting for you to lead it to greatness.

Dullsville is probably the hardest of all the scenarios—at least it would be if it weren't for a bug that makes it much easier than it claims to be. In order to win (properly), you have to know just about everything there is to know about what makes a city an attractive place for a Sim to live.

Win Condition

The claimed goal is to achieve a population of 20,000 Sims and be $5,000 in the black—in only ten years.

Unfortunately—or fortunately, if you like to win easily—the game sometimes forgets to check the money part of the win condition.

General Strategies

Raising a city's population from 1,680 to 20,000 in 10 years is simple, especially given $20,000 to start with and no financial constraints. If you want to take advantage of the bug, just take out a bond or five, build a huge infrastructure, set taxes to zero, and let the simulation run. You'll reach 20,000 in less than two years.

On the other hand, if you want to try to beat the scenario as advertised, and in addition to the 20,000 population have $5,000 free and clear, it's not so easy.

You'll have to build a small, cheap, efficient, dense annex to Dullsville, using as little money as possible and wasting even less than possible.

Step-by-Step Solution

Load the Dullsville scenario, pause it as soon as you can, and select No Disasters from the Disasters menu.

A quick look around the town shows that you have just a little bit of low-density commercial, industrial, and residential zones. You'll need a lot more zones to fit in 20,000 people, especially in the 10 years allotted.

And since you only have $20,000 to start with, and you need to have $5,000 free and clear in the bank (funds minus bonds), you've got to start making back

Dullsville "before"

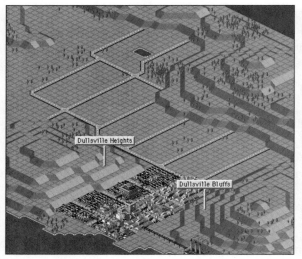

Add a road grid

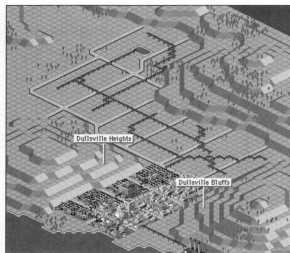

Add a power line

Your area zoned

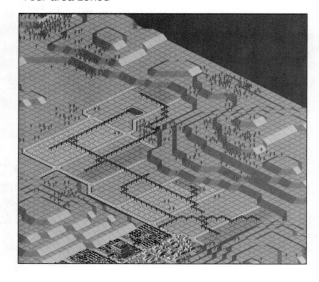

your investment fairly quickly. That means keeping your maintenance costs at a minimum.

The best place to build is just north of Dullsville proper and adjacent to the existing city so you can easily use the existing power plant. Start by laying out a gridwork of roads as the basis of your expansion. Don't make it too big all at once, or you'll be paying for maintenance on unused roads.

Next, you'll need to run power lines from the existing city all through the new grid. Put enough to get things going, but don't waste your money.

Now zone the new grid—all high-density. Go heaviest on residential, next heaviest on industrial, and last commercial. Be sure to mix up the zones for proper trip generation.

In order to get a dense population to move in, you'll need a water system. Place between 10 and 15 pumps by the water. For the most pumping capacity, place them so as many sides as possible are adjacent to water. Run power lines to power the pumps.

Add water pipes, sparingly, but with good coverage of all the zoned areas.

Ideally, if you were careful enough, you should have at least $10,000 left in your treasury

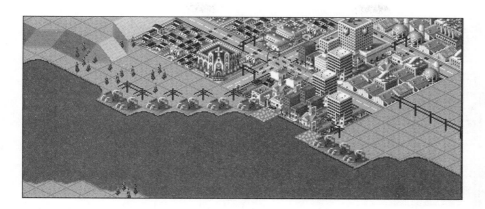

Water pumps placed

at this point. If not, then you may have built too expensive an infrastructure, but as long as you have $4,000 for another coal power plant, you can still get by without taking out a bond issue.

Now open the Neighbors window to keep an eye on the population as it grows:

To give our incoming population a quick jump, turn all property taxes to zero and leave them there for the first year and a half, from June, 1910, until January, 1912.

Once the taxes are shut off, turn the simulation to Llama and watch for a year and a half. In January, 1912, pause the game again. Your city should look something like this:

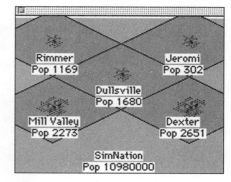

Neighbors window

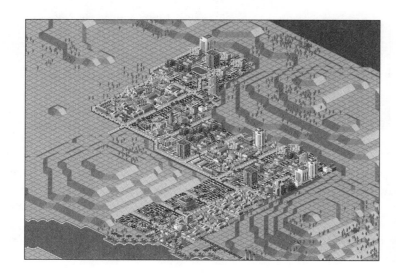

January 1912

Finance		
1% Sales Tax	✓	19
1% Income Tax	✓	67
Legalized Gambling	✓	39
Parking Fines	✓	33

Education		
Pro-Reading Campaign		
Anti-Drug Campaign		
CPR Training		
Neighborhood Watch		

Other		
Energy Conservation		
Nuclear Free Zone		
Homeless Shelters		
Pollution Controls		

Safety & Health		
Volunteer Fire Dept.		
Public Smoking Ban		
Free Clinics		
Junior Sports		

Promotional		
Tourist Advertising		
Business Advertising		
City Beautification		
Annual Carnival		

Estimated Annual Cost	
Finance	160
Safety & Health	0
Education	0
Promotional	0
Other	0

Done	YTD Total$	0	EST Total$	146

Now open the Budget window again and set property taxes back to 7 percent. Since every dollar counts in this scenario, open the Ordinances window and enact all four of the Finance ordinances:

Now set the game back to Llama for another year. By January, 1913, you should be approaching a population of 10,000, and be making a small yearly profit (only a few hundred, but that's OK for now). Pause the simulation.

Now you'll need to expand some more. It might be worth building over by the lake northwest of the city center for high-value residential property. Check the demand indicator to help you choose the zones that are most needed (mostly residential and industrial). Be sure to mix up the zones. Lay roads, power lines, and water pipes. You'll also need another coal power plant. At this point, if you were careful (read that as *cheap*), you should be about broke, but hopefully won't need to issue a bond.

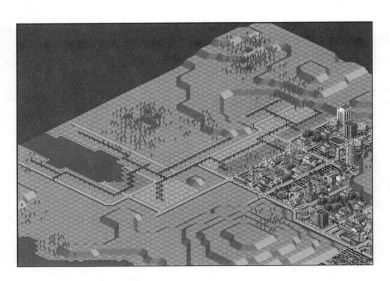

Second wave of
expansion

Now run the simulation at Llama or Cheetah, checking your population and funds every year. In the sample run used for these screen shots, the population was 14,920 in January, 1915, and the city was making a little over $1,000 a year.

By January, 1918, the population was 23,120 with $6,000 in the bank, and the scenario won.

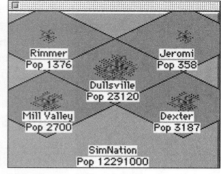

Neighbors window "after"

Dullsville "after"

FLINT, MICHIGAN

Flint, Michigan, the star of the film *Roger and Me*, is the classic case of putting all your eggs in one basket. This town was so dependent on the automobile industry—on *one* automobile company—for its livelihood, that when General Motors pulled out, the town suffered. The moral issue of whether it was right for GM to close down its Flint operation and leave the town in ruins is entirely beside the point. The fact is, they did it. It happened. And it will happen again in other places.

The lesson to be learned from this is: In order to maintain a healthy city through a rocky economy, you can't put all your workers in one industry, much less one company.

Win Condition

Winning the Flint scenario is embarrassingly easy. All you have to do is increase the industrial population from 10,000 to 21,000 in 5 years.

When I confronted Will and Fred with the ease of winning this scenario, their studied response, after due consideration of all the facts, was "Oops!"

General Strategies

What you have to do here is attract industry to move into town. There are quite a number of deserted zones ready for new occupants. If only there was a way to make it an attractive place to be! And what could be more attractive to business than low or non-existent taxes?

Since the only requirement to win is to increase your industrial population, you can win this scenario by doing nothing more than lowering industrial taxes to zero. Sims will flock in by the thousands.

Step-by-Step Solution

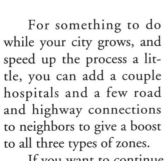

Tax books with
Industry turned to zero

First, lower them taxes. You can either go to the Property Taxes books (from the Budget window) and turn industrial down to zero.

Or you can make a personal statement instead by opening the City Industry window and individually turning all industrial taxes except automotive down to zero. Turn that one all the way up.

Then just open the Graphs window, turn on the industrial population graphs, and watch it rise. Here's what it looks like when it starts:

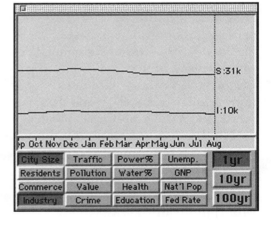

Tax settings in the City
Industry window

For something to do while your city grows, and speed up the process a little, you can add a couple hospitals and a few road and highway connections to neighbors to give a boost to all three types of zones.

If you want to continue playing Flint after winning the scenario, you may want to keep a little bit of taxes coming in by doing a little expansion (zoning and infrastructure building) to bring in those Sims who won't stand for even a low tax rate.

If you want to make Flint more of a challenge, see the instructions in Chapter 10 for modifying scenarios and include an additional financial goal, such as having an unencumbered $20,000 in the bank.

OAKLAND

The Oakland scenario is not an easy one to beat. And the Oakland Hills fire of October 1, 1991, wasn't so easy either! Both authors of this book lived within view of the smoke or flames and two Maxis employees, including Will Wright (one of the designers of *SimCity 2000*), lost their homes in the fire. Signs mark the former locations of their houses in this scenario.

Win Condition

Put out the fire and reach a population of 50,000 within five years.

General Strategies

This is a very hard scenario; in fact, it's probably impossible unless you pause the simulation the instant the fire begins and build a fire block, preferably with water, all around the fire. Do it fast to protect as much of the existing city as you can—and feel extra proud if you can save Will's and Chris's houses.

Once the fire is out, you still have to expand the infrastructure and bring the total population up from 41,000 to 50,000.

Step-by-Step Solution

First, pause the simulation as soon as you can and turn off disasters. At some point during the five-year scenario, one of your oil power plants will reach its old age limit and need replacing. If you don't keep an eye on it, it'll blow and you'll lose some valuable time. If you let the No Disasters setting take care of it, be sure you have enough funds in your account to cover replacement, even if you have to take out a bond. Then zoom in on the firestorm.

The initial firestorm area. See Will's and Chris's houses?

Use the bulldozer to clear a firebreak all around the burning area and deploy your firefighters. As each tile of fire is put out by your firefighters, move them adjacent to another fire tile until it is out—and continue this process to extinguish the fire more quickly. The effectiveness of the

Firebreak and firefighters deployed

firefighters is related to distance, so the closer you can move them in the better.

Use the dezoning mode of the Bulldozer to de-zone the burning area. This will remove the rubble and put the fire out sooner.

Once the fire is out, it's time to build up the population. The biggest clear spot for building is south of Lake Temescal, so start there with high-density zoning.

Empty space below Lake Temescal

Newly zoned area below Lake Temescal

After that, just search for every small, flat spot in the city and zone, power, and water when necessary. There's not much flat land, and modifying the terrain is expensive, so you'll have to search carefully to find small areas to zone. You can always bulldoze low-density areas and replace them with high-density areas.

Issue bonds as you need them; there is no financial requirement in Oakland's win condition.

When you've zoned every nook and cranny you can, turn property taxes down to zero, turn the simulation on Cheetah and watch that population rise. For a closer view, open either the Neighbors window or the Graphs window set to Size.

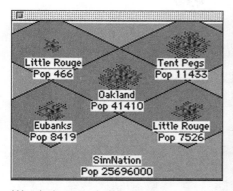

Watch the population rise here . . .

. . . or here.

HOLLYWOOD

Lights. Camera. Action. Cut. Cut! CUT! A UFO-like movie monster gets loose and ravages Tinsel Town. A terrible disaster, but great cinema.

This scenario varies a lot in difficulty every time you play it, due to the randomness of the monster's actions. The monster will always appear, but what it does and how long it stays is impossible to predict.

The monster will always destroy at least some structures, but how many depends on its mood. In the DOS version, whenever the monster blows up buildings, it sets the remains on fire more likely than not. In the Mac version, there are a few options; you'll have a one-in-three chance of whether the monster sets fires, plants trees, or places water. If you run the scenario and it places trees or water, you're in luck.

Win Condition

You need to reach a total population of 100,000 within five years.

General Strategies

Basically, you follow the monster, cleaning up after it, and pay special and immediate attention to fires.

Next you have to attract enough Sims to Hollywood to replace those that left because of the monster and reach a total population of 100,000. Since you're starting with 93,500, increasing to 100,000 is fairly easy. Once again, about all you have to do is lower taxes.

Step-by-Step Solution

Run the simulation at Turtle speed while the disaster is happening and follow the monster. Whenever it sets a fire, pause the simulation and bulldoze a fire-break around the flames. Be ruthless. Clear everything away from the flames completely. If even one fire gets out of control, chances are good that you've lost. Placing firefighters near the flames will make them burn out quicker.

Monster setting fires

Bulldozed firebreak around flames and firefighters ready to place

Set the scenario back to Turtle and repeat until the monster leaves.

Once the monster is gone, clean up after it—clear the rubble and restore power. Depending on the amount of damage, you may need to do extensive rebuilding or nothing at all.

Open the Budget window and lower property taxes. The lower the better.

Open the Neighbors window, set the simulation on Cheetah, and watch the population. It may take a dip at first, but soon it will rise and you will be a star in Hollywood.

HURRICANE HUGO DOES THE CHARLESTON

Charleston, North Carolina, is hit by a hurricane. High winds destroy buildings, then the coastline is flooded and destroyed.

Win Condition

To win Charleston, you need a total population of 45,000 within five years.

General Strategies

You start with $20,000 in cash and a thriving port town with a population of around 35,000. Instantly, a hurricane hits, and floods take out major portions of the city's coastline.

There's no quick and easy solution to this one, just a lot of cleanup work. You can protect particular favorite buildings along the coast by strategically placing your emergency patrols in the path of the flood, but you can't even put a dent in the overall damage.

Wait until the flood subsides, then start repairing, rebuilding, and expanding.

Remember that not only do you have to recover from the disaster and return to your former population, but you have to expand enough to reach a population of around 10,000 more Sims than you started with—all in five years. As with the other scenarios, the best way to get a quick jump in population is to lower taxes and make sure everyone has power and water.

Step-by-Step Solution

As always, load the scenario, pause the simulation, and select No Disasters from the Disasters menu. When the scenario begins, the high winds will damage some buildings, causing a few to explode and fires to break out.

Before the flood

Then the winds will whip up the ocean waves and, along with the precipitation, cause floods. You'll have to let the disaster take its course, but run it at Turtle speed so you have time to try to minimize the damage.

During the flood

After the flood

As soon as the floods subside, pause the simulation again. It's cleanup time. Get in there, clear out the rubble, and restore power lines and roads wherever necessary. Then rezone the recovery area to a mix of high-density residential, industrial, and commercial.

If you want to play it extra safe, you can zone, power, and water the empty land on either or both sides of the Grace Memorial Bridge. If you need more cash to complete the job, issue a bond.

Damaged area cleaned up and rezoned

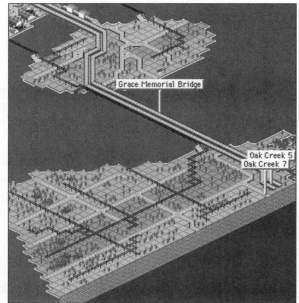

Zoning new territory

Next, make sure there is enough water for the whole city. Look at the underground view. You'll see that there are plenty of pipes, but not enough water to go around.

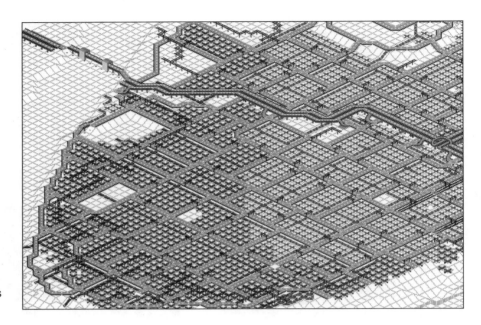

As you can see, there's
a water shortage.

Take advantage of the swamps to place water pumps with as many sides
and corners adjacent to water as possible. Power up the pumps and connect
them to the water system with pipes.

Water pumps in the
swamp

Now all you have to do is lower taxes to zero, open the Neighbors window so you can watch your population rise, and set the speed to Llama. Watch for power outages and build a new power plant if you must.

Charleston completely recovered

Solutions for the Scenarios from *SimCity 2000 Scenarios Volume 1: Great Disasters*

Atlanta

Atlanta has been invaded by a UFO. Your task is to clean up after the invasion and help the city grow larger than it was before. The win condition is to reach a residential population of 72,000 — that's *residential*, not total population, within five years. Luckily, there are no financial constraints, so you can take out as many bonds as you need and worry about the deficit after the next election.

The initial residential population is 57,000. With losses from the UFO invasion, it can fall as low as 51,000. That's a lot of residents to attract in only five years, making this a fairly difficult scenario.

Here's how to win:

- The first chance you get, open the Disasters menu and select No Disasters. The UFO is enough to deal with. Don't let all your hard work be ruined by an earthquake or a nuclear meltdown.

- Set the speed to Turtle and follow the UFO. What the UFO does, how long it sticks around, and how much damage it does are randomly determined, so hope for the best. If it sets fires, you must mercilessly bulldoze firebreaks around the fires to keep them from spreading. If you turn the building layer off, it is easier to see all the fires and keep them from spreading. Also, using the bulldozer to dezone the rubble around the fires will keep the Sims from rebuilding on your firebreaks, which would supply more fuel for the fire.

- Once the UFO leaves, dispatch your six firefighting brigades to help put out the fires.

- When all the fires are out, pause the simulation.

- Rebuild the area that was destroyed by the UFO. Restore the roads and rails, but don't worry too much about the highways. Zone most of the destroyed area to dense residential, with a few small spots of industrial and commercial to keep the commuters happy. Restore power to the rezoned areas.

- You'll need a lot of money, so open the Budget window and take out at least 10 bonds. Don't worry about paying them back until later (if at all).

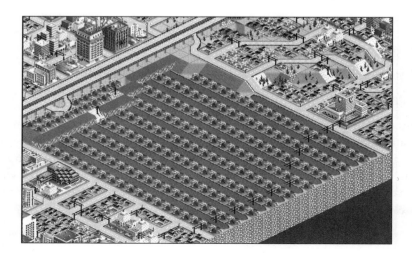

Expanded Atlanta
water supply

- One of the most important requirements for a dense population is an adequate water supply. There are two areas with water pumps and water, but they don't supply nearly enough. One way to fill this need is to expand the larger of the two water sections—the one over by the parks—with more pumps. Be dainty if you wish, but the fastest way to get that water is to clear out all the roads, wipe out the parks, and level the ground, then fill the whole area with alternating rows of water and water pumps. Be sure to supply power to all the pumps.

- Now lay water pipes (underground) throughout the city, connecting everything to the new pumps.

- Zone the open woodlands around Piedmont Lake and that whole corner of the map. Once again, zone mostly dense residential, with just enough industrial and commercial to satisfy the trip generator. Run power through the area.

- Next, slowly and carefully search the map for any unzoned areas. Zone them dense residential and hook them to the power grid.

- To get the population boost you'll need, add at least five roads and five rail connections to neighboring cities.

- Here's where you have to be ruthless. If you're lucky, you may not have to do it, but if you want to win the scenario the first time through, bulldoze those low-density suburbs and rezone them to high-density residential. Make sure they have power connections.

- Set the speed to Turtle to get the simulation going, then check above and below ground to make sure that water and power are routed to the whole city.

- Open the Budget window and set Property Taxes to zero.

- Open the Graphs window; display the Residents graph.

- Set the speed to Llama and watch the graph. As long as the residential population keeps increasing at least every two months, you're OK. If it levels off, pause the simulation, level some more low-density residential areas, and rezone them to high density.

If you followed all the instructions, you should win the scenario with at least a year to spare. Of course, the city will be in deep debt . . . but that's another scenario.

Chicago

In Chicago, the disaster part of the scenario—the chemical spill and general pollution—is a minor hassle. The hard part is to raise your industrial population from 17,000 to 44,000 in 10 years. Since there isn't any open space for adding new zones, this will require some heavy-handed destruction and redevelopment.

Once again, there are no financial constraints, so you can take out all the bond issues you want—and you'll need a lot. Here's how to beat the Chicago scenario:

- The first chance you get, open the Disasters menu and select No Disasters.
- Set the speed to Turtle and surround the pollution clouds with your three firefighting brigades. In just minutes the disaster will end, and your real task—increasing industrial population—will begin.
- Pause the simulation.
- Why wait? Open the Budget window and issue a dozen bonds. You'll need the money. At least $200,000. And don't get too high-minded and try to keep your city out of debt—you've got a number of power plants that are about to expire, and if you don't have the cash to pay for their automatic replacement, you'll lose time, energy, and population. If you have money left after you win the scenario, you can pay some of the bonds back.
- Next, give your population a water supply. You can bulldoze the water near the yacht harbor to create rows of land, then fill those rows with water pumps and power them up.
- Now look over the zoning situation. Turning off the building layer will make this easier to see. There are big, separated clumps of each zone type. You're going to have to mix up those zones and make it easier for commuters to get the density up. And you're going to need more industrial zones. Also notice that a lot of this city's landscape is covered by roads, far more than is actually necessary for happy commuting.

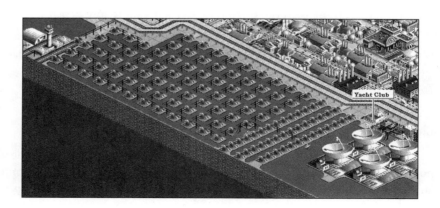

One solution to Chicago's water and power needs

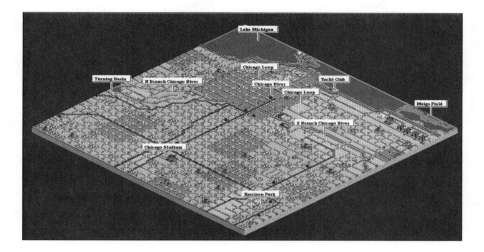

Before rezoning

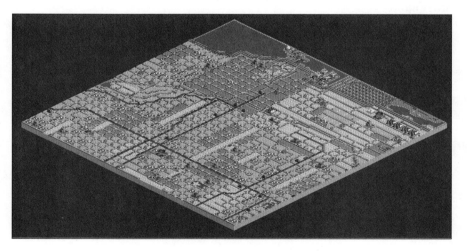

After rezoning

- The cruel but efficient way to win this scenario is to bulldoze areas of the residential-zone section and put in some commercial zones and a lot of industrial ones. Then clear out some areas in the commercial sections and put in a few residential zones and a lot of industrial zones. Then clear out small patches in the industrial areas and add a few residential and commercial zones. Take out unnecessary roads to allow more space for growth. The before-and-after shots show one rezoning possibility.
- Once your zoning is done, add a lot of rail connections to your neighbors—10 ought to do it.

- Watch your money supply! If you don't have the bucks when your power plants wear out, they'll blow. Issue those bonds!
- Open the Budget window and set taxes to zero.
- Set the speed to Turtle and make sure the whole city is getting power and water.
- Open the Graph window and turn on the Industrial Population graph.
- Set the speed to Llama and watch the industrial population grow. If it declines at all, or stagnates for more than three months in a row, pause the simulation, raze more residential and commercial zones, and turn them industrial.
- That should do it.

Davenport

Relax. Davenport is an easy scenario. All you have to do is clean up after a minor flood and raise your population from 106,000 to 118,000 in five years. The amount of damage done by the flood varies each time you play, but usually the major damage occurs on Rock Island, which houses only water and power infrastructure. There is always the chance that the shoreline south of Rock Island will suffer, but it can easily be rebuilt.

Here's how to beat Davenport:

- The first chance you get, open the Disasters menu and select No Disasters.
- Wait out the flood. When it subsides, pause the simulation.
- Restore any power plants and water pumps that were destroyed in the flood. You'll need more later, so either add them here and now, or put them somewhere else. Your choice.
- Clean up, rezone, and hook up power to any mainland areas that were hit by the flood.
- Set the simulation to Turtle and make sure water and power are well distributed.
- Pause the simulation again and add the necessary water pipes.
- Open the Budget window and issue about $100,000 worth of bonds.
- To get the population up, you'll need more zones. There's plenty of open country to develop, so that's no problem. Zone the barren corner near Bettendorf (where the PortVille and Cat's Corner edges intersect) with roads and a mix of the three zone types (all dense, of course). Be sure to supply it with power and hook it to the water grid. Add another power plant and more water pumps if necessary.

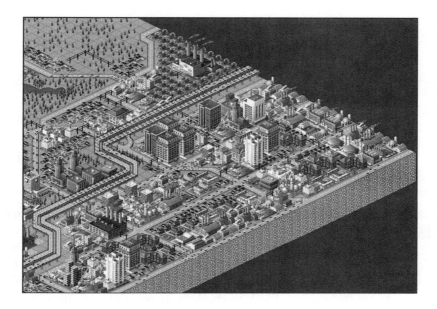

Newly zoned area

- The final thing you need to do is to give your industry a boost. Here's an industry-connection tip: Just place one tile of railroad on any edge of the city. When you're asked if you want to make a connection to a neighboring city, say yes. Repeat this a few times. The simulation counts each of these as a full, working connection. It doesn't check to see if there's any traffic on the tracks.
- Set all property taxes to zero.
- Open the Graphs window and display the City Size graph.
- Set the speed to Llama and watch the population rise. If it stops rising, pause the simulation and add a few more zones. No sweat.

Homestead

I'm going to deal with this one very briefly, because it makes me mad. It's just not fair! The text message that introduces the scenario teases you, leading you to believe that it can be won with only the $20,000 you are given. Balderdash! I ran this one 30 times and every time, there was so much damage to the power plants and the water system that it was barely possible to get Homestead back to its original population of 44,000—much less raise it to 65,000 in five years—without more money.

I tried pausing the simulation instantly, and used the Raise Terrain function of the Bulldozer tool to build a dike around the power plants and water pumps. Didn't help. You just have to ignore the tease and issue a lot of bonds. No tricks to winning this one, just brute force and brute bucks. Here's the process:

- The first chance you get, open the Disasters menu and select No Disasters.
- Wait out the hurricane. When it subsides, pause the simulation.
- Why wait? Issue a whole mess of bonds.
- Restore any power plants and water pumps that were destroyed in the flood; while you're at it, add a few more of each.
- Clean up any spots that have been damaged by winds.
- Pick a big, open spot or two and zone it with a good combination of the three zones—all high-density. Add roads, power, and water. Since you're going for a 50 percent population increase, you'll need to zone a lot of land, but not 50 percent more than the city starts with, because many of the existing zones are low-density.
- Set the speed to Turtle to check the power and water distribution.
- Set all property taxes to zero.
- Open the Graphs window and display the City Size graph.
- Set the speed to Llama and watch the population rise.
- Go back and play the Chicago scenario again. Now there's a challenge that's not a tease!

Malibu

As you read this, keep in mind that I write it with a tear in my eye. I have a lot of good childhood memories of Malibu Beach and the surrounding hills, and here I sit, telling you that you're going to have to flatten those hills and line the beaches with luxury condos to win a computer game. Yes, I know it's only a game—only a simulation—but it still feels like a betrayal of something, somehow. . . .

But enough of that. We've got a challenge to meet. In only five years, we have to raise the population of this small, exclusive little beach community of about 6,000 souls to a bustling city of 27,500. Oh yes, and we have to put out a fire, too. (So what else is new? This is Malibu—floods, fires, and mud-slides are the norm around here.)

Here's the plan:

- As soon as you can get that Speed menu to open, pause the simulation. If you don't get it right away, the fire will spread and burn so many movie stars out of their homes that we won't see any good new movies for years.

- Once the simulation is paused, open the Disasters menu and select No Disasters.

- Deal with the fire: Bulldoze a fire break around it, then dezone the rubble to keep it from being redeveloped and becoming a fire hazard.

- Set the speed to Turtle and deploy your two firefighting brigades.

- When the fire subsides, pause the simulation again, clean up the mess, and restore the damaged areas.

- Before we go on, let's analyze the situation. Basically, we've got to supply infrastructure for an additional 22,000 people. That requires quite a bit of flat, buildable land. Half this city is water and unbuildable. Most of the land consists of mountains without any large enough flat spaces for efficient roads or high-density buildings. Most of the existing flat land is already sprinkled with low-density zones; the rest is a beautiful beach that, if at all possible, should remain a beautiful beach for the sake of posterity. There are a number of approaches you can take, but the one we suggest here is to flatten the mountains and build dense communities. That way we can leave the existing town of Malibu and the beaches as untouched as possible. Besides, with all the floods, fires, and mudslides that happen around here, the average Sim couldn't afford the insurance to live down there.

- This job will take a lot of money, so issue bonds, bonds, and more bonds. But wait! The difference between this scenario and the previous few is that the bank won't let you take all you'll need. Your credit rating is too low. If there's a trick to this scenario (call it a deep understanding of the simulation if you're above tricks), it's knowing that your credit rating is based on the value of the infrastructure. Such a small town as Malibu, with few roads and only one power plant, doesn't have much collateral. The solution is to go ahead and issue whatever bonds you can, then build some roads and maybe a power plant, then issue more bonds, then build more, then issue . . . you get the idea.

- Now's the time to let go of my childhood, set the Bulldozer tool to Level Terrain, and flatten the mountains all along the edge opposite the ocean. The more you lower the peaks, the more flat, buildable land you'll have, and the more likely it is that you'll take out some existing houses. You'll need a *lot* of flat, buildable land. If you don't bite the bullet now and lower the peaks enough, you'll have to zone some of the flat beach area to reach the population goal.

- Once the mountains are flattened, build an efficient infrastructure of roads and zones. Add power plants as needed and run power lines. •

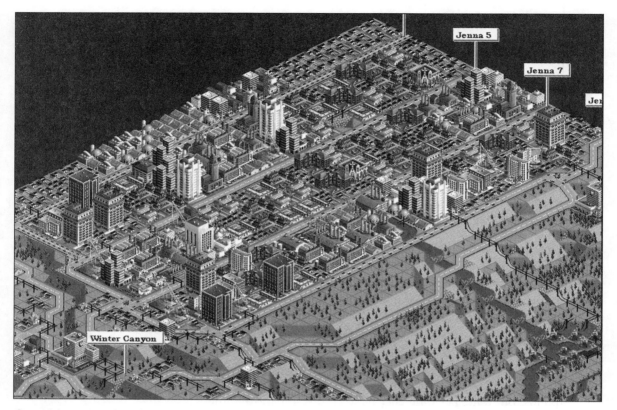

One of the mountains after
leveling and development

- Line Malibu Creek with a dozen or so water pumps and run pipes through the new areas.
- Set the speed to Turtle and make sure you have full power distribution.
- Open the Graphs window and display the City Size graph.
- Set the property taxes to zero, set the speed to Llama, and watch the population rise.
- Check regularly to make sure there's enough water and power for the growing population.
- If you flattened the mountains enough, you shouldn't have to do anything but wait. But if the rise in population slows or stops, you can zone some of the flat beach area for the extra population boost you'll need to win this depressing scenario.

Manhattan

As scenarios go, Manhattan isn't very difficult, but there is a lot of damage control and cleanup work. When the nuclear plant blows, fires and radiation spread far and wide. After the fires have been put out and the damage is as cleaned-up as it can be, you've got to get your population back up to its original 118,000, and then up to 130,000. The 10 years you're given is easily enough time. This one can actually be won in five years or less.

Here's how:

- The very first instant you possibly can, pause the simulation.
- Open the Disasters menu and select No Disasters.
- Fires will already be spreading through the city, so surround each patch of fire with a bulldozed fire break. Dezone the rubble to keep it from being redeveloped and becoming more fuel for the fire.
- Set the simulation to Turtle to let the rest of the explosions (if any) occur, then pause it again and build more fire breaks.
- Back to Turtle again, as you deploy your seven firefighting brigades to put out the fires.
- Once the fires are out, pause the simulation and start rebuilding the damaged areas. While you're out there cleaning things up, go ahead and remove some of the unnecessary roads that take up space but don't contribute to the simulation's commuter requirements.
- Restoring power will take some doing, for a number of reasons. You've lost at least one of your nuclear plants, the city is so big that it takes a while for the simulation to get around to doing its power checks, and those pesky flashing radiation signs make it harder to focus on the pesky flashing power signs. Since this city has had bad luck with nuclear plants and needs lots of power for expansion, go ahead and buy a few fusion plants. They're expensive, but that's what bond issues are for.
- Open the money bag—er, I mean Budget window—and issue a few hundred thousand dollars' worth of bonds.
- Luckily, the city already has a good water supply. If you make sure to restore power to the pumps right away, water becomes a nonissue.
- If you clean up and rezone the damaged areas, and remove enough roads to make up for the land use you lost due to radiation, you'll have no problem getting your population back up to the original 118,000. But to boost it to 130,000, you'll need to develop more land. As always, you have a number of options. The one chosen for this explanation is to use the Bulldozer to create a landfill island in the

The new Hudson River landfill

Hudson River. You'll need to turn at least two-thirds of the river (at least the part of the river that you have access to) to land. OK, OK, I know. All you wonderful people from New York are going to get upset about this, but if I can level the Malibu hills, you can live with a little landfill in your river. After all, it's not as if I'd asked you to develop Central Park (an option I'd rather not even discuss).

- Once you've created your landfill island, give it roads, zones, water, and power.
- Add a few industry connections (highways or rails off the edges of the map), and you're all set.
- Set all property taxes to zero.
- Set the speed to Turtle and make sure the whole city is hooked to the water and power grids.
- Open the Graphs window and display the City Size graph.
- Set the speed to Llama and watch the population rise.
- This one, though it involved a lot of cleanup, was easy. You might say it was a walk in the park (unless, of course, you did develop the park).

Portland

Portland isn't a difficult scenario, but it takes a long time and some tough decisions. When the volcano erupts, it does massive damage to the city center; if you don't get the fires under control right away, the city is doomed.

And once you get that under control, you have only five years to build the city from 102,000 to 115,000.

Here's one solution:

- At the very first possible instant, which will be after the volcano rises from the ground, spewing fire for miles around, pause the simulation.
- Open the Disasters menu and select No Disasters.
- Deal with the fires. You know: Bulldoze fire breaks, dezone the rubble, set the simulation to Turtle, and dispatch your firefighters.
- Once the fires are out, pause the simulation, then go to the Budget window and issue a lot of bonds.
- Set the Bulldozer tool to Level Terrain and flatten the volcano.
- Rebuild the destroyed areas, mixing the three zones (all high-density), and distribute water and power. You should have enough power plants for the whole scenario—unless you lost some to fires—but you'll need more water pumps: at least a dozen, more if they aren't on the water.
- With these repairs made, it's time for the tough decision. In order to entice those extra 13,000 Sims to move in, you'll need more and denser zones. You can get subtle here, but the two sure-fire brute-force methods are these: Flatten the whole Portland Heights corner of the map and develop it, or tear out about half of the existing suburbs. Since we've destroyed so much natural beauty in the last few scenarios, let's redevelop suburbia.
- Get mean. Get ruthless. Get your Bulldozer and clear out at least half of those spread-out, sprawling, low-density single-family residential zones. Wipe them off the map. And get rid of the extra roads while you're at it.
- Once the suburbs are cleared out, rezone them with a good mix of the three zones (heavy on residential). Give them power. They should already have water.
- Set property taxes to zero.
- Set the speed to Turtle until you're sure water and power are well distributed.
- Add a few industry (highway or rail) connections for good measure.
- Open the Graphs window and display the City Size graph.
- Set the speed to Llama and watch the population rise.
- If it slows or stops rising, pause the simulation, clear out more low-density residential areas, and rezone them, or zone the flatlands surrounding Portland Heights.

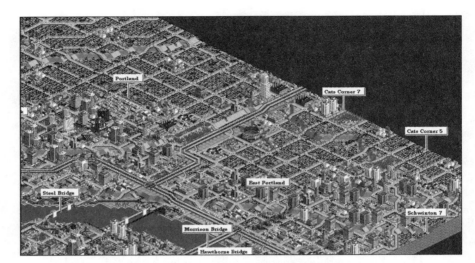

Portland before
redevelopment

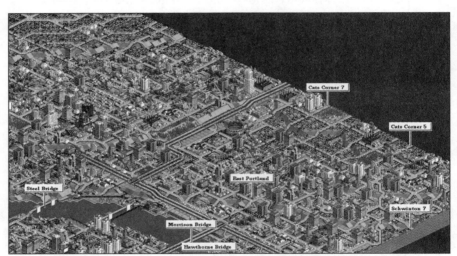

Bye-bye, suburbia!

San Francisco

The original *SimCity Classic* came with a scenario depicting the 1906 San Francisco earthquake. This one is not only updated for *SimCity 2000*, but is also moved to the year 1989 for the Loma Prieta earthquake. In this scenario, you wait out the shaking, then deal with the fires caused by broken gas mains. Then you have to raise the city's population from 54,000 to 68,000. This one isn't very difficult to win, and if you stay open-minded, you won't even have to change the existing city at all. Here's how to win:

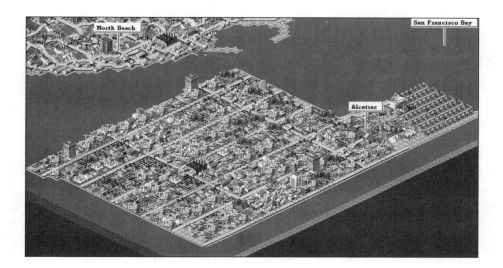

Alcatraz Landfill

- At the first possible instant, pause the simulation.
- Open the Disasters menu and select No Disasters.
- Get the fires under control: bulldoze fire breaks and dezone the rubble.
- Chances are there are still a few explosions ahead, so set the simulation to Turtle, let them happen, pause the simulation again, and get the new fires under control.
- Set the simulation to Turtle again and dispatch your firefighters.
- Once the fires are out, pause the simulation again and rebuild the damaged areas. Make sure power is restored to the whole city.
- To get to the required population level, you've got three choices: Develop every park, including Golden Gate Park; wipe out all the low-density residential areas and rezone them to high-density; or (my choice) build a landfill extension to Alcatraz.
- Go ahead and issue bonds for about $100,000.
- Use the Level Terrain setting of the Bulldozer to create a nice big extension to Alcatraz. About 35 by 45 tiles ought to do it.
- Give it roads and zone it. Supply power and water.
- Set all property taxes to zero.
- Open the Graphs window and display the City Size graph.
- Set the speed to Llama. In just a few years you'll have won.

Silicon Valley

Here's another easy scenario—if you understand the basics of the *SimCity 2000* simulation. You've got your disaster—a minor "oops" that only costs you a power plant and a few other buildings, if you act fast. And you've got to get your industrial population from 33,000 to 48,000 in five years. Since there's plenty of wide-open flat space, this kind of growth is no problem. All you have to do is:

- Pause the simulation as soon as you can.
- Deal with the fire from the microwave beam: fire breaks and dezoning.
- Set the speed to Turtle and deploy your firefighters.
- When the fire's out, clean up the mess.
- Issue about $150,000 worth of bonds.
- Now it's just a matter of expanding the city with roads, zones, water, and power. Though the goal of this scenario is to increase your industrial population, don't just place industrial zones. You need the others for support. You should zone at least 65% of the currently empty ground to ensure quick success.
- Replacing the lost microwave power plant with a single fusion plant will give you all the power you'll need.
- You'll need to add a lot more water pumps and run pipes through the new zoned areas.
- Lower property taxes to zero.
- Set the speed to Turtle until you're sure the whole city has water and power.
- Open the Graphs window and display the Industrial population graph. (You might also want to display the Water percentage graph. If it falls below five percent, add more water pumps.)
- Set the speed to Llama, kick back, put your feet up, and win.

Washington DC

Washington DC is one of the easiest scenarios to beat, even if those martini-besotted lawyers are a pain. Beyond dealing with rioters and their fires, the population goal—raising it from 118,000 to 135,000—is rather simple if you don't mind turning the Capitol into a business park and giving the President a few thousand condo-dwelling neighbors.

Here's the solution:

- As soon as you can, pause the simulation.

- Open the Disasters menu and select No Disasters.
- Those rioters have already set some fires, so deal with them: Turn off the building layer so you can see them all, bulldoze firebreaks, and dezone the rubble.
- Once the existing fires (don't worry, there'll be more) are isolated with fire breaks, and while the simulation is still paused, dispatch all your firefighters to start putting the fires out.
- Dispatch your policemen to surround different groups of rioters.
- Set the simulation to Turtle until more fires start, then pause it again.
- Bulldoze fire breaks, dezone the rubble, redeploy your police and firefighters.
- Repeat the preceding two steps until no more fires start.
- Quench new fires with your firefighters; surround and quell all the rioters with your police.
- Once the fires and the rioters are gone, pause the simulation, clean up the mess, rebuild, and rezone.
- Analysis time. No, not with the president's analyst. We've got to get the population to rise by about 17,000. Not too difficult, considering all the flat, open space we have to work with. Now, I suppose it might be possible to win this scenario without zoning all those parks and patriotic open spaces—if you painstakingly get rid of a lot of the roads, and redevelop all the low-density areas into high-density ones. But I'm getting lazy. This is the fifteenth scenario and my Bulldozer finger is tired out. If you want to be tricky and preserve our national heritage, go ahead. But for the easiest solution, follow the next few steps.
- Issue some bonds. $100,000 ought to do it. And don't worry about taking too much. It's a Capitol expense (some may say a joke like that is a Capitol offense).
- Build roads and zone *all* the empty space. Fill those parks and surround those monuments. Make the Mall a mall. Turn Potomac Park into a planned community. Chop down those cherry trees around the Washington Monument and zone, zone, zone! Leave no open space undeveloped.
- Add a half-dozen industry connections. (Just place rail tiles on the edge of the map and you'll be offered a chance to buy a connection. Go for it. The voters (and the simulation) will never know the difference. A half-dozen connections will do it.
- You'll have plenty of power (unless you lost a power plant to the riots), but you'll need to add a lot of water pumps.

D.C. developed

- Set the taxes to zero.
- Set the speed to Turtle until you're sure there's full water and power distribution.
- Open the Graphs window and display the City Size graph.
- Set the speed to Llama and count your votes.

Solutions for the Great Cities Scenarios from the *SimCity 2000 CD Collection*

These three scenarios are available only on the *SimCity 2000 CD Collection*. Each city has a special replacement building or two that can be displayed in *SimCity 2000* if you use *SCURK* to swap the graphics.

Barcelona

The Barcelona scenario is easy and it's a beautiful city, too. All you have to do is raise your population from 120,000 to 130,000 in five years. Oh, and clean up after an atomic explosion, which is a chore, but nothing to worry about if you act quickly. Here's the scoop:

- As soon as you can, pause the simulation.
- Open the Disasters menu and select No Disasters.

- Deal with the fires: turn off the building layer, bulldoze fire breaks, and dezone the rubble.
- Set the speed to Turtle and deploy your firefighters until the fires are out.
- Pause the simulation again and clean up the mess: replace the roads and zones.
- Make sure power is supplied to the whole city. Unless you lost a power plant to fire, you won't need to build any more.
- What you will need to get this city to grow is an increased water supply. Pick a nice empty corner and place alternating strips of water pumps and water in it. Power up the pumps and add pipes to distribute the water throughout the city.
- Add a few industry connections. A half-dozen "cheater" one-tile rails at any edge will do.
- There's a chance that if you didn't have much fire damage, and if the radiation doesn't make too much of your land unusable, you can now set the property taxes to zero and come close to reaching the 130,000 population goal. But then again, you might not. Let's win this scenario so we can say we did, then go on to creating our own cities instead of picking up after someone else. Some serious money and a bulldozer should get the job done.
- Issue about $150,000 worth of bonds.
- Take a good, close look at the beautiful, rolling green hills, because they won't be there for long. Set your Bulldozer to Level Terrain and flatten a couple of hills. Add roads, zones, and power and water pipes.

Barcelona hills leveled
for zoning

- Set the simulation to Turtle until you're sure water and power are well distributed.
- Open the Graphs window and display the City Size graph.
- Set the speed to Llama and your work is done.

Las Vegas

This is the only add-on scenario that has a goal other than a population level. How refreshing! In this one, you've got to get crime under control—down to 5% in five years. Not too difficult—and there are no fires! Best yet, you can win this one without issuing any bonds.

Here goes:

- Pause the simulation as soon as you can.
- Open the Disasters menu and select No Disasters.
- Open the Ordinances window and turn off Legalized Gambling. Turn on Anti-Drug Campaign, Neighborhood Watch, and Homeless Shelters. (Homeless shelters may not do much to affect crime, but it's a good thing to do.)
- Build two or three prisons.
- Place a dozen or so police stations spaced out all over the city. (You'll have to clear out some other buildings to make room, but be ruthless—this is crime you're fighting.)
- Open the Map window and display the Crime Rate map.
- Set the simulation to Turtle and see how the new stations affect the crime rate.
- With the Map window open, locate the areas that still have high crime; put police stations at the worst spots.
- Before you know it, you'll be a winner.

Paris

This scenario is demanding. You have to make use of every spare square inch of ground and do some redeveloping. You have five years to get a fire under control and raise your population from 152,000 to 169,000.

Here's how:

- As soon as you can, pause the simulation.
- Open the Disasters menu and select No Disasters.
- Deal with the fire in the usual way.

The Jardin du
Luxembourg

- Rebuild the damaged areas.
- If you analyze the city, you'll find that there's plenty of power, unless the fire got out of hand and destroyed a power plant. You'll also find that there are quite a few water pumps, but no water distribution.
- Go underground and run pipes to and from all the water pumps all over the city.
- You've got a lot of pumps, but not enough. One way to add more is to turn the Jardin du Luxembourg into a fountain with pumps and water.
- Set the speed to Turtle and make sure power and water are well distributed. If you need more water, add more pumps. You can find a spot for them.
- Next, pause the simulation and develop every last park with roads, zones, power, and water.
- That still won't be enough, but there is a solution. The RCI indicator tells you that you have a surplus of industrial zones. If you let the simulation run for a while, many of those zones will be abandoned. Clear out these abandoned industrial zones—be careful not to take out any power plants—and rezone them to a mix of residential and commercial. Add roads, water, and power.
- Set all property taxes to zero.
- Set the speed to Turtle to make sure everything is hooked up.

- Open the Graphs window and display the City Size graph.
- Set the speed to Llama and watch the population rise. If it slows or stops, pause the simulation, bulldoze the diagonal highway, and develop the reclaimed space.

CHAPTER
14

Recreating Cities from Maps

One of the first, most common, and favorite things people do with *SimCity* and *Sim-City 2000* is to recreate their home town (or home city). And in order to create the scenarios, the folks at Maxis had first to build models of all those existing cities.

This chapter will help you recreate models of real cities in *SimCity 2000*, choose good cities to simulate, locate the proper maps, and undertake a step-by-step map-to-city procedure.

PICK A CITY, ANY CITY

When choosing a city to recreate, remember that there are limitations to the types of cities that *SimCity 2000* can simulate well.

Scale is a big issue in selecting a city to simulate. The size of the total city limits in *SimCity 2000* is about five miles by five miles. Each tile is approximately one acre. The cities that work best are ones with outer dimensions between one mile by one mile and five miles by five miles.

If you build a town that's only a few acres in size, you won't see very much on the screen to begin with. These can be good starting points and can be used for planning and projecting possible future growth, but trying to scale a tiny town up to fill a *Sim-City 2000* landform doesn't represent the town very well.

And if you try to build a city that's much bigger by scaling it down, you'll lose too many of the important roads. If you want to build a really big city, then do it in five-mile-by-five-mile segments.

If you have a particular reason to choose a city, such as that you live there or just like the place, so be it. If you're just looking for a good city to recreate and play with, try to pick one with some variation in altitude and some water (rivers or lakes). And picking a city that fills between one-half and three-fourths of the total landform is a good idea, so that you have enough of the city to keep its flavor but have plenty of room to grow and make it your own.

USING MAPS TO START YOUR CITY

Once you've chosen a city, you need a map. In general, the best type of map to use (and the easiest to get) is a topographic map. These maps show:

- The terrain, including elevation and water locations
- City infrastructure, including roads, highways, police stations, and fire departments
- Other important civic structures, including hospitals, schools, colleges, and churches
- The shape of the city itself; you can usually guess pretty closely which zones are which.

Topographic maps come in different scales. A 7½-minute topographic map is at a good scale for transferring to *SimCity 2000*.

7½-minute topographic maps are $2.50 each from the United States Geological Survey. You can call or write the USGS (U.S. Geological Survey, Denver, CO 80225 or Reston, VA 22092) and tell them what state you're interested in. They'll send you a booklet that shows the whole state, and you can pick out the individual maps that you want. Sometimes the city you want may be located on a few different maps.

Another good source of maps is the Rand McNally map store. There are about 25 of them spread around the U.S. Their customer service number is 800-333-0136.

Map Link, 24 East Mason St., Suite 201, Santa Barbara, CA 93101, is a map wholesaler and distributor that also does some retail business. You can contact them by phone (805-965-4402) or fax (800-627-7768) to get a catalog.

If you want to get even more detailed, and to be as accurate as possible with the different zones and densities, you can contact the planning commission of the city you want to build. They *may* have a service that will duplicate and send you a copy of their actual up-to-date zoning maps. And then again, they may have only old ones, or none at all. The situation varies from city to city.

Sometimes, when planning commissions are touting their future plans in an attempt to attract new citizens and businesses, they prepare a brochure of what they expect their city to be like in five years or so. (If you call them and tell them that you are a businessperson thinking of locating your business to their town, they'll probably rush it right out to you. But don't tell them we sent you.)

The best thing to do is just call or visit your chosen city's city hall and ask for the zoning department. Eventually you may make your way through the bureaucracy and find someone who can help you.

THE PROCEDURE TO RECREATE YOUR CITY

1. Once you get the maps you need, mark out the outer perimeter of the area you want to simulate. For a good scale match with *SimCity 2000*, mark out a five-mile-by-five-mile square.

2. Divide the square into an 8 × 8 grid, creating 64 equal-sized blocks. Each block will then translate to 16 × 16 tiles in the *SimCity 2000* landform. If you intend to recreate a number of cities, or you don't want to mark up the maps, you may want to make a reusable grid template on a clear plastic sheet that you can place over your maps.

3. Fire up *SimCity 2000* and choose **Edit New Map**.

4. On the Terrain Toolbar, make sure the Coast and River buttons are up and set the three sliders all the way down.

5. Click on Make to create a really boring place.

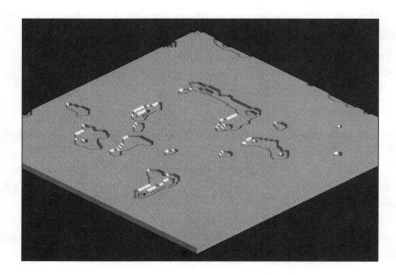

6. Unfortunately, the landform, as generated, will have some features. Use the Bulldozer to get rid of them. No trees, no hills, no water, no nothing. Just flat, barren terrain:

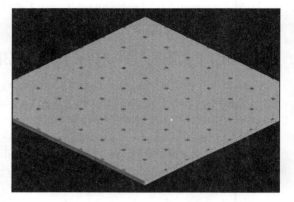

7. Mark off the squares of 16×16 tiles with trees to create a grid that matches the grid on the map, by putting trees at each intersection. You can always remove them later:

8. Square by square, mold the landform elevation on the computer to match the landform on the map. Each tile of elevation represents approximately 100 feet on the topographic map.

9. Add water, square by square.

10. Add major highways, square by square, then roads.

11. Add infrastructure buildings and important civic buildings.

12. To the best of your ability, place zones to match the city.

13. Whether or not the city you're recreating has a power plant, it'll need one in *SimCity 2000*. And power lines, and water pumps and pipes.

14. Turn on the simulation and see if it flies.

In sum, remember: You won't be able to make a perfect copy of the city. You'll have to fudge the data a little to get them to work in *SimCity 2000*. You'll need to leave out the smaller roads, and anything that's smaller than an acre will have to be scaled up to a full acre or eliminated. But that's OK. This is a model, not a real city.

If you've built a city you're proud of, put it up on the BBSs and share it with others. And send along a Readme file that gives your name and explains a little about the city and why you made it.

P A R T
IV

The Making of *SimCity 2000*

Introduction to
The Making of *SimCity 2000*

During the years that the original *SimCity* (now called *SimCity Classic*) has been played, thousands of people who bought and played it contacted the makers and let them know what they thought about it.

Almost unanimously, the cards, letters, faxes, and e-mail messages said something like, "*SimCity* is great—but I want more."

And, unlike many politicians, those *SimCity* mayors not only pointed out the problems but offered good suggestions and solutions. Maxis gathered those suggestions and kept them. Many of them were great, some of them were silly, and a few of them were so complex that they'd work better as complete games.

SimCity 2000 exists because computer entertainment enthusiasts demanded more: more details, more reality, more art, more animation, more sound, more music, and more fun. And now that personal computers with enough memory and disk storage—and sound and color capabilities—are affordable, the time is right for *SimCity 2000*.

So, the time was right . . . What then?

- How do you turn an idea into a game?
- What kinds of personality traits and skills go into the making of such a game?
- How does *SimCity 2000* work?
- Who does the work?
- How long does it take?
- What goes on behind the scenes?
- What are the worst parts of making a computer game?
- What are the best parts?

Part IV: The Making of SimCity 2000 will attempt to give you an idea of what is involved in creating a game like *SimCity 2000*. The subject will be approached from the outside—interviews with the key people involved in the project; from the inside—a detailed description of the simulation model upon which *SimCity 2000* is based; and from the long-term perspective—what the future holds for *SimCity*.

But first, here are a few game design "words of wisdom" gleaned from conversations and personal experience that may help put the following chapters into perspective:

- The *easiest* part of making *SimCity 2000* was coming up with more things to throw into the simulation.

- The *hardest* part was deciding what to leave out: how to have enough elements to make the game complex, interesting, and realistic, but few enough that it will run fast enough to be a fun, challenging game, or even run on something smaller and more affordable than a super computer—and without so many little picky details that it won't be fun for the player.

- The *most complex* part of the design is the balancing, sometimes called game balancing—controlling the system so that little problems don't snowball into huge, unmanageable ones. And that's only the complexity of the inner simulation model. Putting it into a graphical form, hooking together all the different aspects of a city, and keeping it streamlined enough to run on a personal computer (where graphics already consume most of the time and power spent by the processor) is not an easy task.

- The *tedious* part is making sure the complex part is done right. And the only way to do that is through a lot of trial and error, a lot of writing code, testing code, throwing it out, rewriting it, and testing it again, as well as a lot of play-testing by people who are experts at finding problems and bugs in both logic and interface.

15

The Making of *SimCity 2000*

This section of the book is a series of . . . well, they're something between interviews and conversations between Michael Bremer and the various key people who contributed to the creation of *SimCity 2000*. We covered the making of the game, but we also tried to talk a bit about what the different jobs are, and generally what it's like to work in this industry. Sometimes the conversations strayed a bit from the subject, but much of that straying was left in to give you an idea of the personalities of the kinds of people who make games like *SimCity 2000*.

THE PRODUCTION OF *SIMCITY 2000*

Don Walters was the producer for the SimCity 2000 project. The job title of "producer" is a confusing one that means different things in different industries. In the film industry, the producer is the person with primary personal and financial responsibility to get the job done. Producers have lots of power. In the record industry, the producer is more like the director of a film. They have the artistic control, but there are usually financial people watching over. And in the computer entertainment industry, the term producer means very different things in different companies.

So, Don, what the heck is a producer, anyway?

Basically a producer—at least here at Maxis—is a project leader who coordinates all the different parts of the project and makes sure everything happens.

The implementer?

More of a coordinator of the project as a whole. There are other people in charge of the different components: the programmer, art director; documentation writer. . . . They all implement their portion of the project. The producer coordinates all those activities into one unified project.

What are all the different parts of a project?

There are the music people writing music; sound effects people coming up with sound effects; writers writing game text, help text, manuals, addendums, back of box copy, PR materials; people who are designing the box; people who are designing the collateral pieces that go in the box; various programmers to program the game; artists who make all the art that goes into the game; testers to track down the bugs; manufacturing people to make it a product; marketing people; sales people . . . and a few more.

How did you get either blessed or stuck with this gig [depending on the mood for the day]?

I knew somebody. Getting into this whole industry was a compete fluke. I was going to college and ran out of money. A friend who was moving out to California asked me to come along, and I said, "Sure." Once there I met someone who was working at Brøderbund, which ran at that time a division called Kyodai for importing and porting Japanese computer games. He hired me there.

What did you do at Kyodai?

I was in charge of Q.A., customer service, and tech support. Which means I was Q.A., customer service, and tech support. It was a small group. I had three temps that helped me out sometimes.

Then what happened?

After a while Brøderbund shut down Kyodai. At that time, Maxis was expanding and hiring, and I got the job.

What other Maxis projects have you produced or worked on?

RoboSport, *SimAnt*, and *El-Fish* on various different computer platforms.

What's the best part of being a producer?

The chance to work with really interesting people. Especially at Maxis. I've learned so much from working on these products—about things other than computers and computer companies. Like in SimAnt, I learned a lot about ants and other insects—social insects—more than I ever thought about learning. It's an education.

What did you learn from doing *El-Fish*?

I learned a lot about Russians.[1] It was interesting because I hadn't had much interaction with Russians before. They had always been portrayed as the enemy while I was growing up, during the cold war. I had never been there or known anyone from there. And all the information we heard about Russia was pretty much propaganda, from our side or theirs. To meet people that lived through those times, but on the other side, was pretty interesting.

What's the worst part about being a producer—or is there one?

Stress. Basically, you have the responsibility for getting a project out, but since you aren't actually doing all the different pieces, you don't have direct control on when they're completed. Sometimes it's pretty stressful trying to coordinate different types of people and make them work together as a team. Sometimes there's friction between different elements of a project.

You play peacemaker?

I try to. I'm getting a little better at it, but it's the worst part of the job.

What are the hours like?

At the beginning stages of a project, when there's not much going on, it's pretty sweet—six, eight hours a day. And then at the end of a project, it can be 12 to 16 hours a day, seven days a week, 31 days a month for three or four months. That can be pretty stressful, too.

How many projects do you produce at once?

It's different at different companies, but here at Maxis, we have a few projects at a time, but we try to time them so we're in crunch mode on only one at a time.

And crunch mode is . . . ?

The final couple months of the project, when you're trying to get all the bugs out of the code, get the last minute collateral together, just putting the final project together. That deadline is getting close and there are always final details to take care of, and fast.

---

[1]The program *El-Fish*™ was a true child of perestroika—a joint venture between Russian and American companies. It was based on a product and advanced artificial life technology created in Russia by Vladimir Pokhilko and Alexey Pajitnov (designer of *Tetris* and other games), and polished, packaged, and turned into a commercial product by the Maxis team.

Say someone is reading this book, and really likes *SimCity 2000*, and thinks, "Gee, I want to work on a project like that. I want to produce games." What would you tell them to do to prepare for the job?

Buy a lot of Maalox.

Invest in the Tums company?

Definitely invest in the Tums company. And be prepared to spend half of your time on a project at work, away from your family and the rest of your life.

What should somebody who wants a job like this know before applying?

You should have fairly decent people skills, communication skills, both written and oral. You have to be able to mentally multitask and work on a number of different things simultaneously. You should also be pretty familiar with all the different components that make up a game. You need to know everything from a general idea of how computers work to how the printing process works, and even manufacturing. Be familiar with different computer platforms. . . .

Would working for a while as a tester help prepare you for producing?

That helps a lot. Especially if you aren't familiar with all the different computer platforms. After being a tester, you'll know it all. And the testers work pretty closely with producers, programmers, and writers so they learn the whole process by association. Ideally, tester would be a good way to start.

Is it important to like games, or can you look at this as "just a job"?

If you're going to produce entertainment software, you need to know what is entertaining and what is fun. A lot of times, the products that are being designed by someone else may need a push in a certain direction. A fresh set of eyes can help, if the eyes know what to look for. You should have a good idea of what makes a good interface to present the information.

So you're involved with the design?

Pretty much everyone on the team has many different ideas, and all those ideas are evaluated and a lot are implemented. Everyone on the team has input—and the team's big. I'd say I contribute more to interface design than to the game play, but I do what I can.

So it's not like the old days where there's one hacker sitting alone in a room and hands off a finished game?

Some games are still designed that way, but our products are usually pretty large and complex. They're not a side-scrolling, story-boarded decision tree.

These games have millions of possibilities. It's not just a straight-through approach.

So the more freedom you have as a player, the more complexity you have as a developer?

Yeah. It's just not quite as easy to sit down and design everything out beforehand and know it will work the way it will on paper.

What about technology? How much do you have to stay on top of the newest toys and trends?

You have to stay totally on top of it all. Sometimes it seems like that new technology is coming so fast that it's passed over your head and you end up scrambling to try to understand the latest trends. But as the technology advances, so must your products, to take advantage of the new capabilities. And yet you have to support the existing, older technology, too. And platforms—you always want to know what platform to choose for a product. If it takes a year or two or more to create a game, you have to predict what the popular platforms will be that far down the road.

How do you know?

You don't. You can have opinions. You can make educated guesses. But you really don't know.

THE ART FOR *SIMCITY 2000*

Jenny Martin is Maxis' Art Director, responsible for the quality and timing of the on-screen (as opposed to printed) art in SimCity 2000. *Her duties included coordinating all the artwork—setting and maintaining the visual style of the art for the project.*

Tell me about yourself . . . your life in 30 seconds. . . .

I started out working as a photographer, and doing illustrations, somewhat, on the side. Then, I started working at a company that did computer graphics slides. That was my first introduction to computers. At that time we were using a $100,000 system to do what you can now do on the average PC.

So, I started doing illustrations for slides. And then went to work at EPYX, started doing Commodore 64 games, and IBM—what was that ugly four-color mode? . . . CGA, oh boy, I can't even remember that anymore—Apple II, and all that good stuff. I worked at EPYX for about two years. Then I worked at Bally Sente, which was Bally Corporation's California Arcade division [which was previously owned by Nolan Bushnell]. I did arcades for a year, and then I freelanced for three years, working for almost all the companies here in the Bay Area: Accolade, Mediagenic, Brøderbund, and some smaller houses that were doing work for Sega, etc. And then I joined Maxis, three years ago March, as Art Director.

What do you think about the art in *SimCity 2000*?

Out of all the titles that I've worked on over the years, I'm probably the most proud of *SimCity 2000*. I think we've really pushed the envelope. I always loved *SimCity* as a game before I worked here, but I wished it had more detail. The graphics were OK for the time, but I sort of longed for more. So working on the title, in general, was a lot of fun, and I really think that Suzie [Greene] who was lead artist, and Kelli [Pearson] and Bonnie [Borucki] and Eben [Sorkin] did a great job bringing it into a realistic, sort of whole new world.

What [if anything] do you think is special or new about the art in this program?

Other than the view[2] which is pretty obvious, I think just the level of detail, going down to little tiny cars in the parking lots, or having the ad on the screen in the movie theater, or the Maxis building. That sort of thing, it's real personable-like.

How would you describe the artistic style in this game?

I think the style would be classified as realistic. It's not real stylized, it's pretty heavily realistic. Cities don't have one style, so we wanted to make a mix of the deco and the modern and the old style ornate buildings. We didn't want to make it all look the same. We looked at tons of books, tons of building books.

How would you describe the technical style used in *SimCity 2000* art?

We *are* dealing with tiles, although we've had more freedom than typically associated with tile artwork. Usually tile artwork means piecing everything together out of little 16-by-16-pixel tiles, with a limited palette. On this project, we had a strict size for the base of the building, but from there up, it didn't matter. We're not doing the giant, beautifully painted and scanned backgrounds, but we did have a lot of freedom in creating whatever we wanted within the size limitations.

How did working in 256 colors change things compared to Maxis' previous 16 color work? Easier? Harder? Take longer?

It does take longer. But it's such a freeing thing. And you still *do* run out of

---

[2]A simulated 3-D, sometimes called 2½-D, perspective view.

colors. You always think, "If I just had one more color." And then you look at *SimFarm* and remember that you did that with only 15 colors. But 256 colors is nice. We actually only used about 152 colors, because the rest were cycle colors, so we didn't really get the full free range.

How did you do the color cycling?

Thankfully, Will [Wright] did all of it. We didn't do any of it. So it was something that Will did for us—the cars and traffic. He basically figured out if it could work, and he had done so much art work while figuring it out that it was basically done and left that way.

If you look at the final palette, it's pretty confusing what he did and how he made it work on each tile. We were more than happy to let him handle that.

So a lot of the colors out of the total palette of 256 are reserved for the cycling aspect to make animations?

There might even be as many as 100 colors taken out of the palette for cycling colors.

What other technical aspects or limitations or extra flexibility did you deal with?

Drawing the three different sizes of everything was a technical feat. We had to draw them in the largest size, cut them in half, clean them up, cut them in half, clean them up. So by the time you're done with a building, you're pretty sick of that building.

How many different buildings were there?

You know, I haven't even counted how many different buildings there were.

Each one of them had to be done in three sizes?

Yeah, each one was in three sizes.

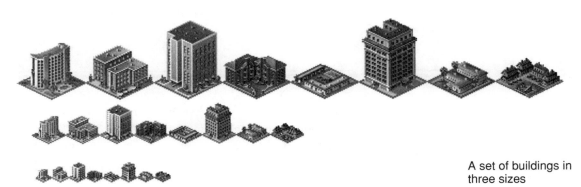

A set of buildings in three sizes

Colors, the Palette, and Color Cycling

These days, Macintosh, DOS, and Windows all support thousands, if not millions, of possible colors, but these systems usually limit the number of those colors that can appear on the screen at a time. Most computer games these days support either 16 or 256 simultaneous colors.

The more colors you want to display at a time, the more memory it requires to hold that information—that's memory in RAM, memory on the hard disk, and memory on the floppy disks the program comes on. In addition to memory requirements [and the cost of extra disks], displaying thousands or millions of colors at once slows down the computer, because it has to move so much more information around in memory and draw it on the screen.

The *palette* is the set of all the colors available in a particular program; it is chosen by the art director, with input from the programmers. You can think of it as an electronic version of the painter's palette, where the artist mixes colors. What it actually is, is a lookup table for the computer. It has one column of numbers, from 0 to 15 for a 16-color palette and from 0 to 255 in a 256-color palette. In the other column are the instructions for mixing that color out of red, green, and blue [RGB].

Programmers don't have to spell out the RGB formula for each pixel [dot] drawn on the screen, they just say make this pixel color 127, and the computer will look up the color on the palette.

The palette can be customized for each program and changed while a program is running. If you change a color definition in the palette, say change color 192 from blue to red, then every instance of color 192 on the screen will change from blue to red. This change happens very quickly—much more quickly than having the computer search every dot to find out which ones are color 192 and changing them to another color—and takes very little CPU time, so it doesn't slow down the action in the game.

Color cycling is a technique that takes advantage of the power, speed, and flexibility of changing color definitions in the palette to create effects or animations. *SimCity 2000* uses color cycling to create, among other things, the animations of traffic on the road and the title screen.

The Mac version was finished first. Was there a lot of extra art, touchup, or conversion work involved in changing it over to DOS?

Since it was 256 colors, it's been almost a straight shot from the Mac over to DOS. The only extra work that was required was the scroll bars and things like that, that we had to recreate for DOS.

There were no palette problems?

With the actual game art, there's been no tweaking.

For Windows?

Windows I think will be the same, but who knows?[3]

Other than the buildings, there were a lot of other tiles, for the landscape and streets. How many other tiles were there?

Between terrain, and water, subway, rails, roads, wires, and so on, there are quite a few. I'd say about 50 of these small tiles for each view size.

What are your favorite buildings or tiles? Any that you're extra proud of or think are extra fun?

I really love the stadium. I love the stadium. My only bummer is that the stadium isn't animated. Oh well. And I really like the Transamerica building—I'm sorry that didn't get in.

Was that for legal reasons?

Yeah, legal reasons. It's part of their copywritten logo, so we couldn't use it without their permission. It's such a cool-looking building . . . but it got axed.

I also like a lot of the larger commercial buildings, like the Theatre Square building [the Maxis building]. I like a lot of the larger zones. I like the construction zones too, I think those are really neat. And the larger residentials. It takes people a lot of playing time to get those big three-by-three zones [zones with a three-tile by three-tile base], you need a big population before you get those.

How many artist hours did it take to do all the work?

I'd say we took, in serious production mode, it was four artists plus myself, full time, for four months.

Describe the artists that worked on the project, and what they did.

OK, Suzie Greene has been an artist in the game industry for about nine years, about the same amount of time I've been in the industry. We've worked together at several other companies. She was the senior artist and lead artist on this project, so she set the style and was in charge of helping the other artists keep to that style. And she sorta coordinated and made sure that

---

[3]At the time of this interview, the DOS version was in final beta and the Windows version was just begun.

Jenny's favorite buildings, including the Sydney Opera House, which appears only in the Australian version of *SimCity 2000*

everybody had zones to work on, buildings to work on, and helped out with that. She was a big force behind the artwork in *2000*. Bonnie Boruki, another Senior Artist, was also instrumental in this project, although she was also doing a lot of work on another product during that time. Kelli Pearson did a lot of the bigger zones, like the zoo, the marina, the large commercial zones, and some of the arcologies. Her style is a good complement to Suzie's. Eben Sorken was here for a short time but did a bit of work—he did the power plants, some of the industrial stuff, and a couple of the arcologies.

How did you go about dividing the work between the different artists?

We started out doing the specialty zones, like the city hall, the stadium, police, fire, schools, and so on. We split them between cultural and civic. They weren't split that way in the game, but it was a way for us to divide the work. Then Kelli took commercial zones, and did those. Suzie focused on cultural zones, Eben worked on power zones, and Bonnie was doing some commercial and residential as well. So it was pretty much, "Well, this is what we have left to do, what do you feel like working on?" I think that's important; if you have a feeling for something, it helps you draw it.

Once you assigned a building or series of buildings to an artist, how did they go about drawing it?

The first thing we would do is find a reference. Especially dealing with the industrial or the power plants or commercial buildings. We looked at a lot of books of aerial photographs of different cities. Just to get a mix of different kinds of architecture. Make it a good blend, but make the buildings look custom.

We started with the reference, then we'd draw the most zoomed in [largest] view. We all looked over the work and decided, "Well maybe we should change that, change this." And the next day Will would have it in the game.

What about the actual drawing process?

It varies. You usually draw an outline and then start filling that in or block it in with solid colors and start detailing it. That's the most common way.

Were there always hand sketches first?

For the larger, more unique zones like stadiums and arcologies, things that were large, those were definitely drawn first on paper. For most of the smaller buildings, we just drew them on-screen. Sometimes it's easier that way.

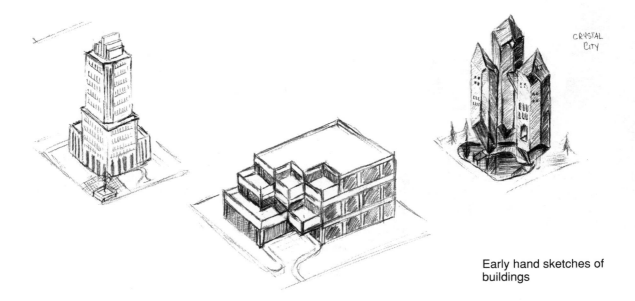

Early hand sketches of buildings

What about the monster?

[*Chuckle*] We went round and round and round about a monster. Everybody had a different idea for the monster. What turned out to be the driving force behind the creation or the actual look of the monster was the fact that it had to be symmetrical. Completely symmetrical and it had to be made out of components. That made the body round and the arms jointed so that Will could take it and build it and move it in the program. It wasn't done in the traditional animation way. Like in the original *SimCity* [now *SimCity Classic*], the monster was animated by four frames. This was one done in pieces, and Will pieced it together on the fly.

It started out as an ant alien, then it became a spaceship, then it became a round orb with legs.

Were there other suggestions along the way?

There were a lot of others. We have a number of early sketches of monster ideas that didn't make the cut.

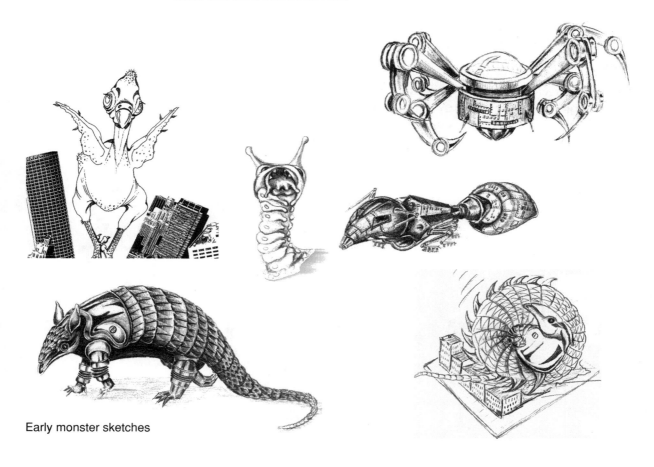

Early monster sketches

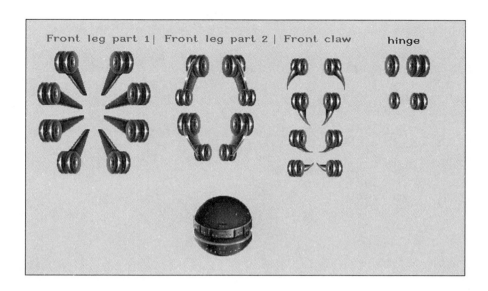

Pieces of the monster

What computers and art programs do you and your crew use?

We use 486 PCs. We use Deluxe Paint[4], which is still the workhorse in this industry. We sometimes used Photoshop[5], but the *SimCity 2000* art was almost entirely created on the PC using Deluxe Paint.

And then transferred over to the Mac with as little confusion as possible?

Right. We used DeBabelizer[6] on the Mac to convert all the Deluxe Paint files to PICT files, and we gave those to Will, and that was the end of that.

What are you looking at for the future as far as art programs and expanding your capabilities and expanding the art in the games you work on?

We're looking at 3D Studio[7] and what we can do with that. We're looking at different paint programs like Photoshop and Painter[8]. At Maxis, we still have the tile-based thing happening, so that keeps us rooted in the heavy-duty pixel-pushing realm. So we'll still have one foot in pixel-based programs and the other foot in 3-D.

---

[4]Deluxe Paint IIe by Electronic Arts, San Mateo, CA.
[5]Adobe Photoshop by Adobe Systems, Inc., Mountain View, CA.
[6]DeBabelizer by Equilibrium Technologies, Sausalito, CA.
[7]3D Studio by Autodesk, Inc., Sausalito, CA.
[8]Fractal Design Painter by the Fractal Design Corporation, Aptos, CA.

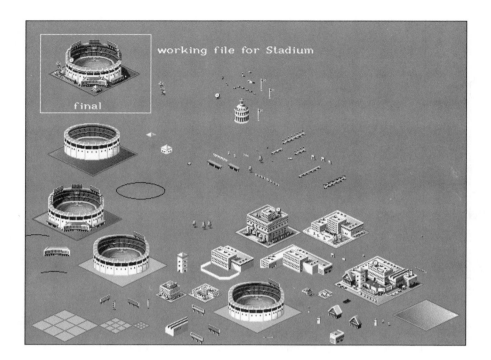

A working screen for assembling the stadium

Is that because of the nature of the games, the simulations that Maxis does?

Right. Our palettes are restrictive, but also a tile area is a lot smaller than doing a big giant background, where you can just be free and paint it. We need to have those tight little pixel-editing capabilities.

What went wrong during the project?

Well, I wouldn't call it something going wrong, more like an experiment tried. It changed our perspective [literally]. The perspective in the current game has what we call a 2:1 view, because it steps sideways two pixels and up one. Originally, we tried a different view, 4:1, more of a straight-on view of building faces.

Closer to the view in the old *SimCity*?

No. Down even more. Less overhead, almost an eye-level look at the buildings. But when the buildings appeared together in the game, the city appeared too flat.

In addition, there were other restrictions on the artwork, the way Fred wanted to do the screen redraws affected what we could draw. It just didn't

Comparing the old perspective
(on the left) with the final
perspective (on the right)

work out, so we had to change it. We had to change art, and the programmers had to change a number of things, too.

**Above and beyond the actual drawing of pictures, is there anything else
that the artists can or should contribute to the development of a game?**

The artist can project, even during the early concept stage, what the final art
will look like, to some extent. The programmers and producers can be looking at the same set of specs and see something totally different. The artist's
perspective is unique.

**So in other words, the artists should get involved in the project as soon as
possible?**

Yes. And they do.

**Any words to budding artists out there who might someday want to do art
for computer games?**

You have to know your beast. If you want to do artwork for games, you have
to know about games. When I interview people, if they have an interest in

games, that weighs a lot more heavily for me than somebody off the street that says, "Wow, I want to be in this industry because I think I can make a lot of money." Or especially if they like our games. Just like with anything, you need to know the industry you're trying to work for.

What about the tools?

The tools now are almost not even an issue anymore. They've become pretty easy to use. If you have strong illustration skills, and a good portfolio, you can pretty much learn the tools.

What do you look for in a portfolio?

I look for really strong, tight illustrative skills, especially things on disk even if they're not created in Deluxe Paint, Photoshop, or any of the other paint programs is OK. I'm not the flying logo type, because you can't always tell from 3-D stuff, or at least flying logos, the level of illustration skill behind that. Usually I look for things created, painted on a computer, or else in their portfolio, traditionally done.

THE MUSIC FOR *SIMCITY 2000*

Sue Kasper, a Bay Area musician, wrote most of the musical soundtrack for Sim-City 2000. Brian Conrad wrote one piece for the game and did the technical programming to implement the music in the DOS version.

Let's start with you, Sue. Tell me about yourself . . . how did you get into music? How did you end up writing music for computer games?

SK: Well, I've been playing music for 16 years. I've been in bands and I wanted to be a famous rock star. It didn't work out, and it was kinda like, "Well, what else can I do with my life?" And I got into computer games because I knew some people in the industry. The doors kinda opened that way, and I just got into a software program that I really like. I've always been a composer, and I've always had these great melodies in my head. This was a great opportunity to be able to do everything, to be a one-man show—or one-woman show, really.

Ultimately, what would you like to do musically? Still wanna be a rock star?

SK: Well, I think I'd like to just write music for other people.

And Brian, your role in this is actually more on the technical side, but you do have an extensive musical background. . . . Tell me about yourself.

BC: I've been playing music, let's see . . . I'm from a musical family—I've seen a picture of me at nine months playing a drum. So it's been with me all my life. I don't even remember my first public performance, since I supposedly sang at a fashion show when I was three years old.

I've played piano since age eight, and drums since age 11 . . . studied with various instructors, majored in music at the University of Washington and played in all kinds of organizations from country bands to symphony orchestras.

And with that musical background, your main job these days is as the Technical Director at Maxis, where you do a lot of programming and managing programmers.

BC: Twiddling bits, right.

I think the software industry is second only to working in a record store for having a high percentage of frustrated or hopeful musicians.

BC: That's correct.

Anyway, what's it like to write for a computer game as opposed to live music?

SK: It's a lot more limiting. You have to take a lot more into account. You can't just freely use whatever you want. Take it, Brian.

BC: Well first of all, you have to take into account the limitations of the particular machines you're composing for. For instance, on the Macintosh, you can use only internal sounds, you're limited to six voices—you can get as many as eight, but most of the time you're limited to six because we need to reserve two of the eight voices on the Mac driver for sound effects.

You're less limited on the PC side, because most of the sound cards can handle anywhere from six voices on up. The majority handle around 12; 24 is not uncommon these days. So you have a full-blown synthesizer with the PC sound cards.

Limitations on the PC are particularly that most of our products are done with general MIDI. It seems to be an easier spec because it defines a specific set of instruments. That in itself imposes limitations. A lot of composers aren't happy with general MIDI because it doesn't have all the instruments they want to use. So it's tradeoffs.

So, with general MIDI you're limited to the instruments that are built into the sound cards?

No. To the instruments in the general MIDI specification. Some sound cards have instruments built into them, most all of them are changeable. The Yamaha series of sound cards are programmable.

For the instrument sounds we use a set of tone banks from the Fat Man, George Sanger's company, for general MIDI. Those tone banks are changeable.

The newer cards can accept samples to create the sound. The newer technology is in the Gravis, Wave Blaster, the multi-sound products from Turtle Beach, Aria, products using the chips from Sierra Semiconductor. Those have sample sounds of the instruments.

So how many different tunes or pieces of music are in this program?

SK: I did 12½ minutes of music. I don't really know how much of that they used . . . but there were about ten tunes.

Were they ten separate moods for different occasions? Did the designers say do you want a tune for when the monster comes and a happy one for winning a scenario, or what?

SK: Moody. Dark and moody was the major theme for this. That's all they kept telling me—moody and dark, moody and dark.

One of the examples they really liked was the movie *Blade Runner*. So I watched that and listened to the music to get an idea of the mood they wanted.

I held out for some more upbeat, jazzy-type music that makes you think of a city. I tried to incorporate, like, industrial sounds into the music. I had this great vision of how I wanted it all to turn out, but because of the limitations. . . .

What held you back?

One of the limitations you're working with is sustain. To have it really moody and dark you need a lot of sustainy-type sounds. That was a real challenge, to make it not sound like, how most computer music sounds . . . how would you put it?

Hop and bop?

SK: Yeah.

BC: Mechanical.

SK: Yeah, mechanical. You have to make it sound more like music.

And you [Brian] wrote one of the tunes?

BC: Yeah.

Which one?

BC: It's in there somewhere. I originally wrote it as a title screen tune, but

Will decided to go with the jukebox approach and randomly select a tune for the opening.

So your main artistic consideration was to keep it musical within the limitations of the medium. And the main technical considerations were . . . ?

BC: It's making the music sound right on all the different cards and platforms.

How is it these days with eight billion new sound cards a day coming onto the market?

BC: Well, first of all, we don't have the problem so much on the Mac, because the Mac has internal sound. There is a line of sound cards coming out for the Mac, and we'll have to deal with that soon. On the PC side, we use Miles Design drivers, which are runtime, loadable drivers that let the user select specific drivers for music and sound.

Two drivers?

BC: Yeah. At home I'll play digitized sound effects through my sound card, and play the music through an external MIDI instrument, a Sound Canvas box. That gives me the best sound quality combination.

Only the DOS version of *SimCity 2000* supports this? Windows too?

BC: Any product that supports an external MIDI driver. For the Windows version, the MIDI Mapper can be set up so digital sounds are handled by one device and MIDI can be handled by another device. Most commonly you can send it on an MPU-401 MIDI interface to another device.

What about the Mac version? Does that have support for external MIDI?

BC: No.

Maybe someday in the future?

BC: Possibly, when the Mac sound cards catch on.

So, Brian, you're the main "technical" music implementer. You use the Miles drivers . . . what else does that involve?

BC: The Miles driver involves translating the API with common calls. . . .

And API is?

BC: Application Program Interface. Anyway we had a set of commands that we used in the Mac version to call music, and the process was adapting those to the PC and linking them to the Miles drivers, which in turn controlled the sound cards.

Also, we included multiple MIDI files. A lot of game companies do this nowadays—include different versions of each MIDI file optimized for various sound cards. Each of the cards is a little different and handles the instruments differently. We have one set of MIDI files for the Sound Blaster family which covers all the cards that use the Yamaha OPL sounds. We have a general MIDI spec which works very well with the Roland Sound Canvas, the SCC-1, the Aria. And there's a set of files for the Wave Blaster, which uses the EMU set of sounds.

And that's because something that sounds great on one card may sound crummy on another?

BC: Right. For instance, the original general sounds Sue gave us sounded great on her system, but when you play those back through a Sound Blaster or Ad Lib Gold, it didn't sound quite right. So we went in and changed the sounds some.

SK [*sincerely*]: Thank you.

BC: It didn't really take a lot of work, but we got it so it sounds really nice on the Sound Blaster. I was surprised we only had to do one set of files that sounded good on both the Sound Blaster and Sound Blaster 16. On the Sound Blaster 16 you can hear it in stereo, and we put panning in so it has a dimension like you're listening to a band on a stage. You don't get that on most of the cheap sound cards, but you do on the Sound Blaster 16, the Pro Audio series, the Wave Blaster, the MPU-401, and I think the Aria has stereo, too. So you hear that panning and it makes it real nice. Especially that one with the drum part [Brian mouths a drum line] you get one drum out of each speaker for effect.

SK: It's like going into a studio, and Brian's the engineer who puts it together and makes it sound the best he can.

BC: That's what we try to do. Michael Perry worked on the sound a bit, too. And it was Justin's [Justin McCormick] role to make the instruments sound the best they could on the Mac.

SK: It's amazing the transformation it goes through from start to finish. When I bring it in, it sounds wonderful because I'm creating it on my synthesizer system. But play it through a little sound card and it's a jumbled mess. It's really a long process to get the final product.

Is there a sound card shakeout coming, or will there be a new or better standard for sound across computer platforms and across all the sound cards?

BC: General MIDI is a start. But many musicians aren't happy with it because they want more sounds.

SK: A lot of it will go CD eventually.

Practically speaking, why didn't you just put Sue with a band in a recording studio and record the whole thing and . . . ?

BC: Put it all on a CD. That's what would happen, You'd have to put it on a CD. It takes 10 MB to store one minute of music. And at 12½ minutes, that's 125 MB.

So it's either on a CD or you'd have to buy a new hard drive for each game, and install the game from 80 floppies.

BC: Right. And nobody would do that. The logical extension is to use CD-ROM for delivery and have live tracks on there.

But in the mean time, for floppies, the way to go is to use MIDI files to tell the synthesizer what to do.

BC: It takes 10 Megs for a minute of digitized music, and 10K for a minute of MIDI. That's a 1000:1 difference in space requirements.

Did anything in particular go wrong in this project? Any interesting anecdotes? Or did it just go so smooth that it was boring?

SK [*giggling*]: The truth would take too long to explain. At times it was very stressful because of all the technical problems. Fortunately for me, I got to do the fun stuff, create the music, and hand it over to "them" to make it work in the program.

And Brian had the headaches of the implementation.

BC: Justin had the headaches of the implementation on the Mac.

So Justin McCormick did the Mac music implementation. . . .

BC: You should have invited him to this interview, too.

Well, I knew that it was going to be before noon, and Justin lives programmers' hours and wouldn't be awake. . . . OK, so who else in the computer game industry is doing good music, or is there anybody?

BC: Well, of course there's the Fat Man Team. They've done interesting music for Origin. The music for The Incredible Machine [by Dynamix], was great if you play the original MIDI files through a good system. I like that, but don't know who the composer was.

If the composer of the music for The Incredible Machine reads this book, three cheers to you. Anyone else?

BC: LucasFilms does a lot of good music in their games.

And who's doing good technical support software for music?

BC: Miles Design makes good drivers for the PC. And we have Hilstrom drivers.

These are things that developers use. What about good MIDI software for composing?

SK: I have my own personal preference. It's called Bars and Pipes.[9]

What's your process? How do you do what you do? It's computerized, so you don't record the music and hand over a tape. . . .

SK: I have an Amiga computer and I use Bars and Pipes [MIDI software]. I like it a lot. I'm a guitar player, a lead guitar player, and although they have MIDI guitars now, they don't really work well for writing MIDI music as of yet. And I'm not an incredible keyboardist. I hear all the melodies in my head and it's just a matter of getting it down. I can go in there and manipulate it any way I want.

By that you mean. . . .

SK: I can plot the melody note by note. I play them in, sometimes in slow motion. I can loop it and go over and over it in small sections. Then I can edit it on the screen to really fix it up. After all that I can sound as good as an accomplished keyboardist.

So the software actually records the music as you play it. . . .

SK: Yeah, then I can go in there and manipulate it any way I want, change the time signatures, the notes, everything. Mainly, I'm a very creative person, and it's a great tool that lets me play something I wouldn't be able to do, something that normally I wouldn't be able to play on my own, and do all the instruments.

Sounds like fun. Is that a power thing?

SK [*laughs*]: Yeah. It's great. I don't know how to play drums either, but I can put down rhythms. I don't know how to play flute or sax, but I can use all those sounds and create a whole arrangement.

---

[9]Bars and Pipes by Blue Ribbon Soundworks, Ltd.

So what do you actually turn in to Brian and his crew?

SK: A floppy disk with general MIDI files. Then they had to do a lot of conversion to get it to the Mac.

And Brian, how do you compose? I know your main instrument is drums, but I've heard you play great keyboards.

BC: I use a Roland D-10 as my controller. I use a Vox Dr. Synth or a Sound Canvas general MIDI module. I use Cakewalk for Windows as my sequencer software.

How much of it do you actually just play, and how much do you go back in and modify?

BC: On a good day or bad day?

In general.

BC: MIDI is like anything else. If you practice and practice until you can play the whole tune forward and backwards, then hit the record button, you'll still make endless mistakes. Fortunately with MIDI, as long as everything is kept fairly well in rhythm, you can go back in and change those one or two bad notes on the screen. You can adjust velocity, the volume of the notes, the attacks. So you can pretty well edit your performance. You don't want to get into a loop where you're spending a lot of time editing your performance when you'd be better off learning to perform better on the keyboard. Certainly keyboard players have an advantage. They can just play in arrangements very fast.

And a lot of times scores don't sound quite right, so you have to quantize to make them sound tighter. We're used to hearing recordings with the ambiance of the recording studio, but you lose that with the computer. It's too clean. So it's tricky. It's a very interesting form of performance. There's a lot to be learned about it yet.

What would you say to musicians or potential musicians that might want to get into soundtrack for games or other multimedia projects?

SK [*laughs*]: Ask for a lot of money up front. There's a lot involved. There's always new equipment to buy. It's a lot to learn technically. I was lucky to work for Maxis where it's like a team effort, which made it all possible to me because I'm not a programmer. I'm learning that now, taking classes. And it's hard to find classes that teach you how to play MIDI music. But really, it's like in any other industry, it's who you know. Of course, you have to have the talent to back it up, but getting in the door is really hard.

BC: Probably the best thing you can do is know as much as possible about

MIDI, how to really use your MIDI tools effectively. Definitely you want to know as much as you can about the Macintosh sound environment and the PC sound card environment. Fortunately, I think we're going to be seeing a lot more sound cards, even on the Mac, so the main focus is to understand how those work, what kinds of sound and limitations they have.

From the composition side, I'd recommend that the individual read up on film and TV scoring. It's the same approach. You'll be scoring animations, or miniature cartoons.

Learn to develop a wide range of styles. Many submissions that I get from composers in the business often present a demo tape, either of projects they've worked on, and/or examples of various styles of music they are capable of composing. Some composers are limited, they can do either rock or jazz. Others can do everything: country, symphonic, eastern music, jazz rock, a wide range. The more varied you are, the more creative, the more innovative you are, the better your chances are in the business.

Any last words?

BC: You really ought to listen to the music from *SimCity 2000* on a PC with a MIDI interface playing through a good system to hear what Sue's done in a proper light.

THE DOCUMENTATION FOR *SIMCITY 2000*

The documentation for SimCity 2000 was written by Michael Bremer, one of the authors of this book.

Since you are one of the authors of this book—and are interviewing yourself—let's skip over all that background stuff to avoid being accused of grandstanding. So, what is game documentation?

As far as writing goes, the manual is the biggest part of it, but there are lots of other things, too. Like writing the package copy, writing and/or editing screen text and the collateral stuff [addenda, catalog copy, etc.]. Plus, in many cases for Maxis games, there will also be a teacher's guide.

What is the "purpose" of documentation?

The way I see it, there are three main purposes: to help the player get up and running and playing as quickly, easily, and painlessly as possible; to add flavor and mood to the game's atmosphere, and to minimize tech support calls as much as possible.

Why are Maxis manuals so darn big?

It all depends on the game. In many games, like role-playing games, the actual "game" is to figure out how the world works. If you give too much information in the docs, then you spoil the player's fun. So you give the very basics, then add flavor and enhance the mood.

But the usual Maxis type game has a different approach. The "game" isn't trying to figure out where you are and how the world works, it's creating your own world. We give you all the tools to build something . . . in *SimCity 2000*, that something is a city. The game is to build that city, not to figure out how to use the tools. Besides, those tools are powerful, and a power tool without proper instruction is a dangerous thing.

Basically, the more possible choices, the more opportunity for creativity rather than reaction, the more freedom the player has—the more the documentation has to explain how to go about doing it. It's almost more like documenting an application than a game. Would you want a word processor or paint program—creativity-enhancing applications—that expected you to figure out how to find the hidden commands and controls? No. You want to be able to look them up and use them.

Also, we've traditionally put "added value" material into the manuals. Background information that's useful for playing the game, but beyond that, too. A ready-at-hand source of more information about a subject that's interesting enough to have a game made out of it.

What is the ideal size for a manual?

Ideally, there would be no manual. The game would be designed so intuitively that the players could instantly figure everything out on their own—with on-line help for the tricky parts. Maybe just the added value stuff would be printed, like a coffee table book, that you could look at away from the computer.

Why hasn't this happened yet?

The main limiting factors are industry mind-sets and display technology. It's still a drag to read a lot of text on a screen—and a real hassle to open a help window that covers up the thing you're reading about. But it'll come. With time.

And at that time you'll be out of a job?

No. I'll be there, writing the equivalent of the documentation right into the program design.

So what's involved with writing a manual? What's the whole process?

You start looking at the game as early as possible, preferably in the earliest design stages. You read the design specs, you look at the sample art, you try out the early alphas, and think about it. You might take some notes, but you can't start really writing yet.

Once the game gets to the point where it's actually playable, you start writing. But you have to keep in constant contact with the programmers and the producer to make sure you know what's final and what's probably going to change. And count on a lot of things changing at the last minute.

Once the first draft is written, you run it by as many eyes as you can. We have staff editors here, and they're great. But it also has to go to other eyes. The programmers, producers, and testers need to see it. They can warn you of impending changes. And tech support needs to give it a once-over and have the chance to point out anything that should be added to help out the customer and minimize calls for help. And you need to find people that haven't seen the game before to play through the tutorial to see if it really does the job.

Then you take everyone's edits, look them over, and change or rewrite as necessary. Of course, at this point the program is still changing, so you have to keep up with that.

Once you've got it all "finished," you run it by the editors again, then take and crop all the screen shots. At this point, the final art may not be in, so you might have to take temporary screen shots and find out from the Art Department when the final art will be done. Sometimes you have to mock up screen shots, either yourself or with the help of the artists.

Then you prep the manuscript for the layout department. Clean up any notes to yourself or others. Put in any captions for graphics. List and define the functions of all the different heading levels and styles. Make a list of all the graphics, their names, descriptions, which are temporary, and so forth.

Then layout does their thing. I'm lucky here at Maxis to be able to work closely with the layout group. I think it's best that way. You can explain what you meant by different comments and suggestions. You can answer important questions about how important a graphic is, or how big it'll have to be to serve its intended purpose. When layout is done, you and the editors give it a once-over, to make sure the headings are all at the right levels, that the graphics are with the right text, and a thousand other details. And of course, the program has continued to change during layout, so you'll have to rewrite a few sections.

Once the layout has been edited and perfected, it goes to lino [a high quality photographic printing process]. The linos need to be checked over, then they go to the printer.

A week later the printer sends back the blueline master that also needs to be checked. Then you get to work on the addendum.

But what about the actual writing process?

It would take at least a whole book to cover the tech stuff, and maybe another book each for the marketing and education writing. But I can say this: once you start writing, you have to separate your brain into two parts: the nerd and the new kid. One part has all the game and computer knowledge you've gathered for years, and the other has to forget everything you already know about the program and about games and about computers. You have to write from your knowledge and experience, but you have to keep that new kid around to remind you that everyone who's reading the manual hasn't been playing the game or following it's progress for the last year or two.

What's the most fun part?

Starting. Thinking it over and coming up with the right approach for the product. Planning all the bits and pieces and how they're going to fit together.

What's the hardest part?

The actual writing. I love coming up with ideas. I love planning what I'm going to write. I love having written. But the actual writing is hard work. As jobs go, I can't complain, but it is hard work.

What are the problems?

The basic problem is that this job is impossible to do perfectly. And it all comes down to two things: the program is the star, and it takes a lot longer to print manuals than it does to duplicate disks.

Since the program is what people buy, if shipping is delayed, even by months, because the program wasn't ready, that's life. But if the product is delayed even a day because of the documentation, that's inexcusable. Even at Maxis where the founders have, from the beginning, believed in the importance of good documentation, you better not be the cause of a shipping delay.

Add to that the fact that you can duplicate tens of thousands of disks overnight, and you can keep changing the code and adding features until the last second. But it takes two to three weeks to print a manual, plus at least two weeks for layout and proofing, plus at least a week or two for editing and tutorial testing. That means you have to have the manual written five to eight weeks before the program is done. You can do a good job, but it'll never be perfect.

Quit whining. Beyond the manual, what are the contributions of the doc worker?

There's the screen text: messages and help text. It has to be written or at least edited . . .

We often get involved in interface design, especially where words and names of things are concerned, but in other ways, too. You're the one coming at the project with fresh eyes—the new-kid half of your brain—just as a player who just bought the game would. If there are things that are confusing or non-intuitive to you, chances are those things will be confusing and non-intuitive to anyone else coming to the game.

And you have to be ready early to pass on some writing, especially the intro chapter stuff, to the PR and marketing departments so they have something to work with.

A very important function is putting together the list of unknowns. As you get near the end of the manual, you compile a list of all the questions you have, all the features you don't understand. You'll find that your list of unknowns becomes the programmer and designer's list of things to do—everything they either haven't or couldn't decide yet. Then you have to sit down with everyone involved and go through the list, forming a consensus and getting the decisions made. When nobody can come up with a good decision, you have to be ready to make it. Your best bet is to choose a path that will be easiest for you to explain to the readers, since that will be the easiest and least confusing for the player.

What about the newspapers? How was that done?

That was a monumental part of the whole project. I had very little to do with it. Fred set up the system. He listed what the necessary stories would be and set up lists of interchangeable variables. Debra Larson, another writer here, wrote most of the stories and came up with the lists of variables. A lot of the stories are really funny—I'm jealous that I didn't have time to work on them. But it was a lot of work. It took weeks of writing and editing and getting contributions from others around the company, and testing each story in the newspaper to make sure it made sense with all the changing variables.

Can you summarize your approach to documentation writing?

Be the advocate for the player. Be the translator between all the people who are so close to the game that they take too much for granted. Set aside part of your brain to be the new kid. Get the information across as quickly, as easily, as painlessly, and as enjoyably as possible. Even if you have to break all the rules. And avoid sounding academic at all costs — even in educational materials.

I notice you refer to it as documentation writing, and not technical writing—why?

Partly because the writing we do here includes tech stuff, but it also includes a lot of marketing and educational stuff, too. And fear is a factor, too.

Tech writers have a bad rep. I meet people at parties and they say, "I hear you do technical writing. I've been wanting to meet one of you guys for a long time." All I can do is cover my vulnerable areas and beg the guy not to hit me.

Really, for the most part, that rep is deserved. There's a lot of really boring, incomplete and badly translated tech writing out there. A lot of it isn't written for the right audience. You write for engineers, sound like an engineer. You write for normal people, sound like a normal person. You write about games, sound fun. But then again, tech writers faces those impossible deadlines, so it's not all their fault.

But it's getting better. Especially in the computer game industry. We're pushing the hardware to its limits in the games, and we're pushing the envelope in quality, enjoyable docs. By golly, we're trendsetters!

Do you have any words of wisdom for people wanting to write in this industry?

If you're writing about entertainment, you have to be entertaining. Forget every paper you wrote for your college professors. Forget every contract you ever tried to read. Write the way you'd talk to a friend.

Read lots of children's books. The good ones are masterpieces of communication without big words for the sake of big words. They do the job— tell the story or get the point across—in the simplest, most direct way. I make the writers that work for me read children's books, just to show them that it can be done.

Read and write screenplays. They're all action and dialog, no waste, no fluff. A good class in screenplay writing will help you be entertaining yet stay to the point.

Work with a good editor.

Learn to use humor. It is a good tool. But it takes practice.

On the subject of humor, other than this interview, your stuff often has a few laughs in it. . . .

It's a defense mechanism for the reader. . . . OK, when you get to the essence of writing, whether it's sales or marketing materials or step-by-step procedures in a tutorial, what you are really doing is teaching. You're telling people about a place, then taking them there and teaching them about it; where and why it is, how to survive there.

I've always found that people don't learn when they're scared or even uncomfortable. And face it, to many people, computers are frightening. And to any sane person, the minds of the people who make these games are very scary places.

Humor conquers fear and puts people at their ease. Once you can laugh at something, it isn't scary any more. I've experimented with this a lot. I've taught a number of classes over the years, lately, mostly about computers. No matter how well you design your course or how well you explain things, if the students are scared or uncomfortable, they won't learn. But if you get even the worst computerphobe to the point where they can laugh at the computer, they're ready to dig in and play with it and learn about it.

So, if that's what you believe, why aren't this book and this interview funnier?

Who asked you?

How do you rate the *SimCity 2000* manual?

I'm proud of it. It's complete, it's clear, it's readable . . . fun even.

If the manual is so complete, why does this book even exist?

A manual should—and this one does—have all of the information that a person shelling out money for the game deserves: enough of an intro to get the feel of the place, enough tutorials that those who want step-by-step instructions can get comfortable with the game, and a reference section that answers most questions about the simulation and how the whole thing works. Anything less is confusing, maybe even a rip off.

But a game shouldn't come with *all* the answers. Players should have the chance to explore and figure out *some* things on their own. After a while of trying, or after they gain some real mastery of the game, they can get more—hints, tips, details, inside info, ways to win—from an after-market book like this.

Besides, a lot of the information in this book wasn't available until after the program was done and shipped; until we had a chance to play it for a while ourselves and figure it out a bit; until the programmers were done and could relax a while and had enough time to answer our questions.

What's the Gallery at the back of the manual all about?

I'm glad you asked. . . . We've always put something extra in our manuals. Something for "added value," like a history section, or a science section. To give some added value to the city experience of *SimCity 2000,* I originally started to put together a piece on modern trends in city planning, but when I got into the research, I kept coming up against the fact that all the great cities in the world weren't planned at all. They evolved from the lives and needs and dreams of the millions of people that lived there over many years. So, instead of one person's opinion about something, I decided to include a number of people's opinions, in words and pictures, of what "city" means to them. There're a few poems, some drawings, some photos, a couple of essays. . . . I think it all turned out great.

To sum it all up, you can write a really good, very complete manual, and give it added value, but it can never be perfect. . . .

That just about sums it up.

TESTING *SIMCITY 2000*

This conversation/interview with Alan Barton, Maxis Q.A. manager and lead tester on the DOS version of SimCity 2000, *and Chris Weiss, lead tester for the Macintosh version, took place on a short break, late at night in the Maxis testing room while* SimCity 2000 *DOS was in full-tilt testing crunch time. They were just a little bit burnt out. . . .*

Tell me in your own words what your contributions to *SimCity 2000* have been. . . .

[*Silence.*]

I'll help you out here. Alan, you're the lead tester on the DOS version, and Chris, you're the lead tester on the Mac version.

CW: That's right.

So how'd you get here? What happened? Why are you here? How did you get to be hotshot gamester lead testers?

AB: Kind of fell into it.

That sounds traumatic. Chris, can you outdo that story?

CW: Oh, hell yeah. I used to be involved in telecommunications a lot and made a lot of friends through computer networks. And one of those friends was Steve Smythe, who was in this industry. He knew my affinity for games and hacking on hardware and whatnot, and he introduced me to the people here and got me a job. It was through friends.

In your background, did you guys play a lot of computer games before you came here?

AB: Yep.

How about a little enthusiasm here guys?

CW: Back in the beginning when I had an Apple II, I used to love hacking on games.

OK, I give up. What exactly does a tester and/or lead tester do on a project? It sounds like you just sit around all day playing games and having fun.

CW: If only it were so good. We only have fun half the day. For a tester, the job is to find new and exciting ways to break the program. To try to do things that they think a bored user would do, or a user that doesn't know what's going on, or how to play. Try to press the wrong buttons at the wrong times. Trying to do limits testing. Like try to make the city as large as you can or as small as you can. What happens if I drag this piece of work off the world that I'm on or what happens if I try to assign too many troops to this group. That kind of thing.

So you're trying to find anything that the programmers and designers may not have thought people would think of.

CW: Find things they don't already have a contingency for. You know, in a lot of cases, it's not that a programmer didn't think of something, they might have made a typo somewhere in the code that might only show up as a problem during certain times. Also making sure that the programs work on all kinds of different hardware combinations. One of the biggest things we have to deal with is compatibility, especially in the DOS market. You have to test on a lot of different video cards and sound cards, different brands of CPUs, different BIOSs, all kinds of fun stuff. All the different versions of all the different drivers for mice and sound cards, different versions of DOS, and all the possible combinations of cards, drivers, and DOS versions.

So you have a big supply of all that stuff here?

CW: We wish we did.

So how do you cover the rest of it?

AB: We call up the manufacturers and get the cards on loan. We use our or our friends' machines at home. We also use third-party testing houses that have a wider variety of cards and stuff.

What about independent beta testers. Do you want everybody who reads this book to call and say, "Hey, I'll test your next game!"

AB: No. We don't do that.

CW: Some companies do, but we don't anymore.

AB: Out-of-house beta testers are too risky. We've had a lot of security problems in the past.

So you only deal with official bonded businesses for outside testing. . . .

AB: Or bring people in house on a temporary basis to test.

What's the "lead" in lead tester?

AB: In addition to the regular tester duties, the lead tester has to create the test plan and work closely with the programmers and producers. They have to schedule the rest of the Q.A. resources.

What's a test plan?

AB: It's the plan that testers follow to work every function in the program. Everything the program is supposed to do, we write it in the test plan. When the product is about two weeks away from release, we'll go through that very carefully and make sure everything is working. All the buttons click, there're no frags. When you click this button, the right menu pops up or that window pops up. And there's some stress testing in there as well as configuration testing.

Is this the greatest job in the world?

[*AB laughs.*]

CW: So far. It isn't that bad. I don't have too many complaints.

AB: A lot of people think we sit here and just play games and play with our hardware all day, but there's a lot of documentation, a lot of communication with other departments, a lot of meetings. A lot of headaches and a lot of time.

And of course those jerks who write the manuals come by at the last minute and say, "You gotta read this right now and make sure I got all the latest changes in there right."

AB: Yeah. [*Glaring menacingly at the innocent manual writer.*] You got an hour. Hurry up. Here's 50 pages.

Gee, I'd never do that more than twice a week. . . . So you guys get paid to play games?

CW: It's not just a matter of playing the game, because once you've found all these bugs, and you give the programmer the list of bugs, and he goes and works on them and gives you back the list indicating which ones have been fixed, then you have to go back through and play the game the exact same way you did before to try to recreate the bugs to make sure they're really fixed. So half the time you're duplicating your effort.

So what's the basic process? Say you're a tester, not a lead tester, and you find a bug. What do you do?

CW: First you try to reproduce the bug. You try and duplicate the exact steps that produced the bug and then try to track down the cause. Is it something about that particular machine or any of the drivers or memory resident anything that's causing the problem? Then you write up the whole thing, how it happened, what it did, when it happened, all the steps to recreate it. That way the programmer can look at the bug report and either know what's causing it or at least be able to narrow down the part of the code responsible. They have to be able to find the problem as quickly as possible so they can fix it.

So testing isn't just finding bugs, it's trying to find the cause.

CW: There's a lot of Sherlock Holmes stuff.

So are you guys the absolute masters of the game?

AB: Not really. We never have the time to play for very long at a time. We never had the chance, until recently, to even build large cities. The file format kept changing during development, so we'd have to keep starting over and rebuild our cities. We're really not masters. We know a lot, and can build a good city, but a lot of the public is going to be able to build cities better than we can.

CW: Our job isn't to be masters, it's to be destroyers and trouble-finders.

What kind of hours do you guys work?

CW: I had a day off last month.

AB: I think we all did. Once.

CW: When it gets down to the wire . . . when it gets to the last couple of weeks before release, we put in 12- and 15-hour days pretty consistently, and when we get down to the last couple days, it's around the clock. We've got people there for 20, 25, 30 hours.

So when you finish testing one of these games—I know that by the time I finish the manual, and the Teacher's Guide, and a third-party book, and whatever else there is, I'm pretty sick of a product. I never want to see it again — for a while at least. How do you feel? Do you go home and play it at home when you finally get a day off?

CW: Usually, right after the program releases, we have a blowout [party], but then we jump right back into it, because we always think that maybe we missed something. Or things show up. It gets out on the shelves, and onto thousands of machines with new video or sound cards, or even new machines. Or old ones with different combinations of hardware and software that we couldn't test.

Why would a customer find a problem that you guys—you professionals—don't?

CW: 'Cause we can only spend 15 man-hours a day on it for a few months. And we've only got about four full-time testers to a game. Once it's out in the real world with tens or hundreds of thousands of people banging on it, they're bound to come up with a combination of circumstances that we didn't. They're bound to have hardware that we don't have, or driver versions that we don't have.

At the rate that new stuff is coming out, it's impossible to keep up with it all.

AB: Just the way their machines are configured software-wise can be a big issue. Different TSRs, different memory managers.

So people shouldn't take it too personally if they find a bug in a software program version 1.0?

CW: No.

What kind of bugs do you consider absolutely inexcusable to miss?

CW: Anything that crashes. Anything that we think we should have found that somehow got missed. Inevitably there's one or two of those. Things that crash, things that are obvious, things that somebody should have caught but didn't. Two testers may discuss a bug then both think the other one is going to write it up, but neither does. Late-night communication errors.

Sometimes you put so much effort tracking down a tricky hard-to-duplicate bug that you might let some of the more obvious ones go, thinking someone else will report it.

And typos—and not having our names in the credits.

[*Chuckle*] That's an inexcusable bug. What are the total testing hours on either a typical project or on a project like *SimCity 2000*.

CW: *SimCity 2000* was in testing for like a year.

AB: Not full time, but the whole testing process took that long. At least for the first version, the Mac, there was always at least one tester assigned to it for the entire time.

CW: So you're talking thousands of hours.

AB: I'd say over 5,000 man-hours.

For the Mac version, or all versions. . . .

AB: Just the Mac. That's for the initial first platform development of the game.

CW: When you have an original version, versus a port, there's a lot more testing that goes into that. Because you have to deal with the simulator, getting that all ironed out smooth; is it reacting the way you want, balancing it for fun gameplay. With a port, you're mainly dealing with the interface and the hardware, so there's not nearly as much work.

AB: It generally goes quicker.

Briefly describe the process of testing a product. . . . When do you first see it?

AB: We first see it in early alpha.

CW: Too late.

AB: Yeah, too late as far as we're concerned. We'd rather get involved in the early design stages. Help with the general interface.

CW: That may be more of an ego thing. . . .

AB: Well. . . .

CW: We usually get it when all the major features are there. You can place zones, the city builds, but you still have to struggle to keep it from crashing.

And at that point you're throwing in interface suggestions and hoping they'll listen?

AB: Yeah, but mainly at that point we're getting familiar with the product and what it's supposed to do. Trying to catch the major loopholes.

So you're keeping an early eye on it during alpha.

AB: Sometimes we see it even before that, just to boot it up and see what's done so far. But it's not ready for testing.

Then what happens?

AB: When it goes to beta it means that all the features of the game are working. The load, save, sound, the sound support. All the windows work and the model is functioning semi-normal.

And that's when you guys really kick in?

CW: That's when we start up the bug list and start people really working on it.

AB: We start putting in a lot more time on it at that time, once it's fairly stable.

And then near the end of the beta, you jump in and bang away at it.

AB: Yep. Start with the 20-hour days seven days a week. You get everyone in the company who can to put in whatever time they can spare, day or night, to help.

I remember quite a few of those sessions. So what kind of training and/or personality do you need to be a good tester?

CW: It helps if the person has hardware experience. At least for us.

AB: A decent understanding of hardware. You can't be afraid of it. You have to be able to open it up, swap cards, change drivers, change mice, change IRQs on sound cards and video cards, that kind of thing.

CW: And knowing the software. Especially if it's a Windows product, you have to know Windows fairly well.

AB: Yeah, you have to know what the .INI files are all about.

CW: And for DOS an all-around knowledge. How to mess with CONFIG.SYS and AUTOEXEC.BAT files.

And then beyond that, what about gaming?

It helps to be an avid gamer. I'd say a good well-rounded gaming experience is best. Not just all one type of game like role-playing or flight simulators. We all have our preferences—I like flight sims, but I like and play a lot of other types of games as well.

Aside from Maxis [speaking politically, here], what do you guys think are the best games you've seen and played in a while?

AB: I haven't seen one.

CW: You know, it's kinda weird, now that I see so much stuff, since it's part of my job to check out the competition, nothing captures my attention for very long any more. I think the last thing that spent more than two weeks on my hard disk was *Syndicate*.

AB: *Syndicate* probably caught all of our eyes for at least two weeks.

Who made that?

AB: Bullfrog, released through Electronic Arts.

CW: Baseball was another one, *Tony La Russa's Ultimate Baseball*. It was a multi-player game that worked out kinda nice. I don't think there's enough good multi-player games out there for the PC. Most are single-player.

In closing, what would you say to somebody who is thinking they might want to get into the industry as a tester. What's your suggestion? Get a real job?

CW: Well, first, make connections. Then, you have to get to know your hardware.

AB: Know a little about programming. It helps to have an understanding of what's going on inside the machine, what the code is doing.

CW: On the Mac you should know ResEdit, DOS people should know Windows, you should know DOS, and all about memory managers. And you need writing skills. You have to be able to write up some fairly technical procedures in a way that others can understand it.

And it doesn't hurt to have proofreading skills, 'cause you'll be asked to read over manuals and all the screen text.

CW: You have to be pretty retentive.

PORTING *SIMCITY 2000* TO DOS

Jon Ross and Daniel Browning were the two main programmers involved in taking SimCity 2000 *as developed on the Macintosh and porting or converting it to work on DOS machines. At the time of this conversation, both programmers were in high gear working against some serious deadlines, and had been working long, late hours, especially Jon.*

So, Jon, you're the "lead programmer" on the DOS version of *SimCity 2000*?

JR: I guess, yeah. When we started the port nine months ago, I was the only programmer on the project. As the windowing system started coming together and the Mac version kept adding features, we realized that it was a little large, so we recruited Dan. So I guess I'm the lead programmer by default.

'Cause you've been at it longer?

JR: Yeah.

Any other programmers been helping out?

JR: Yeah James Turner has been helping out, doing odds and ends; he's also doing the port to the Windows version. Brian Conrad did a lot of the music stuff. He's our Technical Director, he's a musical type of guy. Some of the tools and utilities have been done by various other people around.

How did you get into this position?

JR: I got hired, and they said, "You're gonna do the *2000* port." And for the first few months we spent a lot of time deciding what windowing system to use, and there were some lying around that Maxis had [from other projects], and after working with them all, we realized that none of them were really gonna work for *2000*. So we had to sit down and write one from scratch.

And that's because DOS has no "official" windowing system, and unlike Mac and Windows, you have to do everything yourself.

JR: Roll your own everything, yeah. Then this project turned into more than a port, it was a whole windowing system design job. So we stole pieces of the various systems that we had around, and modified it to work in protected mode, which none of the other ones did, which is running the machine in it's native 32-bit environment, and also made it to support Super VGA graphics. Very few games have done that, actually. This is sort of rare to have Super VGA only. . . .

SimHealth[10]. . . .

JR: Yeah *SimHealth*.

So we're either trendsetters or doing things that everybody else knows better than to do.

JR: Well, Marketing wigged when they finally found out. We'd been telling them for months that we're doing this in Super VGA only in protected mode 16-bit machines only and they said, "Uh huh, yeah, OK, whatever." And then they found out what that meant in non-technical terms and realized that not all the IBM computers out there could handle those specs.

DB: But the installed base is growing quickly for those machines. Almost anything sold now can handle it.

JR: Yeah, that's true.

---

[10] *SimHealth* is a custom simulation, a design-your-own national health care system, that Maxis created at the request (and payment) of The Markle Foundation. It has been available in college book stores and through direct mail since February, 1994. At this time there aren't plans to distribute it through the usual software channels.

Before we get into more details, let's jump over here to Dan. . . . How did you get involved in this . . . life?

DB: OK, let's see, I was an architecture major at U.C. Berkeley, at the College of Environmental Design, and that's where I got a lot of my design experience. But I graduated and realized that I didn't want to be an architect, because I'd taken a computer graphics course from Jim Blin and Ed Catmul, two of the leaders in the graphics field. So I got a job with Synapse Software as a video game programmer and worked on this video game called *Vyper* for the Mindset computer. The Mindset computer went under, so *Vyper* didn't do too well. And then I got into 3-D graphics, working for a company called Cubicomp that did 3-D production video graphics, things like flying logos and TV commercial stuff. I did some graphics programming there, and from there I worked for Autodesk and did some CAD programming for that company, and then I went over to VPL Research, which was a virtual reality company, and I worked on some virtual reality applications. Then I started my own business, and that was interesting. I completed the software—I was working on a software product—but the funding fell through, so I thought I better look for a job. A friend of mine named Joel Dubiner, a video game producer, heard about some openings here and told me to get in touch with Brian Conrad. I faxed him my résumé, and I got the job. I like the atmosphere and the people and the products, especially the products, because they're not the typical video game products. So I joined.

So as far as programming, are you self-taught, or did you take classes?

DB: I took classes. My minor at U.C. Berkeley was computer science. I took the whole set of classes. I also took a lot of logic design and breadboard design.

Hardware?

DB: Yeah. I designed a frame buffer, a medium-resolution frame buffer to fit into an S-100 bus. That was a lot of fun. I got a lot out of it; I think it helps me as a programmer.

And you, Jon, did you learn your programming in college?

JR: No, I guess I'm self-taught.

Being self-taught is kind of hacker chic. In some game industry circles, people tend not to admit that they went to college for programming. There's still the "kid sitting alone in his room" mystique. But the technical demands of the job are changing that. Back to you, Jon. . . .

JR: I was doing electronics, which I didn't go to school for either . . . that was fun. I was really fascinated by electronics. I got into it from musical equipment, taking it apart and putting it back together. I got a job as a tech at this company that did navigation systems for missiles. I started doing some of the design of that stuff, and then they asked me to write a program to control this box that I built. That's where I first learned to program. I actually got more interested in the programming than the electronics. I had a friend, Paul Schmitt [formerly of Raxsoft, now of PhotoDex], who worked on the *SimEarth* Mac to DOS port for Maxis with Daniel Goldman. I called him up one day and he said he was doing another port for Maxis, *A-Train*, and asked me if I wanted to help him with it. I figured, missiles, video games, perfect match. I though how hard could programming games be? But the games are way more difficult, incredibly more complicated than navigating missiles.

So I did *A-Train* and the *A-Train Construction Set* with Paul, and when that was over he went off to do the Photodex thing and didn't really know what I was going to do. So I called Joe [Scirica, Maxis V.P. of Product Development] and said, "Wanna give me a job?" and he said, "OK." And now I live here.

Let's jump over to the process of doing a port. How much of the original Mac code can be used as is, how much had to be touched up, and how much had to be totally rewritten?

JR: Well first, we wrote the windowing system. We tried to make it generic and stand alone so it can be used for future projects. Then we started moving the Mac code over. Anything having to do with any of the drawing code from the Mac, any of the way the windows moved, buttons, mouse, all that was rewritten from scratch. The only Mac code that we tried to keep as pristine as possible was the simulator. It was written in generic C and we literally moved it across and recompiled it, and it pretty much worked.

What percentage of the program is the simulator?

JR: Not very much. It's interesting, 90 percent of programming for a commercial product is user error trapping. Preparing for errors in user input. The actual simulator takes up less than 10 percent of the code.

DB: I'd say it's about a 50/50 split between original code and new code.

How did you divide up the work? You [Jon] started and were going to do the whole thing, then as the project got bigger, more people came on board. . . .

DB: Jon's the "core man." I'm the dialog box guy.

JR: When we realized that this project was getting really large, I looked at the code to see what parts could be split off and could be worked on separately without having to know the whole rest of the system. I feel that more than one person dealing with the same thing . . . when programmers overlap sections of code, it tends not to work out very well from my experience. It seemed like the dialogs—and there are a lot of them—could be split off pretty easily from the rest of the program, and the interaction between the dialogs and the whole rest of the program was pretty minimal. So Dan sat down and mimicked almost the entire Mac library and built the dialogs.

So what's your goal on a port? Do you try to make it as close to the original [Mac in this case] as possible? You can't really try to make it as DOS-like as possible, because there is no such thing.

JR [with evil glint in his eye]: Well first of all, we were going to make it all command line and text based to keep it as close to the DOS platform as possible, but decided that that wasn't going to work.

DB [*chuckling*]: The marketing department came back with a few suggestions.

JR: As far as functionality goes, for us that's almost secondary. My whole focus in the port was to do it in the smallest amount of time and with the least energy possible, so my concern was, make a platform so the Mac code could have as little change as possible in moving over to DOS. The byproduct of all this is that the windowing system is very close to the way *SimCity 2000* works on the Mac. That wasn't the goal, but that's the way it ended up.

How's the performance of the DOS version as opposed to the Mac version?

JR: Oh, it's fifty billion times better.

DB: It is. A lot faster.

JR: There are pros and cons. The simulator is, oh, ten times faster.

Comparing what machines?

JR: Compare a 16 MHz Mac vs. a 16 MHz PC. In Cheetah mode, the fastest mode, the simulator goes as fast as the machine can go. If you compare the two, the simulator runs a lot faster on the PC. Some of the graphics stuff happens a bit faster on the Mac, because there is no 1 MHz bus between the CPU and the video card like there is on the DOS machine. That seems to be a big bottleneck, especially for a game this graphically intense. So portions of the graphics stuff work a little faster on the Mac, or maybe about the same.

DB: Jon has done a lot of work to optimize the graphics speed.

JR: I've always felt that the user should get immediate gratification for whatever they do. If they hit a button, something should happen. Even if it's stupid, something should happen. That's one of my big concerns.

So part of the big technical challenge is you're working with the DOS extender, using a lot of memory, running in protected mode, which is, for those non-techies out there in the universe . . . ?

JR: DOS, when it started, was running on 8088 machines, which had a certain architecture which could only use 640K of memory. As machines progressed, the hardware got to the point where you could use as much memory as you had in your machine, but DOS did not progress accordingly.

That was to keep backward compatibility.

JR: Right. So what we do is sort of ignore DOS and throw the machine into its native mode—protected mode—where it can use all this memory and leave DOS behind. That posed a lot of technical challenges. Actually, it was the first real protected-mode software I've done, and there are some interesting quirks to it. And there's a very big lack of standards as far as protected mode goes.

DB: Jon, again, was the core man, leading us into the realm of extended DOS.

What about support for all these new accelerated graphics cards?

JR: Way back when, I decided that that was something I would not do—sit and write drivers for a hundred different cards. It's so much work. I've seen it done. So we decided to license somebody's auto-detection and video card drivers, and the drivers that we're using have support for a lot of the accelerated video cards, the S3 and the 8514, and the Mach 32 chips. We support all those in their native modes, so there's a significant graphics speed increase when you're running on those cards. That's something I really wanted in there, because I wanted to encourage people to go buy accelerated video cards. If more people have them, we can take advantage of them and put more stuff in our games and still have them run fast enough to be fun. If you don't have one, go buy one.

Did you guys make any special changes or add any sneaky hidden things to the DOS version of the program? I won't tell anyone, I promise.

JR: Actually, one of the early pre-beta versions, where I first got the simulator hooked up, had this bug in it where it kept putting down churches about every other house. It was Jerry Falwell–land. A mass of churches. I'm gonna hook it up so if you type in a bad word, it'll do that.

You're just gonna pick a few bad words, and have it do that.

JR: Yeah a few four-letter words.

DB: We should do the llama, when you press the Maxis logo on the file dialog. . . .

JR [*laughing*]: Yeah we should do that, have a sound effect. In the file dialog there's a thing that looks like a button, but isn't. We should give it a sound effect. Maybe.

Note to readers: Alas, the llama sound didn't make it into the first release.

Did you learn any big lessons from working on this project?

JR: Don't do your own windowing system. Well, actually, I learned a lot technically. A wealth of programming knowledge was gained doing this project. And I learned how sewers worked. I never knew before how sewers worked.

What more could you want out of a job? Technical stuff and how sewers work?

JR: One more thing. We're so keyed into this thing, looking at it line-by-line, chasing down the bugs, my vision of it was becoming dark and depressing. You start thinking it's ugly, it's bug-ridden, just because you're so used to looking for things that are wrong with it. I took a version home and showed it to my roommate, who had never seen it before. I watched him play for about a half an hour. The guy was just floored. He was so amazed at how in-depth it was and how good it looked. That was a really eye-opening experience. I came back to work the next day and actually played it for a while. It's really a good game.

So the lesson is, "When you're programming, you have to concentrate on the bad stuff, but every so often take some time, step back, and sniff the good parts"?

JR: Yeah. People ask what it's like to work on this really big project, and it's not fun, because you're so keyed into the negative all the time. Because you want it to be so good. You have to find and kill all the problems. You walk away at the end and never want to look at it again. So it's not a happy, joyous experience the whole time. But if you can watch someone else, with a fresh attitude, play it, it can brighten things up.

WILL AND FRED ON *SIMCITY 2000*

Will Wright is one of the founders of Maxis and the creator of SimCity *(now* SimCity Classic*). Other games he has designed for Maxis are* SimEarth *(with Fred Haslam) and* SimAnt *(with Justin McCormick). His business cards have proclaimed him to be everything from Living Legend to Llama Consultant. He is also a real wise guy. Fred Haslam . . . well, read on and see for yourself.*

Warning: this interview/conversation gets out of control and leaves the intended subject matter far behind.

Will, would you like to tell us how you rose to fame and fortune as a game designer?

WW: No.

No? OK. Fine.

FH [*laughing*]: He started out in a cheap rock band called the *Dazzlers*. Just before they hit it big, they kicked him out. His last words to them were, "You guys don't know how to party."

What? His nose wasn't big enough and his drumming wasn't loud enough?

WW: They didn't appreciate bongos.

OK, Fred, in slightly more detail and truth than Will's story, how did you get involved with *SimCity 2000*?

FH: I was born in a small log cabin in Kentucky.

WW: No he was born in Petaluma.

FH: No I wasn't, I was born in SF [*Michael's note: this could either refer to San Francisco or Science Fiction*]. I had just finished another job and I was broke. I sent out 50 résumés and one of them happened to land at Maxis right on the day that they started looking for a Macintosh programmer to work with Will on *SimEarth*.

I went over and talked to Will, and we had a little synergy going talking about the *SimEarth* project, and that was fun.

You may not know this, but I think the thing that clinched the job for you was the fact that you already knew about plate tectonics. I remember Will talking about you and he was really excited about plate tectonics.

FH: I was pretty happy with the *SimEarth* plate tectonic model.

WW: Me, too.

FH: We got the continental drip action going.

WW: Out of all the models we've built I think that *SimEarth* is the most impressive. . . .

Wait a minute. Fred, did you say "continental *drip*"?

FH: Yeah continental drip is one of my favorite theories. I read about it once. It was presented as a joke, but I think there's really something to it. If you look at the globe of the planet, you'll see all these little things dangling down toward the south pole.

Hmmm. . . .

There's the bottom of Africa, the bottom of South America, Baja, Florida, India, Italy. Everything points down, except of course Australia, which is always backwards. And I thought about it and there's actually a reason for that.

WW: No. . . .

FH [*to Will*]: I told you this before. There's actually a reason for that. You know these things are all created by plate tectonics; the magma underneath the earth, pushing things around and spreading things out and squeezing them and pulling them.

WW: Yeah. . . .

FH: There are currents down there. What would affect those currents? Do you think the earth's rotation might affect those currents? Wouldn't it tend to make them go sideways? If you look at most of the major plates, they're moving sideways towards each other like the center of the Pacific, the center of the Atlantic—they go generally up and down.

My theory is that, given the earth's rotation, it affects the magma so that you tend to get currents that run parallel to the equator. And that's what causes continental drip.

Ladies and gentlemen, you heard it here first.

WW: I don't buy it.

FH: You don't think the earth's rotation would affect magma currents?

WW: Oh, I think it very well could, I think there's a Coriolis effect there.

FH: Which way do you think those currents would flow as a consequence?

WW: I don't think those currents have anything to do with all those little appendages pointing down. I would think they would have a lot more to do with the surface erosion. Like the global ocean currents would have a much bigger effect than the magma currents. Because when you look at it, like the north Atlantic, it's spreading right there. So you basically have this other plate over here where it's subducting, that's California, and the Pacific plate rotating. I mean, you look around the whole edge, you're getting every range of motion. You're getting spreading this way, spreading that way, rotation . . . so I don't see any consistency. . . .

FH: Look at South America. I think that's a classic case of continental drip occurring. South America. You have that mountain range that goes straight down the middle and creates that little thing at the bottom.

WW: That's from the collision between the. . . .

FH: Right! Exactly, the collision this way [hand gesture]. Continental drip.

WW: Well, you have a collision here, but in the Atlantic you have a spreading there. It always has to balance out. For every spreading zone there has to be a subduction zone.

Is that continental suck?

WW [*chuckling*]: That's conservation of continents.

FH: That's a given. Try to make a ball-shaped field, there's always a place where nothing's moving. . . .

WW: What you're saying, I think, has a lot more to do with the directions that the continents broke apart in. So there was this huge Gondwanaland, and basically the world is spreading out from that now. It's still in this giant global expansion, continental expansion thing.

FH: Well actually, the Atlantic is opening and closing. It just goes like that. [*hand gestures*]

WW: Yeah, historically. It's starting to subduct also. Maybe it's stopping, maybe it's reversing, I don't know.

FH: Do you know how many times the Mediterranean has dried up?

No. . . .

FH: Many times. Dozens. Hundreds. I don't know. It's dried up so many times that there are huge salt formations underneath the Mediterranean. I got that from Scientific American.

WW: Do you know what the big theory was before continental drift? How people explained it? Global expansion. They thought the whole planet was expanding slowly. They said that's why South America fits into Africa, because they used to be one continent before the earth got bigger and they spread apart.

FH: Sort of the raisin bread theory. That's the way they explain how the stars move away from each other. You have the dough for the raisin bread, you got the raisins. As it expands because of the yeast action, the raisins move away from each other.

WW: Oh. I had heard that as the balloon theory, with dots on a balloon.

[*This went on for a bit with a lot of hand gesturing and incomprehensible terms. Cut to a while later, back on the subject of SimCity 2000. For more information on plate tectonics, see the* SimEarth *manual.*]

FH: . . . and then after finishing *SimEarth*, I was so excited about being a real computer game programmer, that they talked me into doing *SimCity 2000* before I knew what was going on.
WW: So I wouldn't have to do it.

So Will, you came up with the original *SimCity*. I'm sure you're sick of telling that now-famous story of how it came about, but one more time, please.
WW: Aliens abducted me and put a chip in my brain.

Gee, I thought it had something to do with enjoying making the buildings more than blowing them up when you were designing *Raid on Bungling Bay* for Brøderbund. . . .

FH [*out of nowhere*]: I stick to my continental drip theory. I also think I know what Nemesis is.

WW: Is this going to go in the book?

Unless you'll pay blackmail to keep it out.

FH: After I came to the conclusion as to what Nemesis was, there was an article in *Scientific American* that make me think about it. . . .

WW: The black hole orbiting?

FH: No. The incredible upwelling.

WW: Oh, the volcanic. . . .

FH: Yeah, we're talking massive upwellings. A hundred to a thousand times the size of Krakatoa.

WW: Well, you know the KP boundary stuff, how the dinosaurs died? Basically there was Alvarez's theory that it was a giant meteor, but then there was all this contradictory evidence that it was volcanic activity. And now they're beginning to link the two, that perhaps these meteors caused the volcanic activity.

FH: The massive upwellings that they were talking about, the ones that they have evidence for, occurred in the middle of the Atlantic. They threw up so much magma that they found rocks that were similar on both sides of the Atlantic.

WW: Yeah, but imagine a giant meteor hitting the middle Atlantic, that's the thinnest part of the crust.

FH: That would do the trick. But it's happened regularly over time, approximately every 20 to 30 million years.

WW: But, see, it could very well be meteorite showers starting the tectonic event.

FH: But anyway, if it was the massive upwelling, remember Krakatoa lowered the earth's average temperature by two degrees. And we're talking about something a thousand times the size of Krakatoa. . . .

WW: Mount Pinatubo, they're saying two or three degrees. Mount Pinatubo, the one that blew in 1989 or so.

FH: Which then brings us to why the theory of nuclear winter is complete bull. If you want to go into it. . . .

Well, let's wait until *SimEarth 2000*. . . .

FH: The theory of nuclear winter was based on two pieces of evidence, the fact that Krakatoa lowered the earth's temperature by two degrees, and the amount of soot that was generated by the firebombing of Dresden. Then they went ahead and assumed that every nuclear device dropped would generate as much soot as the firebombing of Dresden. That's where the nuclear winter theory came from.
WW: I think it's far too complex to even analyze.

[*Desperately trying to get the conversation back under control . . .*] **OK. So the aliens implanted a chip in your brain and that's how *SimCity* began. Now, back to *SimCity 2000*.**
FH: Well, OK.

So Maxis said, "Fred, go to it. Make *SimCity 2000*."
FH: Basically, they said "go to it," but they had some ideas. They gave me this list of things from off the networks.

WW: It had to be 3-D.

FH: Not at first. When it started out, it was still the overhead view, and I had a really complex water model so you could build dams and the water would flow out. I finished off the highways; I'd just done the first step on the "free zoning," which is what I call it. And then at about the eight-month point, they said it had to be 3-D. When we got *A-Train* from ArtDink, that's when things started to hit the fan.

WW: Then there was the four-to-one perspective.

FH: I did it that way and absolutely refused to listen to anybody else, and eventually . . . well, Will was working on another project that had the 2 to 1 perspective, and when he joined me on this project, he brought that code over wholesale to get it looking good.

Do you still wish it was 4-to-1 perspective?

FH: No. I went back and looked at what I was doing. And [*whistle*].

So you were working on *SimCity 2000* on your own for about a year and a half. What kind of research did you have to do, other than learning the original *SimCity* code through and through?
FH: Uh. . . .

WW: I gave you a bunch of books.

FH: I glanced through them. Basically, Will already had all the research in his head; it didn't seem to me like it was worth doing it all over again.

So you took his word for it.

WW: Yeah, we have lots and lots of city planning books.

FH: Will gave me a book called *Trip Generation*, which is over a thousand pages and weighed more than both my cats. And it was nothing but graphs and numbers. And he'd never read it.

[*Lots of laughing.*]

FH: I was thinking of keeping it as a car jack.

When and why did Will get involved in the project?
FH: At the year-and-a-half point.

Which is about a year ago?
WW: About a year ago.

When you started on the project, Will, what did you do?

WW: I sort of dived into the interface stuff. We kept the model. Fred just moved the model right in. I just rewrote all the graphics, with the code I had been working on for a few months for another project. And of course, we had to talk to the artists about redrawing everything they had already drawn.

FH: Yeah, but we had already done that like three times. They were going insane.

WW: Really.

I already interviewed Jenny about the project and asked her if anything went wrong and she said, "I don't think you want to hear about it."

FH [*laughing*]: The proper question is what went right. . . .

Anybody else help on this, programming- and designing-wise?

WW: Justin [McCormick] helped on the music and on a few hairy bugs. Mick [Foley] did the shape-draw stuff that all the graphics rely on.

What were the biggest challenges for you?

FH: Oh God, the networks were evil. Putting down roads, putting down wires, putting down highways, putting down rails, putting down subways, putting down tunnels, putting down pipes, putting down bridges.

WW: Really, it was the highways. I tried fixing that highway code a couple of times and that was godawful.

FH: Well it was working, and we moved the tiles around just a little. All the tiles shifted down by one, and that screwed up the highways significantly. I think I finally got that worked out, didn't I? There are four types of bridges, so we're talking about 11 things that have to interact, connect, overlap, over-run, go underneath each other, detect each other. It was a lot.

WW: A combinatorial explosion.

FH: Will made the first whack at it, and I went back and tried to improve what he had and came up with something that, well, worked. And we left it at that.

WW: I never would have gotten the highway code.

FH: People complain about how stupid the roads are when they try to go over hills. But making it smarter would have been an incredible problem.

WW: That was the hairiest code in the whole thing.

What tools did you guys use?

FH: Hammer, saw, chain saw, ball peen hammer. . . .

Programming tools.

FH: Think C[11], ResEdit[12], Tmon[13]. . . .

WW: Think Debugger[14], Mick's [Mick Foley] shape shoot stuff, Steve Hales' sound stuff.

FH: And both my brothers.

They're tools?

FH: They're my private debuggers. My private testers.

WW: And Cassidy [Will's daughter] for user interface.

How old is she now? Seven?

WW: Yeah, seven. She likes Captain Hero a lot.

Captain Hero? Where'd he come from?

FH: I had this list of things I wanted to throw into the game right from the start. I had to get rid of about half of them. But the one thing I held onto, I was true to myself, I didn't back down, was Captain Hero. I put him in at the last second. We had one tile left over and I thought, "Yes! It's mine!" and Captain Hero is one tile.

WW: I found one tile later and put in the Loch Ness monster. That was the last tile.

So back to Captain Hero . . . what, why, and when?

FH: Oh, I've been role-playing for years. I've been running Champions, which is a superhero role-playing game. It's the most fun of any role-playing game. Most games you have to worry about getting killed. But superheroes, they're nigh immortal. The game master drops safes on them, blows them up, and shoots them with tanks, and they come back for the next adventure.

But what does Captain Hero do in *SimCity 2000*?

FH: He runs around and stops disasters. He'll put out fires, he'll back off flood waters, and he fights the monster. He fights tornadoes, too.

---

[11]Think C by Symantec, Cupertino, CA.
[12]ResEdit by Apple Computer, Inc.
[13]Tmon by Viacom New Media, Inc., Wheeling, IL.
[14]Think Debugger by Symantec, Cupertino, CA.

Is he random, or. . . .

FH [*to Will*]: Should we tell him?

WW: I don't know if anyone's figured that out yet.

FH: Maybe we shouldn't tell him.

WW: They'll figure it out eventually, so we might as well. . . .

FH: OK. If you don't take a military base, he becomes available. If you take a military base and they can't find a place to put one, he becomes available. He'll show up for a quarter of your disasters.

WW: You'll hear a cheering when he appears.

FH: Oh, and also it switches to the closest-in view and centers on him, so you can't miss him.

In a new city, before you reach the option of having a military base. . . .

FH: You need a population of 60,000 before you have the option.

And you won't see him until after you get the military base offer. And what about Nessie?

WW: Nessie you almost never see. She eats boats.

FH: You need a marina.

[*At this point Jeff Braun, cofounder of Maxis, walks into the room, and he and Will talk about some scheduling stuff for a couple of minutes.*]

Since I've already lost control of this interview, and you're here, Jeff Braun, do you have anything profound to say about *SimCity 2000*?

FH [*whispering to Jeff*]: Buy it!
[*Lots of laughing.*]

That's professional, but not profound. Anything, Jeff?

JB: No. [*He leaves.*]

What does it take to be a game designer and/or game programmer?

WW: Selective brain damage.

FH: What does it take?

Yeah. What kind of person, what's the lifestyle. . . .

FH: You have to love games and you have to be smart. At least the programmer has to be smart.

How much of the job is technical, programming and math stuff, and how much is more artsy design stuff.

FH: As Edison said . . . what did Edison say?

WW: 99 percent perspiration and 1 percent inspiration.

FH [*laughing*]: Well we did about 99 percent inspiration as well and tossed out 98 percent of it.

What was your working method here? How much do you design ahead of time before you actually start programming?

FH: Well, we had the original *SimCity*, and that's where it started. I wrote up the stuff we talked about, and we put in the shape-shooter stuff. It's basically at the point where the game is stable enough that you were getting income and were putting things down, and Will had the interface going, that we started designing again.

WW: We did it more by accretion than. . . .

FH: Well, at the point where you had the interface stable, where you were actually able to grab things and put them down, that's where we started putting things in again.

WW: I'd say that within a couple months we had about 90 percent of the design. We knew what we wanted. We wanted highways, underground. . . .

FH: We knew everything we wanted at the start, worked on implementing it for two and a half years, then spent the last six months putting in everything else. Putting in all the disasters. Like the volcano was so much fun. We put it in at the last second.

WW: All the fun stuff was done in the last month.

FH: Actually, you can't get the volcano as a random event. You can only get it as a part of a scenario.

And a new set of add-on scenarios is on the way. [Blatant plug.]

WW: What, Krakatoa?

Portland. I wanted to call the scenario "Mounting St. Helen" on the box, but they made me change it. So now it's "Mountains that lava too much and the Mayors that have to deal with them."

[*Groans and a discussion of personal earthquake experiences that led into hurricanes.*]

WW: I was camping on the coast of Louisiana when Camille hit.

FH: All right!

Speaking of Camille, are you guys believers or not of massive design documentation ahead of time, before programming?

WW: I'm not. [*During the last few minutes, Will has been manhandling a calendar and tearing it up. He hands me three days in December.*]

So you just try it. If it works keep it, if it doesn't, toss it?

WW: Yep.

So what advice do you have for people who want your jobs—or other jobs like them.

FH: Learn how to program.

WW: Be weird.

FH: Learn how to program and play lots of games. If you find yourself capable of writing a game, someday you'll be capable of writing a really good game. My dad's a writer, and when you ask him how to learn to write, he says, "write." So basically, do it and keep doing it until you get good.

WW: I'd say you should read a lot, too. Read a lot of stuff that's not about computers. There's imagination, but there's also exposure.

FH: Know the world. I bet you could write a really good game if you watch nothing but MTV.

WW: I think I've seen a few.
[*Lots of chuckles.*]

Is there anything else about the making of *SimCity 2000* that you would like to say, that's interesting and at least somewhat coherent?

FH: I can't believe how impossible the credits were.

WW: I think the music too. I think this is the first program we did where I really like the music. Not to dump on our other programs, but, you can take anything and listen to it four or five times, but when you have to hear it over and over, every day, every five minutes, at some point. . . .

FH: It wasn't only the music. It was the way you had it laid out, so it wasn't always coming up.

WW: It was sort of random, but Justin did a good job of getting it into the right instruments, and Sue did a good job of composing. I thought the pieces were really nice. They weren't obnoxious. That was the main thing.

FH: If you're sitting and watching your city and touching none of the buttons, you won't have to listen to the music. But as soon as you start doing stuff, the music pops up. I think that was a good idea.

WW: That's what keeps it from becoming annoying. It only starts when you click on buttons. And then it picks random songs, sometimes based on the button you're clicking on. If you stop interacting with it, the music stops. So it's actually the user interacting that causes the music. That way, if you're just letting it run in your office, you won't hear the music all the time.

Anything else?

FH: Yeah. If Ren and Stimpy's so commercial, when are they going to make another cartoon?

C H A P T E R
16
Inside the *SimCity 2000* Model

This chapter describes the inner workings of the simulation behind the game. A lot of this information is repeated elsewhere in this book, chopped into discreet pieces, and spread out in various chapters on various subjects. But it is all *here*, in one place, for a serious dose of simulation surfing. And for your reading pleasure.

Note: We have attempted to divide the explanations of the different parts of the model into discrete sections for ease of dealing with one thing at a time and ease of finding the area of the model you want to read about. But in the actual simulation, all the elements of the model are so interrelated that each section has some overlap with at least one other section.

Another Note: The explanations in this chapter assume that the goal of the game is continued growth. Things that promote growth are described as desirable and things that prevent growth are considered problems to be solved. This single point of view was taken to give consistency to the explanations, not to dictate that you must always strive for growth in the cities you build. Choose your own goals and build what you want. If you prefer smaller cities, look for those things that block growth and put them to your own use.

THE SIMULATION TECHNOLOGY

When asked what simulation technique was used in *SimCity 2000*, Will Wright shrugged and said to give it a fancy name, like System Dynamic CA Hybrid Discrete Stochastic Monte Carlo Thing. Right.

What *really* goes on inside the model is close to 100 different variables interacting in a hybrid simulation, half-based on cellular automata and half-based on system dynamics.

Cellular automata (often called CAs) are explained in a sidebar; they are used to calculate all the local variables and statistics. Each tile in the map is a CA—actually a whole stack of CAs, one for each of the variables that describes what's going on in that tile, including pollution level, crime level, land value, presence of power, and so forth.

During each simulation cycle, each tile calculates all these factors based on its neighbors. For example, if all your surrounding neighbors are highly polluted, you're bound to catch the overflow and be polluted, too. All the information that shows up as charts in the Map window is handled with a modified CA technique.

SimCity 2000 departs from the classic CA rules in two ways:

- Different CAs can affect each other; for instance, the pollution CA can affect the land-value CA, which in turn can affect the crime CA, and so on—in effect making a three-dimensional CA array.
- The values in the CAs are affected by global variables.

The system-dynamics part of the simulation deals with the global, overall variables and functions, like the demand for different zones. These global functions drive the lower-level, spatially distributed CAs.

FROM *SIMCITY* TO *SIMCITY 2000*

Everything in the old *SimCity* (Classic) model is in *SimCity 2000*, but a lot more features have been added:

- You can build your own hospitals, and they have an effect on the game.
- You can build schools and other educational facilities, and they will have an effect on the game.
- The industry model is much more varied and complex.
- You can get a number of population breakdowns.
- There is a water system.
- There are a lot more power sources available.
- There are more transportation options, including subways and highways.
- There are kudos (special reward buildings or zones).
- There are now rail stations where passengers embark and debark.
- There are arcologies.

Cellular Automata

Cellular automata are a method of computation. They are often used as an exploration of artificial life. One of the best-known examples of a CA is the game *Life*, based on the work of the mathematician John Horton Conway.

In its simplest form, the CA has for its basic parts a grid, a starting condition, and a set of rules:

- The grid is two-dimensional, like graph paper. Each square in the grid is called a *cell*.
- At the starting condition, some of the grids are blank and some are filled in.
- The rules determine what will change.

Here's the process: At the starting condition, each cell on the grid looks at all eight of its surrounding cells and, following the rules, figures out whether to change or not. All the cells figure out what they're going to do, but they don't do it until they have all done their calculation. Then they all change at once. Once they have changed, the grid starts over with the new state as a starting condition.

In the game of *Life*, the following rules hold, assuming that filled-in cells are living and blank ones are dead:

- A living cell with fewer than two living neighbors dies of isolation.
- A living cell with more than three living neighbors dies of overcrowding.
- A dead cell with exactly three living neighbors spontaneously springs to life.

This game is pretty simple in theory, but it can get quite complicated when you add different colors, more complex rules, and various starting patterns on the grid. In theory, any calculation that a computer can do can be represented in a CA.

The important thing to remember about CAs and their use in simulations is that, strictly speaking, they are a local phenomenon—they only react to their eight neighbors. *SimCity 2000* breaks that rule. It uses a system of CAs to represent each of the tiles on the map, but it breaks the local isolation rule. Sometimes rules are meant to be broken.

For a chance to play with creating your own CAs on your computer, see the game *Life Genesis*, which is included in the Microsoft Entertainment Pack for Windows. On the Mac side, there is something even better—CASim by Ken Karakotsios.[1]

---

[1] *CASim*, Algorithmic Arts, P.O. Box 20191, San Jose, CA 95160. $29.95 plus tax. Write or e-mail him at Karakots@netcom.com for more information.

THE CORE OF THE MODEL

The central core of the model is the balance between residential, commercial, and industrial demand:

- Residential demand is driven by the presence of commerce and industry, because you need someplace for the workers to live.
- Commercial demand is driven by the overall population size. The more people you have, the more you need stores and pet shops and the like.
- Industrial demand is driven by the external national model (more on this later), because you need to sell the bulk of your industrial goods to consumers outside your city. The demand indicator is at left.

In general, the residential demand will equal the sum of the industrial and commercial demands.

In a small city, there is more demand for industry than for commerce. Initially there is an industry-to-commerce ratio of 3:1. As the city grows and the population nears 100,000, the ratio approaches 1:1. Beyond that, commercial demand continues to grow and outstrips industry.

But no matter the demand, there are three major limits on city growth:

- There is no growth without power.
- There is no growth without transportation.
- Growth is severely limited unless there is a water system.

If these conditions are met, your city will grow—subject to quite a number of complications.

ZONE DEVELOPMENT

Unlike the original *SimCity*, where all zones were the same size and shape and all Sim-built buildings (other than single residences) were the same size (3×3 tiles), *SimCity 2000* has buildings that are 1×1 tile, 2×2 tiles, and 3×3 tiles.

Low-density zones, whether commercial, residential, or industrial, support only 1×1 buildings. These buildings keep your land value high, your crime low, and your population happy.

In general, high-density zones, as they develop and continue to grow, first fill with 1×1 buildings, then are replaced by 2×2 buildings (there are two steps or densities of 2×2 buildings), and then eventually become 3×3 buildings—if all the other conditions are met.

Low-density zones are financially and aesthetically desirable. They keep land values higher and bring in more money from property taxes. High-density zones allow a greater population, which increases revenues through sources other than property taxes. There's always a tradeoff.

CAPS

There are also a number of "caps" that prevent you from growing beyond a certain point. But don't worry, the Sims will let you know when they've hit a cap and what to do about it.

Residential growth hits a cap at a population of about 15,000. At this point, you need some entertainment centers, such as stadiums and zoos and marinas, before the residential population will break through that cap.

Up to a point, the more you build, the more population you can get.

The commerce cap is broken by the presence of airports or roads off the edge of the city to reach your neighbors. These represent your ability to get goods for commerce and generally carry on business. If you don't have enough commercial transportation, the Sims will let you know, and you'll have to either enlarge your airport or add roads to your neighbors.

The industry cap is broken by the presence of seaports, highways, or rail connections off the edge of the city. These enable you to ship your industrial goods to market. The amount of industrial trade capacity required is based on the amount of industry in your city—the more industry, the more capacity you need. When you don't have enough, the Sims will raise a stink (by sending out an Industry Needs a Seaport message), and you must add some more. This message can flash by quickly and be easily missed, so if you notice your industry lagging behind the other two zones and unemployment rising, add more industrial carrying capacity. If you don't have a river or coastline, a seaport is useless. Also, the carrying capacity of a seaport is dependent on the number of docks it has. But docks won't be built unless you have the warehouses and support structures to back them up. So make sure that your seaports have plenty of inland area as well as actual coastline.

While carrying capacity is carrying capacity as far as the simulator is concerned (and as far as your costs are concerned, since the cost of running a road, rail, or highway off the edge of the city is roughly equivalent to an airport or seaport of equal carrying capacity), there are some reasons to consider one over another:

- Aesthetics is one reason. You may like or dislike the look of roads going off the edge. Or you may be prone to seasickness and not want a seaport anywhere near you or your city.

- A road, rail, or highway can perform double duty. It can provide the carrying capacity that you need to bust the caps, and it can be used for successful trip generation to promote edge-zone growth. (See "Transportation" next in this chapter.)
- While it makes no difference to your city—as far as carrying capacity goes—as to whether you have multiple roads (or rails or highways) all going off one edge or whether they are spread out and go off two or more edges, it *will* make a difference to those neighboring cities. If they are well-connected, they will grow faster, and their growth will feed back into the national model, which will grow faster and create more industrial demand for your city.

TRANSPORTATION

The physical layout of the city has a major effect on growth because of the city's transportation needs. Zones will not develop at all unless they are within three tiles of some form of transportation.

For a zone to develop or a building to "grow" to a larger building that will support a bigger population, it must be useful to the citizens. And the way it is useful is through access. The Sims will build or customize the building to suit their needs—if they can get there.

The access needed is an easy, preferably short trip from any one type of zone to both of the other types of zones:

- Residential to commercial
- Residential to industrial
- Commercial to residential
- Commercial to industrial
- Industrial to residential
- Industrial to commercial

The way this is tested is through *trip generation.* A trip or journey is simulated from each building in search of the other two zones. There is a limited amount of time and distance allotted for each trip. If the trip is successful within the limits, the building has the opportunity to develop. If the trip is not successful, the building will stagnate or decay. The number of successful trips is used to calculate the traffic density, as shown in the Map window.

Trip Generation

Here's how trip generation works:

1. The simulation starts from a zoned tile.

2. It heads off in one direction, looking for a mode of transportation (road, subway station, or rail station—but not tracks without a station). If it doesn't find it in three tiles or less, it will go back to the zone and try another direction. If after trying four directions it still can't find what it's looking for, the trip is a failure.

3. If it does find a mode of transportation within three tiles, it will hop on and follow it in search of the desired destination zone.

4. If it finds the destination zone within the time and distance limits, the trip is considered successful.

5. If the simulator runs across another type of transportation on the way, it will flip an electronic coin to decide whether or not to transfer over to it.

The actual time and distance limits of a trip amount to 100 steps—that's *steps*, not tiles. Cars on roads take three steps per tile. Cars on highways take one step per tile. Buses on roads take two steps per tile. Buses on highways take one step per tile. Rails and subways take one step per tile. There is also a four-step trip charge to use a station, which simulates the hassle of getting there, parking, waiting in line, and so on.

There is some limited opportunity for backing up and trying another route during the 100 steps, but if the steps are taken and the target zone isn't found, the zone gets a no-trip rating.

Trips prefer to follow the non-diagonal roads, so even though you may want diagonal roads in your city for design and aesthetic purposes, be sure to have plenty of orthogonal roads, especially around bus stations.

The only time a trip will cross non-transportation tiles in search of transport is at the very beginning of a trip. Once on a road, rail, or subway, the trip can only transfer from one means of transport to another if their access points are adjacent.

One thing that some people have questioned about the model is the fact that a trip is considered successful if it reaches the desired type of zone, whether or not the zone is developed. It can be argued that reaching an empty zone is about as useful as reaching no zone. The counterargument is that if this weren't the case, a new city could never develop—you would need to have developed zones before you could develop zones. In addition, if a zone is conveniently located as the destination of a developed zone's trip, it itself becomes a prime candidate for development.

Trips are only generated one way. The model assumes that if you can get there, you can get back.

Traffic—the number of cars that travel over any particular section of road at a particular time—is a by-product of trip generation.

Modes of Transportation

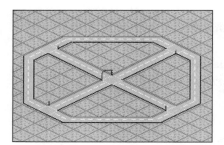

Road section

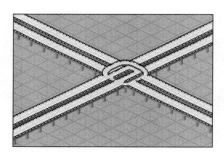

Highway section

Bus depot

Rail and subway depot

There are five modes of transportation in *SimCity 2000*: roads, highways, bus lines, rails, and subways.

Roads are the bare-bones basics of transportation. They are inefficient and lead to a lot of pollution and traffic, but they are cheap to build and cheap to maintain.

Highways allow cars to go further in search of their destinations than roads, and they also have double the carrying capacity. Of course, for your highways to be used, you have to have roads leading to them and on-ramps to provide access to them.

Buses are a major boon to *SimCity 2000*. They lower both the traffic density and pollution from automobile exhaust on both roads and highways within a given radius of a depot. The busier the traffic around the station, the more effective the bus line will be. It has the highest effect close to the depot and a gradually decaying effect as you get farther away. The maximum radius of effect around a depot is about 10 tiles, depending on the roads and traffic in the area.

You must place a bus depot to institute a bus line. Passengers can only get on a bus at the depot, but they can get off buses all along the line. This fact actually makes buses about twice as efficient as subways and railways. In *SimCity 2000*, about twice as many Sims will take a bus as will take subways or rails, assuming that they can get where they want to go with the bus.

Rails and subways are identical as far as the simulator is concerned, except that subways can't make connections to neighboring cities (and therefore don't affect industrial carrying capacity. The only other difference is that one is above the ground and the other is below. Unlike buses, Sims can get on and off of rails or subways only at stations and depots, so you need at least two depots or stations for them to serve any purpose at all. A rail-only series of trips from one zone to the two destination zones requires three stations.

Transportation Strategies

In general, one of the main things that keep cities from developing is that the different zones are too far away from each other and the simulated trips fail. You have to mix your three zone types to get good growth.

You *can* mix your transportation systems. A successful trip, though limited in time and distance, can take two or three different types of transport. You can run rails or subways from outlying communities into the city center where the Sims can then take buses (or taxis or rental cars) the rest of the way. Or the other way around. Of course, this is more hassle for the poor Sim, having to switch modes of transport all the time, so it isn't as efficient as a single line. It does work; not perfectly, but it does work.

One of the features that you can take advantage of in your layouts is that the model assumes that all types of zones are accessible just beyond the edges of the city. If you run roads, highways, or rails off the edge, any nearby zone will have successful trips to neighboring cities. It is expensive to build a transport line off the edge of the city, but it can be useful. You can use this fact, for instance, to segregate your heavy industry away from your city center and your high-land-value residential areas. Heavy industry at the edge—with a road off the edge—will have successful trips and will develop. Of course, you have to have industrial zones near enough to your city center and your high-land-value residential zones, but these can be smaller, lower-density, less polluting industrial zones. A highway or train off the edge of the map will serve the double duty of providing industrial capacity and ensuring completed trips. A road off the edge serves the double duty of providing commercial capacity and ensuring completed trips.

LAND VALUE

Land value has a major impact on growth and is very important to consider when growing a city. There are a number of things that affect land value:

- Proximity to the city center—the closer the better. Good access to the attractions of the city is something CitiSims will gladly pay more for.

- Size of the city—the bigger the city, the more the land value increases as you approach the city center. This is because bigger cities have more attractions (restaurants, clubs, and so on).

- Proximity to trees, water, and parks—the general amenities of life—adds value.

- Proximity to hilly terrain increases land value.

- Pollution has a negative effect on the value of surrounding land.
- Crime has a negative effect on the value of surrounding land.

Land value has a direct affect on crime. High land value tends to deter crime. Low land value areas tend to have more crime. Land value and crime have a small feedback effect, where one going up (or down) makes the other go down (or up), in turn pushing the first one even further, and so on. It is possible to get such widespread low land value that crime will get completely out of control. But by placing police well, spreading out your city, and adding some water or green areas, you can both increase land value and decrease crime.

POLLUTION

Pollution is caused by automobiles, industry, power plants, ports, and military bases. It directly affects land value—the higher the pollution, the lower the land value. This indirectly affects crime, since low land value breeds crime in *SimCity 2000*.

Different zones and buildings produce different amounts of pollution, measured in "pollution units." Exactly how these units fit into the math of the simulation is beyond the scope of this book and not really needed. Table 16-1 will help you plan prevention strategies for pollution.

All other buildings and structures have no effect on the pollution model in *SimCity 2000*, including four of the power plants: hydro, wind, solar, and microwave.

Residential and commercial zones do not pollute at all in *SimCity 2000*. This is one area where the model really steers clear of reality, for our homes and offices and gas stations produce a lot of pollutants, garbage, and waste. We can only assume that since industry and the other special zones produce so much more pollution, residences and commerce would, in comparison, just produce a nuisance amount of pollution and not make that big a difference in the overall simulation. Either that or it was a decision for the sake of speeding up the simulation by limiting the number of calculations and sticking to integer values. Or maybe the programmers got lazy.

CRIME

According to *SimCity 2000*, crime breeds and spreads in areas of low land value and high population density. High crime also lowers the local land value, forming a feedback effect that can get out of control and lead to riots.

Table 16-1 Polluters and Their Relative Pollution Units

Building or Structure	Pollution Units
Industrial 1 x 1 building	6
Industrial 2 x 2 building, low density	12
Industrial 2 x 2 building, high density	18
Industrial 3 x 3 building	24
Natural gas power plant	10
Oil power plant	25
Nuclear fission power plant	2
Nuclear fusion power plant	2
Coal power plant	50
Stadium	4
Prison	10
Water pump	2
Runway	10
Pier	10
Crane	5
Warehouse	5
Airplane on runway	10
Subway station	5
Bus depot	3
Rail depot	4
Civilian parking lot	2
Military parking lot	2
Loading dock	2
Military airplane hangar	2
Port loading zone	10
Water treatment plant	10
Civilian airplane hangar	5
Plymouth arcology	15
Forest arcology	10
Darco arcology	12
Launch arcology	15

Providing law enforcement, lowering the population density, and raising the land value are actions that defeat or at least lower crime in an area.

Law enforcement consists of prisons and police stations.

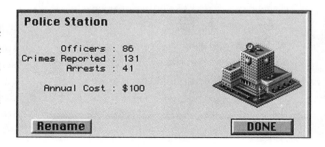

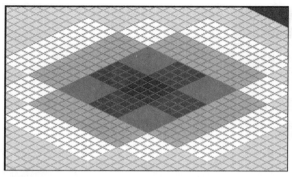

Single police station

Police stations lower crime in their immediate vicinity. There are five bands of effectiveness around a station, with the most powerful effect closest to the station. The maximum radius that a station can affect is about 14 tiles. Placing stations so that their effect overlaps provides better coverage. The figure to the left shows the effectiveness of a single police station.

And here's the effectiveness of overlapping police station areas:

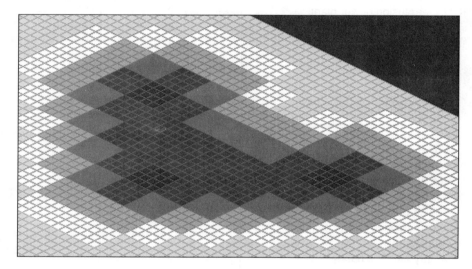

Three overlapped
bands of effectiveness

Since police must patrol their entire areas of effectiveness, it is not a very efficient use of your police force to place a station on the outskirts of the city. Put your stations right in the middle of a problem area (or an area you want to prevent becoming a problem) so that the police that patrol the entire radius around the station are earning their keep.

A police station's actual effect on crime in each band of effectiveness depends on the amount of crime in the area and the funding of the police department. And stations must be powered to have more than a token effect.

The main function of a prison is to make your police stations more efficient and more effective; it frees officers from having to guard prisoners at the stations so that they can go out on the beat and catch bad guys. Its effect on the simulator is to cause an citywide decrease in crime—as long as it isn't overcrowded.

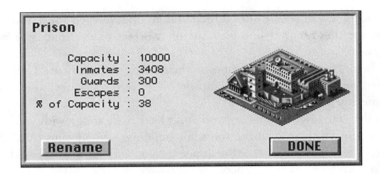

There is no set population level at which a prison becomes necessary. A police chief may recommend it when he thinks it's a worthwhile investment. When you need a prison the actual effect it will have on crime depends on your crime level, the number of police you have, how efficient your police are, and how well they are funded.

Prisons can hold up to 10,000 prisoners, but they can handle only a certain throughput of prisoners before they become overcrowded. They release 25 percent of their prisoners every year to simulate different term lengths and to make room for new prisoners. As (and if) your prison population grows and 25 percent are continually released, eventually it will level off at a stable prison population. If you have more criminals than the prisons can handle, there will be an overflow of criminals back into society and crime will run rampant.

Beware that prisons inspire the NIMBY (not in my back yard) factor among your citizens.

THE POWER MODEL

Electric power is necessary for all development. *SimCity 2000* doesn't even allow the stray SimHermit to build a shack with a potbelly stove for heating and kerosene lamps for light. You gotta be hooked to the power grid.

During every simulation cycle, the power model looks at each power plant, checks its possible power output, and then follows the power lines and connected buildings, adding to the power available when it meets another power plant and taking away from the power availability when it meets a developed zone. When the available power reaches zero, any other buildings on the grid will be unpowered and decay.

Power travels through power lines and through powered buildings. It will not travel through an undeveloped area of a zone.

Placing lots of power lines throughout an undeveloped zone, as opposed to just running a power line into one or two tiles of the zone, will help it grow faster.

The only cost for power lines is their original placement. There is no maintenance fee for power lines, and they have zero resistance, so they don't dissipate any power.

Unlike the original *SimCity*, you don't have to be stingy with your power lines or remove them to make room for buildings. When Sims build buildings, they will move the power lines underground and build on top of them.

You can have multiple, unconnected power grids.

Power is measured in megawatts (MW).

Developed areas consume ±⅓ MW per tile, depending on the population density, the year (the technology level that can lead to more efficient use of power—or blatant waste and overuse), and certain city ordinances.

All power plants (other than wind and hydro) have a 50-year life span, after which they need to be replaced.[2] This fact represents wear and tear and makes up for the fact that you don't have to pay any maintenance on power plants. As the power plants approach their age limits, you will receive warnings in the newspapers. If you don't replace one in time, it will blow up. When it blows up, it doesn't cause any fires or damage to surrounding buildings, but it does stop delivering power, and the loss of power can cause city decay.

Wind and hydro don't need replacement every 50 years for two practical, if not realistic, reasons. First, since they are so small and you need so many to produce a useful amount of power, it would be a real pain to go around replacing them all the time. Second, for memory-saving reasons, the simulation lumps all hydro plants together and all wind plants together and can't track the age of each individual plant.

The availability of different power sources depends on the year in the city. As new technologies—including new power sources—are invented, they will be announced in a newspaper.

Upon starting a new city in the year 1900, you will have only coal, hydroelectric, and oil power at your disposal. The other plants become available over time.

Table 16-2 lists gives important information about the power plants in *SimCity 2000*.

---

[2]Selecting No Disasters in the Disasters menu will automatically replace power plants every 50 years and deduct the cost from your funds.

Plant Type	Year Available (±10 Years)	MW	Cost ($)	Pollution Unit
Coal	1900	200	4,000	50
Hydroelectric	1900	20	400	0
Oil	1900	220	6,600	25
Gas	1950	50	2,000	10
Nuclear fission	1955	500	15,000	2
Wind	1980	4	100	0
Solar	1990	50	1,300	0
Microwave	2020	1600	28,000	0
Fusion	2050	2500	40,000	2

Table 16-2 Power Plant Vital Statistics

THE POPULATION MODEL

SimCity 2000 is populated by Sims—electronic life forms that move in and out of cities. They have a maximum life span of about 90 simulated years. Sims between the ages of 20 and 55 are considered employable, and given the chance, they will work and pay taxes.

The model divides Sims into different age groups, each of which is treated differently and reacts differently. There are three main ways that the population model can influence the simulator and city growth (and non-coincidentally enough, three views in the Population window):

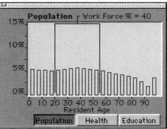

Population view of pop. window

- Overall population and age distributions give the statistics you need to track trends in the ages of your Sims—the percentage that are potential taxpaying workers, retired, and children—the hope for the future.

- The health level affects the life expectancy of your Sims.

- The education level of your Sims directly affects which industries you can support in your city.

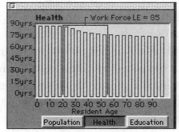

Health view of pop. window

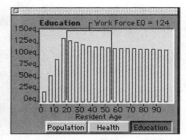

Education view of pop. window

When your city is first created and Sims move in from other places, every Sim is an immigrant. Simmigrant population is weighted towards people of working age, primarily between 20 and 55. There will be some older Sims and some younger, but most will fall in the 20–55 year-old range.

Simmigrants come into town with an average life expectancy of 59 to 65 and an average education quotient of 85 or slightly below. What this means and how *SimCity 2000* models health and education will be explained in detail in the next two sections.

THE HEALTH MODEL

For those familiar with the original *SimCity*, health is a brand new factor. Where once hospitals appeared on their own in residential zones, they—and the health of your Sims— are now your responsi-

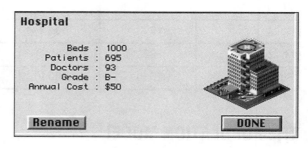

bility. Health is expressed as life expectancy (LE). The Health graph shows the life expectancies of each age group.

As mentioned, the life expectancy of a Simmigrant is set at 65. That's not very good considering a possible LE of 90.

The way the health model works is not only functional for the game but fairly realistic, within limits. Taking the long-term-care wellness approach, hospitals primarily affect the youngest Sims—children from 0 to 5 years of age.

At the time a Sim is born, its life expectancy is set. This life expectancy is primarily affected by the presence or absence of hospitals. It is also very slightly increased if the Free Clinics, Public Smoking Ban, or Pollution Controls city ordinances have been passed. Raising the life expectancy of your Sims is a slow process that takes many years.

As the Sims age and move up to the next age group, a little bit of time is subtracted from their life expectancy, depending on your city's pollution value. The higher the pollution, the more time they lose.

As the Sims continue to age and reach maturity, they beget little Simlings who then move through the age ranges and eventually beget their own Simlings. The Sims' reproductive age range is about the same as the workforce age range—20 to 55.

As Sims continue to age, the older ones die off.

THE EDUCATION MODEL

The education quotient (EQ) of your Sims is the measure of the amount of education your population has received. It is closely interrelated to both the health model and the industrial model, and it has a great impact on city growth. It affects a number of things, especially including what type of industries you can support in your city.

An EQ of 85 is the equivalent of a high school education. An EQ of 100 is the equivalent of the current United States average. The maximum EQ in *SimCity 2000* is 150.

A Sim's EQ is raised by attending school. After school, the EQ will decay slightly. This decay can be negated by the presence of libraries and museums and by enacting the Pro-Reading Campaign ordinance. Libraries serve a population of 20,000, and museums serve 40,000.

When working-age Simmigrants enter a new city, their EQ is fixed at 85 or slightly below. The few children that come with them have a marginally lower EQ.

Children in the 0-to-5 age range get their education from their parents through association and home preschooling. The EQ given to newborn children is calculated by taking the average EQ for all the working-age Sims and dividing it by five. So Sims of the first generation to be born in a city receive an EQ of 85 divided by 5, which is 17.

Simlings of the next two age steps, 5–10 and 10–15, get an additional amount of education from schools. The amount that they get depends on how many schools you have and how well they are funded. If you have enough schools to cover the entire population, the children will receive 35 EQ points in each of the two age groups.

In *SimCity 2000* there is a single school that provides elementary, middle, and high-school education to Sims from ages 5–15. The overall capacity of a school is 1,500 students, which serves an overall population of approximately 15,000, more or less, depending on the population's age distribution in your city. Using the Query tool on a school reveals, among other things, the student population, the number of teachers, and a grade. The grade is a measure of how well the school is serving its purpose, not the average grade of the students in the school (actually the two might be very close).

So under the best of circumstances, that first generation can increase their EQ to 17 + 35 = 52 by age 10 and 52 + 35 = 87 by age 15.

Then with a little bit of educational decay over their working years they're back to around 85, where their parents were. So if you build

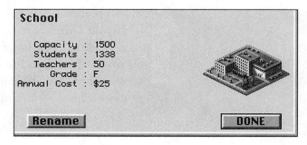

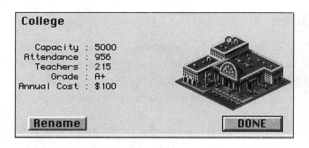

enough schools and keep them funded, you can maintain a population with, on the average, a high-school education.

Colleges in *SimCity 2000* serve a maximum capacity of 5,000 students, which serves an overall population of roughly 50,000, more or less, depending on the population's age distribution in your city. Using the Query tool on a college reveals, among other things, the student population, the number of teachers, and a grade measuring how well the college is serving its purpose.

If you have colleges ready and funded when the Sims hit college age, then the average EQ of the people served is multiplied by 1.5. So assuming that our first-generation Sims go to college right out of high school and enter with an EQ of 87, they'll graduate with an EQ of about 130, which is the limit for the first generation of Sims born in your city.

When these Sims have children of their own, they'll start out better then their parents did. They get an EQ of one-fifth of 130, or 26, to start their lives with. As they go through school, pick up 70 points, and increase that by 50 percent in college, they can reach an EQ of 144.

And the next generation can emerge from their 0-to-5 years with a starting EQ of 28.8, and so on.

Eventually your city can hit and maintain an EQ of 150, assuming you have enough well-funded schools and colleges for all, along with plenty of libraries and museums to prevent EQ decay.

The Education model ties in directly with life expectancy and the health model—EQ is affected by how long the Sims live. If they die very young, before they can finish their education, then the average EQ goes way down. Also, if your Sims are dying, say in their late 50s or 60s, then that means that a larger portion of the total population is found in the younger ages, which require schooling. This fact makes the schools and colleges less effective, since they have to serve a higher percentage of the population (as opposed to only 10 percent).

If your citizens are dying young, that means you don't have enough hospitals. Adding a few hospitals can reduce the number of schools and colleges you need to build and maintain by making the ones you have serve a larger overall population. Keeping your Sims healthy is more efficient than building more schools—and more humane.

EQ is very important to city growth, because it leads directly into the Industrial model.

THE INDUSTRIAL MODEL

The Industrial model determines what types of industries are in demand and desired in your city. It is based on three controlling factors:

- The external demand for industries
- Tax rates
- Current ratios of existing industries

The external demand for industries is based on a historical model and a national model. The historical model approximates the actual U.S. industrial demand for the years from the beginning of the simulation in 1900 to the time that the simulation was finished in late 1993, with an added random element to make it more of a challenge and less of a history lesson. The national model is a simple growth model that generates populations for the surrounding cities and for SimNation as a whole. The size of the nation partly dictates the demand for different industries in the nation as a whole. As a rule, the national model grows at about the same rate as your city, so you don't really have to worry too much about what it will do.

Adjusting the tax rates that individual industries are charged lets you modify the demand for and success of various industries in your city. For instance, if you want to discourage certain polluting industries, raise their tax rate. If you want to encourage industries, lower theirs. It is a good idea to hedge your bets by making sure that your city isn't entirely dependent on only one or two industries. (Learn the lesson of Flint, Michigan.)

The current ratio of different industries in your city affects demand. If you've got a zillion automobile plants, you might satiate the national demand.

Those three factors control the national demand for various industries, but not your ability to support them in your city—that depends on your Sims' EQ. High-tech jobs will only come to your city if you have an educated labor base, so the industrial model ties in with the education model.

As far as *SimCity 2000* is concerned, high-tech industries are the best, because they produce less pollution. Less pollution has a number of

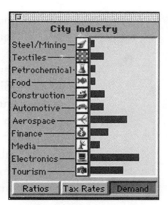
Industrial demand window

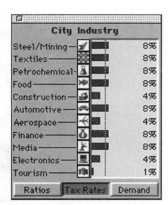
Industrial taxes window

Industrial ratios window

positive effects on the city and its citizens, including longer life expectancy, higher land value, and, indirectly, lower crime.

In general, high-tech industries will grow slowly even with a low EQ, but they receive a growth boost if your city's average EQ for working-age Sims is above 100. Maintaining an EQ of 100 requires the placement and funding of colleges, but not necessarily for the entire population. You can maintain this level with colleges for about half the population.

There are a couple industries that are very demanding of a high EQ, above and beyond the others: aerospace and electronics. Like other high-tech industries, they receive a growth boost at an EQ of 100. They also get another boost if your EQ is above 130. In addition, they receive a curtailment if your EQ is below 80.

The industries available in *SimCity 2000* can be divided into three categories: heavy-polluting industries, low-polluting industries, and the tourist industry. Table 16-3 (and the Industry window) lists these industries from the heaviest polluters at the top to the lowest polluters at the bottom.

The tourist industry is affected by ordinances and land value and a few other minor factors. In spite of what the manual says, hospitals do not help the petrochemical industry. So sue us.

Table 16-3 Tech and Pollution Levels of Industries

Industry	Tech Level	Pollution
Steel and mining	Low	Heavy
Textiles	Low	Heavy
Petrochemical	High	Heavy
Food	Low	Heavy
Construction	Low	Heavy
Automotive	High	Heavy
Aerospace	Double-high	Low
Electronics	Double-high	Low
Finance	High	Low
Media	High	Low
Tourism	High	Almost none

THE FINANCIAL MODEL

Finance in *SimCity 2000*, like finance everywhere, consists of getting money and spending it. There are three ways to get money:

- Collect property taxes
- Issue bonds
- Enact ordinances

There are also three primary reasons to spend money:

- Build infrastructure
- Maintain infrastructure
- Enact ordinances

Most of this is pretty straightforward and is listed in tables and charts elsewhere in this book, but bonds and interest rates are worth mentioning here under the Financial model.

Bonds were the most demanded feature that was left out of the original *SimCity*. They enable you to keep playing and keep trying even after you run out of money, much as real cities do.

When you issue a bond, you receive $10,000. You pay the yearly interest on the bond until you pay it off. You have to pay bonds off all at once, and you have to pay them back in the order they were issued. This means that if you have a number of bonds at varying interest rates, you can't pick and choose which ones to pay off; they have to go in order.

The number of bonds you can issue depends on your loan rating. This rating ranges from AAA (good) to F (stinky). It depends on the current city value—all the infrastructure you've built—and the number of bonds you currently have outstanding.

The interest rate you pay on bonds is calculated as follows:

$$\text{prime rate} + 1\% + x\%$$

where x is an additional percentage based on your credit rating.

The prime rate can range from 1 to 12 percent, depending on the current economic trend. There are four economic trends: depression, recession, steady, and boom. The standard cycle is to go from recession to steady to boom to steady to recession every five years. Occasionally, a recession will become a depression. (Historically in the real world, depressions tend to happen every 60 years. They happen randomly in *SimCity 2000*.)

The way the cycle is generated is fairly simple: low interest rates cause a boom, and a boom causes interest rates to rise. Kinda like a dog chasing its tail.

THE WATER MODEL

The Water model in *SimCity 2000* is fairly complex.[3] You can ignore it completely when you are first beginning, but you'll need a water system before you can grow your population very large.

The elements of the water system that you have control over (other than the water mains) all need power, and all need to be connected to the water network. They are:

- Water pumps
- Water mains
- Water towers
- Treatment plants
- Desalinization plants

Water pumps can be put anywhere to produce water. The actual amount of water they pump depends on the water table of the city, which is created when the terrain is generated. Since this is random, you'll have to experiment with each city to see how much water you get from a pump. In addition, pumps will produce more or less water depending on the weather model and the season. When it is raining or snowing, you'll get more water out of a pump—up to twice as much as otherwise. Of course, during dry times, your pump's output can be reduced by half.

Beyond these considerations, the more sides and corners of a pump that are adjacent to fresh water (not ocean water) the more the pump will produce. A pump with one side or corner adjacent to fresh water will supply about 50 percent moe than a pump or well totally surrounded by dry land. With two sides or corners adjacent to water, it will pump 100 percent more. With three sides or corners adjacent to water, it will pump 150 percent more, and so on.

There are eight possible adjacent sides to any pump. So if you can put your pump on a one-tile island surrounded by water, it will pump massive quantities of water. You can customize the landform in New City terrain-editing mode to create these islands, or you can modify the land in city-building mode.

Water pipes under buildings are supplied by Sims when they build. You have only to place water mains and to connect them to sources and to each other.

---

[3]In early prototypes, it was even more complex: It had the ability to model water flow, so you could block rivers and create reservoirs. This option was taken out because the value it added was far exceeded by the amount of CPU time and simulation speed that it cost.

Water towers store excess water when your pumps are producing more water than your city is using. Then during the dry season, if there isn't enough new water being pumped, they put that water back into the system.

Each water tower will store enough water to supply 62 tiles for one month. You'll never see your water towers fill until the water grid is totally blue, and then they will fill slowly. You can see how full a tower is by clicking on it with the Query tool.

Also as a water tower fills, the bottom portion of the tower will animate.

Treatment plants clean sewage, *theoretically* increasing the efficiency of your system (but not really). In addition, if you have enough treatment plants to cover the city population—approximately one treatment plant for every 20,000 Sims—the overall pollution level of your city will be lowered by 10 to 15 percent. Treatment plants create their own pollution (10 pollution units), but this is insignificant compared to the overall positive effect they produce.

Desalinization plants are totally useless unless you have a coastline and the plants are adjacent to the water. The pumps that are built into a desalinization plant won't work on fresh water. On the other hand, if you place the desalinization plant on the coast, it treats and pumps about as much water as two regular pumps. As with pumps, its output is affected by the number of sides adjacent to water. If you build it on an island in the ocean, entirely surrounded by water, you'll get a lot of water from your plant. Desalinization plants are also slightly affected by the water table and the weather.

One possibly confusing aspect of the water system is that when you place pumps in an area where there isn't water flowing through the pipes, the new water from these pumps sometimes shows up elsewhere in the city. To remove unnecessary complexity from the simulation, all the output from all the pumps is connected to one water network, and all the water tries to enter the city water system from one place and spread out from there. The backward justification for this is to say that some pumps pump, while others "suck."

MICROSIMS

The final aspects of the model are the microsims, or microsimulations—"little simulations"—that track local statistics and, when appropriate, feed information into the other parts of the model. Microsims track most of the special buildings or structures that you can build. Their information is displayed in the query boxes that appear when you use the Query tool (or shift-click) on the building. They are updated yearly at the end of January.

Some of the microsims and their statistics have a great effect on the model and the city (and output their information to other microsims and to the global simulation), some have very little effect, and quite a few exist just for the fun of it. Some of the statistics trigger newspaper stories.

There are four types of information displayed by microsims: actual calculated statistics, built-in names and numbers (constants), the date the structure was built, and a random number or name. Not all types of data are displayed in every microsim.

A microsim is created and updated for each of the following buildings or structures:

- The Mayor's House
- City Hall
- The Statue
- The Llama Dome
- Each hospital
- Each police department
- Each fire department
- Each school
- Each stadium
- Each prison
- Each college
- Each zoo
- Each treatment plant
- Each desalinization plant
- Each arcology
- Each individual power plant (other than wind and hydroelectric)
- All wind power plants combined*
- All hydroelectric power plants combined*
- All bus stations combined*
- All rail stations combined*
- All subway stations combined*
- All parks combined*
- All museums combined*

- All libraries combined*
- All marinas combined*

For items marked with an asterisk, most of the structures each have their own microsim, but some are grouped for memory efficiency. There is only one microsim to cover each of these types of structures, no matter how many of the structures you have.

Because of memory limitations, you can have a maximum of 150 microsims in any one city. (It is possible that more memory may be allocated to microsims in future revisions.) Once you have the total 150 microsims, when you add another structure that normally requires one, it won't get a microsim. You can build and place the structure, it will still have its global effect on the city and the simulator, but it won't track or display the local statistics in the query box.

Arcologies have precedence in the microsim hierarchy. If you're out of microsims and place an arcology, it will steal the microsim from the first structure you created. Arcologies won't, however, take a microsim from another arcology, and they can't take over any of the *combo microsims* (wind power, hydro power, marinas, and so forth).

Here are the statistics contained in each microsim and a little explanation of what it affects (if anything) in the model.

> Ports (both sea and air) are zones and do not have microsims.

Power Plants (Not Hydro or Wind)

- Maximum Output is determined by the type of power plant.
- Running at *n*% of Capacity is calculated from the number of developed tiles attached to the plant, with a slight random factor thrown in to allow for line loss.
- Age is set to zero when the power plant is established and incremented every year. When the age reaches 48, it triggers a newspaper story, warning you that the plant is near the end of its usefulness. When it reaches 50, the microsim checks to see if No Disasters is set in the Disasters menu. If it is set, then the plant is automatically rebuilt and the cost of the plant is deleted from your funds (if you have it) and the Age variable is reset. If No Disasters isn't set, or if you don't have enough to pay for a new one, the plant will blow up.

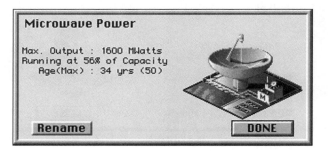

City Hall

- Employees are calculated as one employee for every 900 total citizens but limited to 200.
- The Built In value is the year when the city hall has was built; it doesn't change.
- The Analysis button at the bottom brings up a small window that displays a count of all the tiles (acres) for each type of structure and calculates the percentage of the city that each type of structure occupies:

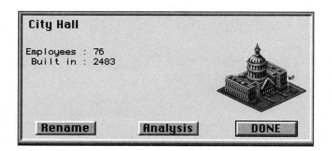

LAND USE		ACRES		% of CITY
Transportation	–	2312	–	%33
Power	–	251	–	%3
Water	–	124	–	%1
Residential	–	1812	–	%26
Commercial	–	695	–	%10
Industrial	–	831	–	%12
Ports/Airports	–	216	–	%3
Education	–	152	–	%2
Health/Safety	–	142	–	%2
Recreation	–	301	–	%4
Arcologies	–	0	–	%0

Hospitals

- Beds are set to 600 or 1,000 for each hospital, depending on your computer.
- Patients are calculated as a function of the total population, the number of hospitals in the city, and a slight random factor, capped by the 600- or 1,000-bed limit.
- Doctors are calculated as a function of total population and hospital funding (with an additional random number added as a fudge factor to make the number look more realistic).

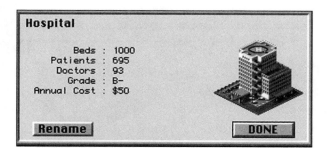

- The Grade value rates how well the hospital is serving its purpose. It is calculated as a function of the patient-to-doctor ratio. The grade, or quality, of the hospital feeds into the overall health model, affecting the LE.
- Annual Cost is the amount of funding you've provided.

Police Departments

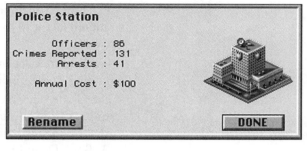

- Officers are calculated as a function of total population and police funding, limited to one-fiftieth of the total population per station.
- Crimes Reported are calculated from the citywide crime model and the total number of police stations.
- Arrests are calculated as a ratio of crimes and officers, an added random factor to allow for luck of both police and criminals, and an added efficiency bonus if there are prisons. Once arrests are calculated for all the different police departments, the microsim adds up total arrests and tries to distribute them to prisons, if there are any. If the prisons get full, criminals are released, which increases the crime rate for the next simulation cycle.
- Annual Cost is the amount of funding you've provided.

Fire Departments

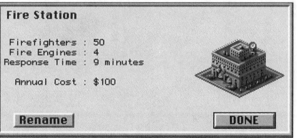

- Firefighters are calculated as a function of total population and fire department funding, limited to one-fiftieth of the total population per station.
- Fire Engines are calculated as a percentage of firefighters.
- Response Time is just for show. It's totally random and doesn't affect the simulation in any way.
- Annual Cost is the amount of funding you've provided.

Schools

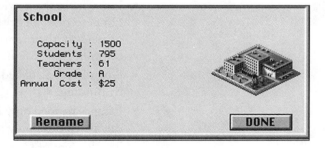

- Capacity is set at 1500 for all schools.
- Students are the total number of citizens between 5 and 15, limited to one-twentieth of the total population, divided by the number of schools, and

then limited again to the capacity of 1500. There is also a slight random factor (0 to 16) added to make the number look more realistic.

- Teachers are calculated as a function of the total population, school funding, and a small random factor.

- The Grade value rates how well the school is performing, not the students. It is calculated as a function of the student-to-teacher ratio: 12.5:1 or below is an A+, 27:1 or above is an F, and the other grades (A, B, C, D, and E) are equally distributed between 12.5 and 27. The grade, or quality, of the school feeds into the overall Education model, affecting the EQ.

- Annual Cost is the amount of funding you provide your school system. If funding is too low, a newspaper story is generated.

Stadiums

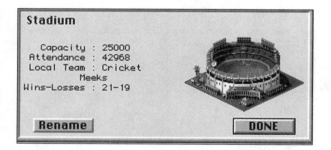

- Capacity is set at 25,000 for each stadium.

- Attendance is calculated as a function of the total population, the number of stadiums in the city, and a random factor, capped by the 25,000 limit.

- The Local Team is picked randomly from a list.

- Wins-Losses are calculated randomly and don't affect anything—not even attendance.

Prisons

- Capacity is set at 10,000.

- Inmates are the previous year's prison population, minus 25 percent (25 percent of all prison inmates are released every year, as they reach the ends of their sentences) plus captured criminals transferred from the police microsims.

- Guards are calculated as a percentage of the total population, affected by funding.

- Escapes happen only if the prison is full, in which case they are calculated randomly with the funding level as a minor factor.

- The Percent of Capacity value is the number of prisoners

incarcerated, divided by the total capacity of 10,000. If prisons are below full capacity, they send an efficiency bonus to the police department microsims. If they are full, the microsim triggers a newspaper story and takes away the police efficiency bonus.

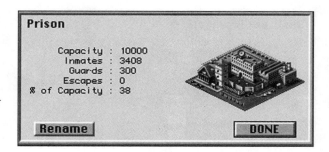

Colleges

- College Capacity is set at 5,000.
- Attendance is the total number of citizens between 15 and 20, divided by the number of schools and then limited to the 5,000 capacity. There is also a slight random factor (0 to 32) added in to make the number look more realistic.
- Teachers are calculated from the city population, funding, and a random factor.
- The Grade value rates how well the college is performing, not the students. It is calculated as a function of the student-to-teacher ratio: 12.5:1 or below is an A+, 27:1 or above is an F, and the other grades (A, B, C, D, and E) are equally distributed between 12.5 and 27. The grade, or quality, of the college feeds into the overall Education model, affecting the EQ.
- Annual Cost is the amount of funding you are providing.

Zoos

- Peruvian Llamas have a random number changed yearly.
- Andean Llamas have a random number changed yearly.
- Alpacas have a random number changed yearly.
- Other Dromedaries have a random number changed yearly.[4]

---

[4]To set the record straight, llamas are *not* dromedaries, and Peruvian llamas are *also* from the Andes. But that's getting picky . . .

The Great Bremgahi Statue

- Height is fixed at 65 feet.
- The Material is always bronze.
- The Built In value is the date the statue was erected.
- The Number of Pigeons perched is a random number changed yearly.

(Wonder why it's called Bremgahi? . . .)

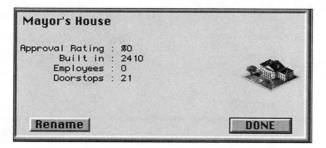

The Mayor's House

- The Approval Rating is read in from elsewhere in the simulation and displayed.
- The Built In value is the year the house was erected.
- Employees are a random number that is set when the mayor's house is built and then decremented by one each year until it reaches zero.
- The Doorstops value starts at zero when the mayor's house is built and is incremented by one each year until the Employees value reaches zero.

Note: In beta versions of SimCity 2000, Employees used to be Llamas and Doorstops used to be Dead Llamas. It seems that the llama lovers at Maxis struck a blow for something or other.

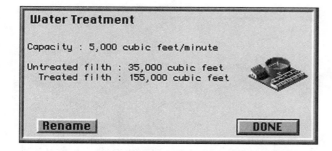

Water Treatment Plants

- Capacity is set at 5,000 cubic feet per minute.
- Untreated filth is a random number.
- Treated filth is mostly random but limited by the number of employees (calculated but not displayed).

Desalinization Plants

- Running at *n*% of Capacity is the amount of water being processed versus the total water that can be processed, with a random factor thrown in.
- Salt/tons removed is a random number.
- Employees are based on the overall city population.

Arcologies

- Design Capacity is the population that the arcology was built to hold. It is a different preset number for each of the four arcologies.
- Residents are calculated from the design capacity, the residential tax settings, and an internal birthrate.
- The Built In value is the year the arcology was erected.
- Conditions describe the quality of life inside the arcology. The factors involved are crime, pollution, land value, power, and water. Conditions start as a number representing an A+ rating. Then the number may be lowered by crime, lowered by pollution and raised by land value. (Each of these factors is equally weighted.) If there is no power, then the rating is divided in half. If there is no water, it is divided in half again.

Llama Domes

- Weddings are a random number that can change every year.
- Visitors are mostly random but limited by the total city population.
- Llama Sightings are random.
- Complaints are random.
- Bungee Jumps are random.

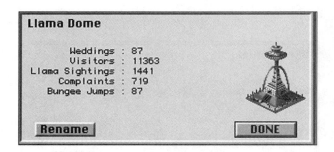

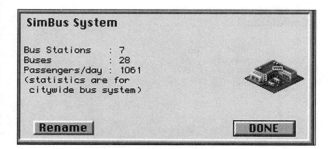

The Bus System

- Bus Stations are the total number of bus depots in the city.
- Buses are calculated at four per station.
- Passengers/day are the total citywide number of bus trips taken by Sims, passed from the trip generator.

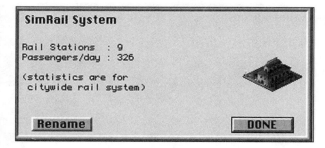

The Rail System

- Rail Stations are the total number of rail depots in the city.
- Passengers/day are the total citywide number of rail trips taken by Sims, passed from the trip generator.

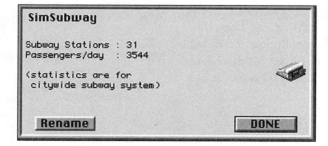

The Subway System

- Subway Stations are the total number of subway stations in the city.
- Passengers/day are the total citywide number of subway trips taken by Sims, passed from the trip generator.

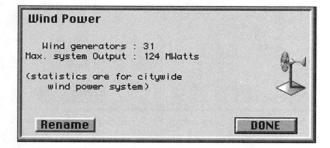

Wind Power Plants

- Wind generators are the total number of wind generators in the city.
- Max. System Output is calculated by multiplying the total number of wind generators by their power output (4 MW).

Hydroelectric Power Plants

- Hydro Generators are the total number of hydroelectric generators in the city.
- Max. System Output is calculated by multiplying the total number of hydroelectric generators by their power output (20 MW).

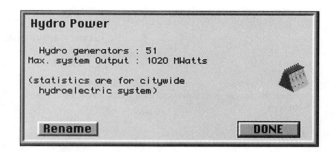

```
Hydro Power

  Hydro generators : 51
Max. system Output : 1020 MWatts

(statistics are for citywide
  hydroelectric system)

   Rename                    DONE
```

Parks

- Attendance (last year) is calculated from the total citywide park acreage and a percentage of the total city population
- Acres (citywide) are the total land area of all parks in the city. (One tile is approximately one acre.)
- Employees are calculated as a function of the total city population and the total park acreage.

Note: Park microsims are only available for big parks.

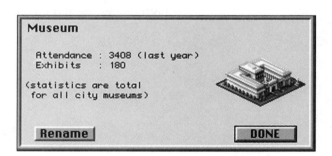

```
SimPark System

  Attendance : 11335 (last year)
       Acres : 198 (citywide)
   Employees : 22
(statistics are for
 citywide park system)

   Rename                    DONE
```

Museums

- Attendance (last year) is based on total population, funding, and the number of museums.
- Exhibits are based on the number of employees (calculated from the total population, funding, and the number of museums, but not displayed), the number of museums, and attendance.

```
Museum

  Attendance : 3408 (last year)
  Exhibits   : 180

(statistics are total
 for all city museums)

   Rename                    DONE
```

Libraries

- Attendance is based on total population, funding, the number of libraries in the city, and the number of employees (calculated from the total population, funding, and the number of libraries, but not displayed).

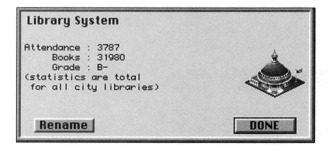

```
Library System

Attendance : 3787
    Books : 31980
    Grade : B-
(statistics are total
 for all city libraries)

   Rename                    DONE
```

- Books are based on funding and the number of libraries.
- The Grade value is based on the ratio between total population and attendance.

Marinas

The Boats value is calculated from the total population and the number of marinas.

INFORMATION FROM NON-MICROSIMS

Not all of the data that show up when you use the Query tool are from a microsim. The information you see when you inquire about water pumps, for instance, consists of direct readouts of local statistics from the model at large, mostly from the CA-based map and terrain info. This information is both interesting and useful, but it has no microsim of its own.

C H A P T E R

17

The Future of *SimCity*
(Truth, Predictions, and Rumors)

Maxis gave *SimCity 2000* the tag line The Ultimate City Simulator, and they're right—at least for now. But, as always, you can expect the *SimCity* simulations to keep pace with expanding technology.

A NEVER-ENDING PROCESS

SimCity itself, like the real cities it simulates, is a growing, evolving thing.

Over the years, the game has been constantly modified in response to player requests (and demands), eventually evolving into *SimCity 2000*. And though the new *SimCity 2000* is perhaps the ultimate city simulator, there is, in keeping with the nature of the game, always room for expansion.

NEW MACHINES, NEW VERSIONS

When *SimCity* was first conceived, it was created on a Commodore 64. The first version of the program to be released was written on a Macintosh SE, and was designed to work on Macs as lowly as the 512e. When it was ported to the DOS platform, it was made to work on a bare-bones XT (8088) with literally any graphics card (even CGA) and as little as 512K RAM.

SimCity 2000 on the Mac requires a near-top-of-the-line machine, with plenty of memory, a hard drive, and a color monitor. The DOS version requires a high-end machine: 386 or above (486 recommended), 4 MB memory, and Super VGA graphics (no monochrome, no EGA, no vanilla VGA). And *SimCity 2000* stretches the graphic, sound and calculating abilities even on these new, powerful machines. The Windows version of *SimCity 2000* pushes the hardware capabilities even further, so that the Pentium now becomes the platform of choice!

Once the next generation of computers is out there en masse—possibly the Power PC (or its successor), or maybe Pentium 2—you can be sure that *Sim City*, in some form or another, will again be pushing the next wave to its limits.

But in the meantime . . . rumors abound about versions of *SimCity 2000* for a number of other platforms, ranging from OS/2 to UNIX to a number of new (and not so new) game console machines. In addition, there are many online possibilities for *SimCity 2000*. Expect to wait at least a year, but it looks as if a multiplayer version (Windows- and/or Mac-based) has a high probability of surfacing. And don't be too surprised if one fine day you find that the great information superhighway has brought an interactive multiplayer *SimCity 2000* to your TV set.

WHITHER GOEST THE CLASSIC?

SimCity 2000 requires a lot of hardware to run, but most computers sold these days, both Mac and IBM, can handle it. Now that 2000 is out, what's going to happen to the original, now dubbed *SimCity Classic*?

Multiplayer *SimCity Classic* on a UNIX workstation

As far as the DOS, Windows, and Mac versions go, it pretty much depends on the demand. People with these platforms who would still want *SimCity Classic* are those with older, slower, and/or monochrome computers; those with laptops that can't display 256 colors; younger folk who might be confused by the complexity and number of choices in *2000*; and even us hard-core *SimCity 2000* city-builders who, on occasion, long nostalgically for simpler days.

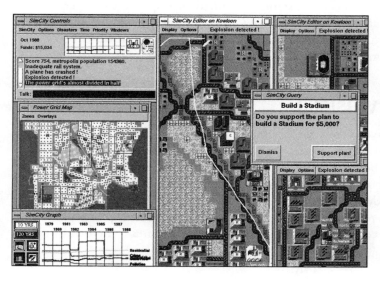

But wait! There's still a lot of life in the old Classic. An OS/2 version has recently been released. There's also a UNIX version, which runs on Silicon Graphics Iris, SPARC SunOS, and other UNIX workstations. Taking advantage of the vast

power of these workstations, this version allows multiple Edit windows—
and multiple players for collaboration on city-building.

Multiplayer SimCity is available directly from DUX Software; a demo
version is available via anonymous ftp from ftp.uu.net (192.48.96.9), in the
directory vendor/dux/*SimCity*. For more information, contact DUX Software, 4906 El Camino Real, Suite 1, Los Altos, CA 94022; tel., 1-800-543-
4999 or 1-415-967-1500; fax, 1-415-967-5528; e-mail, simcity@dux.com.

And a DOS (and perhaps a Macintosh) online multiplayer version of
SimCity Classic is about to be launched by a new online gaming network
called TEN (Total Entertainment Network). This version will include features such as buying and selling plots of land, tak-
ing out loans from a bank, and voting on
proposals for changes that will affect more than
one player. It also provides the ability to chat with
other players during games (both publicly and
secretly—for making those private deals).

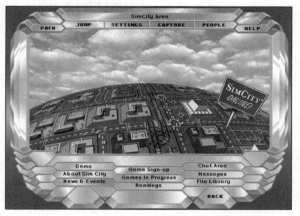

For more information on this version of *Sim-
City Classic*, and on the Total Entertainment Network, contact Planet Optigon, Inc. (formerly
Optigon Interactive), 5901 Christie Avenue,
Suite 208, Emeryville, California 94608; tel., 1-
510-596-8700; fax, 1-510-547-4324; Internet,
ten@ten.net; America Online, TENetwork.

SimCity Classic Title
Screen on TEN

ADD-ONS

This book covers all the add-ons available at press time: *SimCity 2000 Scenarios Vol. 1: Great Disasters* and the *SimCity 2000 Urban Renewal Kit*. In
addition, the *CD Collection* contains at least a couple of extra scenarios and
lots of extra cities (see Appendix C). Other scenario collections may be
released if the demand is there. Other than these, there are no other add-ons
in the works (at least no *small* ones).

FUTURE POSSIBILITIES

SimCity 2000 is a deep program. You can build and rebuild a million cities.
You can invent and test out thousands of designs. You can grow and shrink
and run and rule and play for years and never do the same thing twice.

But do you ever want more? For instance, imagine that after building the
perfect city in *SimCity 2000*, you could hop into a pink Cadillac or a Corvette

and race through the city's streets. Or fly a helicopter between the buildings, or even fly a plane over it. And bomb it if you want. Or use *SimCity* to build the sites for role-playing or battle games. Or even convert one of your cities to full 3-D and take a virtual-reality walk through it.

If you'd like to take *SimCity 2000* beyond its limits and try any or all of these things, all it'll take is a little patience. Things are cooking in the back rooms of Maxis that will once again show us all just how much you can do — and how much fun you can have—with a home computer.

CONTESTS AND SO FORTH

Also, be on the lookout for various city-building and design contests around the country, sponsored by Maxis, a number of local newspapers, and by cities, schools, and educational groups.

A number of newspapers have worked in conjunction with Maxis on *SimCity*, and even more will be working with *SimCity 2000*; holding contests, opinion polls, and other promotions. They'll pass out computerized copies of the local city—sometimes as it is, sometimes just the barren landscape that was there first—and let the local citizens either design, redesign, or renew the city. Then they show the results to local politicians and get their reactions. Sometimes they even set the mayors down in front of the computer and see what they can do.

Keep an eye out. You might win something nice, or at least get your picture in the paper.

Maxis has also stepped up its online profile, and will be setting up contests and other promotions on most of the popular networks.

EDUCATIONAL VERSIONS

Of course, for the educators out there, *SimCity 2000* is available in special education versions, including multiple-use site licenses and teacher's guides.

C H A P T E R

18

SimCity 2000
Urban Renewal Kit (SCURK)

If you ever experienced any unwanted limitations in *SimCity 2000*, the *SimCity 2000 Urban Renewal Kit* (*SCURK*) will remove them. It gives you total freedom to do just about anything you want (in *SimCity 2000*). That's freedom from cost, simulation, and artistic constraints.

SCURK has three modules: *Paint the Town*, *Pick and Copy*, and *Place and Print*.

- **Paint the Town** makes it easier to modify existing buildings and structures in your graphics tile set by drawing, painting, or even importing your own design from a PCX file format. This utility also allows you to control the palette color cycling, so you can create unique special effects, such as motion and blinking lights. Before you can see your creations in *SimCity 2000*, however, you'll need to use the Pick and Copy utility to transfer the tile object into the *SimCity 2000* tile set.

    Notice that we say easier, not easy. Face it—no matter how simple, convenient, powerful, or wonderful a paint program is, it won't do the painting or drawing for you. Of course, even those of us who can't draw can still load in a building or monument and play with it, change it around, add graffiti, and generally have a lot of fun. But to create a complete new graphics set with a consistent scale—and one that looks good—requires a lot of time, energy, and artistic talent. We artless artisans are counting on the truly talented out there to post some great graphics sets on the boards.

- *Pick and Copy*—an easy (yes, this time we do mean easy) way to mix and match individual buildings from different graphics sets to create a new graphics set, then copy it into the *SimCity 2000* program so you can see the new art as you play the game.
- *Place and Print*—the ultimate city-building power tool. *Place and Print* lets you open an existing city, or start a new one, and do anything you want to it. No costs, no limitations, no pesky Sims to get in your way. You have access to all the regular building, zoning, and land modification tools that *SimCity 2000* offers, and it doesn't cost you a thing. Also, you have control over things that you can't touch in *SimCity 2000*. You can place individual buildings and other objects that are normally under the control of the Sims—even individual seaport, airport, and military base buildings.

And once you're created the perfect city, the city without limitations, the city only you could conjure up from the depths of your imagination, you can print it out, all or part of it, to color, grayscale, or black-and-white printers—in three different zoom sizes—and display your perfect creation for all the world to see.

Of course, once you load your idealized city into *SimCity 2000*, the simulation will kick in and the Sims will start rearranging things to their own liking, so be sure to keep a pre-Sim copy of your city for posterity.

In the DOS version of *SCURK*, you can start any of these three utilities by clicking on any of the three corresponding buttons onscreen. Windows users can open these utilities through the Windows menu.

The *SCURK* version you purchase will only work if you've previously installed *SimCity 2000* for the same operating system. So the DOS *SCURK* will work only with the DOS version of *SimCity 2000*, the Windows *SCURK* will work only with the Windows version of *SimCity 2000*, and the Macintosh *SCURK* will work only with the Macintosh version of *SimCity 2000*.

The recently released DOS *SCURK* also includes some new extended sound and music drivers that were not available when *SimCity 2000* for DOS was released. These sound and music drivers are automatically copied to your hard disk during *SCURK* installation, but you'll still need to run the *SimCity 2000* INSTALL.EXE program to reconfigure *SimCity 2000* to use them. These drivers will show up in the installer, under the Configure Sound and Configure Music options. It is strongly recommended that you check to see if there is a new driver for your sound card, because you might be missing out on the advanced capabilities of your sound card. This particularly applies to owners of the SoundBlaster 32Awe, which has a new driver that enables you to make use of the wave-table synthesis-sampled MIDI instruments.

SCURK must be installed in the same directory as *SimCity 2000*; during installation, it will create a backup of your original *SimCity 2000*'s SC2000.DAT file, which is the file that stores your building images for *SimCity 2000*. The new backup file, which is called SC2000.SAV, will be created from scratch if *SCURK* cannot find the original one, or if the original is damaged. The SC2000.SAV file is used to create the ORIGINAL.TIL file, which you can then copy into other sets. If *SCURK* finds that ORIGINAL.TIL is missing, it will create a fresh copy of it from the SC2DAT.SAV file. Unfortunately, if your SC2DAT.SAV file becomes corrupted, you'll have to reinstall both *SimCity 2000* and *SCURK*.

DIFFERENT VERSIONS OF *SCURK*

This chapter is based primarily on the DOS version of *SCURK*, since it was the first version that was ready. The Windows and Macintosh versions are almost identical to each other and are very close to the DOS version. If you have the Windows or Macintosh version of *SCURK*, don't worry—this chapter will still be worth your while. Here are the basic differences between the DOS version and the Windows and Macintosh versions:

- The menus are worded slightly differently and a few things are rearranged. Everything you'll need is there somewhere, so if you don't see it, try another menu.

- The DOS version has a Main screen with three big buttons to access the three modules. The other versions don't have the Main screen. In Windows, all modules are accessed through the Windows menu.

- In the DOS version, only one of the three modules can be open at a time. In the other versions, all three modules can be open at once in their own windows.

- The DOS version has an Import screen for importing PCX files. The Mac and Windows versions don't have this screen, but they will import anything you can get into the Mac or Windows clipboard.

- In the DOS version of *Paint the Town*, the color cycling palette is separated from the noncycling palette. In the Mac and Windows versions, they're combined.

As this book goes to press, Windows and Macintosh versions of *SCURK* are set to ship.

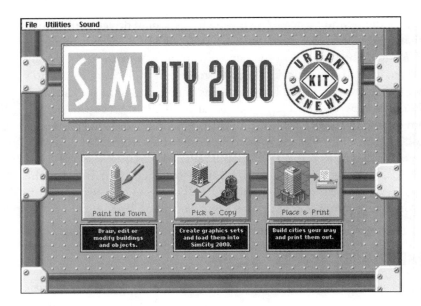

Figure 18-1 Dos
SCURK Main Screen

STARTING *SCURK*

To start the program, type in **SCURK** at the DOS prompt (if you have problems with your video card, you can also type in **SCURKVESA.COM**). Macintosh and Windows users need only double-click on the *SCURK* icon. If you have the DOS version of *SCURK*, you'll wade through some opening title screens and then see the *SCURK* Main Screen, illustrated in Figure 18.1, which lists the three *SCURK* utilities.

PAINT THE TOWN

In this section, you'll learn how to use the Paint the Town tools by creating your own custom Drive-In Theater, complete with onscreen movie. But before starting, let's first go over the basic tools and define some terms that will help you understand the process of creating new buildings.

Definitions and Onscreen Tool Descriptions

When you first start Paint the Town, a screen will open up that looks like Figure 18.2. We'll list the functions of some of the tools you see on the screen here, and define some terms that are used in *SCURK*.

Menu Bar: Using the File menu, you can open new tile sets, open existing tile sets, create new tile sets, save tile sets, and export or import PCX graphics files. Under the Edit menu, you can Undo a drawing action you just performed, Revert to the version of your building that you had saved before you started making changes, and Rotate or Flip your copied images in the Drawing Area. Using the Object menu, you can select a new or blank group of objects from the currently loaded graphics Tile Set. The selected Object Group (such as commercial buildings, residential buildings, industrial buildings, and so on) will then be displayed in the Active Object Group display, to the right of the Object Selector. The Preferences menu allows you to display the Clip Grid, and choose whether or not you want to see color cycling in your Drawing Area and Color Cycle Palette (this is useful if you're annoyed by flickering colors on your screen). The Windows menu allows you to open the color Palette, the color Cycle Palette, and the Import Screen for imported PCX graphics that you want to paste into your drawings. If you haven't yet imported a graphic using the File/Import PCX menu, the Import Screen menu option will be "ghosted out" and unavailable.

Status Area: The following references may be displayed in the Status Area:

- *Import:* Tells you that you have an imported PCX file that you can paste into your Drawing Area.
- *Copy:* Tells you that you have a picture in your clipboard that you can paste into your Drawing Area.
- *x and y:* Coordinates of your horizontal (x) and vertical (y) coordinates in the Drawing Area. The x values range from 0 to 128 from left to right in the Drawing Area; the y values range from 0 to 256 from top to bottom.
- *File Size:* Size in KB of your current Tile Set.

Tiles and Tile Sets: Tiles are the individual squares that define a city block in *SimCity 2000*. Each tile measures approximately 200 feet by 200 feet, or approximately one acre. Most buildings in *SimCity 2000* are 3×3-tile blocks or smaller, but some are 4 x 4, including the arcologies.

A Tile Set is a collection of buildings and other objects that are kept in one file. An example of a tile set is the ORIGINAL.TIL file, which is 935 KB long and contains all the original artwork for the *SimCity 2000* buildings and objects. Note that you can't change the ORIGINAL.TIL file (it is marked Read Only on your hard disk), but must use the File/Save As menu option to save your edited changes to a new tile file, such as MYNEW.TIL (or whatever name you wish to call it, as long as it has the file extension .TIL). You also can't overwrite the FUTURE.TIL tile set on your hard disk, but must use the File/Save As menu option to save your edited changes to a new file name (also with the extension .TIL).

Objects: Objects are the buildings, roads, rubble, animations, and other objects you see in *SimCity 2000*. Not all objects can be edited or changed by you. The following is a list of objects in *SCURK* that you can't edit:

- Road
- On-Ramps
- Rails
- Trains
- Power Lines
- Bridges
- Water Tiles
- The Alien
- Small Boats
- Helicopters

- Police, File, and Military Dispatch Icons
- Zone Indicator Colors
- Highways
- Tunnels, Subways
- Sub-to-Rail Connectors
- Water Pipes
- Ground Tiles
- Signs
- Small Parks

Object Selector: The Object Selector allows you to scroll through the available objects in the current Active Object Group that you have selected from the Object Group menu. To pick a particular building object, click on the arrow buttons until you see the building displayed, then just click on its picture and it will then be displayed in the Drawing Area.

Active Object Group: The group of objects that are currently displayed to the right of the Object Selector. By using the Object Group menu, you can choose from among the following Object Groups:

- *Residential:* All residential buildings.
- *Commercial:* All commercial buildings.
- *Industrial:* All industrial buildings.
- *Specials:* Arcos, city hall, Llama Dome, water facilities, marinas, zoos, prisons, schools, hospitals, police and fire stations, parks, and statues.
- *Power:* All power facilities.
- *Transport and Military:* Bus stations, subway stations, rail stations, cranes, loading bay, cargo yards.
- *Misc. Ground:* Rubble, trees, radioactive tiles.
- *Animated 1:* Tornado clouds, Maxis Man, rioters, explosions, fire.

- *Animated 2:* Bulldozer, ships, airplanes.
- *Construction:* Construction facilities, abandoned buildings.

Base Size: Each object has a fixed and unchangeable Base Size, meaning that you can't make the object larger than the tile size you see in the Drawing window for the objects in the ORIGINAL.TIL set. Some objects have a Base Size of 1 × 1, some are 2 × 2, others are 3 × 3, and some are even 4 × 4. Animated objects that don't stay on the ground (like planes and ships) are limited to their base tile size. Thus, even though the Drawing window can display 4 × 4 objects, you can't use the whole 4-x-4-tile Base Size for all your objects, because some objects are only 1 × 1, 2 × 2, or 3 × 3. Another limitation is height: For all objects except the arcologies and the Braun Llama Dome, the height limit is half the full height of the Drawing Area (except in the Windows version of *SCURK*).

Clip Grid: The Clip Grid defines the area that you can draw in for the particular object and the Base Size that you've selected for it. Although the Clip Grid is always active, meaning you can't draw outside of the object's Base Size boundaries, you can only see the Clip Grid if you toggle it on from the Preferences/Clip Grid menu. Turning on the Clip Grid will reveal a shaded portion of your Drawing Area screen that allows you to see what the actual boundaries are for your object's Base Size.

Drawing Area: The Drawing Area is the portion of your screen where you make changes to your buildings and draw your new designs. After opening the Tile Set file that you wish to edit (File/Open), you select the Object Group menu, pick the class of objects you wish to open (Residential, Commercial, Special, and so on), then use the Object Selector to choose the object you wish to edit in the Drawing Area. You'll see all your edited changes instantly reflected in the smaller windows to the right of the Drawing Area; these windows show you what your finished product will look like at the three *SimCity 2000* zoom levels. Note that you can't draw in these other windows.

Toolbar: The Toolbar contains all the drawing tools that you'll need to edit, draw, erase, and color in your objects in the Drawing Area. Once you have an object displayed in the Drawing Area, you can click on a tool you want to use in the Toolbar, then move your mouse pointer over the Drawing Area to begin making your changes. Note that some of the tool buttons have multiple tools available, which you can see onscreen by clicking and holding down the mouse button or by double-clicking.

In the Windows version of SCURK, there is no height limitation, but if you import your creation into the DOS version of SimCity 2000, the top of the building will be chopped off if it exceeds the height ceiling.

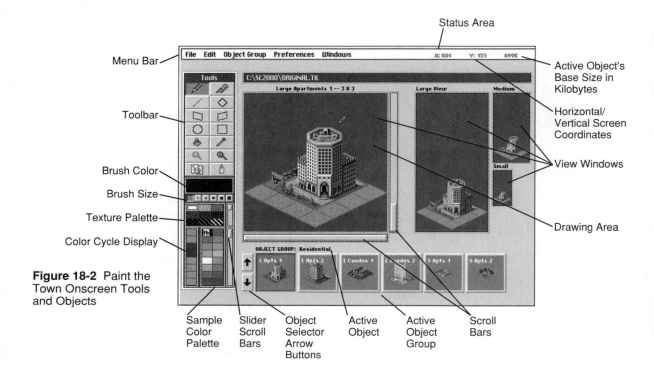

Figure 18-2 Paint the Town Onscreen Tools and Objects

Palettes: Just below the Toolbar, you'll find the Palettes controls, which you use to change colors, texture patterns, and color cycling for both the foreground and background of your objects.

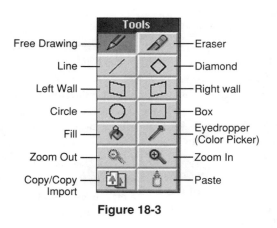

Figure 18-3

Using the Toolbar

The drawing tools found on the Toolbar are very similar to the tools used in other computer paint programs. To use a tool, click on it, then drag the mouse into the Drawing Area to use it. For some of the tools, the cursor will assume the image of the current tool you have selected, but for most tools, the cursor will appear as a pair of crosshairs.

All the drawing tools, which are shown in Figure 18.3, are discussed in the next section.

Free Drawing Tool

You can use this tool to color individual pixels in the Drawing Area, or you can use it to draw as you would a pen or pencil. The color of the Free Drawing Tool's brush can be changed by clicking on the Color Palette to select a new color. The current color is displayed in the Brush Color box. You can also change the size of the Drawing Tool's brush by picking one of the Brush Size buttons just below the Brush Color box.

While you're using the Free Drawing Tool, the left mouse button draws and the right mouse button functions as an eraser.

Eraser

The size of the eraser is determined by the current Brush Size. Just click and drag to erase swatches of your Drawing Area.

Line

Draws a straight line at any angle. Click and hold to begin the line, then drag the mouse to define the direction of the line. Finally, release the mouse button to actually draw the line.

Diamond

Draws diamond shapes. Click and drag to create different-sized diamonds. The thickness of the diamond depends on the current Brush Size. Two Diamond tools are available: If you click and hold down the mouse button on the Diamond tool, a submenu will pop open that lets you choose between a hollow diamond and a filled diamond.

Left Wall

Draws a parallelogram that makes it easier to draw left walls of buildings. The thickness of the wall depends on the current Brush Size. Two Left Wall tool options are available: If you click and hold down the mouse button on the Left Wall tool, a submenu will pop open that lets you choose between a hollow wall and a filled wall.

Right Wall

Draws a parallelogram that makes it easier to draw right walls of buildings. The thickness of the wall depends on the current Brush Size. Two Right Wall tool options are available: If you click and hold down the mouse button on the Right Wall tool, a submenu will pop open that lets you choose between a hollow wall and a filled wall.

Circle

Draws circles and ellipses. The thickness of the circle's outline depends on the current Brush Size. Two Circle tool options are available: if you click and hold down the mouse button on the Circle tool, a submenu will pop open that lets you choose between a hollow circle and a filled circle.

Box

Draws squares and rectangles. The thickness of the square or rectangle depends on the current Brush Size. Two Box tool options are available: If you click and hold down the mouse button on the Box tool, a submenu will pop open that lets you choose between a hollow and a filled box shape.

Fill

This tool fills an area with the current brush color, cycle, or texture. The fill starts wherever you click in the Drawing Area, and then fills in all directions until it comes to another color.

Eyedropper (Color Picker)

Using this tool, you can set the brush color by clicking on any area of your Drawing Area. This is useful when you're trying to match colors for an existing object or building and you don't want to try to find the matching color in the Color Palette.

Zoom Out

Zooms out from the view in the Drawing Area.

Zoom In

Zooms in toward the view in the Drawing Area.

Copy

The Copy tool allows you to copy any portion of your Drawing Area, so that you can paste it into another object, or any other image you want to create. To use it, just select the Copy tool, then click and drag the cursor to outline the portion of the Drawing Area you want to copy. When you release the mouse button, the outlined area you copied will become a "brush" that you can then use to paint the image into any other area or object. Note that after copying an image, *SCURK* automatically changes to the Paste tool, and you can just click the mouse button to paste in the copied image. Also, the image that you copy can be rotated or flipped by using the Edit menu commands for rotating and flipping copied objects. The copied image is kept in memory until you copy another image.

Copy Import

This tool allows you to copy any part of an imported PCX graphics file so that you can paste it into the Drawing Area. This tool is unavailable unless you already have imported a PCX graphic using the File/Import PCX menu command. To use this tool to import a portion of a PCX file, follow these steps:

1. Select the File/Import PCX menu command.
2. Select the PCX file that you wish to import. (SAMPLE1.PCX and SAMPLE2.PCX come with *SCURK*; they have some pretty cool buildings you can import.)
3. After the file has been loaded and you've clicked on OK to acknowledge that fact, click on the IMPORT button on the Toolbar (the Copy tool now displays "IMPORT" in the button).
4. You'll see the PCX graphic file open up onscreen. Click and drag the mouse pointer over the area you wish to copy and import into *SCURK*. After you release the mouse button, you'll return to the Drawing Area of *SCURK*.
5. The Paste tool will be automatically activated, so position your "brush" over the Drawing Area and click the mouse button to paste in the image.

Your PCX image will then be pasted into the Drawing Area.

Paste

This tool becomes activated only when you have already copied an image from the Drawing Area, or have imported a PCX file image and have copied an area of the PCX image (using the COPY/IMPORT button) that you wish to paste into your Drawing Area.

Using the Color Palettes

The color palettes are used to change brush, fill, and texture colors, as well as to choose color cycling effects.

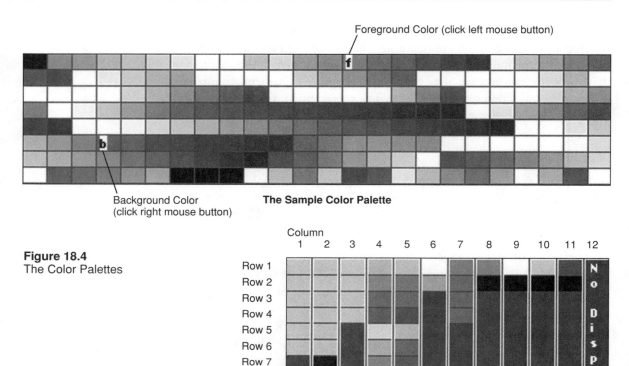

Foreground Color (click left mouse button)

The Sample Color Palette

Background Color
(click right mouse button)

Figure 18.4
The Color Palettes

The Color Cycling Palette

Brush Color

This area shows you what your current brush color and texture will look like when you apply the brush, or other tool, to your Drawing Area. You pick your color using the Sample Color Palette, and your texture from the Texture Palette.

Brush Size

You select the size, or thickness, of the dots, lines, or shapes you can draw or erase. The size of the brush increases from left to right: The leftmost button is a one-pixel square, the next is a two-pixel square, and so on.

Texture Palette

You can pick various textures from the Texture Palette that will make use of the foreground and background colors. The foreground and background colors are defined as follows:

- *Foreground:* The foreground color is always the color of solid colors that you use in your drawings. A solid color is one without a texture pattern in it.
- *Background:* The background color is the color that is used to create the texture pattern for fills, and other large portions of color that you paint in. Background colors can be used *only* with textures, not with solid colors.

Use the scroll bars to pick a texture pattern you want to use, then choose the foreground and background colors from the Sample Color Palette. You'll get a preview of what your texture looks like in the Brush Color box.

Sample Color Palette

Click and hold down the mouse button to open up the entire Sample Color Palette (or use the scroll bar to scroll through the available colors). This palette allows you to choose a much larger array of colors. Click the left mouse button to set the foreground color; click the right mouse button to set the background color. You'll see an f in the Color Palette to indicate which color you've selected as your Foreground, and a b to indicate which color you've selected as your Background.

Color Cycle Display

Click and hold down the mouse button to open up the entire Color Cycle Display. This palette allows you to use cycling colors so that you can create animated patterns and other illusions of movement. There are 12 columns in this display: the first 11 columns, starting from the left, have different color cycling effects; the last column, on the right, allows you to choose no color cycling. Each color square alternates colors as it cycles from top to bottom for each of the 11 columns. You choose the color square from one of the columns that you want to use for your cycling, then click in the Drawing Area to place that color's cycling sequence in the Drawing Area. Then you repeat the task, selecting the next color down from the same column, and so on. You'll notice that your drawing will alternate colors in the same sequence in which you chose them from the color squares in the cycling column you're using.

Tutorial: Create a Sci-Fi Flick at the Drive-In Movie Theater

Let's create a new movie at the Drive-In Movie Theater to demonstrate how to use some of the color cycling abilities found in *Paint the Town*. What we'll do is open up the ORIGINAL.TIL graphics tile set, then select the Drive-In

Theater as our object to be modified in the Drawing Area. Next we'll erase the Sim-Ant movie that is currently playing, and substitute a flying saucer firing a laser beam at the ground. Finally, we'll add a new marquee with strobe-like tracer lights advertising our exciting new motion picture.

Don't worry if you make any mistakes; you can always use the Edit/Undo or Edit/Revert menu command to restore your object to the condition it was in before you made the mistake.

Follow these steps:

1. Once you've started *SCURK*, click on the *Paint the Town* icon button.

2. After the Paint the Town screen opens, select the File/Open menu command. From the files that are listed, click on the ORIGINAL.TIL file. Then click on the Open button to open this graphics tile set, which contains all the original *SimCity 2000* artwork.

3. Using the Object Group menu, select Commercial. After doing this, you'll see some of the commercial buildings appear in the Active Object Group display below.

4. In the Active Object Group display, click on the Drive-In Theater. It should then appear in the Drawing Area.

5. Because the movie screen is too small to edit at this magnification, you'll want to enlarge the screen by clicking twice on the Zoom In tool. Next, center the screen in the Drawing Area, using the Scroll Bars.

6. Select the Preferences/Clip Grid menu command. This will display a shaded portion of your Drawing Area where you can actually make changes to the Drive-In Theater. Any changes outside this area will be clipped off.

7. Using the Eyedropper tool, click on a gray portion of the movie screen where no color cycling is occurring. The Eyedropper tool will "capture" this color and use it as your Brush Color.

8. Click on the Free Drawing Tool, then click on the far-left button of the Brush Size tool to create a brush that is 1 pixel square. Now move the Free Drawing Tool over the Drawing Area and carefully draw over the entire gray portion of the movie screen, including the Ant and the color cycling. If you hold down the left mouse button and drag down the Free Drawing Tool column by column in the Drawing Area, you'll be able to quickly erase all the color cycling pixels without having to individually delete each one. When you are finished, the movie screen should be completely blank with a gray screen, and no color cycling going on, as illustrated in Figure 18.5.

9. Click and hold down the left mouse button on the Circle tool. A submenu will pop up, in which you'll click on the Solid Circle tool.

10. Click and hold down the left mouse button on the Color Palette to open the entire palette display. Next, click the left mouse button on the color yellow. The Color Palette will snap shut, and you'll see an *f* appear in the Color Palette to indicate that this is now your foreground color. The Brush Color box will also be yellow.

11. Using Figure 18.6 as your guide, click and drag the mouse pointer over the movie screen to create a yellow flying saucer. If you make a mistake, don't sweat it; just use the Edit/Undo menu to undo your error, or use the Edit/Revert menu to revert to the original theater image.

12. Click the left mouse button on the Color Palette to open it up again, then click the left mouse button on the color red. This will be your new foreground color; to indicate this, you'll now see an f in the Color Palette inside the red box.

13. Click and drag the mouse pointer over the top of the flying saucer to create a tiny red top. Do the same for the bottom of the flying saucer, so that it appears to have red bulbs on its top and bottom.

Now let's add some color cycling effects to create a laser bolt hitting the ground. We'll choose a color cycle pattern using a brown, brown, yellow, red sequence that is available from the Color Cycling Palette's sixth column.

Erase Ant Movie with Blank Gray Screen

Figure 18-5 Erase the Current Ant Movie

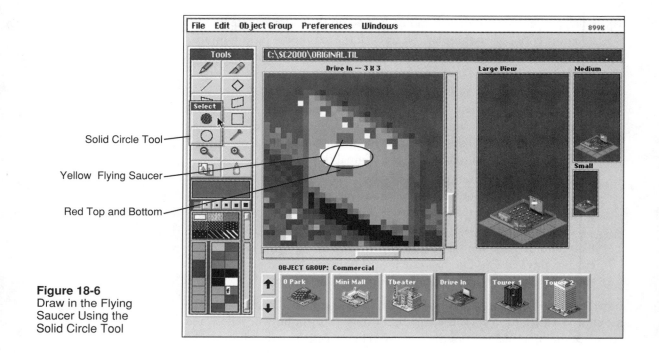

Solid Circle Tool

Yellow Flying Saucer

Red Top and Bottom

Figure 18-6
Draw in the Flying
Saucer Using the
Solid Circle Tool

Follow these steps:

1. Click and hold down the left mouse button on the Color Cycling Palette to open up the available cycling options.

2. In the Color Cycling Palette, move the mouse pointer over the sixth column from the left, where you'll see a color cycling pattern of brown, brown, yellow, and red.

3. In the sixth column from the left of the Color Cycling Palette, move the pointer over the first row, then click the left mouse button. Next, move the mouse pointer just off the lower right side of the flying saucer, and click the left mouse button once. You'll see the pixel onscreen begin to color-cycle.

4. Now we'll add the second color-cycling pixel of our laser bolt. In the sixth column from the left in the Color Cycling Palette, move the pointer over the second row, then click the left mouse button. Next, move the mouse pointer so that it is positioned diagonally off the lower right side of the pixel you placed in step 3 above, then click the left mouse button. You'll see a second pixel begin to color-cycle.

5. Continuing, we'll now add the third color-cycling pixel of our laser bolt.

In the sixth column from the left in the Color Cycling Palette, move the pointer over the third row, then click the left mouse button. Next, move the mouse pointer so that it is positioned diagonally off the lower right side of the pixel you placed in step 4 above, and click the left mouse button. You'll see a third pixel begin to color-cycle.

6. We'll now add the fourth color-cycling pixel of our laser bolt. In the sixth column from the left in the Color Cycling Palette, move the pointer over the fourth row, click the left mouse button. Next, move the mouse pointer so that it is positioned diagonally off the lower right side of the pixel you placed in step 5 above, and click the left mouse button. You'll see a fourth pixel begin to color-cycle.

7. Since you've used up the four color-cycling pixels that are available in the sixth column of the Color Cycling Palette, you'll want to repeat the cycling sequence again using the first, second, third, and fourth rows. This will create the effect of a continuous stream of red and yellow pulses emanating from the saucer. Again, move the mouse pointer over the first row of the sixth column in the Color Cycling Palette, then click the left mouse button. Next, position the pointer diagonally off the lower right side of the last color cycling pixel you placed in step 6, then click the left mouse button. You'll see that this pixel will begin to color-cycle, but in synchronization with the first pixel you placed in step 3.

8. Repeat steps 4, 5, 6, and 7, continuing the path of the bolt from the saucer to the ground.

When you are finished, the laser bolt should look like a red-and-yellow pulse that travels diagonally down and to the right from the saucer until it finally reaches the ground, as illustrated in Figure 18.7.

Finally, let's add the Drive-In Theater's new flashing-light marquee. Follow these steps to do this:

1. Scroll the Viewing Area until you have the Drive-In Theater's marquee centered in the window.

2. We'll be using the brown, brown, then blue color cycling found in the first row of the Color Cycling Palette. Position the pointer over the first row of the first column on the left in the Color Cycling Palette, then click the left mouse button.

3. Move the mouse pointer over the left edge of the top of the Drive-In Theater's marquee, then click the left mouse button to place the first color-cycling pixel.

4. Select the second row from the first column of the Color Cycling Palette, then place the second pixel of the marquee's lights just to the right of the previous light you placed in step 3.

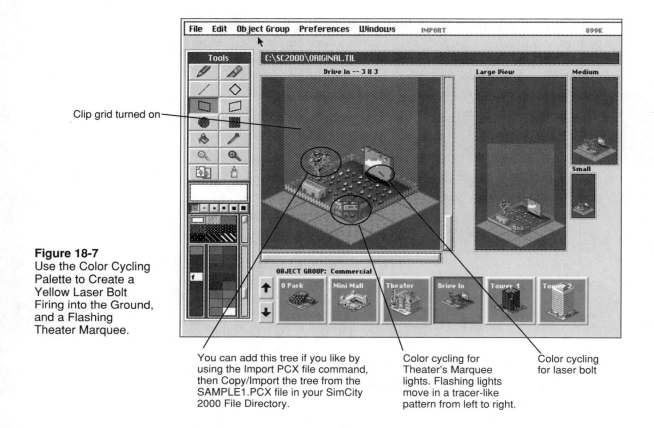

Figure 18-7
Use the Color Cycling
Palette to Create a
Yellow Laser Bolt
Firing into the Ground,
and a Flashing
Theater Marquee.

Clip grid turned on

You can add this tree if you like by
using the Import PCX file command,
then Copy/Import the tree from the
SAMPLE1.PCX file in your SimCity
2000 File Directory.

Color cycling for
Theater's Marquee
lights. Flashing lights
move in a tracer-like
pattern from left to right.

Color cycling
for laser bolt

5. Select the third row from the first column of the Color Cycling Palette, then place the third pixel of the marquee's lights.

6. Continue adding new lights to the marquee, using the fourth, fifth, sixth, seventh, and eighth rows of the first column of the Color Cycling Palette.

7. Since we want to continue the color-cycling sequence, again select the first row of the first column of the Color Cycling Palette, then continue adding marquee lights as you did in steps 4, 5, and 6 above. When you are finished, the marquee's lights should appear to flash from left to right, like a tracer bullet.

Let's now save our changes to a new graphics tile set, so that we can import the new Drive-In Theater to *SimCity 2000*:

1. Select the File/Save As menu.

2. In the Save As dialog box, give your tile set the name MYNEW.TIL, then click on the Save As (or Save) button. After saving your tile set in

the DOS version of *SCURK*, you'll see a dialog box telling you whether or not your file was successfully saved. If it was saved properly, click on the OK button to continue.

3. Select File/Exit to return to the Main screen of *SCURK*.

In the next section, we'll learn how to import the new graphic tile set we just created into *SimCity 2000*.

PICK AND COPY

The Pick and Copy utility within *SCURK* allows you to exchange objects from any graphics set to another graphics set. You can create a new graphics set out of buildings you've created, then exchange them with the original graphics set. When you next run *SimCity 2000*, instead of seeing the original default buildings and scenery, you'll see your newly designed buildings. For your viewing enjoyment, *SCURK* also comes with a Future Cities tile set that you can use in place of the original *SimCity 2000* tile set. The Future Cities

> Note that you can't save your new graphic tile sets to ORIGINAL.TIL or FUTURE.TIL. These files are read-only files, and cannot be overwritten. Therefore, if you're editing either the ORIGINAL.TIL or FUTURE.TIL graphics tile set, you must use the File/Save As menu command to save your creations to a *new* file name of your choice.

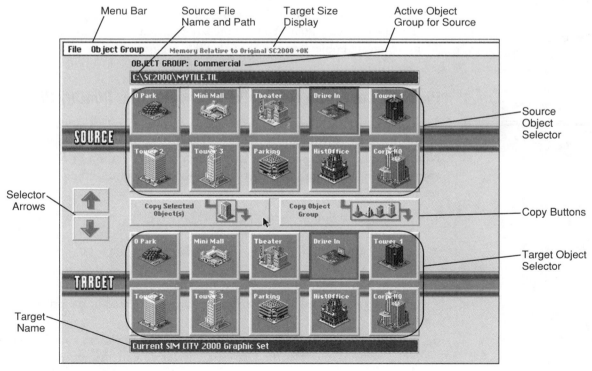

Figure 18.8 Pick and Copy

With the Windows version of *SCURK*, you can select more than one object in the Object Selector by pressing Ctrl at the same time as you click the mouse button. This allows you to pick and copy multiple building objects into your tile sets, and into the *SimCity 2000* program.

Very important note: In order to see your redesigned city buildings in *SimCity 2000*, you must choose *SimCity 2000* as the Target Graphics tile set.

tile set functions exactly the same as the original tile set, but it has futuristic buildings, monorails, and other cool structures.

To use Pick and Copy, follow these steps:

1. When you first start Pick and Copy, you'll be asked to pick a Source Graphics tile set. The Source Graphics file is the tile set that contains the objects you want to copy.

2. Next, you'll be asked what Target you want. You can:

   • Create a new Target Graphics tile set, or
   • Select an existing Target Graphics tile set, or
   • Export the Source Graphics tile set directly to *SimCity 2000*.

   The Target Graphics file is the tile set where you wish to put the newly copied objects; it can include either a file that you create, or the actual tile set that's used in the *SimCity 2000* program.

3. Using the Source Object Selector, copy the objects, either one by one or in groups, from the Source Graphics tile set to the Target Graphics tile set. You can pick a different Object Group and Object for your Target from the ones you chose for your Source.

4. Save the Target Graphics tile set to a file, or export the Target Graphics tile set to *SimCity 2000*. You use the latter option if you want to see your newly created objects in the *SimCity 2000* program itself.

Pick and Copy Your New Drive-In Theater into *SimCity 2000*

To demonstrate the way you import an object into *SimCity 2000*, let's try importing our newly designed Drive-In Theater from the preceding section. Note that the following steps are meant for the DOS version of *SCURK*, so your actual instructions will differ slightly for the Macintosh and Windows versions.

1. Assuming that you've already saved MYNEW.TIL, start up the Pick and Copy utility.

2. In the dialog box that opens next, you'll be asked to select your Source Graphics Set. Pick the MYNEW.TIL file, then click on the Open button. You'll remember that the MYNEW.TIL graphics tile set contains our newly redesigned Drive-In Theater that was created in the previous section.

3. Next, in the next dialog box that opens, you need to choose your Target. Since we want to export the Drive-In Theater directly into *SimCity 2000*, choose *SimCity 2000*.

4. The Pick and Copy main screen will open. At the top of the screen, you'll see some objects that belong to your MYNEW.TIL source file. At the bottom of the screen, you'll see the objects that currently exist in your *SimCity 2000* tile set. From the Object Group menu, select Commercial and you'll see your Drive-In Theater appear in the Source Object Selector.

5. Click the mouse pointer on the Drive-In Theater, then click on the Copy Selected Object(s) button. Your redesigned Drive-In Theater will now be in the Target Object Selector.

6. To save your changes and copy them it into the *SimCity 2000* program, you must select the File/Copy to *SimCity 2000* menu command.

7. You'll be prompted to verify that you want to overwrite the existing tile set for the *SimCity 2000* program. Click on Yes to continue.

8. After a few moments, you should see a confirmation message letting you know that the tile set was successfully copied into *SimCity 2000*.

If you now start *SimCity 2000*, you'll find that any existing Drive-In Movie Theaters will now be playing your new sci-fi flick.

PLACE AND PRINT

Place and Print, the third module/utility, is so open, and gives you so much power and freedom to make and mold your city, that you can either look at it as the cheater's dream (if you play *SimCity 2000* for the game) or the ultimate city-sculpting tool (if you're into *SimCity 2000* for the model-making, creative aspect).

Let's take a quick look around the Place and Print opening screen. If you haven't already, click on the Place and Print button (or select it from the menu). You should see a screen like Figure 18.9 open up.

As you can see in the figure, you have a typical Menu bar. There's also a Toolbox, where you make your tool selections. (In the DOS version it's divided into two toolboxes, one for Edit Tools and one for View Tools. In the other versions all the tools are combined in one toolbox, but all the tools are the same.) The Work Area is where you build your city, and the Object Selector is used to select different building types.

The Edit Tools

Here are some descriptions of the tools found in the Edit Tools box, pictured in Figure 18.9.

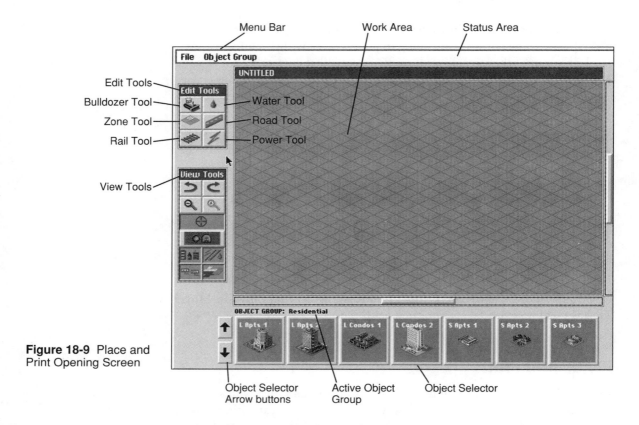

Figure 18-9 Place and Print Opening Screen

- The Bulldozer Tool works the same as it does in *SimCity 2000*.
- The Water Tool can place bodies of water and water pipes. This includes the trees that are grouped with water in *SimCity 2000*, as are the water pumps and other water-related buildings and structures.
- The Zone Tool lets you choose light or dense for all three basic zone types—residential, commercial, and industrial—plus seaports, airports, and military zones. (To actually place military bases, use the Object Selector.)
- The Road Tool is the same as it is in *SimCity 2000*, except that it has no bus depots. (Buildings are placed with the Object Selector.)
- The Rail Tool is the same as it is in *SimCity 2000*, except that it has no rail or subway stations. (Buildings are placed with the Object Selector.)
- The Power Tool only allows you to place power lines. (To place power plants, you'll need to use the Object Selector.)

The View Tools

All the view tools are identical to those in *SimCity 2000*, as shown in Figure 18.9.

For the purposes of this tutorial, we'll assume that you already know how to use all these tools. If you don't know how to use all of them, you haven't played *SimCity 2000* yet. If you haven't played *SimCity 2000* yet, stop what you're doing right now and go play. You'll have more fun learning how things work by playing a game than by using a utility.

Object Selector

Now that that's out of the way, let's look at this new thing, which opens the inner workings of *SimCity 2000* and lets you choose and place almost every building, structure, and landscape tile (a.k.a. the objects): the *Object Selector*.

Actually, the Object Selector works the same in Place and Print as it does in the rest of *SCURK*. The only difference is what you do with the object after you've selected it. In this case, we'll be taking that selected object and plopping it down in the city just the same as we'd normally plop down a police station, library, or power plant. But it's free.

Placing Objects in Your City

Placing things in a city is nothing new. So what's so special about this Object Selector thing? No limits, that's what's so special. There are a number of buildings that you can only get one of in *SimCity 2000*. With *SCURK*, you can have all you want.

Let's learn how to use these tools by creating our own private flock of mansions. Follow these steps to do this:

1. Open the Object Group Menu and select Special.
2. Scroll through the Object Selector until you find the Mayor's House.
3. Click on the Mayor's House.
4. Place three, four, or five Mayor's Houses in the Work Area.

Now how about erecting a few statues in our honor? Follow these steps:

1. Scroll through the Object Selector until you find the Statue.
2. Click on the Statue, then place a few in the Work Area.

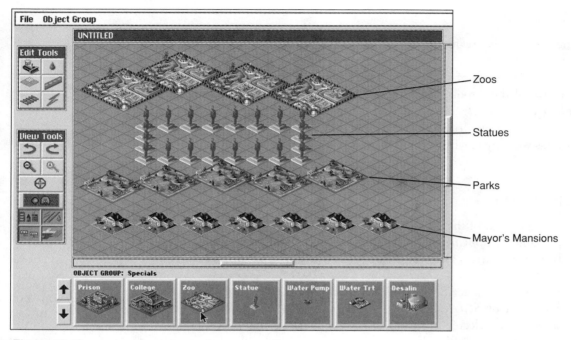

Figure 18.10
Zoos, Mansions, Parks
and Statues Placed
Using *SCURK*'s Place
and Print

As long as we're on the personal-possession-and-power kick, how about a couple of private parks and zoos? Follow these steps:

1. Scroll through the Object Selector until you find the Large Park. Place a couple of Large Parks in the Work Area.

2. Scroll through the Object Selector until you find the Zoo. Place a couple of Zoos in the Work Area.

This little demonstration of power and greed isn't much as cities go, but it does show that you can put anything you want into your cities.

That's all there is to the Place part of Place and Print. Now let's learn how to use the Print feature.

First, we'll need to set up the program to work properly with your printer. These next four steps are for the DOS version only:

1. Open the File menu and select Print Setup.

2. Click on the button for the closest match to your printer.

3. Click on the LPT1 button (unless your printer is hooked to another port).

4. Click on Save. From now on, your printer selection will be saved so that you don't need to configure it again.

Now let's print your city. Follow these steps for the DOS version of *SCURK* only:

1. Open the File menu and select Print.
2. Click on the Large button to print the city on the largest scale.
3. Move the cursor over the small city map and position it so it surrounds the structures you just placed.
4. Click on the Selected button at the bottom of the Print dialog box.

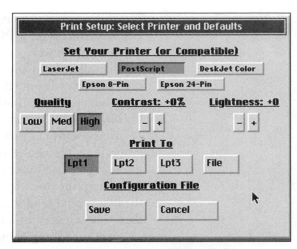

Figure 18.11
Print Setup Dialog Box

In the Mac and Windows versions, the Print Dialog box works a little differently; we're sure you can handle it on your own!

Wait patiently, and a printout of the map will eventually emerge from your printer.

Printing Notes

The DOS version supports disappointingly few printers in its first incarnation. We can only hope that it will be updated to include both the non-color DeskJets and the color PostScript printers (at present only grayscale Postscript is supported in the DOS version). If you really want to print to these printers, then (if it's not too late) get the Windows version of *SCURK*. It will read and write the same city files as DOS *SimCity 2000*, and will print to any printer you've installed.

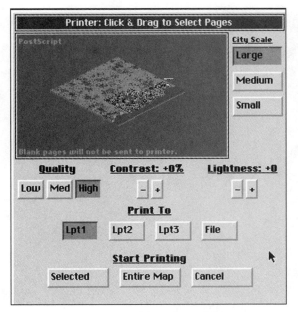

Figure 18.12
Print Dialog Box

Saving and Printing Your Cities in Adobe Acrobat 2.0 Format

If you own Adobe Acrobat Exchange 2.0, or Acrobat Distiller 2.0, you can "print" your maps to an Acrobat pdf file (pdf = Portable Document Format), and then distribute your cities to anyone with a copy of Acrobat Reader 2.0, which is a free shareware program that allows you to read and print any pdf file, regardless of your computer platform.

Thus, if you create a city on your Macintosh, and create a pdf file of your city, someone with a PC—or even a UNIX workstation—can view your city exactly the way you printed it! Of course, you can always just send your city files directly to anybody who already owns a copy of *SCURK*, and then they can print it out. But if you would like to circulate your cities so that others can print them out without having to purchase *SCURK*, Adobe Acrobat is the way to go, since the Reader program is free.

Acrobat works just like a fax print driver, such as WinFax Pro. For example, while you're in the Windows or Macintosh version of *SCURK*, instead of your current printer, you'd select the *Acrobat PDFWriter on Disk* and then print your city. The city would be saved in an Acrobat pdf file, and then you could send it to anybody who has Acrobat Reader 2.0. They could then view it and print it out.

The nice thing about Acrobat files is that soon, Web browsers on the World Wide Web will be able to display Acrobat files, just like HTML documents. You can then easily post your cities on Web pages, and people will be able to see them onscreen.

Appendix

A

Running the DOS Versions of *SimCity 2000* and *SCURK* Under OS/2 and Windows 3.1

The DOS versions of *SimCity 2000* and *SCURK* will both run under Microsoft's Windows 3.1 as DOS applications and, with some tinkering, will work under the OS/2 2.1 operating system.[1] This brief appendix gives you some vital installation tips you'll need to follow in order to get these programs to work with both OS/2 2.1 and Windows 3.1.

INSTALLING DOS VERSION OF *SIMCITY 2000* UNDER OS/2 2.1

The DOS version of *SimCity 2000* can easily be made to run in a full-screen DOS session under OS/2 2.1, subject to the same basic hardware requirements as in native DOS.

1. To install *SimCity 2000*, use the INSTALL.EXE program on your installation disk while running a full-screen DOS session in OS/2.

2. If you're using a sound card that requires a driver to be loaded (such as the PAS 16), you'll get an error message from the INSTALL program saying that your card

---

[1]Some users may find that they cannot get *SimCity 2000* or *SCURK* to run under OS/2, despite removing all TSRs (TSR means *Terminate but stay resident*) in memory. Norton Commander for DOS is a TSR, as are any drivers you install in your CONFIG.SYS and AUTOEXEC.BAT files.

is not found. Ignore the error message and continue to answer the INSTALL questions based on your current sound card.

3. After installing *SimCity 2000*, open the Templates folder and drag a program object onto a clear part of the desktop. The Settings Notebook will open automatically for this new object. Enter the path of your *SimCity 2000* directory and the file name SC2000.EXE in the box provided.

4. Now, in the second box, marked Parameters, enter the following: NO_MEM_CHK (NO_MEM_CHK simply disables *SimCity 2000*'s memory-checking scheme, and allows the program to run in multitasking operating system environments such as OS/2 and Windows 3.1.

5. Turn the Settings Notebook to the next page, marked Session on the tab marker, and click on DOS Full-screen. At this point, the game should run if you click on the new program object.

If you would like to improve the performance of *SimCity 2000* under OS/2, or are not getting sounds while running the game, click on the DOS Settings button on the Sessions page (in the Settings Notebook) for the new object you created, then make the following changes:

1. DOS_DEVICE: If you're using a sound card, such as the PAS 16 card, that ordinarily uses a driver such as MVSOUND.SYS, type in the path, the file name, and any parameters that would normally go in the CONFIG.SYS file in DOS for your sound card's configuration.

2. INT_DURING_IO: Turn this switch on. This allows OS/2 to perform interrupts while reading or writing to files on disk. It also makes a noticeable improvement in the smoothness of the music being played.

3. DPMI_MEMORY_LIMIT: Adjust this to a level above 4 megabytes of RAM. If you have plenty of RAM, raise this setting higher. The higher RAM settings seem to help speed up the simulation.

SETTING UP THE DOS *SCURK* TO RUN UNDER OS/2

Since *SCURK* was mostly developed under OS/2, it will run quite well in a full-screen DOS session. You'll need to make sure that your DOS session settings have DPMI ENABLED, HW_TIMER ON, and RETRACE-EMU-LATION OFF, and give at least 8 to 16 megabytes of DPMI RAM for the DPMI_Memory Limit. Also, when running *SCURK*, you'll need to use the NO_MEM_CHK command-line option when you first start the program, since OS/2 doesn't report the correct amount of memory available when *SCURK* checks at startup.

WINDOWS 3.1 SETTINGS FOR THE DOS VERSION OF *SIMCITY 2000*

Setting up *SimCity 2000* to run in Windows 3.1 as a full-screen DOS application is a snap. All you need to do is, after installing the program, create a program icon for the SC2000.EXE program, then make a few minor changes to the Windows Program Item Properties dialog box for SimCity.[2]

Here's how to do this:

1. After installing the DOS *SimCity 2000* (check to make sure the program runs under DOS before proceeding), start up Windows 3.1.

2. In the Program Manager window, select the program window where you want the SimCity program icon to appear.

3. While still in the Program Manager window, pull down the File menu and select the New option.

4. In the New Program Item dialog box, click on the Program Item radio button, then click on the OK button.

5. In the Program Item Properties dialog box that next opens up, click on the Browse button.

6. In the Browse dialog box, change your directory and drive, if necessary, to the directory and drive where you've installed *SimCity 2000*. For example, if you've installed it on your C drive, in the SC2000 directory, select your C drive and the SC2000 directory.

7. While still in the Browse dialog box, select the SC2000.EXE program name so that it is highlighted, then click on the OK button.

8. In the Program Item Properties dialog box that next appears, you'll see the SC2000.EXE program name listed in the Command line box. After the SC2000.EXE, type in **NO_MEM_CHK**, so that your command line will look something like this:

   C:\SC2000\SC2000.EXE NO_MEM_CHK

   Adding the NO_MEM_CHK switch disables *SimCity 2000*'s memory-checking routine and allows it to run under Windows 3.1.

9. In the Working Directory box, type in the drive and directory where you installed the *SimCity 2000* program. For example, if you installed Sim-City on your C drive in the SC2000 directory, you'd type C:\SC2000.

---

[2]Some users may find that they can't get the DOS *SimCity 2000* or DOS *SCURK* to run under Windows 3.1 using the technique outlined in this appendix. If this happens to you, try removing all TSRs (see the previous footnote for a definition of TSR), non-Microsoft memory managers, and second-party shells (such as the Norton Commander and so on), which may be causing conflicts with *SimCity 2000* or *SCURK*.

10. When you're finished, click on the OK button and you'll return to the Program Manager window. You should see a new *SimCity 2000* DOS icon for the *SimCity 2000* program.

11. Just double-click on the *SimCity 2000* icon to start up *SimCity 2000* while in Windows.

RUNNING THE UNIVERSAL VESA VIDEO DRIVER BATCH FILE

In some instances, you may be forced to run the DOS version of *SimCity 2000* using the universal VESA video driver that is supplied with the program. Maxis provides the batch file SC2VESA.BAT for this purpose, and it loads the universal VESA driver before starting *SimCity 2000*. If you're using this batch file to run *SimCity 2000*, you'll need to make a few changes to the above procedure for running the program under Windows 3.1. Here's what you'll need to do:

- Repeat steps 1 through 6 in the preceding section.

- In step 7, instead of selecting SC2000.EXE in the Browse dialog box, select instead SC2VESA.BAT, then click on the OK button.

- Instead of performing step 8 in the preceding section, do this: In the Program Item Properties dialog box that next appears, you'll see the SC2VESA.BAT program name listed in the Command line box. After SC2VESA.BAT type in the following switch:
  NO_MEM_CHK
  Adding the NO_MEM_CHK switch disables *SimCity 2000*'s memory-checking routine and allows it to run under Windows 3.1.

- Follow steps 9 and 10 in the preceding section.

- Just double-click on the *SimCity 2000* icon to start up *SimCity 2000* while in Windows.

WINDOWS 3.1 SETTINGS FOR THE DOS VERSION OF *SCURK*

To set up *SCURK* to run as a DOS application under Windows 3.1, you'll perform the same steps shown above for setting up the DOS *SimCity 2000* to run under Windows. In each step, just replace SC2000.EXE with *SCURK*.EXE, or, if you need to run the universal VESA video driver, use *SCURK*VSA.BAT instead of SC2VESA.BAT.

Appendix

B

Windows Version Installation Tips

Installing *SimCity 2000 for Windows* (either the original floppy version or the *CD Collection*) is a simple matter of running the standard Windows Setup program:

Start Windows.

Open the Program Manager.

Put the *SimCity 2000 for Windows* (floppy) Disk 1 or CD into the proper drive.

Open the File menu and select Run.

Type **[drive]:\SETUP**, press [Enter] where [drive] is A, B, D, E, or whatever drive is holding the diskette or CD.

If you have the room on your hard drive (about 7 MB for the floppy version and at least 12 MB for the CD Collection), installation will proceed with no problems.

In some cases, getting it to run may be a little trickier.

To make *SimCity 2000 for Windows* run smoothly, two requirements must be met:

You must have your video card set to 256 colors

Depending on your graphics card, *SimCity* may or may not actually run under 16 colors. But if it does, it will look ugly and run slowly because it has to dither (fake) the rest of the colors. It may also run under more than 256 colors. If it does, fine. But setting your video card to 256 colors may save you time and energy.

To find out if you've got 256 colors, double-click on the Windows Setup icon. If it says SVGA or contains the words "256 colors," you're fine. Go play. If it just says "VGA" after the word "Display," you're running under 16 colors and will need to update your driver.

If you need to change your driver, the best thing to do is to use a new driver made specifically for your video card. The docs and disks that came with your video card will tell you whether that driver exists and how to install it if it does. If you have a fancy new graphics card, it will have a special Windows program or control panel that will make it easy to change the driver.

If you don't have the docs and disks for your card, you *might* be able to use the generic SVGA driver that comes with the later versions of Windows (3.11 and beyond). If you need it and have it, here's how to install it: Run Windows Setup, open the Options menu, and select Change System Settings. Click on the down arrow to the right of the word "Display," select the SVGA driver, then click on OK. You'll have to restart Windows for the SVGA driver to take effect.

If you don't have the generic SVGA driver, call the place where you bought the computer. They should be able to tell you what kind of card you have and even supply you with the proper drivers. You can also call the card or computer manufacturer (a lot of numbers are listed in the *SimCity 2000 for Windows Quick Start Guide*) and get the information you need. Most of these companies have BBSes (also listed in the *Quick Start Guide*) that you can log onto for free (except for the phone call, if it's long distance) and get the latest drivers. Most companies also make their drivers available through the major online services, such as America Online and CompuServe.

You need enough free RAM

SimCity 2000 for Windows needs a lot of RAM. If you only have 4 MB on your machine, then there's only room for DOS, Windows, and *SimCity*

Warning!!!
Don't install the wrong driver! Windows ships with a number of drivers for a number of different video cards. Even if it says 640 x 480 x 256 colors, that doesn't guarantee that it will work with your card. In fact, if you install the wrong driver, Windows will stop working completely. According to the technical support gurus at Maxis, a lot of people install the Video 7 drivers that come with Windows—and very few people have Video 7 cards. It's very important that you know what video card you have before you mess with the drivers.

2000. If *SimCity 2000* won't run, close every Windows program—except the Program Manager—and try again.

If that doesn't work, quit Windows and disable any TSRs that you don't absolutely need, then restart Windows and try again.

If you have 8 MB or more, then memory shouldn't be a problem unless you try to run too many programs or a couple of big ones along with *SimCity 2000.*

The SimCity 2000 Readme File

Books like this one can be updated once a year at most, so we can't stay totally up to date with every small program change or the latest tech support tips, much less each new video or sound card that enters the market. That's where the Readme file comes in.

This is an important resource that tells you the latest changes to the program, and the latest installation and troubleshooting tips from the tech support front line—the men and women who spend their working lives on the phones solving people's problems.

As they learn new things about how the program works (or doesn't) with various new computers and new video and sound cards, they put that information into the Readme file on the distribution disks. This is standard industry practice, so always check the Readme files on every program, game or otherwise, that you get.

Appendix

C

The SimCity 2000 CD Collection

The *SimCity 2000 CD Collection* is a single CD-ROM containing:

- *SimCity 2000* (available separately)
- The *SimCity 2000 Urban Renewal Kit*, a.k.a. *SCURK* (available separately)
- *Scenarios Volume 1: Great Disasters* (available separately)
- *Great Cities of the World Scenarios* (not available separately)
- A lot of interesting extra cities, mostly contest winners, submitted by *SimCity 2000* players all over the world (mostly available separately and individually on various online services)

At press time for this book, the DOS version of the *CD Collection* is shipping, and the Windows and Mac versions are close behind. All versions will be pretty much identical in their contents, allowing for the slight differences between the different versions of SimCity 2000 and *SCURK* on the different platforms.

Each of the *Great Cities of the World Scenarios* comes with one or two special landmark buildings that, with *SCURK*, can be substituted for the Braun Llama Dome or any other existing building.

If you don't have *SimCity 2000* or are thinking about it as a gift for a friend, go for the *CD Collection*. It has everything, all on one (almost) indestructible disk. If you already have *SimCity 2000* and you're frugal, you could just get *SCURK*, but you can't beat the *CD Collection* for completeness.

Index

Computer Game Books

The 7th Guest: The Official Strategy Guide	$19.95
Aces Over Europe: The Official Strategy Guide	$19.95
Aegis: Guardian of the Fleet—The Official Strategy Guide	$19.95
Armored Fist: The Official Strategy Guide	$19.95
Alone in the Dark: The Official Strategy Guide	$19.95
Betrayal at Krondor: The Official Strategy Guide	$19.95
CD-ROM Games Secrets, Volume 1	$19.95
Computer Adventure Games Secrets	$19.95
Donkey Kong Country Game Secrets the Unauthorized Edition	$9.95
DOOM Battlebook	$14.95
DOOM II: The Official Strategy Guide	$19.95
Dracula Unleashed: The Official Strategy Guide & Novel	$19.95
Dragon Lore: The Official Strategy Guide	$19.95
Front Page Sports Baseball '94: The Official Playbook	$19.95
Harpoon II: The Official Strategy Guide	$19.95
Hell: A Cyberpunk Thriller—The Official Strategy Guide	$19.95
The Legend of Kyrandia: The Official Strategy Guide	$19.95
Lemmings: The Official Companion (with disk)	$24.95
Lode Runner: The Legend Returns—The Official Strategy Guide	$19.95
Master of Orion: The Official Strategy Guide	$19.95
Microsoft Arcade: The Official Strategy Guide	$12.95
Microsoft Flight Simulator: The Official Strategy Guide	$19.95
Microsoft Golf: The Official Strategy Guide	$19.95
Microsoft Space Simulator: The Official Strategy Guide	$19.95
Might and Magic Compendium:	
The Authorized Strategy Guide for Games I, II, III, and IV	$19.95
Myst: The Official Strategy Guide, Revised Edition	$19.95
Outpost: The Official Strategy Guide	$19.95
Pagan: Ultima VIII—The Ultimate Strategy Guide	$19.95
Panzer General: The Official Strategy Guide	$19.95
Prince of Persia: The Official Strategy Guide	$19.95
Quest for Glory: The Authorized Strategy Guide	$19.95
Rebel Assault: The Official Insider's Guide	$19.95
Return to Zork Adventurer's Guide	$14.95
Shadow of the Comet: The Official Strategy Guide	$19.95
Sherlock Holmes, Consulting Detective: The Unauthorized Strategy Guide	$19.95
Sid Meier's Civilization, or Rome on 640K a Day	$19.95
Sid Meier's Colonization: The Official Strategy Guide	$19.95
SimCity 2000: Power, Politics, and Planning, Revised Edition	$19.95
SimEarth: The Official Strategy Guide	$19.95
SimFarm Almanac: The Official Guide to SimFarm	$19.95
SimLife: The Official Strategy Guide	$19.95
SSN-21 Seawolf: The Official Strategy Guide	$19.95
Star Crusader: The Official Strategy Guide	$19.95
Strike Commander: The Official Strategy Guide and Flight School	$19.95

Stunt Island: The Official Strategy Guide	$19.95
SubWar 2050: The Official Strategy Guide	$19.95
TIE Fighter: The Official Strategy Guide	$19.95
Ultima: The Avatar Adventures	$19.95
Ultima VII and Underworld: More Avatar Adventures	$19.95
Under a Killing Moon: The Official Strategy Guide	$19.95
Wing Commander I and II: The Ultimate Strategy Guide	$19.95
X-COM UFO Defense: The Official Strategy Guide	$19.95
X-Wing Collector's CD-ROM: The Official Strategy Guide	$19.95

Video Game Books

Behind the Scenes at Sega: The Making of a Video Game	$14.95
Boogerman Official Game Secrets	$12.95
Breath of Fire Authorized Game Secrets	$14.95
Complete Final Fantasy III Forbidden Game Secrets	$14.95
EA SPORTS Official Power Play Guide	$12.95
Earthworm Jim Official Game Secrets	$12.95
The Legend of Zelda: A Link to the Past—Game Secrets	$12.95
Lord of the Rings Official Game Secrets	$12.95
Maximum Carnage Official Game Secrets	$9.95
Mega Man X Official Game Secrets	$14.95
Mortal Kombat II Official Power Play Guide	$9.95
GamePro Presents: Nintendo Games Secrets Greatest Tips	$11.95
Nintendo Games Secrets, Volumes 1, 2, 3, and 4	$11.95 each
Parent's Guide to Video Games	$12.95
Secret of Mana Official Game Secrets	$14.95
Sega CD Official Game Secrets	$12.95
GamePro Presents: Sega Genesis Games Secrets Greatest Tips, Second Edition	$12.95
Official Sega Genesis Power Tips Book, Volumes 2 and 3	$14.95 each
Sega Genesis Secrets, Volume 4	$12.95
Sega Genesis and Sega CD Secrets, Volume 5	$12.95
Sega Genesis Secrets, Volume 6	$12.95
Sonic 3 Official Play Guide	$12.95
Super Empire Strikes Back Official Game Secrets	$12.95
Super Mario World Game Secrets	$12.95
Super Metroid Unauthorized Game Secrets	$14.95
Super NES Games Secrets, Volumes 2, and 3	$11.95 each
Super NES Games Secrets, Volumes 4 and 5	$12.95 each
GamePro Presents: Super NES Games Secrets Greatest Tips	$11.95
Super NES Games Unauthorized Power Tips Guide, Volumes 1 and 2	$14.95 each
Super Star Wars Official Game Secrets	$12.95
TurboGrafx-16 and TurboExpress Secrets, Volume 1	$9.95
Urban Strike Official Power Play Guide, with Desert Strike & Jungle Strike	$12.95
Virtual Bart Official Game Secrets	$12.95

TO ORDER BOOKS

Please send me the following items:

Quantity	Title	Unit Price	Total
_____	_____	$_____	$_____
_____	_____	$_____	$_____
_____	_____	$_____	$_____
_____	_____	$_____	$_____
_____	_____	$_____	$_____
_____	_____	$_____	$_____
	Subtotal		$_____
	7.25% SALES TAX (CALIFORNIA ONLY)		$_____
	SHIPPING AND HANDLING*		$_____
	TOTAL ORDER		$_____

By telephone: With Visa or MC, call 1-916-632-4400. Mon.–Fri. 9–4 PST. By mail: Just fill out the information below and send with your remittance to:

PRIMA PUBLISHING
P.O. Box 1260BK
Rocklin, CA 95677-1260

Satisfaction unconditionally guaranteed

Name_____

Address_____

City_____ State_____ Zip_____

Visa /MC#_____Exp._____

Signature_____

*$4.00 shipping and handling charge for the first book, and $1.00 for each additional book.

Ten Great Disasters
for only $9.95

Requires
SimCity 2000

MAXIS

SimCity 2000 Scenarios enhance your city building experience with new cities and urban challenges that load right into SimCity 2000. With Volume I: Great Disasters, you wrestle with 10 different cities on the brink of destruction and tackle everything from an alien invasion in Atlanta to a misplaced microwave beam in Silicon Valley.

 Yes, I want to enhance my city building experience.
Please send me "Scenarios Volume 1: Great Disasters"
for just $9.95 – including shipping and handling!
Remember to specify format (DOS, Windows or Macintosh)

To order, call:
1-800-33-MAXIS
Monday – Friday 8:00 a.m. to 6:00 p.m., PST

Offer expires 3/31/96   Please refer to the following discount code when placing order: C5AZ664